WOLVERINE

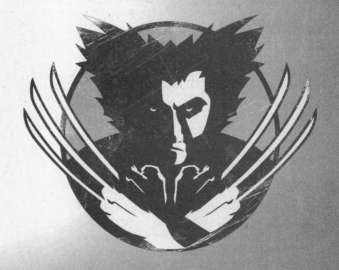

WOLVERINE

PRODIGAL SON

1

Story by Antony Johnston
Art by Wilson Tortosa
Lettering by Zach Matheny

DEL
REY

Ballantine Books · New York

A Del Rey Trade Paperback Original

Published in the United States by Del Rey, an imprint of The Random House Publishing Group, a division of Random House, Inc., New York.

DEL REY is a registered trademark and the DEL REY colophon is a trademark of Random House, Inc.

ISBN 978-0-345-50516-3

Printed in the United States of America

www.delreymanga.com

9 8 7 6 5 4 3 2 1

CONTENTS

Introduction

In 1975, Marvel Comics released *Giant-Size X-Men* #1, introducing a new lineup to the mutant team that would soon join the ranks of the most popular superheroes in the world. The first issue of the regular *X-Men* comic that featured these characters—including the über-popular Wolverine—followed later that year with the banner "ALL-NEW, ALL DIFFERENT" over the masthead. And comics were changed forever…. No, really, they were. You hear those kinds of sweeping pronouncements about new storylines in comics all the time, but this affected the American Super Hero in ways that no one really anticipated when the issues first came out.

The book you're holding in your hands right now is also ALL-NEW, ALL-DIFFERENT, although not at the same level as *Giant Size X-Men* #1. It's another view of Wolverine, Marvel's short, Canadian antihero appearing in manga form. And it brings together two amazing talents from across the globe, as British writer Antony Johnston and Filipino artist Wilson Tortosa work their magic together. Certainly these attributes would be enough to constitute "new" and "different" by anyone's standards.

But what really makes this comic so unlike any Wolverine story that has come before is that it uses the conventions of manga to tell an entirely original tale. Forget what you think you know about Logan, X-Man, ex-member of the Weapon X program, one-time agent of S.H.I.E.L.D. *Prodigal Son* reimagines Wolverine as a completely different person, in a new setting and with a different history and goals. In fact, whether you've read X-Men comics or you're coming to this book from seeing Logan in films, it doesn't matter much. You're going to find something entirely new here.

Our goal is to entertain you; at the very least, we hope to surprise you. We don't expect this "ALL-NEW, ALL-DIFFERENT" story of Wolverine to forever change the way superhero stories are told…

…but we can dream, right?

The Del Rey Manga Team

Chapter One
Quiet Earth

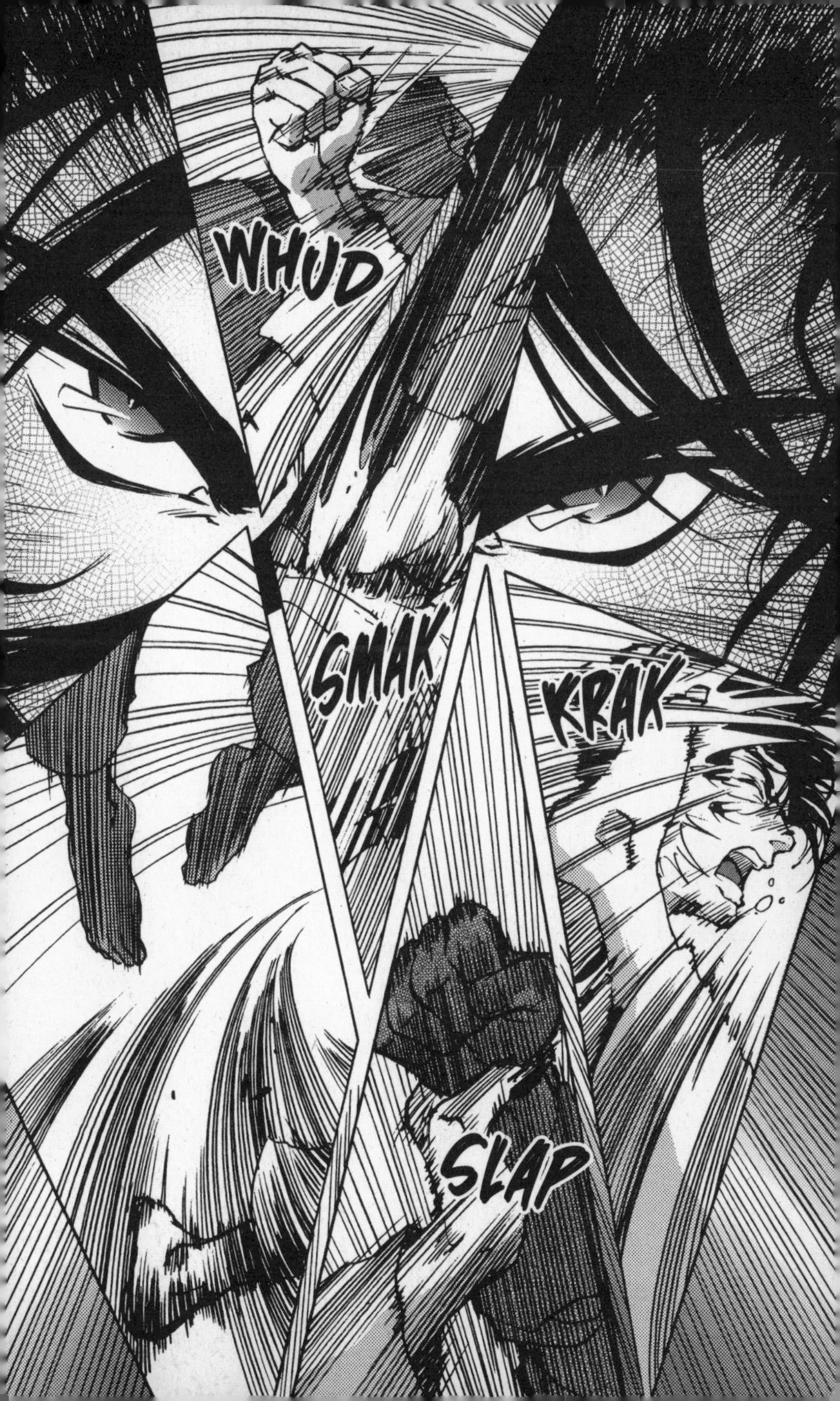
WHUD
SMAK
KRAK
SLAP

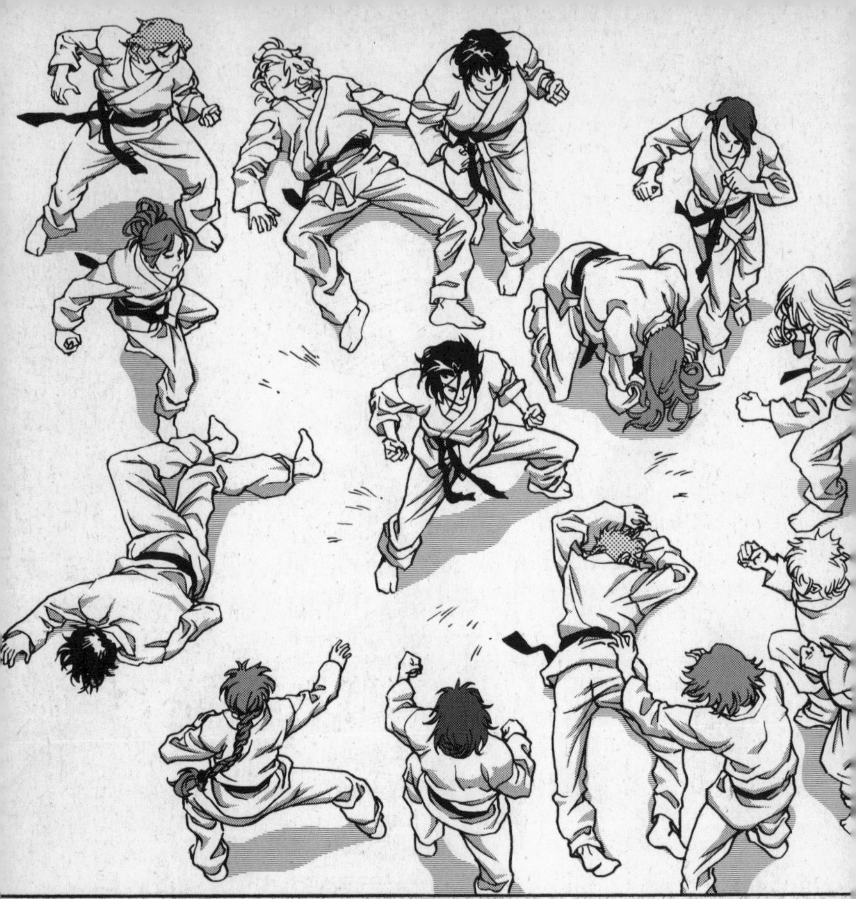

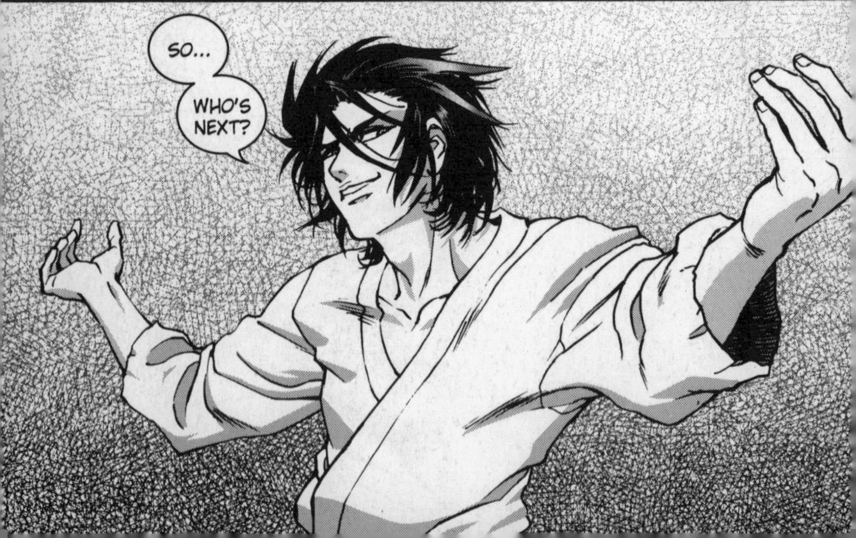
SO...
WHO'S NEXT?

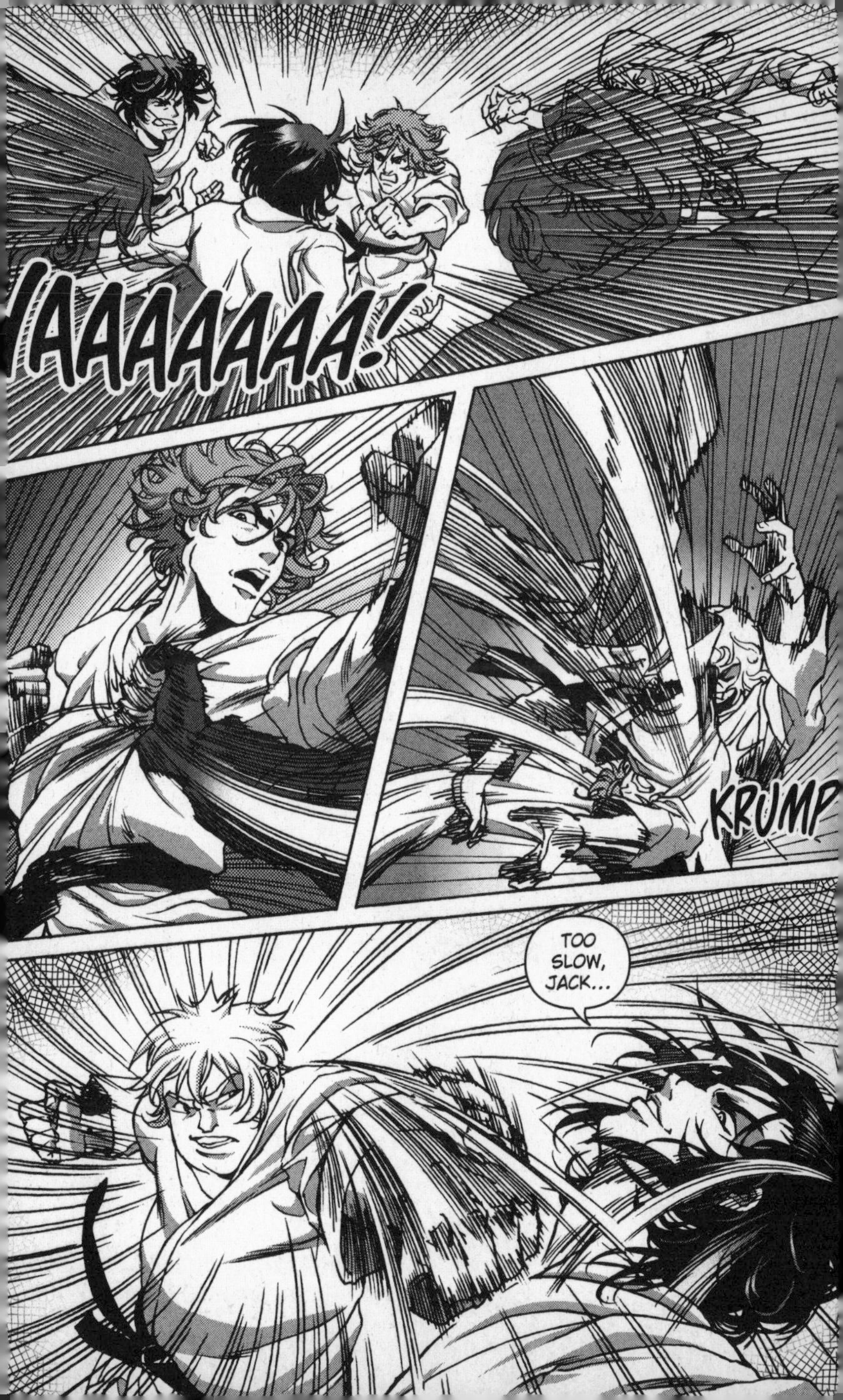
AAAAAAAA!
KRUMP
TOO SLOW, JACK...

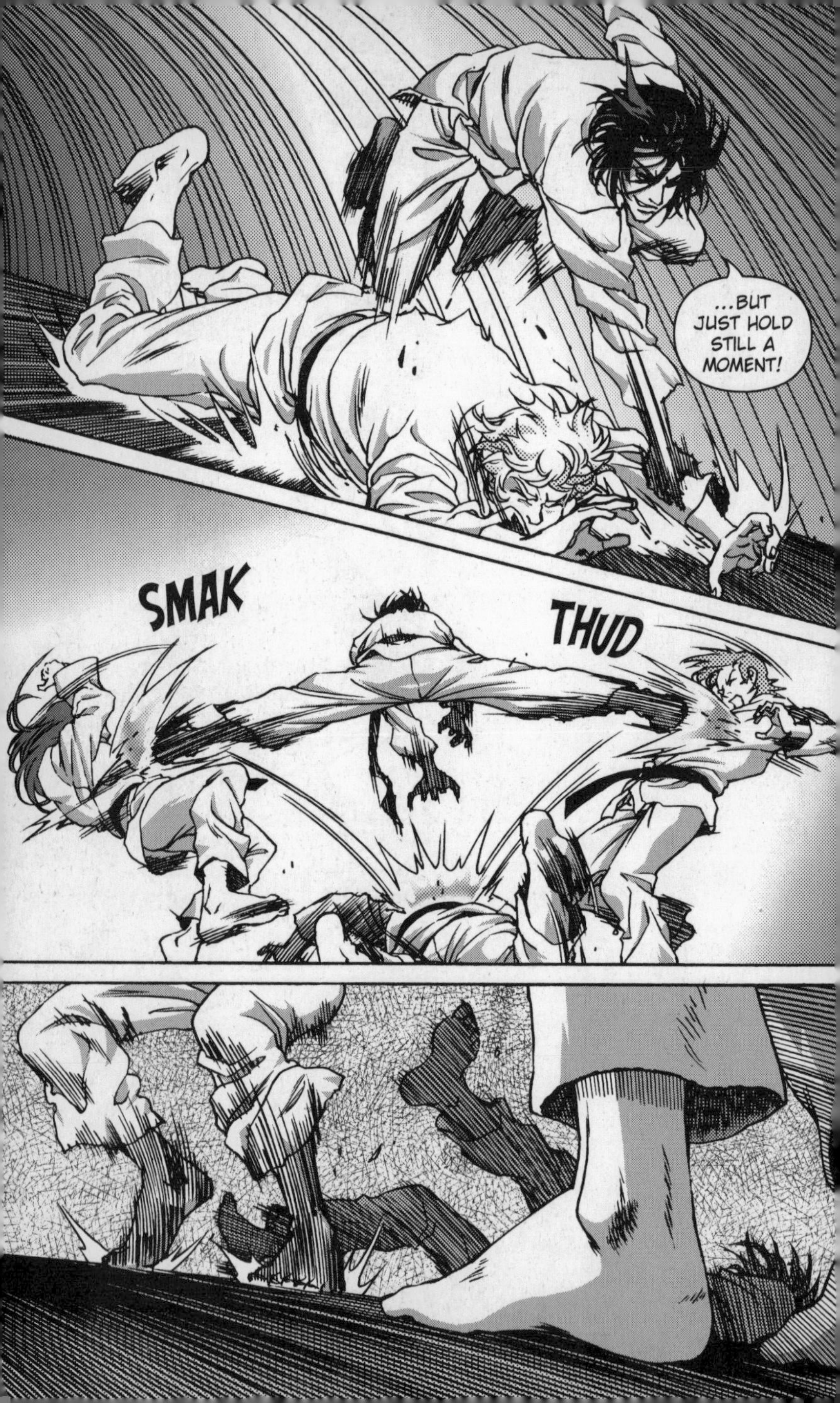
...BUT JUST HOLD STILL A MOMENT!
SMAK
THUD

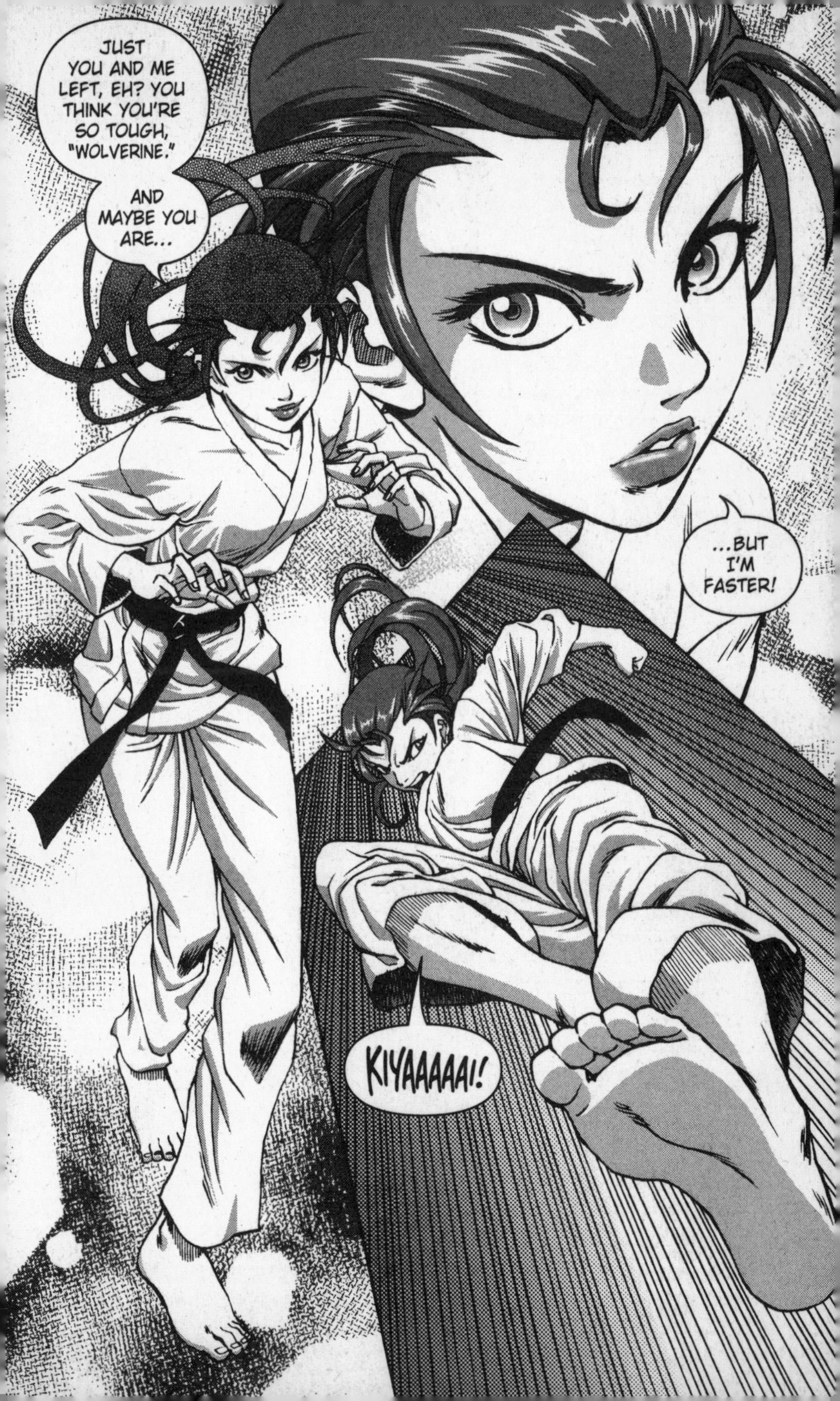
JUST YOU AND ME LEFT, EH? YOU THINK YOU'RE SO TOUGH, "WOLVERINE."
AND MAYBE YOU ARE...
...BUT I'M FASTER!
KIYAAAAAI!

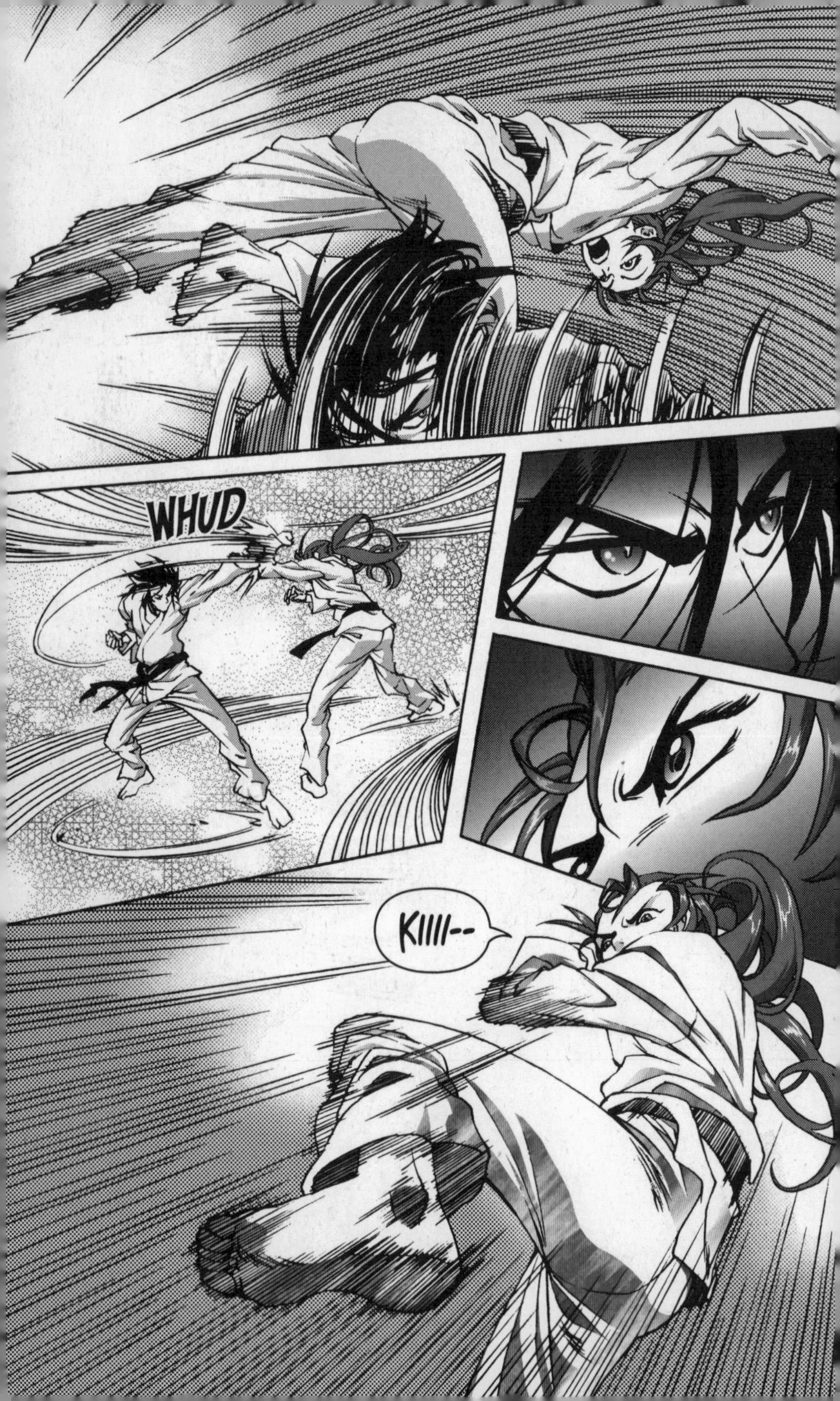
WHUD
KIIII--

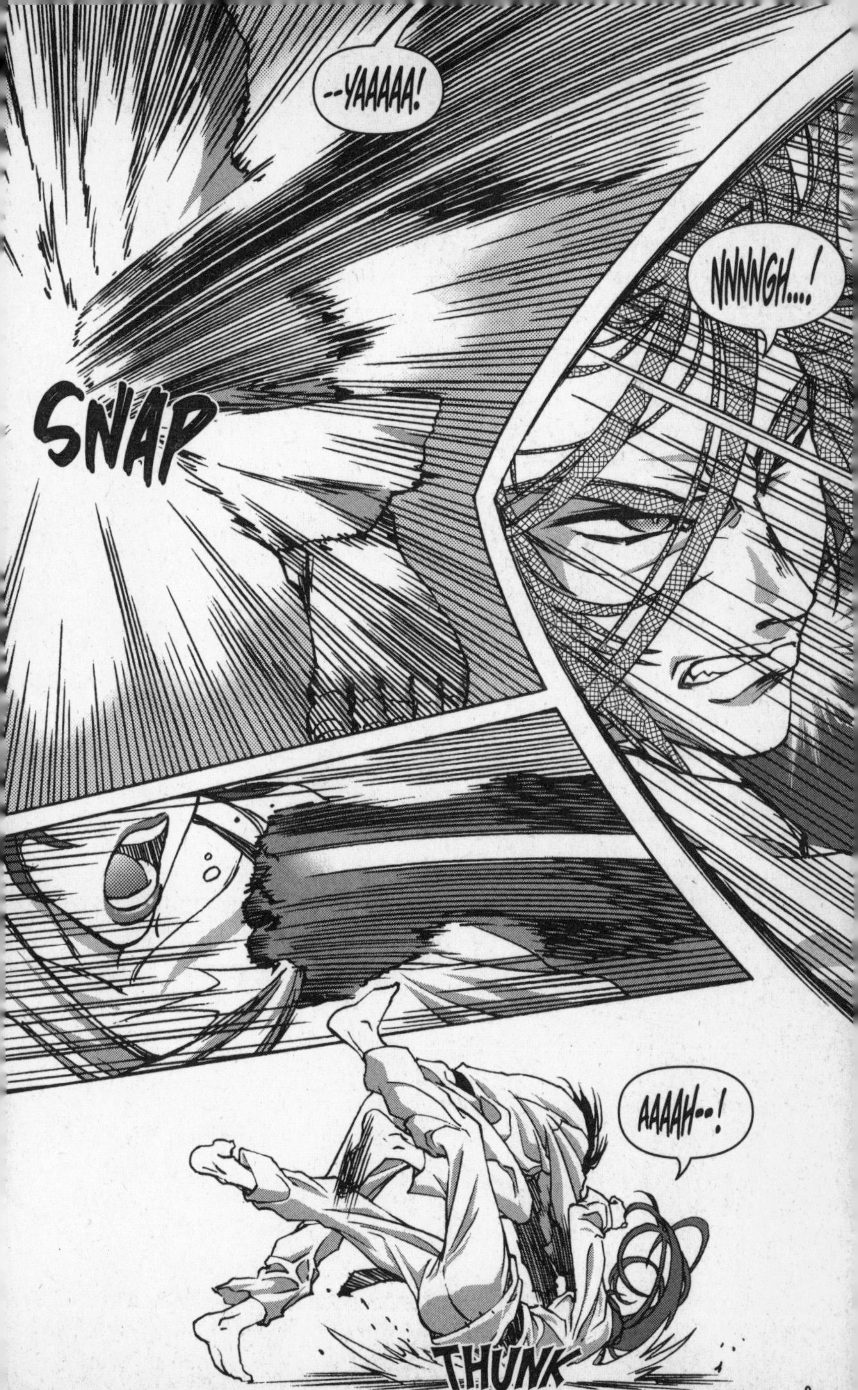
--YAAAAA!
SNAP
NNNNGH...!
AAAAH--!
THUNK

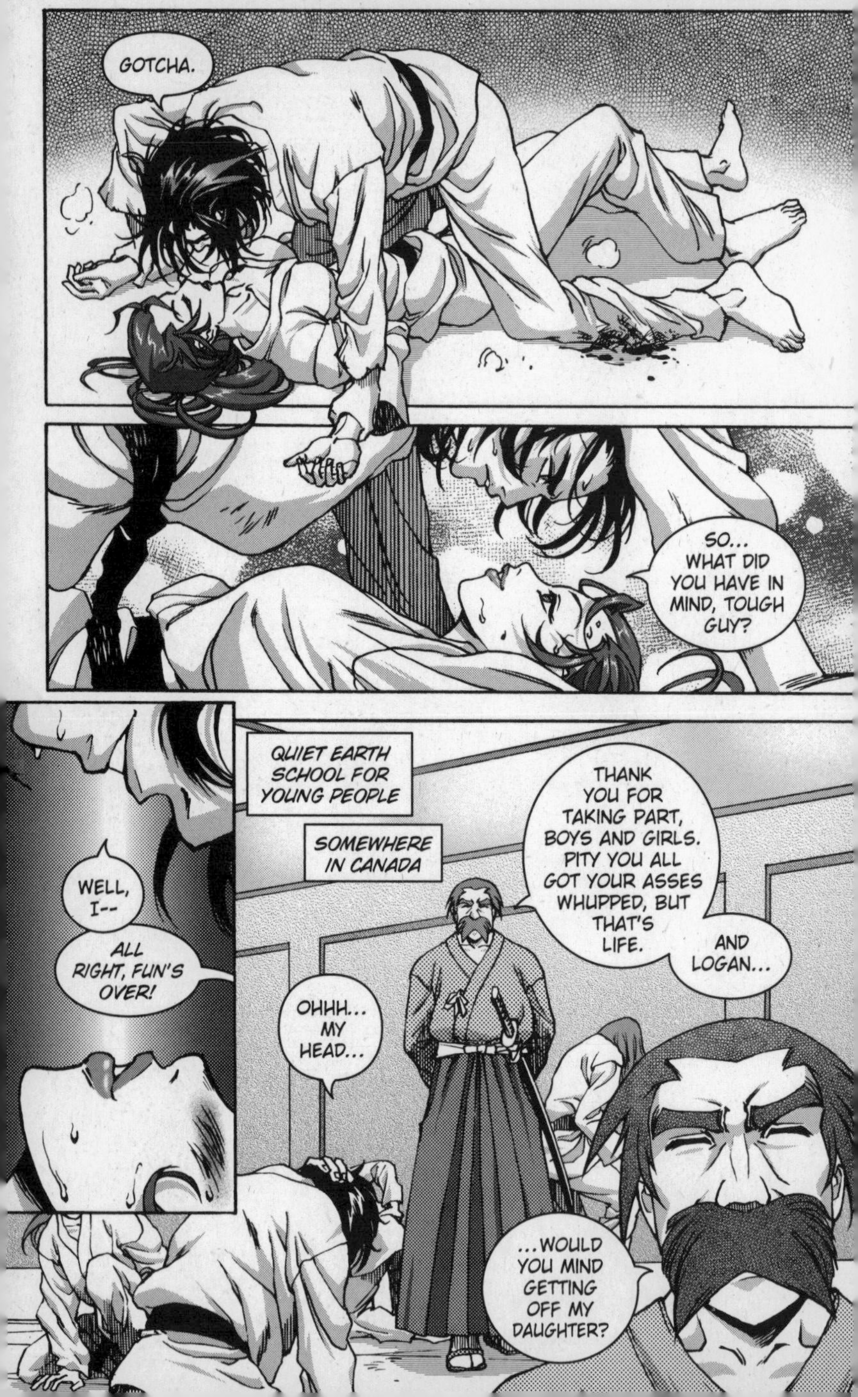
GOTCHA.
SO... WHAT DID YOU HAVE IN MIND, TOUGH GUY?
WELL, I--
ALL RIGHT, FUN'S OVER!
QUIET EARTH SCHOOL FOR YOUNG PEOPLE
SOMEWHERE IN CANADA
THANK YOU FOR TAKING PART, BOYS AND GIRLS. PITY YOU ALL GOT YOUR ASSES WHUPPED, BUT THAT'S LIFE.
AND LOGAN...
OHHH... MY HEAD...
...WOULD YOU MIND GETTING OFF MY DAUGHTER?

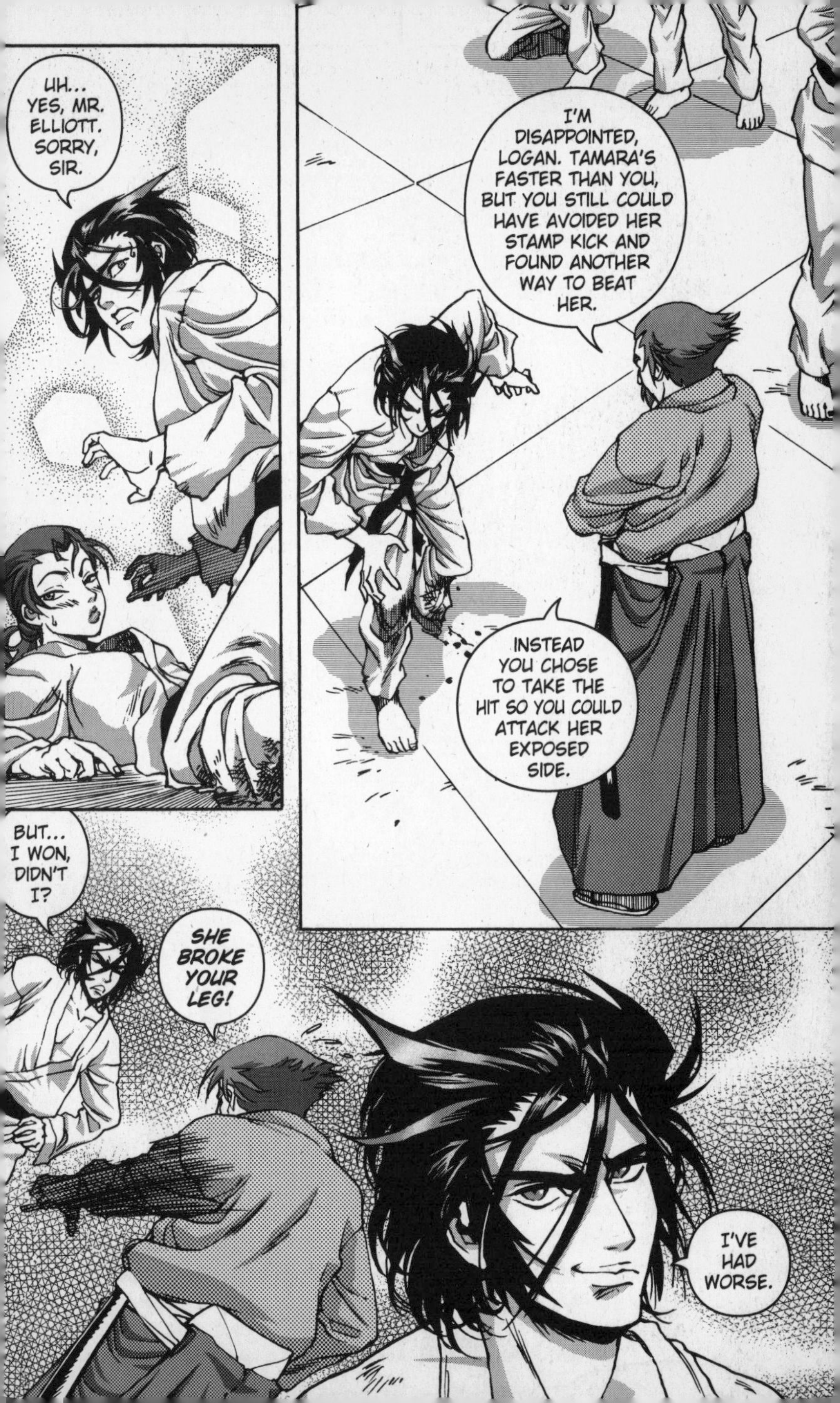
UH... YES, MR. ELLIOTT. SORRY, SIR.
I'M DISAPPOINTED, LOGAN. TAMARA'S FASTER THAN YOU, BUT YOU STILL COULD HAVE AVOIDED HER STAMP KICK AND FOUND ANOTHER WAY TO BEAT HER.
INSTEAD YOU CHOSE TO TAKE THE HIT SO YOU COULD ATTACK HER EXPOSED SIDE.
BUT... I WON, DIDN'T I?
SHE BROKE YOUR LEG!
I'VE HAD WORSE.

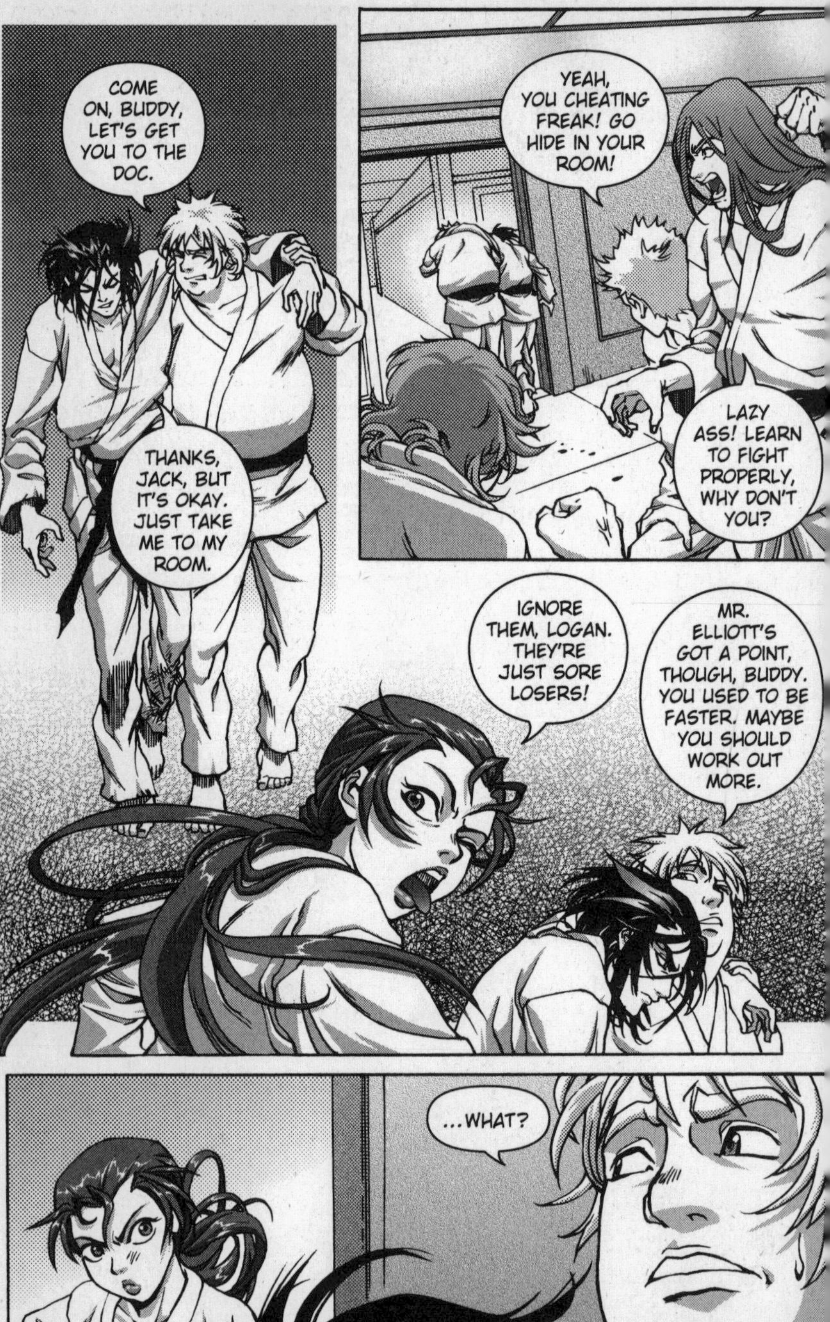
COME ON, BUDDY, LET'S GET YOU TO THE DOC.
THANKS, JACK, BUT IT'S OKAY. JUST TAKE ME TO MY ROOM.
YEAH, YOU CHEATING FREAK! GO HIDE IN YOUR ROOM!
LAZY ASS! LEARN TO FIGHT PROPERLY, WHY DON'T YOU?
IGNORE THEM, LOGAN. THEY'RE JUST SORE LOSERS!
MR. ELLIOTT'S GOT A POINT, THOUGH, BUDDY. YOU USED TO BE FASTER. MAYBE YOU SHOULD WORK OUT MORE.
...WHAT?

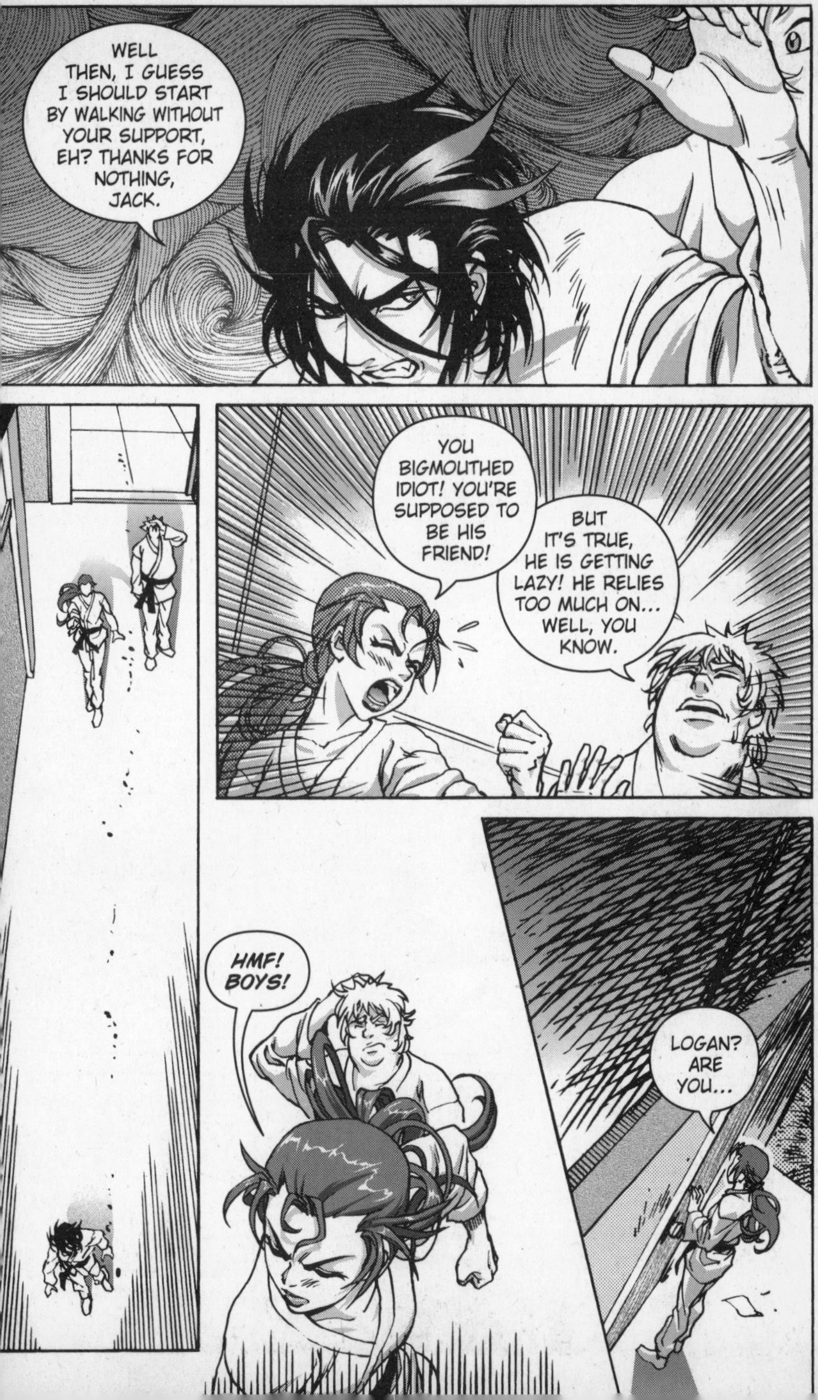

WELL THEN, I GUESS I SHOULD START BY WALKING WITHOUT YOUR SUPPORT, EH? THANKS FOR NOTHING, JACK.
YOU BIGMOUTHED IDIOT! YOU'RE SUPPOSED TO BE HIS FRIEND!
BUT IT'S TRUE, HE IS GETTING LAZY! HE RELIES TOO MUCH ON... WELL, YOU KNOW.
HMF! BOYS!
LOGAN? ARE YOU...

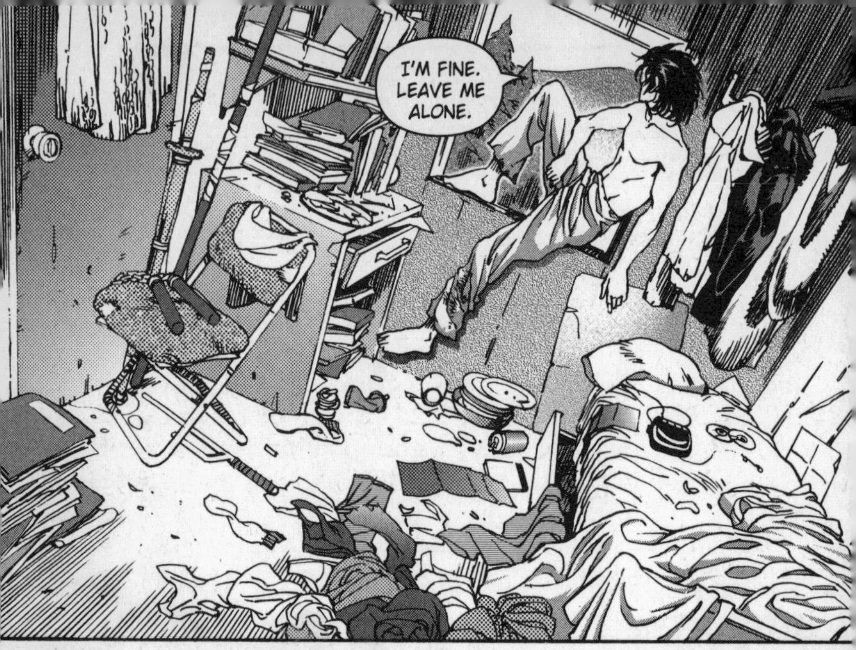
I'M FINE. LEAVE ME ALONE.

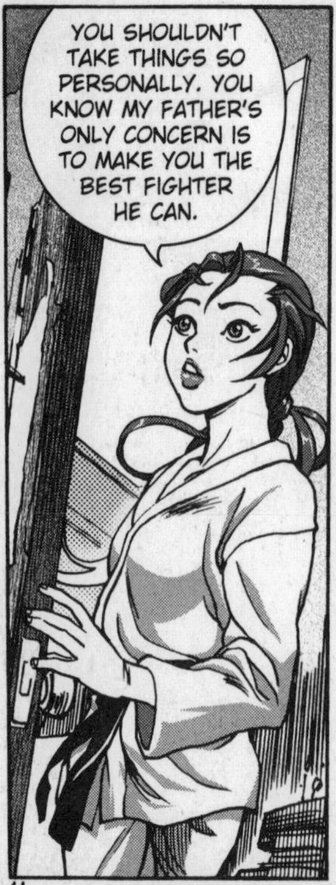
YOU SHOULDN'T TAKE THINGS SO PERSONALLY. YOU KNOW MY FATHER'S ONLY CONCERN IS TO MAKE YOU THE BEST FIGHTER HE CAN.

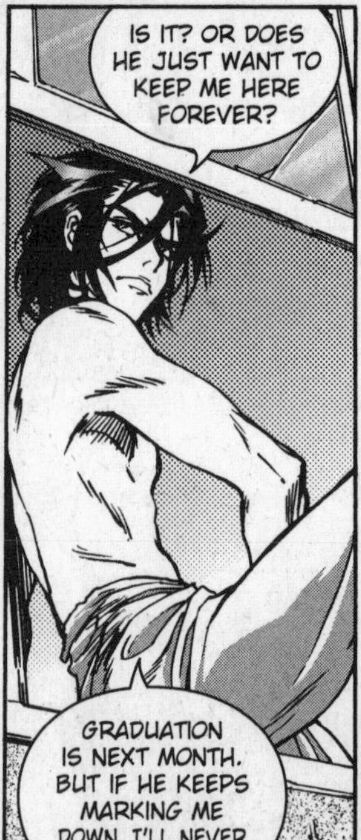
IS IT? OR DOES HE JUST WANT TO KEEP ME HERE FOREVER?
GRADUATION IS NEXT MONTH. BUT IF HE KEEPS MARKING ME DOWN, I'LL NEVER GRADUATE.

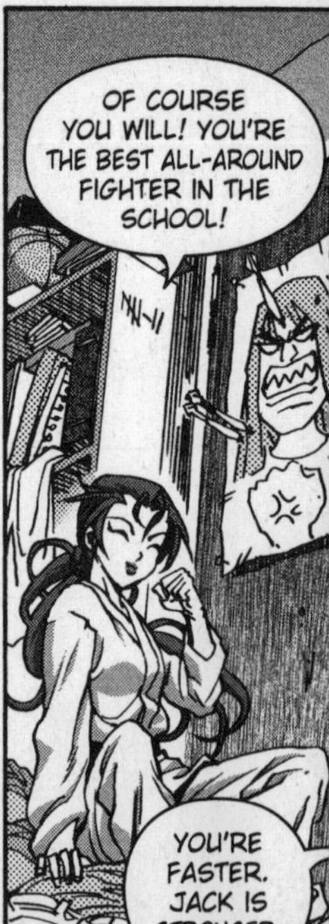
OF COURSE YOU WILL! YOU'RE THE BEST ALL-AROUND FIGHTER IN THE SCHOOL!
YOU'RE FASTER. JACK IS STRONGER.

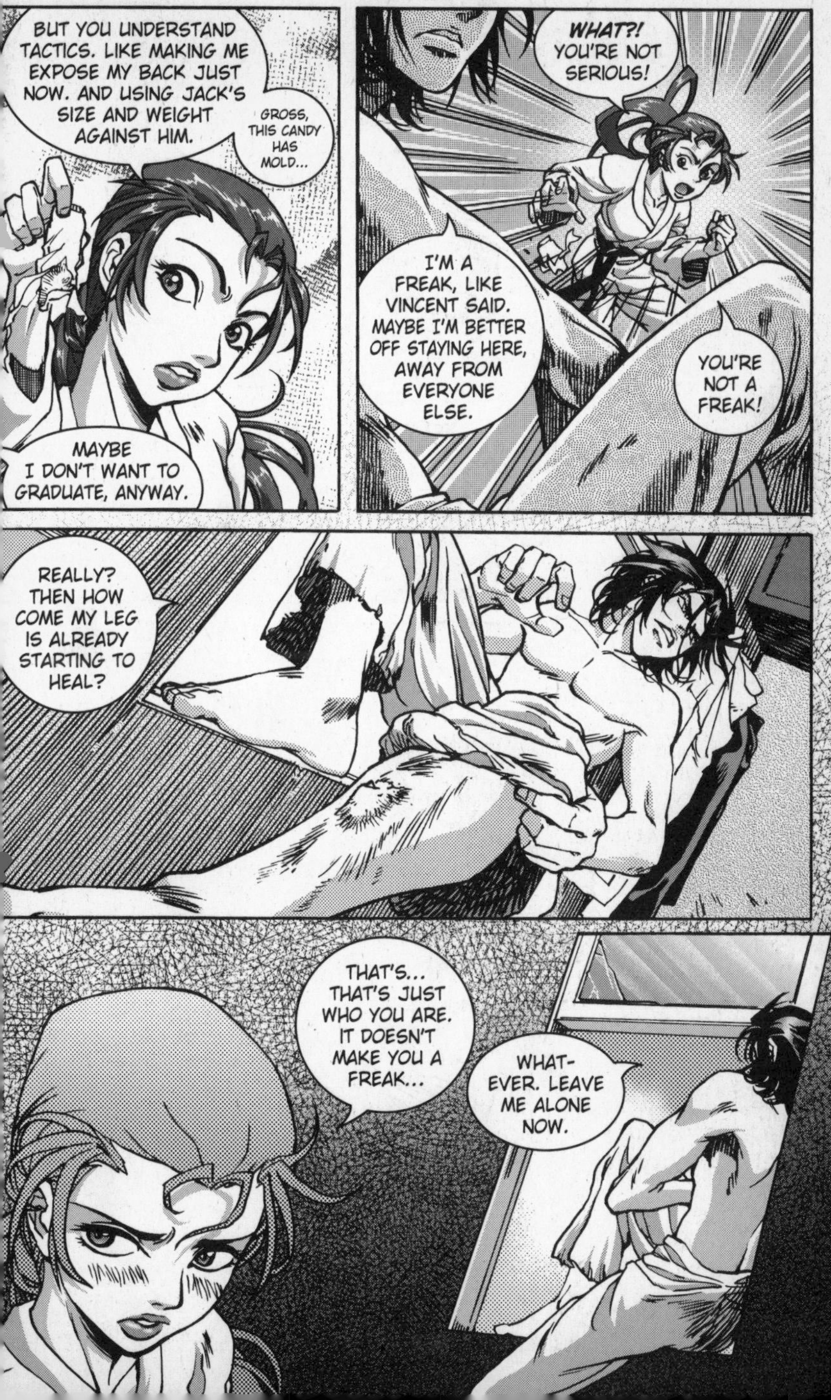
BUT YOU UNDERSTAND TACTICS. LIKE MAKING ME EXPOSE MY BACK JUST NOW. AND USING JACK'S SIZE AND WEIGHT AGAINST HIM.
GROSS, THIS CANDY HAS MOLD...
MAYBE I DON'T WANT TO GRADUATE, ANYWAY.
WHAT?! YOU'RE NOT SERIOUS!
I'M A FREAK, LIKE VINCENT SAID. MAYBE I'M BETTER OFF STAYING HERE, AWAY FROM EVERYONE ELSE.
YOU'RE NOT A FREAK!
REALLY? THEN HOW COME MY LEG IS ALREADY STARTING TO HEAL?
THAT'S... THAT'S JUST WHO YOU ARE. IT DOESN'T MAKE YOU A FREAK...
WHAT-EVER. LEAVE ME ALONE NOW.

Chapter Two
No Regrets

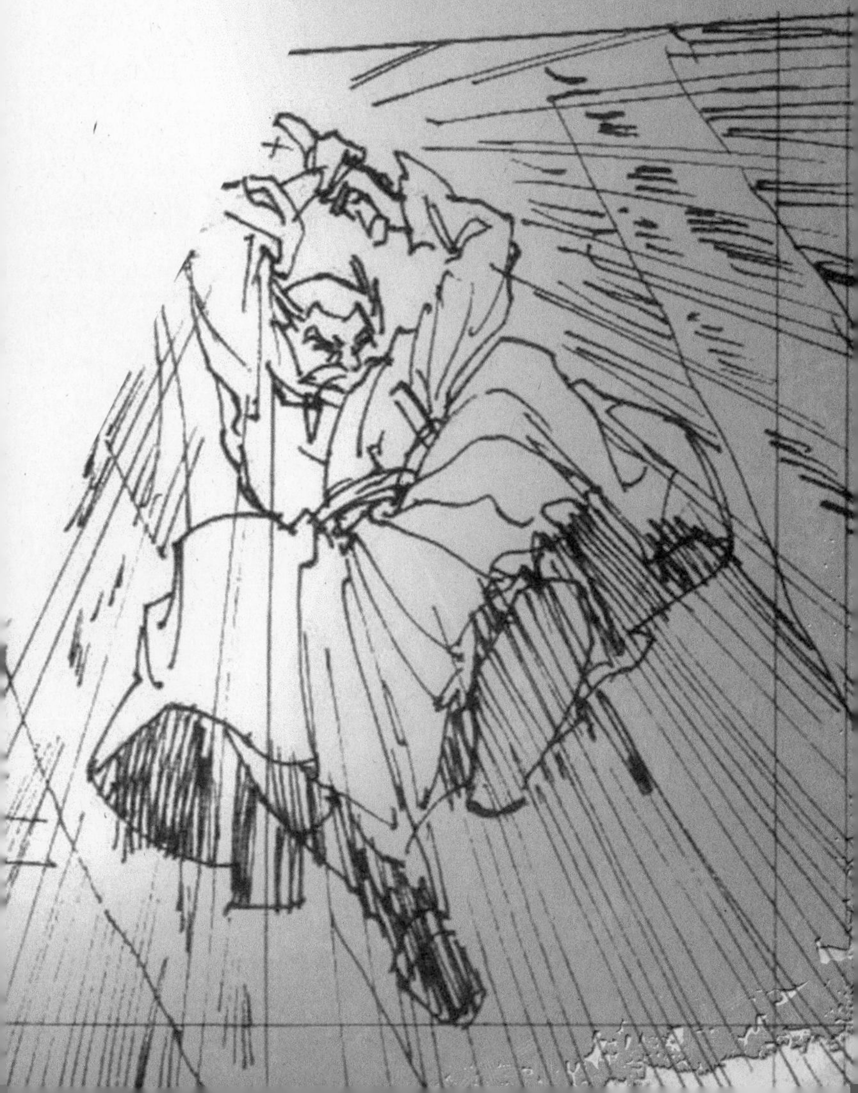

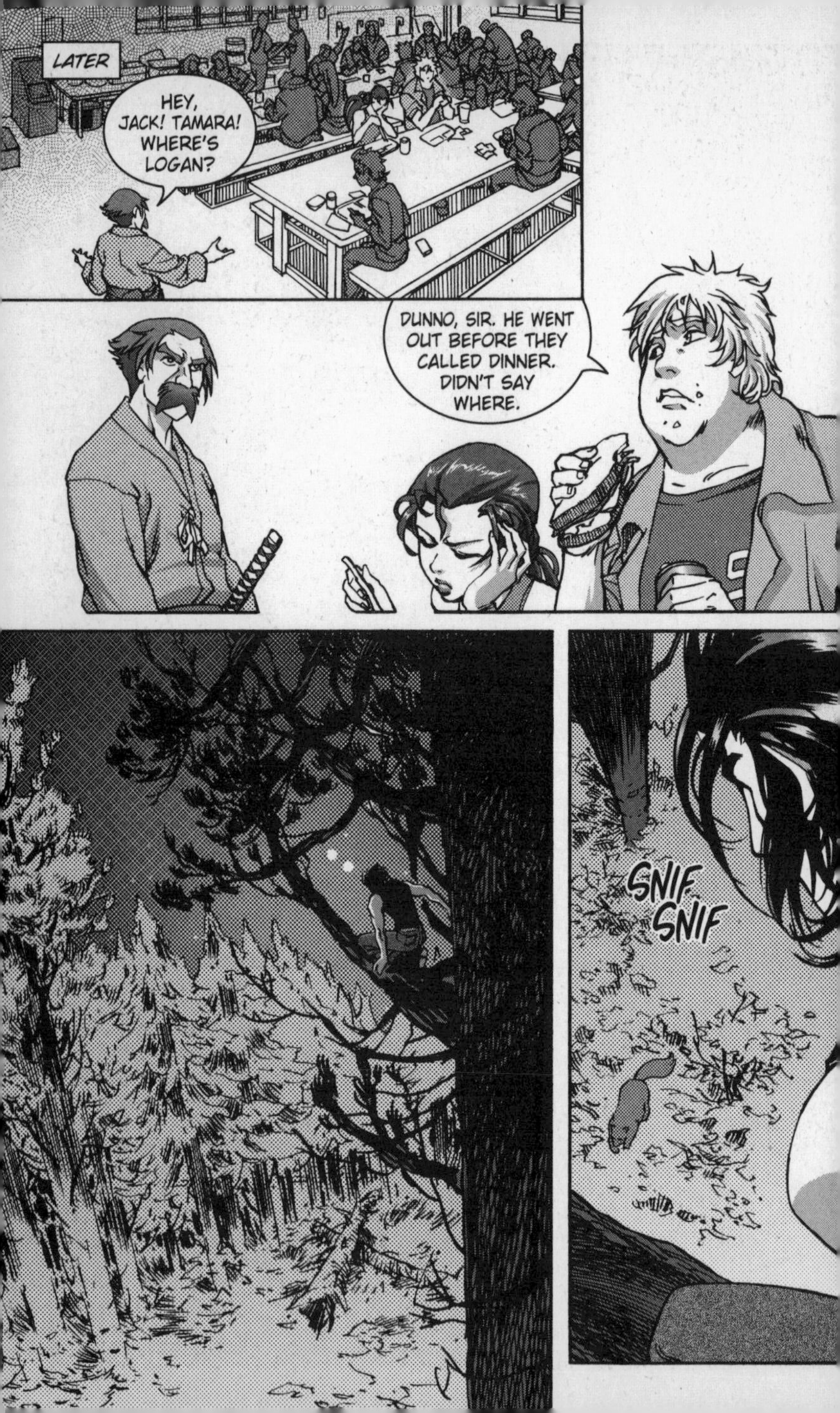

LATER
HEY, JACK! TAMARA! WHERE'S LOGAN?
DUNNO, SIR. HE WENT OUT BEFORE THEY CALLED DINNER. DIDN'T SAY WHERE.
SNIF SNIF

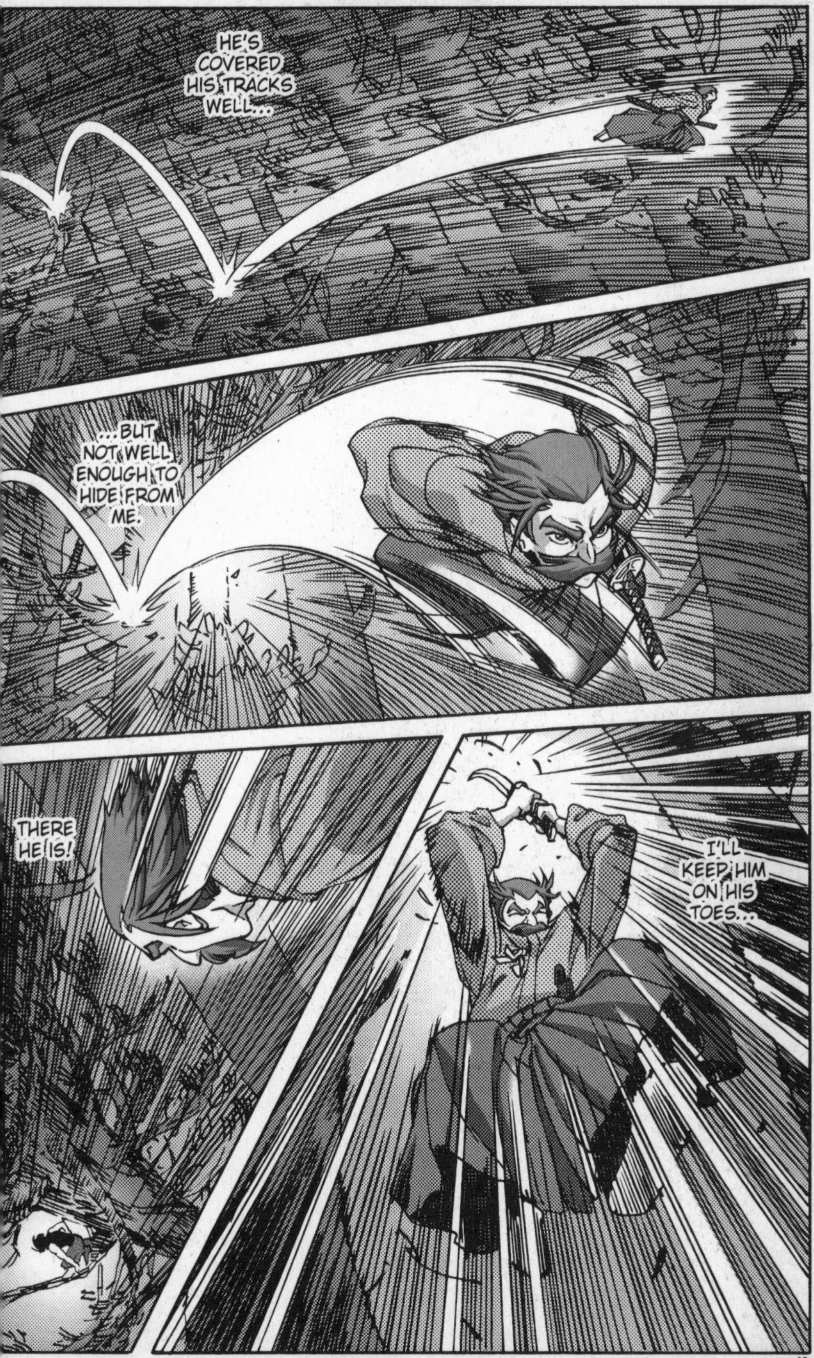
HE'S COVERED HIS TRACKS WELL...
...BUT NOT WELL ENOUGH TO HIDE FROM ME.
THERE HE IS!
I'LL KEEP HIM ON HIS TOES...

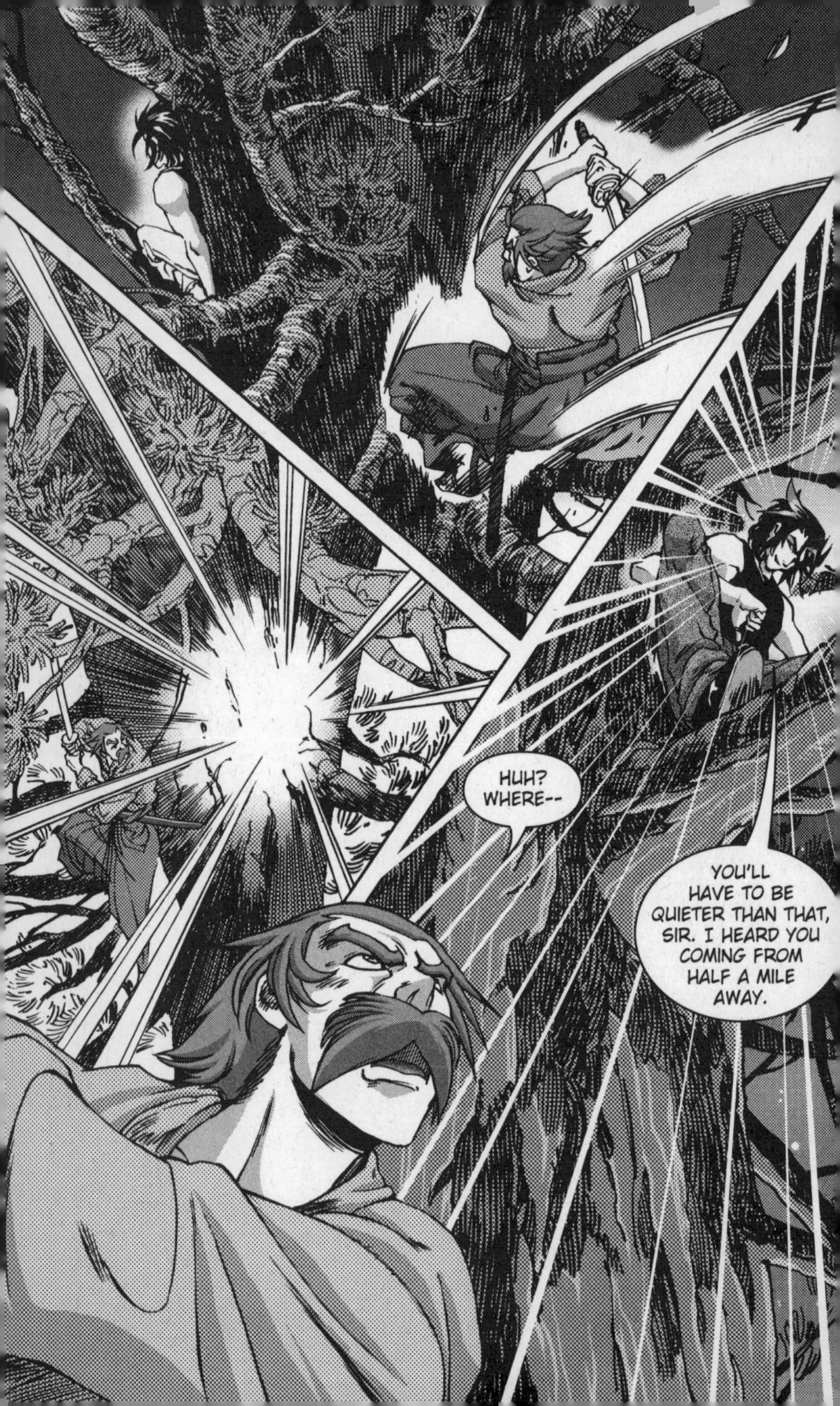
HUH? WHERE--
YOU'LL HAVE TO BE QUIETER THAN THAT, SIR. I HEARD YOU COMING FROM HALF A MILE AWAY.

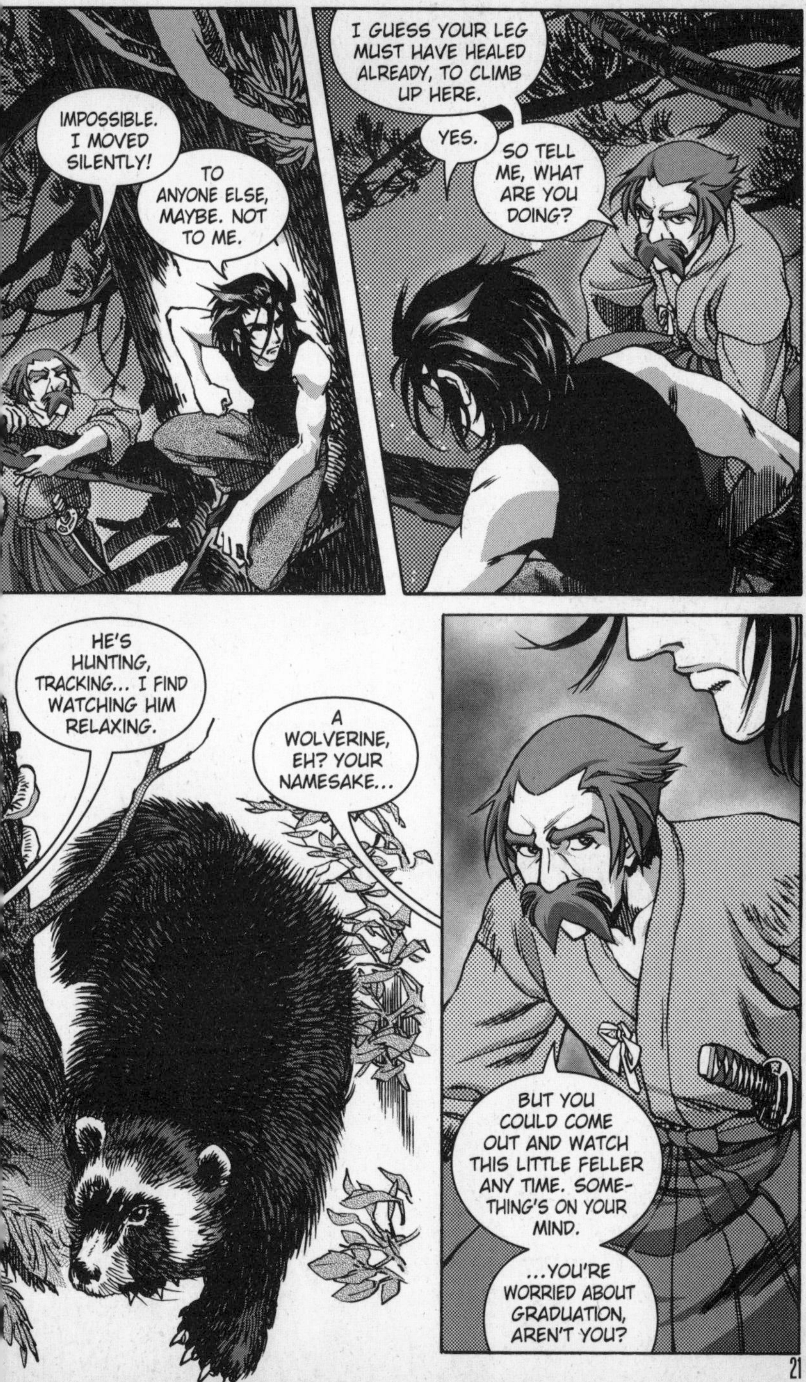
IMPOSSIBLE. I MOVED SILENTLY!
TO ANYONE ELSE, MAYBE. NOT TO ME.
I GUESS YOUR LEG MUST HAVE HEALED ALREADY, TO CLIMB UP HERE.
YES.
SO TELL ME, WHAT ARE YOU DOING?
HE'S HUNTING, TRACKING... I FIND WATCHING HIM RELAXING.
A WOLVERINE, EH? YOUR NAMESAKE...
BUT YOU COULD COME OUT AND WATCH THIS LITTLE FELLER ANY TIME. SOME-THING'S ON YOUR MIND.
...YOU'RE WORRIED ABOUT GRADUATION, AREN'T YOU?

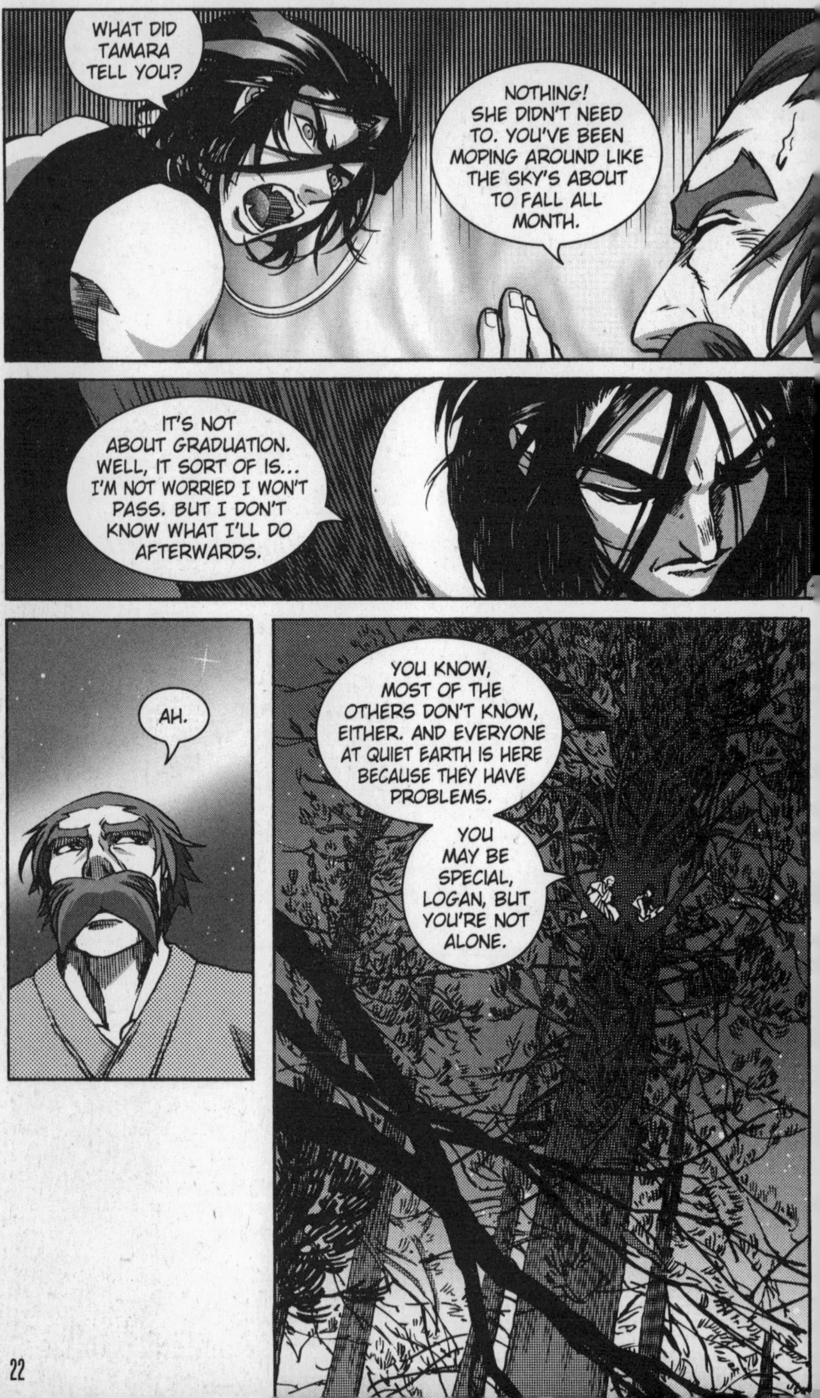
WHAT DID TAMARA TELL YOU?
NOTHING! SHE DIDN'T NEED TO. YOU'VE BEEN MOPING AROUND LIKE THE SKY'S ABOUT TO FALL ALL MONTH.
IT'S NOT ABOUT GRADUATION. WELL, IT SORT OF IS... I'M NOT WORRIED I WON'T PASS. BUT I DON'T KNOW WHAT I'LL DO AFTERWARDS.
AH.
YOU KNOW, MOST OF THE OTHERS DON'T KNOW, EITHER. AND EVERYONE AT QUIET EARTH IS HERE BECAUSE THEY HAVE PROBLEMS.
YOU MAY BE SPECIAL, LOGAN, BUT YOU'RE NOT ALONE.

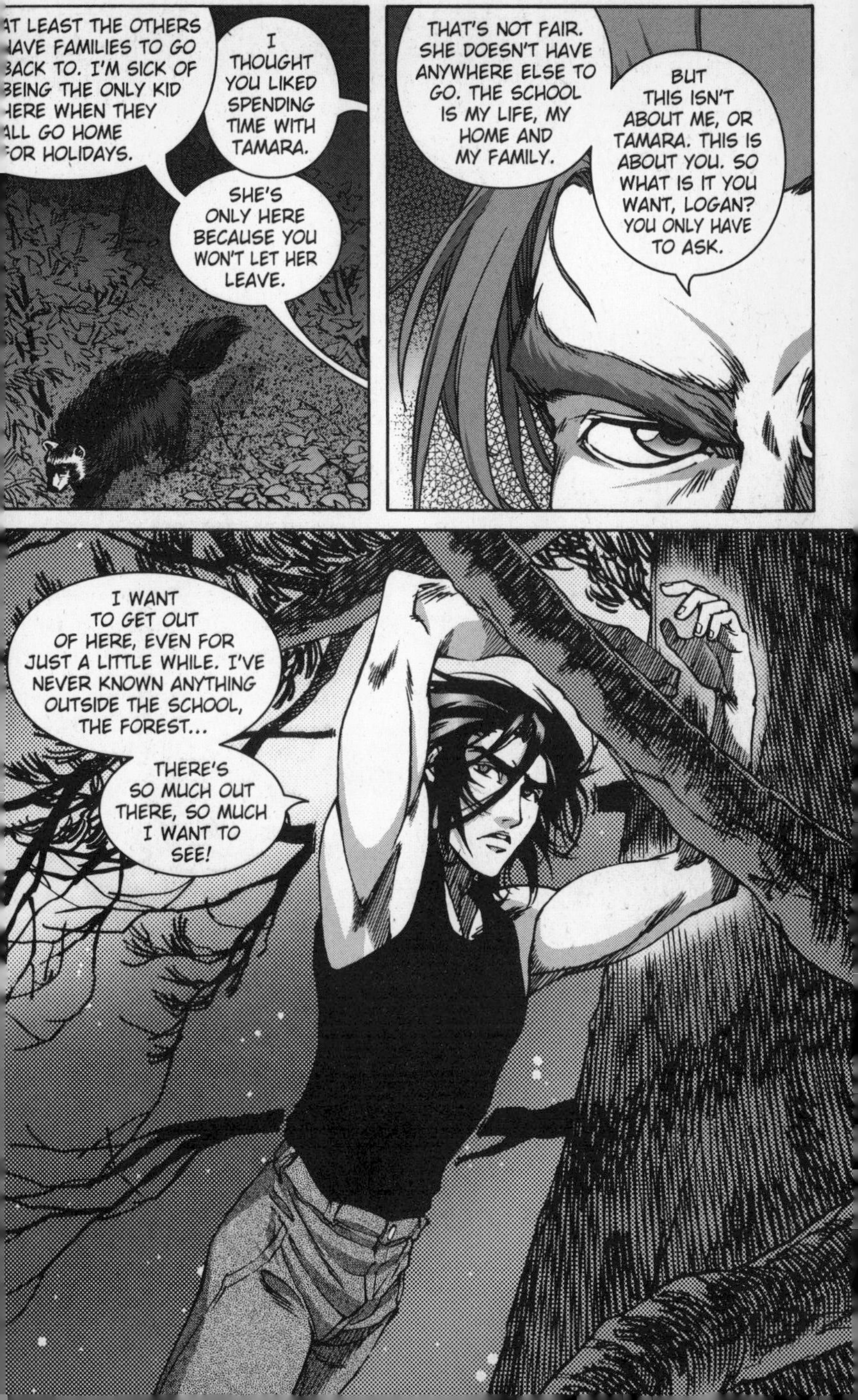
AT LEAST THE OTHERS HAVE FAMILIES TO GO BACK TO. I'M SICK OF BEING THE ONLY KID HERE WHEN THEY ALL GO HOME FOR HOLIDAYS.
I THOUGHT YOU LIKED SPENDING TIME WITH TAMARA.
SHE'S ONLY HERE BECAUSE YOU WON'T LET HER LEAVE.
THAT'S NOT FAIR. SHE DOESN'T HAVE ANYWHERE ELSE TO GO. THE SCHOOL IS MY LIFE, MY HOME AND MY FAMILY.
BUT THIS ISN'T ABOUT ME, OR TAMARA. THIS IS ABOUT YOU. SO WHAT IS IT YOU WANT, LOGAN? YOU ONLY HAVE TO ASK.
I WANT TO GET OUT OF HERE, EVEN FOR JUST A LITTLE WHILE. I'VE NEVER KNOWN ANYTHING OUTSIDE THE SCHOOL, THE FOREST...
THERE'S SO MUCH OUT THERE, SO MUCH I WANT TO SEE!

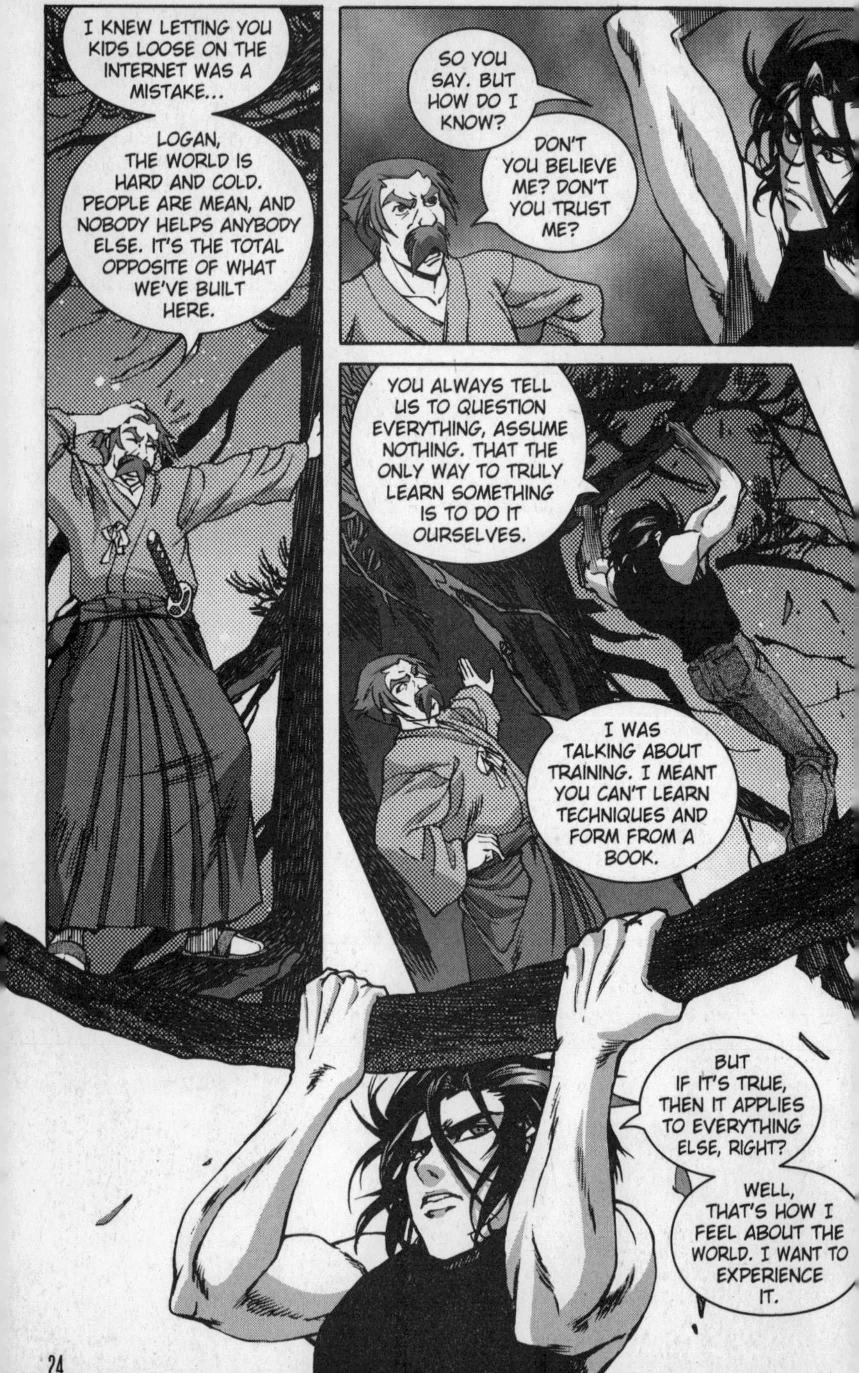
I KNEW LETTING YOU KIDS LOOSE ON THE INTERNET WAS A MISTAKE...
LOGAN, THE WORLD IS HARD AND COLD. PEOPLE ARE MEAN, AND NOBODY HELPS ANYBODY ELSE. IT'S THE TOTAL OPPOSITE OF WHAT WE'VE BUILT HERE.
SO YOU SAY. BUT HOW DO I KNOW?
DON'T YOU BELIEVE ME? DON'T YOU TRUST ME?
YOU ALWAYS TELL US TO QUESTION EVERYTHING, ASSUME NOTHING. THAT THE ONLY WAY TO TRULY LEARN SOMETHING IS TO DO IT OURSELVES.
I WAS TALKING ABOUT TRAINING. I MEANT YOU CAN'T LEARN TECHNIQUES AND FORM FROM A BOOK.
BUT IF IT'S TRUE, THEN IT APPLIES TO EVERYTHING ELSE, RIGHT?
WELL, THAT'S HOW I FEEL ABOUT THE WORLD. I WANT TO EXPERIENCE IT.

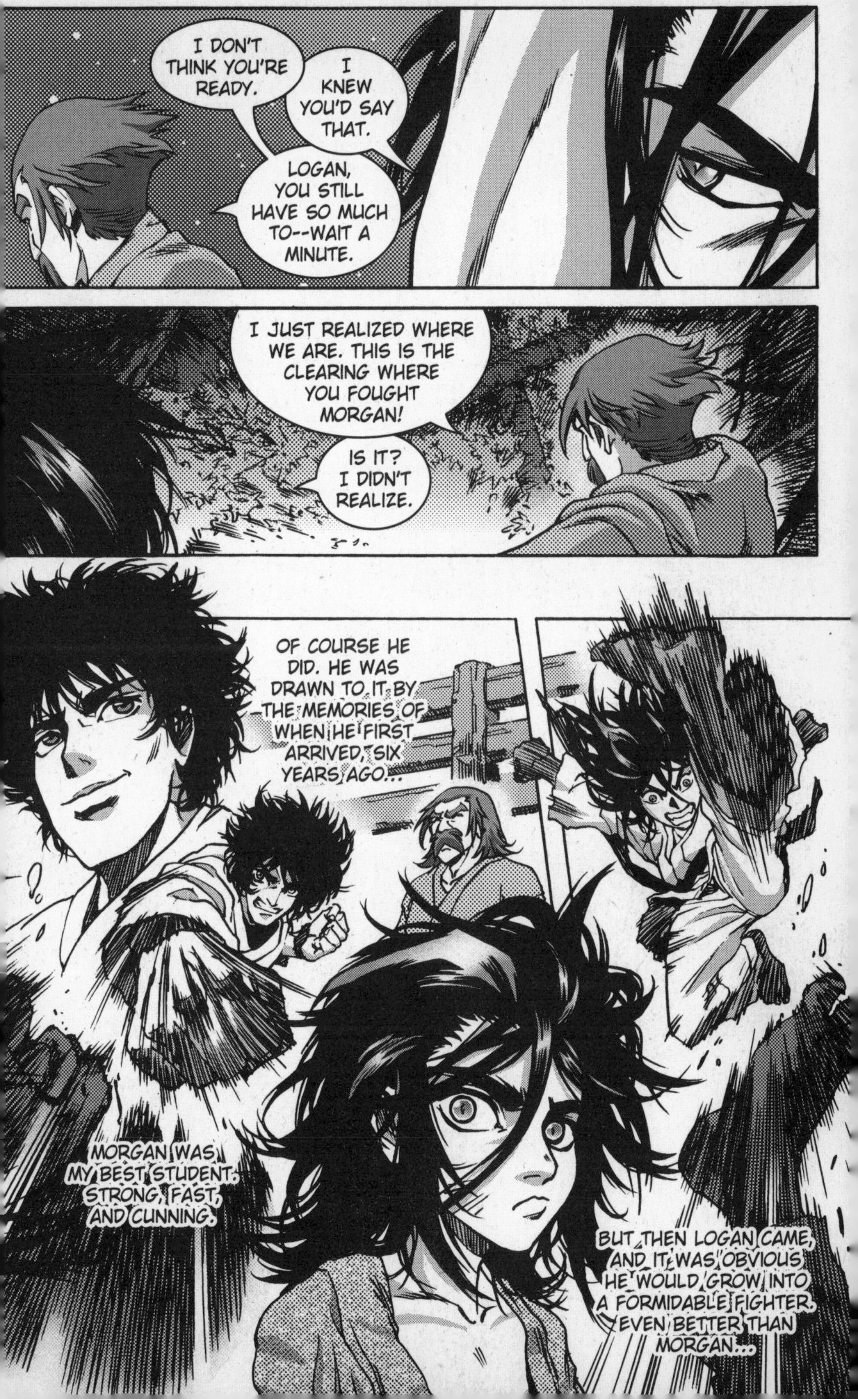
I DON'T THINK YOU'RE READY.
I KNEW YOU'D SAY THAT.
LOGAN, YOU STILL HAVE SO MUCH TO--WAIT A MINUTE.
I JUST REALIZED WHERE WE ARE. THIS IS THE CLEARING WHERE YOU FOUGHT MORGAN!
IS IT? I DIDN'T REALIZE.
OF COURSE HE DID. HE WAS DRAWN TO IT BY THE MEMORIES OF WHEN HE FIRST ARRIVED, SIX YEARS AGO...
MORGAN WAS MY BEST STUDENT. STRONG, FAST, AND CUNNING.
BUT THEN LOGAN CAME, AND IT WAS OBVIOUS HE WOULD GROW INTO A FORMIDABLE FIGHTER. EVEN BETTER THAN MORGAN...

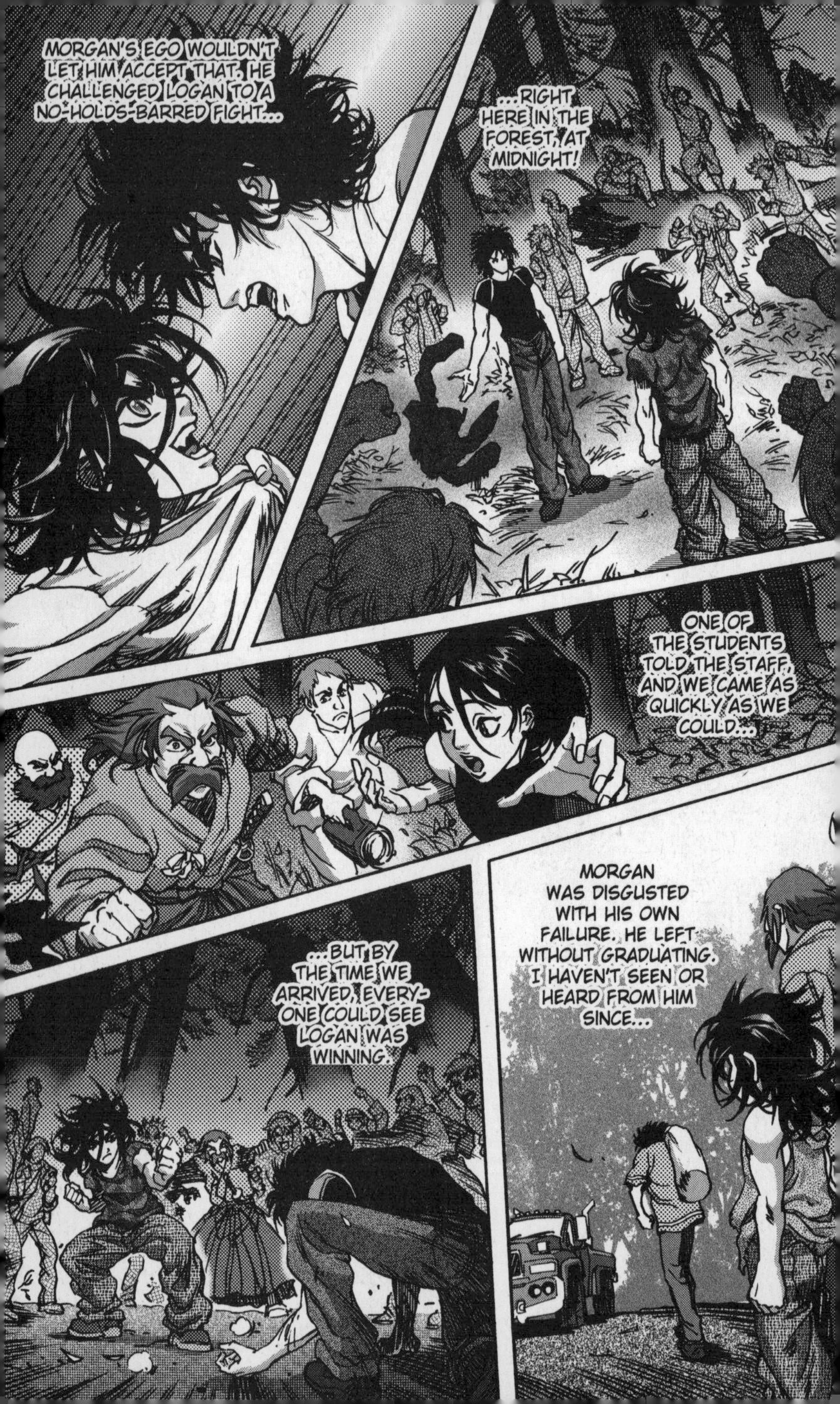

MORGAN'S EGO WOULDN'T LET HIM ACCEPT THAT. HE CHALLENGED LOGAN TO A NO-HOLDS-BARRED FIGHT...
...RIGHT HERE IN THE FOREST, AT MIDNIGHT!
ONE OF THE STUDENTS TOLD THE STAFF, AND WE CAME AS QUICKLY AS WE COULD...
...BUT BY THE TIME WE ARRIVED, EVERY-ONE COULD SEE LOGAN WAS WINNING.
MORGAN WAS DISGUSTED WITH HIS OWN FAILURE. HE LEFT WITHOUT GRADUATING. I HAVEN'T SEEN OR HEARD FROM HIM SINCE...

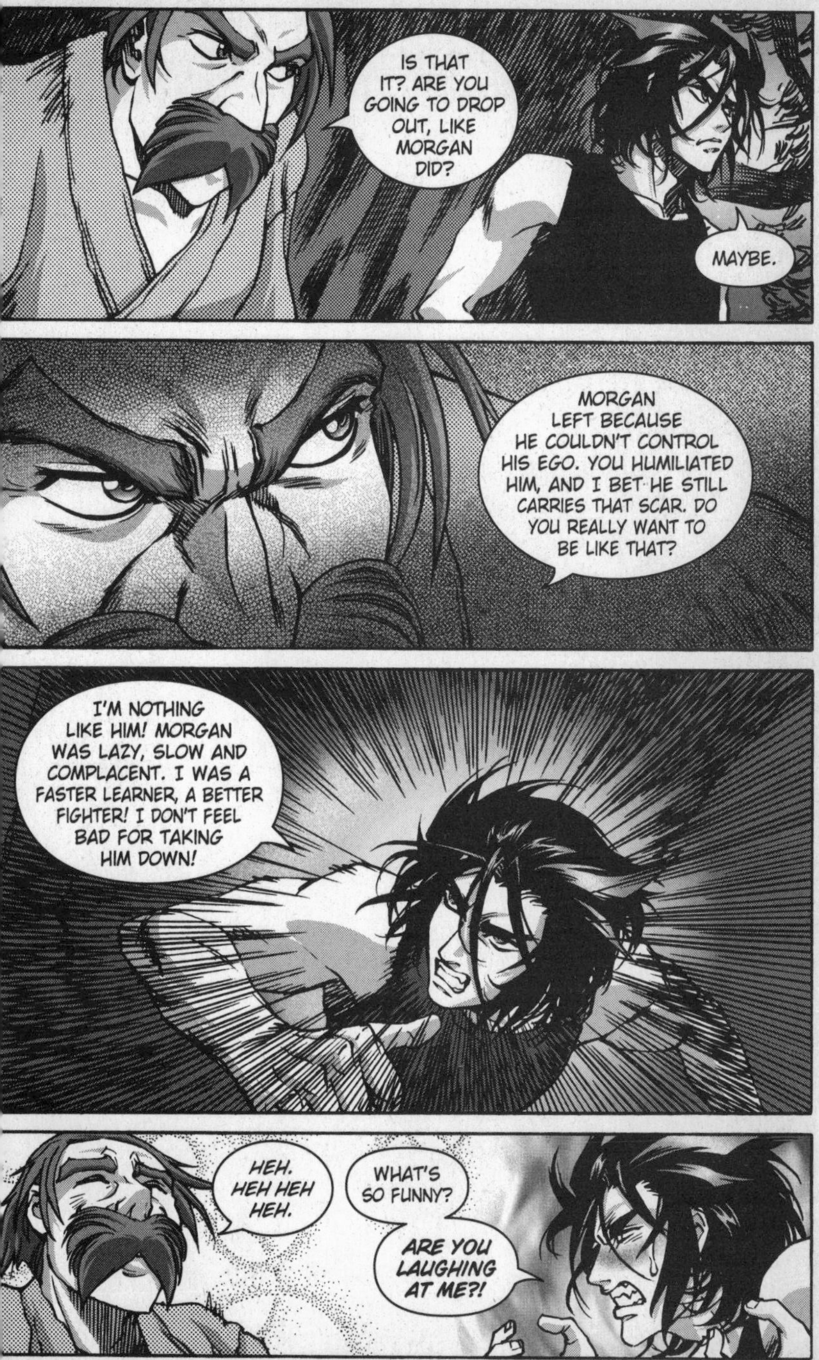
IS THAT IT? ARE YOU GOING TO DROP OUT, LIKE MORGAN DID?
MAYBE.
MORGAN LEFT BECAUSE HE COULDN'T CONTROL HIS EGO. YOU HUMILIATED HIM, AND I BET HE STILL CARRIES THAT SCAR. DO YOU REALLY WANT TO BE LIKE THAT?
I'M NOTHING LIKE HIM! MORGAN WAS LAZY, SLOW AND COMPLACENT. I WAS A FASTER LEARNER, A BETTER FIGHTER! I DON'T FEEL BAD FOR TAKING HIM DOWN!
HEH. HEH HEH HEH.
WHAT'S SO FUNNY?
ARE YOU LAUGHING AT ME?!

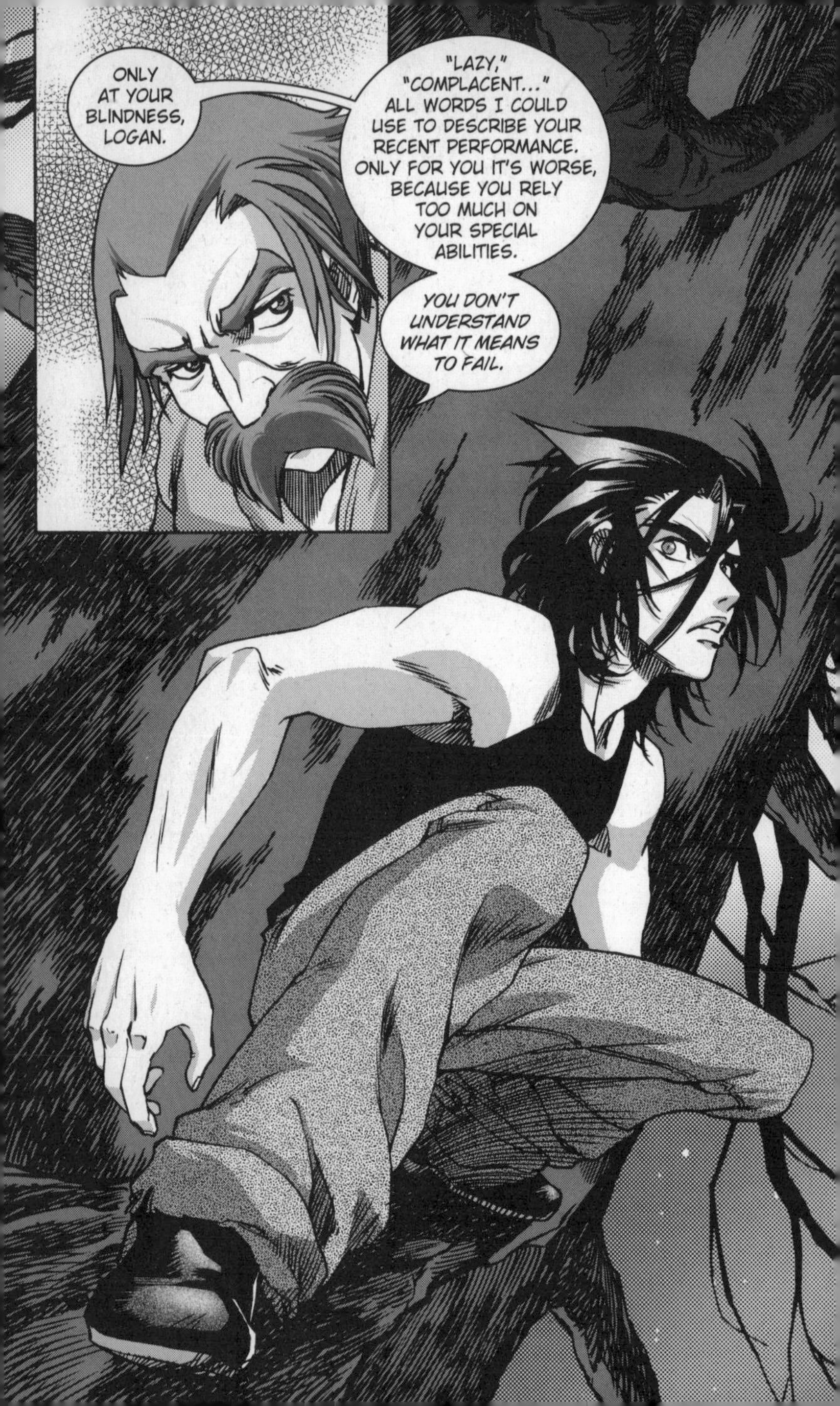
ONLY AT YOUR BLINDNESS, LOGAN.
"LAZY," "COMPLACENT..." ALL WORDS I COULD USE TO DESCRIBE YOUR RECENT PERFORMANCE. ONLY FOR YOU IT'S WORSE, BECAUSE YOU RELY TOO MUCH ON YOUR SPECIAL ABILITIES.
YOU DON'T UNDERSTAND WHAT IT MEANS TO FAIL.

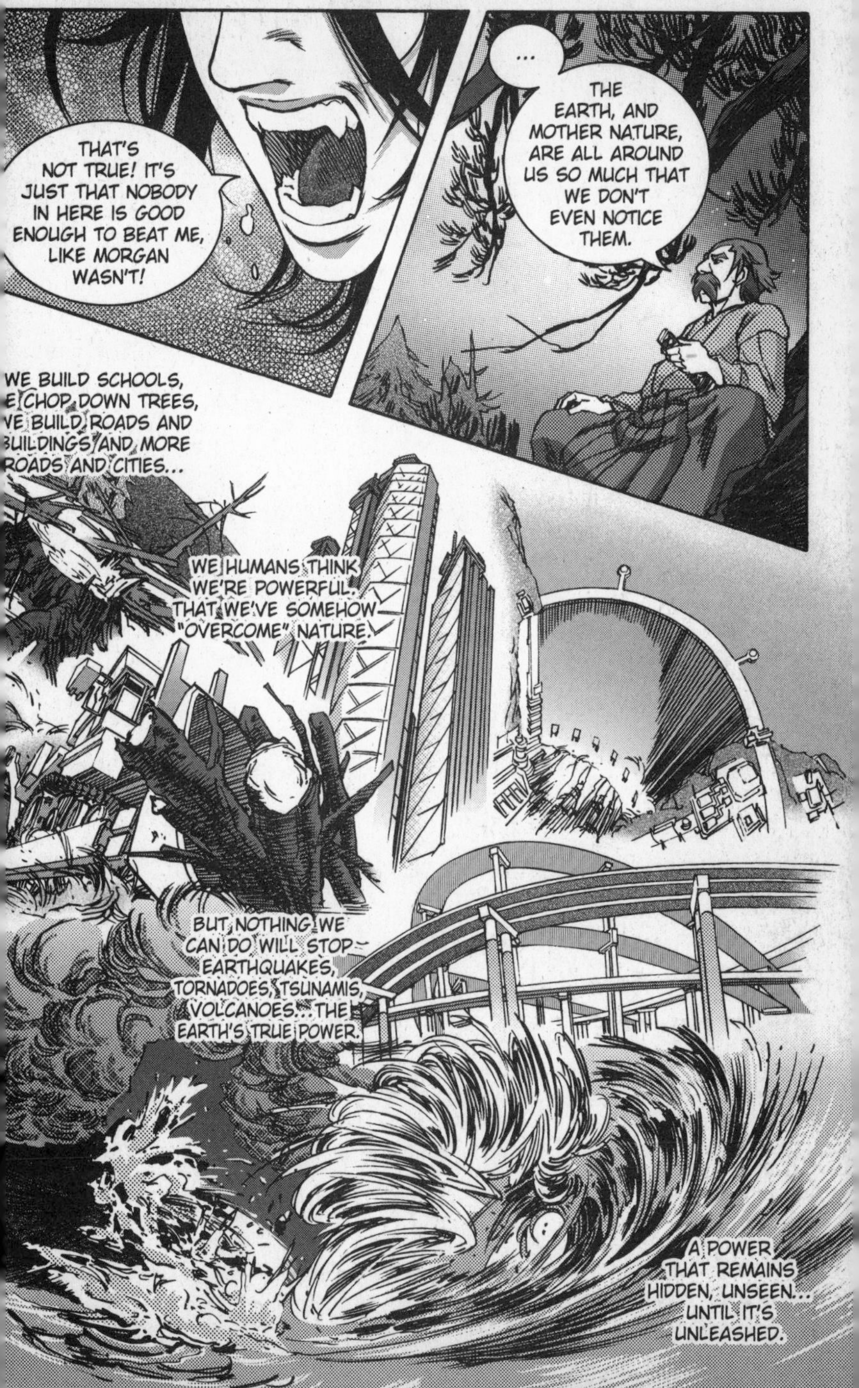

THAT'S NOT TRUE! IT'S JUST THAT NOBODY IN HERE IS GOOD ENOUGH TO BEAT ME, LIKE MORGAN WASN'T!
...
THE EARTH, AND MOTHER NATURE, ARE ALL AROUND US SO MUCH THAT WE DON'T EVEN NOTICE THEM.
WE BUILD SCHOOLS, E CHOP DOWN TREES, VE BUILD ROADS AND UILDINGS AND MORE ROADS AND CITIES...
WE HUMANS THINK WE'RE POWERFUL. THAT WE'VE SOMEHOW "OVERCOME" NATURE.
BUT NOTHING WE CAN DO WILL STOP EARTHQUAKES, TORNADOES, TSUNAMIS, VOLCANOES... THE EARTH'S TRUE POWER.
A POWER THAT REMAINS HIDDEN, UNSEEN... UNTIL IT'S UNLEASHED.

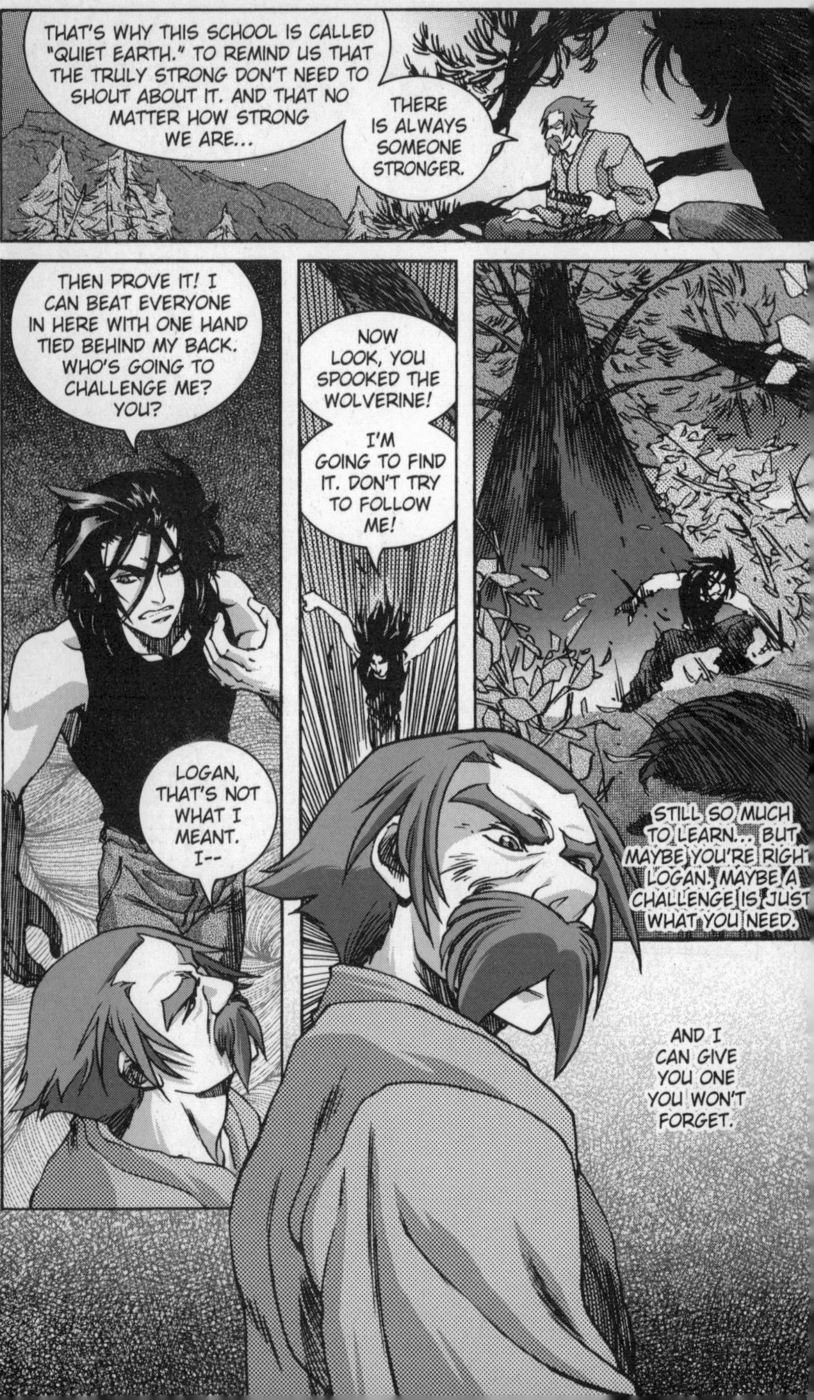
THAT'S WHY THIS SCHOOL IS CALLED "QUIET EARTH." TO REMIND US THAT THE TRULY STRONG DON'T NEED TO SHOUT ABOUT IT. AND THAT NO MATTER HOW STRONG WE ARE...
THERE IS ALWAYS SOMEONE STRONGER.
THEN PROVE IT! I CAN BEAT EVERYONE IN HERE WITH ONE HAND TIED BEHIND MY BACK. WHO'S GOING TO CHALLENGE ME? YOU?
LOGAN, THAT'S NOT WHAT I MEANT. I--
NOW LOOK, YOU SPOOKED THE WOLVERINE!
I'M GOING TO FIND IT. DON'T TRY TO FOLLOW ME!
STILL SO MUCH TO LEARN... BUT MAYBE YOU'RE RIGHT LOGAN. MAYBE A CHALLENGE IS JUST WHAT YOU NEED.
AND I CAN GIVE YOU ONE YOU WON'T FORGET.

Chapter Three
Careful What You Wish For

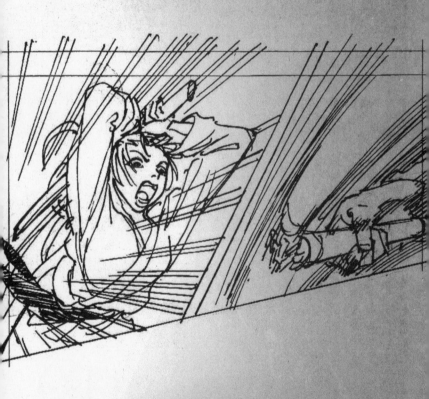

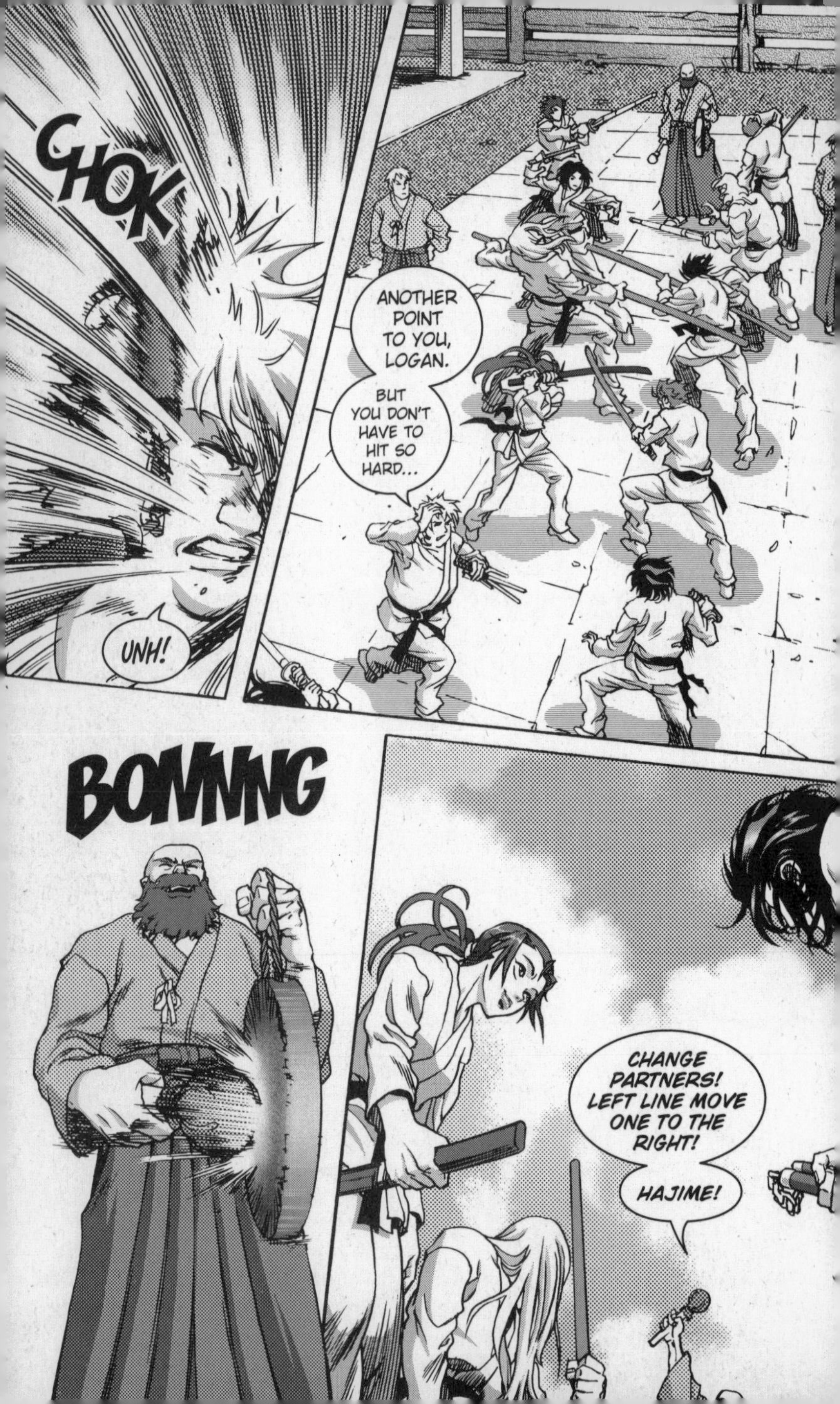
CHOK
UNH!
ANOTHER POINT TO YOU, LOGAN.
BUT YOU DON'T HAVE TO HIT SO HARD...
BONNNG
CHANGE PARTNERS! LEFT LINE MOVE ONE TO THE RIGHT!
HAJIME!

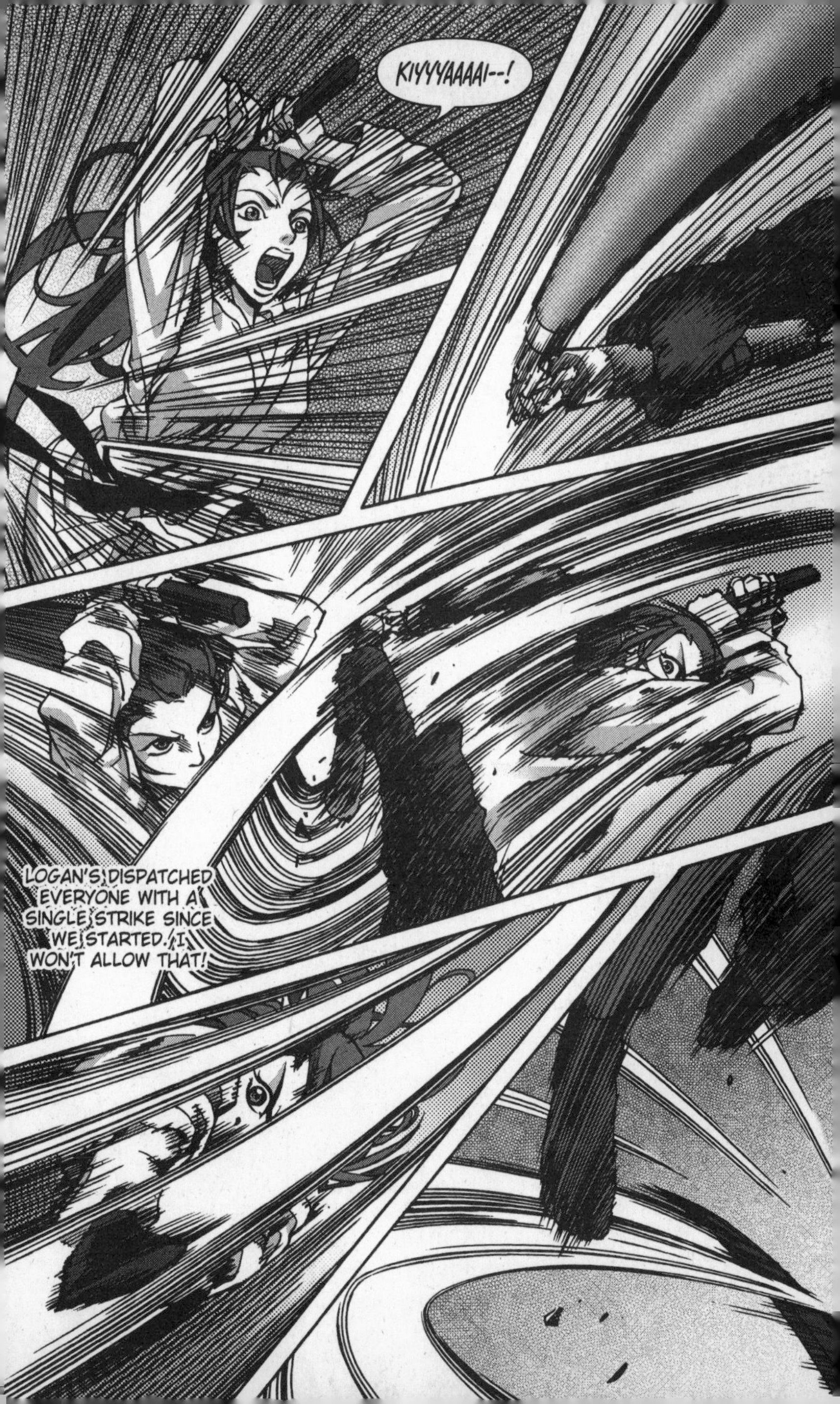
KIYYYAAAAI--!
LOGAN'S DISPATCHED EVERYONE WITH A SINGLE STRIKE SINCE WE STARTED. I WON'T ALLOW THAT!

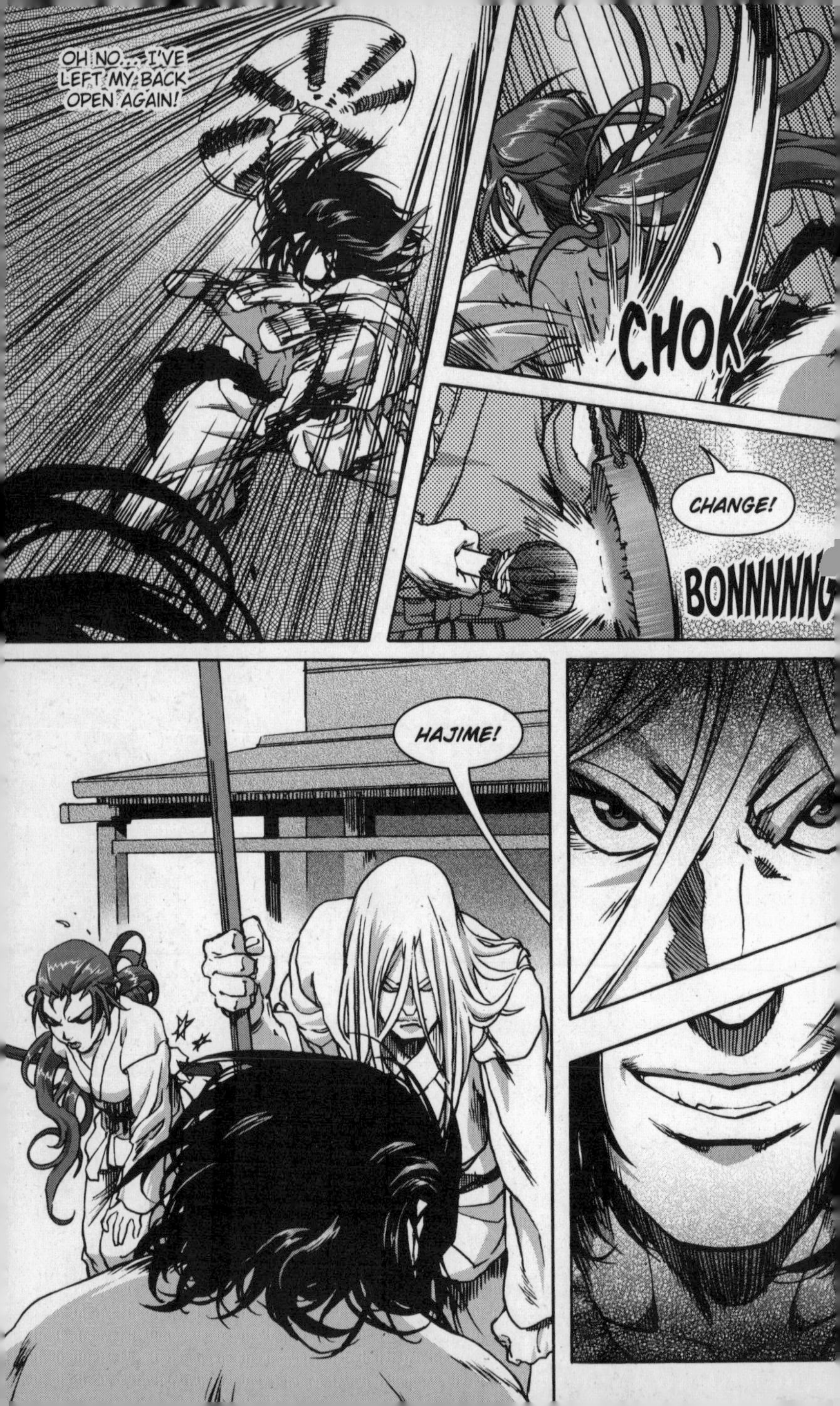
OH NO... I'VE LEFT MY BACK OPEN AGAIN!
CHOK
CHANGE!
BONNNNNG
HAJIME!

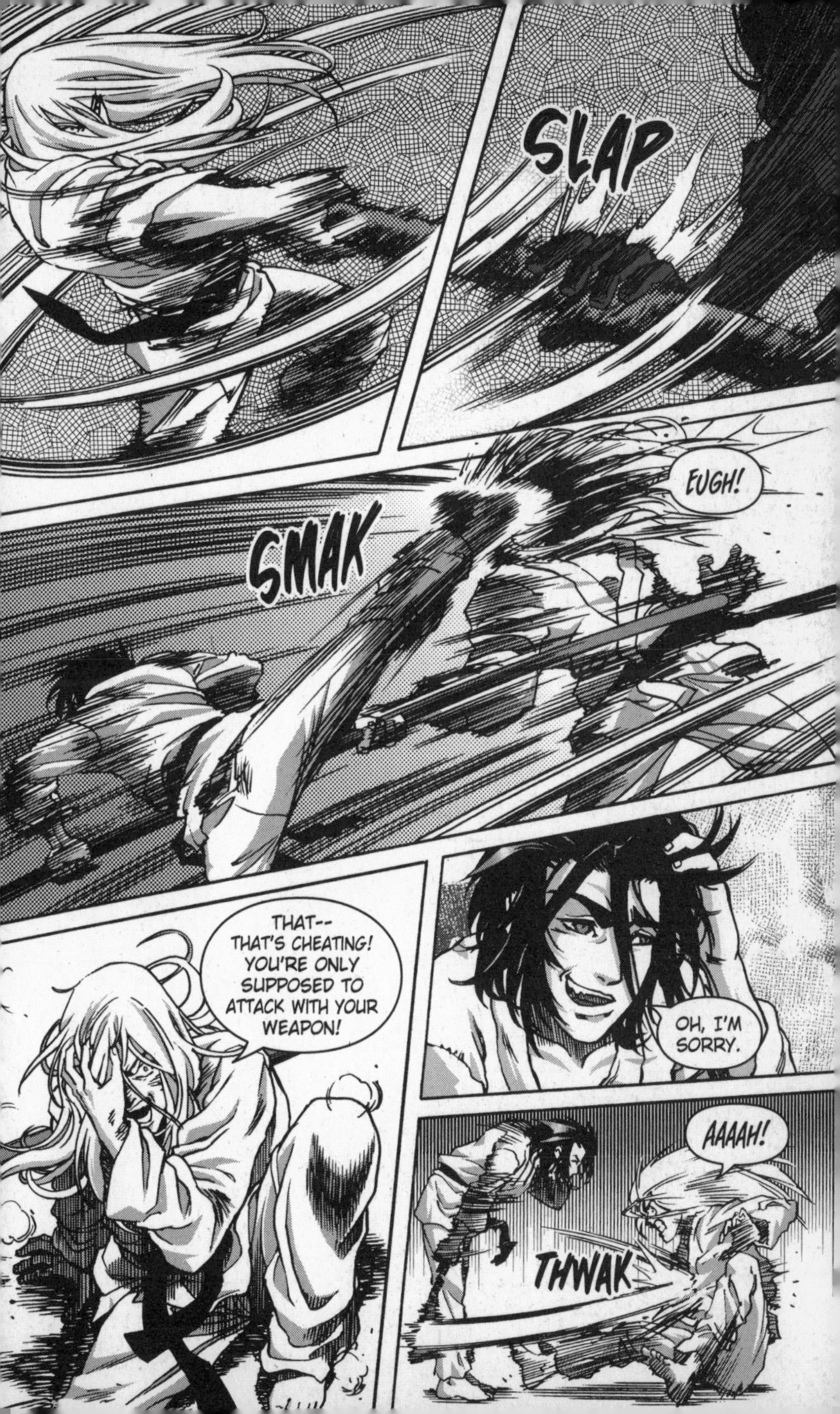
SLAP
EUGH!
SMAK
THAT--
THAT'S CHEATING! YOU'RE ONLY SUPPOSED TO ATTACK WITH YOUR WEAPON!
OH, I'M SORRY.
AAAAH!
THWAK

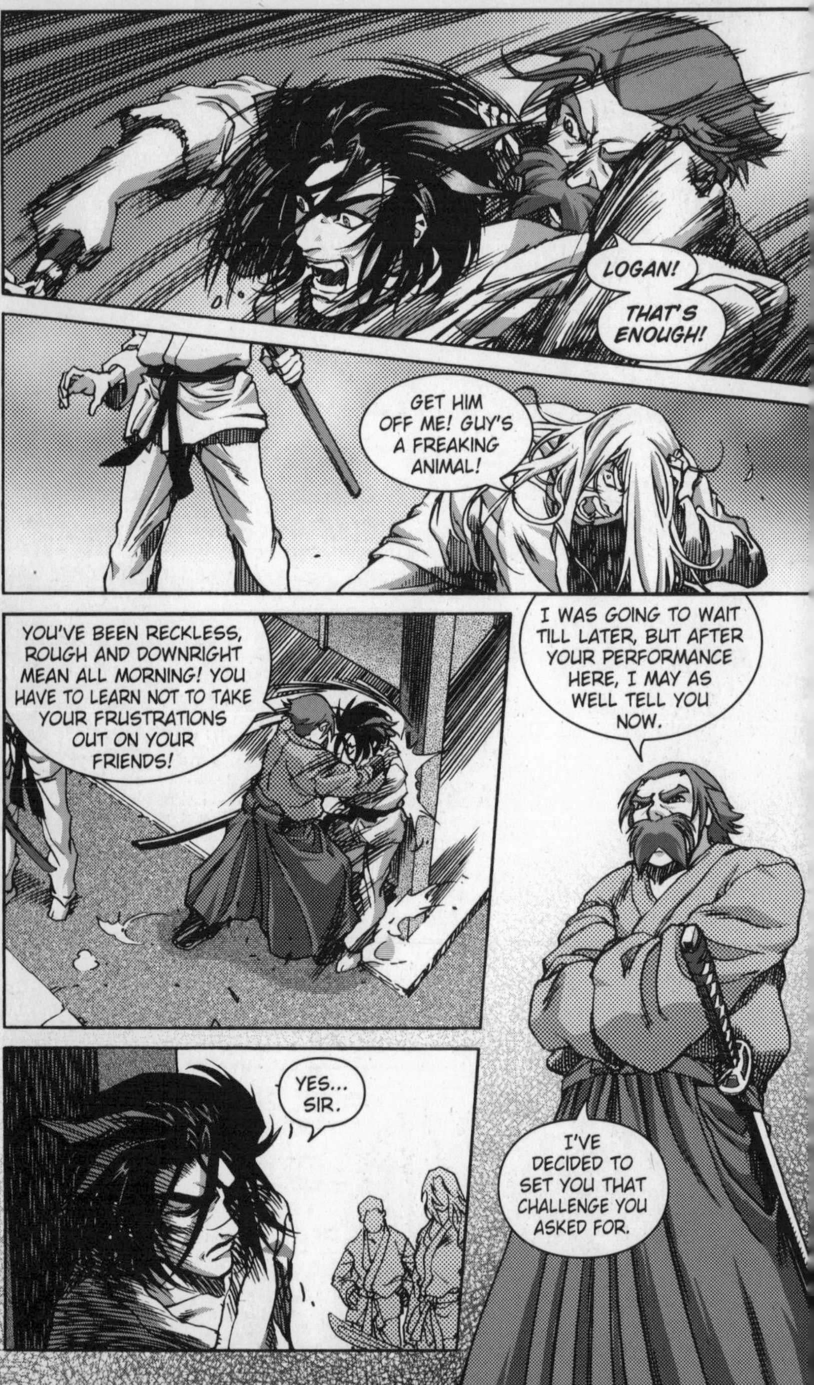
LOGAN!
THAT'S ENOUGH!
GET HIM OFF ME! GUY'S A FREAKING ANIMAL!
YOU'VE BEEN RECKLESS, ROUGH AND DOWNRIGHT MEAN ALL MORNING! YOU HAVE TO LEARN NOT TO TAKE YOUR FRUSTRATIONS OUT ON YOUR FRIENDS!
YES... SIR.
I WAS GOING TO WAIT TILL LATER, BUT AFTER YOUR PERFORMANCE HERE, I MAY AS WELL TELL YOU NOW.
I'VE DECIDED TO SET YOU THAT CHALLENGE YOU ASKED FOR.

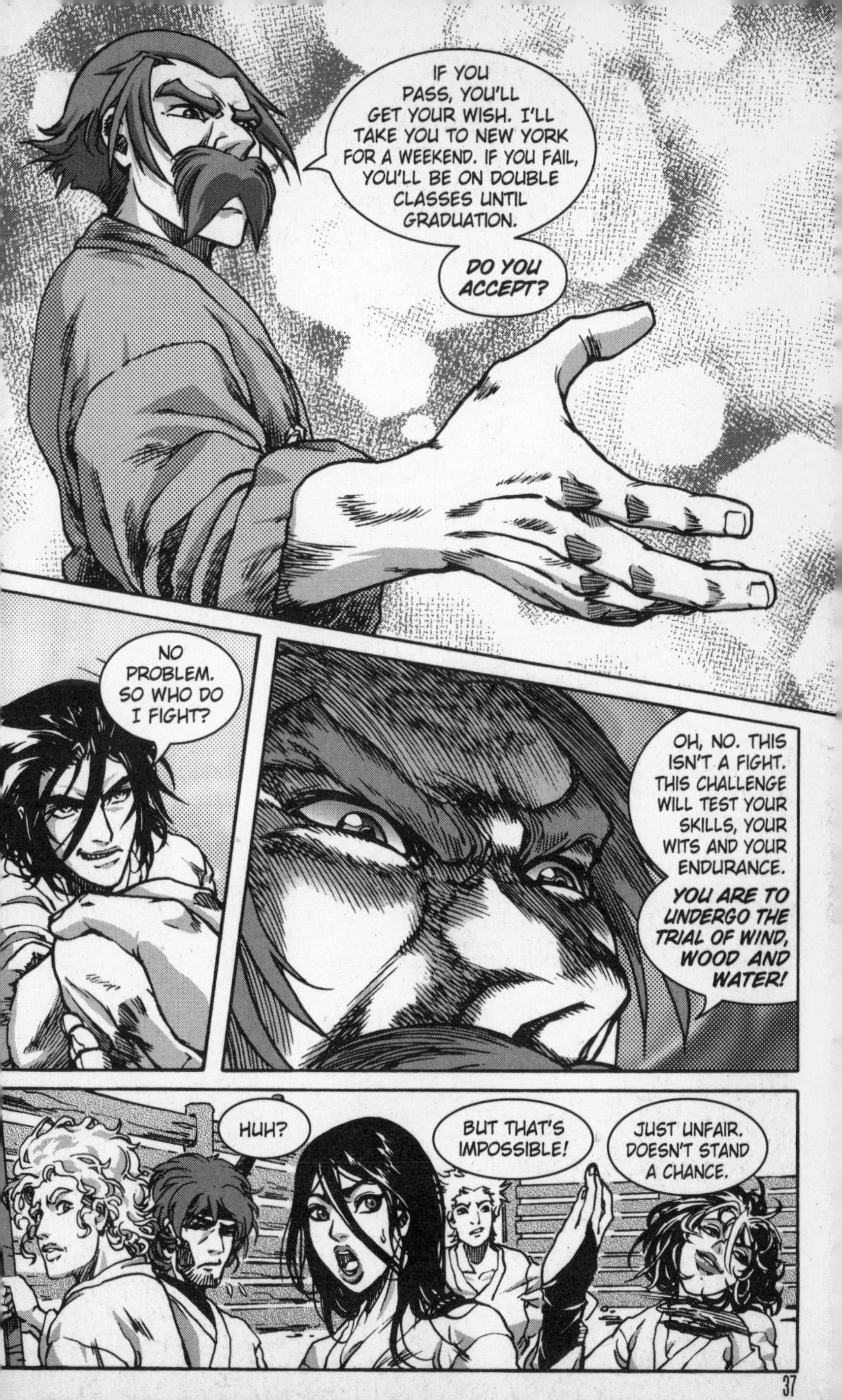
IF YOU PASS, YOU'LL GET YOUR WISH. I'LL TAKE YOU TO NEW YORK FOR A WEEKEND. IF YOU FAIL, YOU'LL BE ON DOUBLE CLASSES UNTIL GRADUATION.
DO YOU ACCEPT?
NO PROBLEM. SO WHO DO I FIGHT?
OH, NO. THIS ISN'T A FIGHT. THIS CHALLENGE WILL TEST YOUR SKILLS, YOUR WITS AND YOUR ENDURANCE.
YOU ARE TO UNDERGO THE TRIAL OF WIND, WOOD AND WATER!
HUH?
BUT THAT'S IMPOSSIBLE!
JUST UNFAIR. DOESN'T STAND A CHANCE.

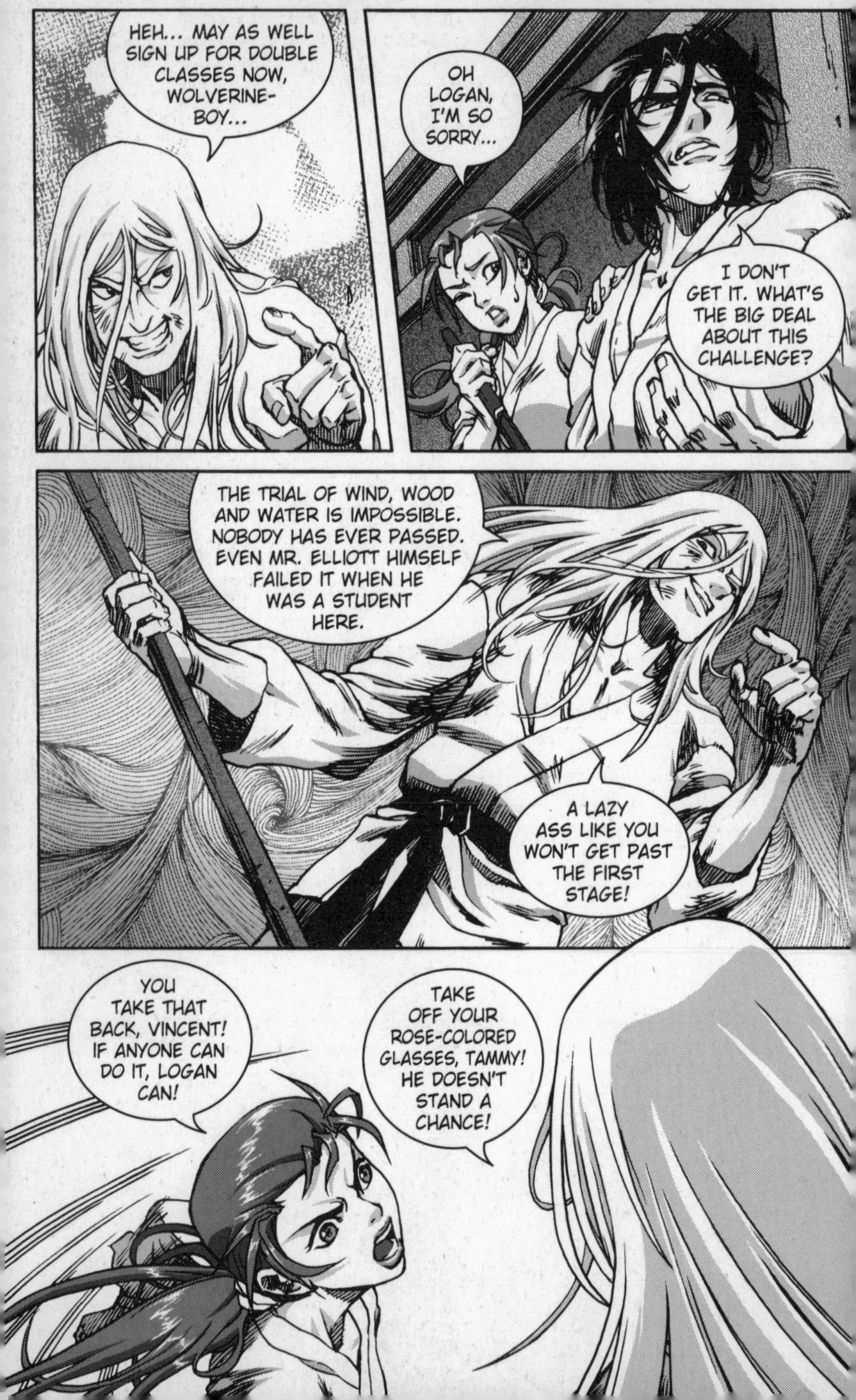
HEH... MAY AS WELL SIGN UP FOR DOUBLE CLASSES NOW, WOLVERINE-BOY...
OH LOGAN, I'M SO SORRY...
I DON'T GET IT. WHAT'S THE BIG DEAL ABOUT THIS CHALLENGE?
THE TRIAL OF WIND, WOOD AND WATER IS IMPOSSIBLE. NOBODY HAS EVER PASSED. EVEN MR. ELLIOTT HIMSELF FAILED IT WHEN HE WAS A STUDENT HERE.
A LAZY ASS LIKE YOU WON'T GET PAST THE FIRST STAGE!
YOU TAKE THAT BACK, VINCENT! IF ANYONE CAN DO IT, LOGAN CAN!
TAKE OFF YOUR ROSE-COLORED GLASSES, TAMMY! HE DOESN'T STAND A CHANCE!

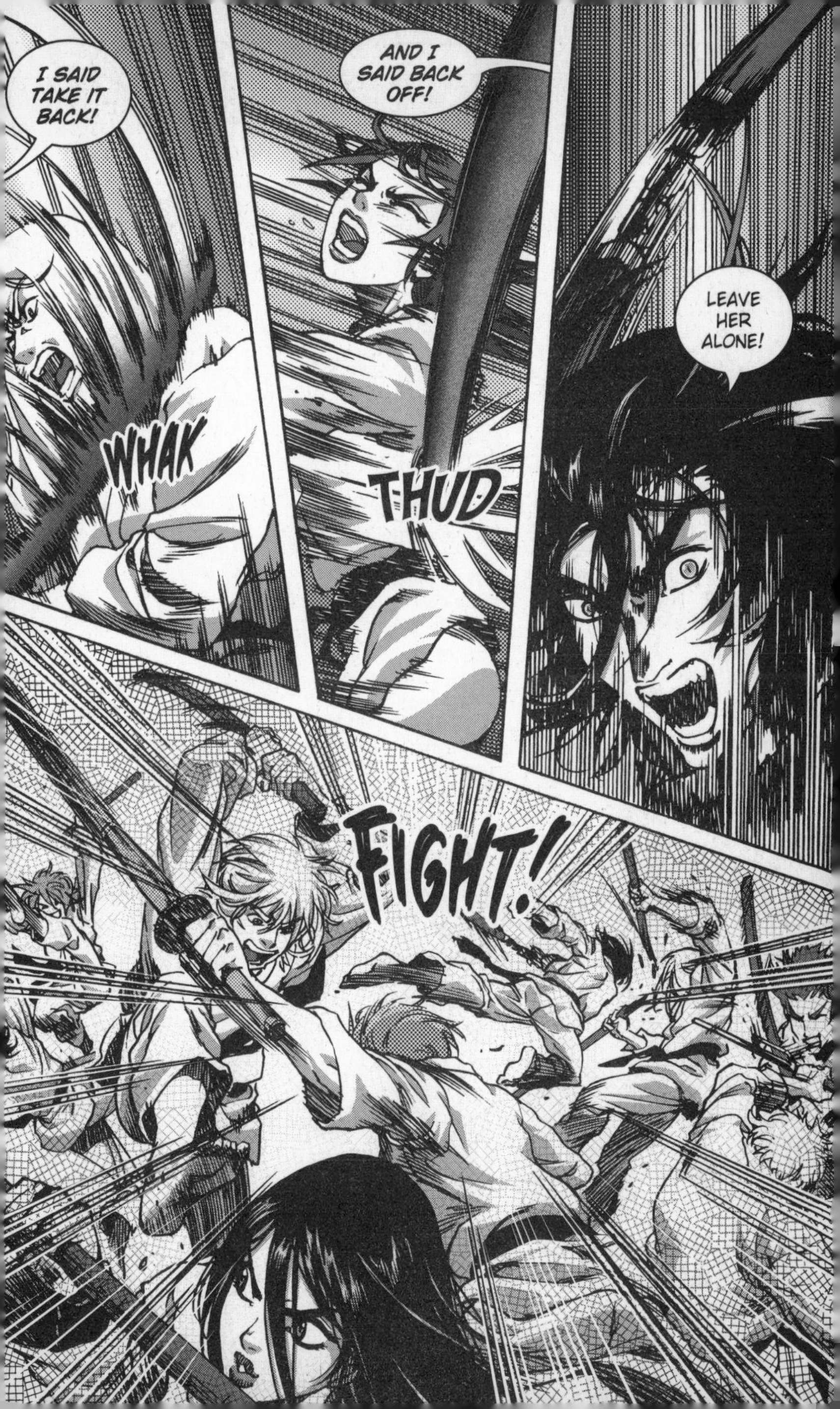
I SAID TAKE IT BACK!
WHAK
AND I SAID BACK OFF!
THUD
LEAVE HER ALONE!
FIGHT!

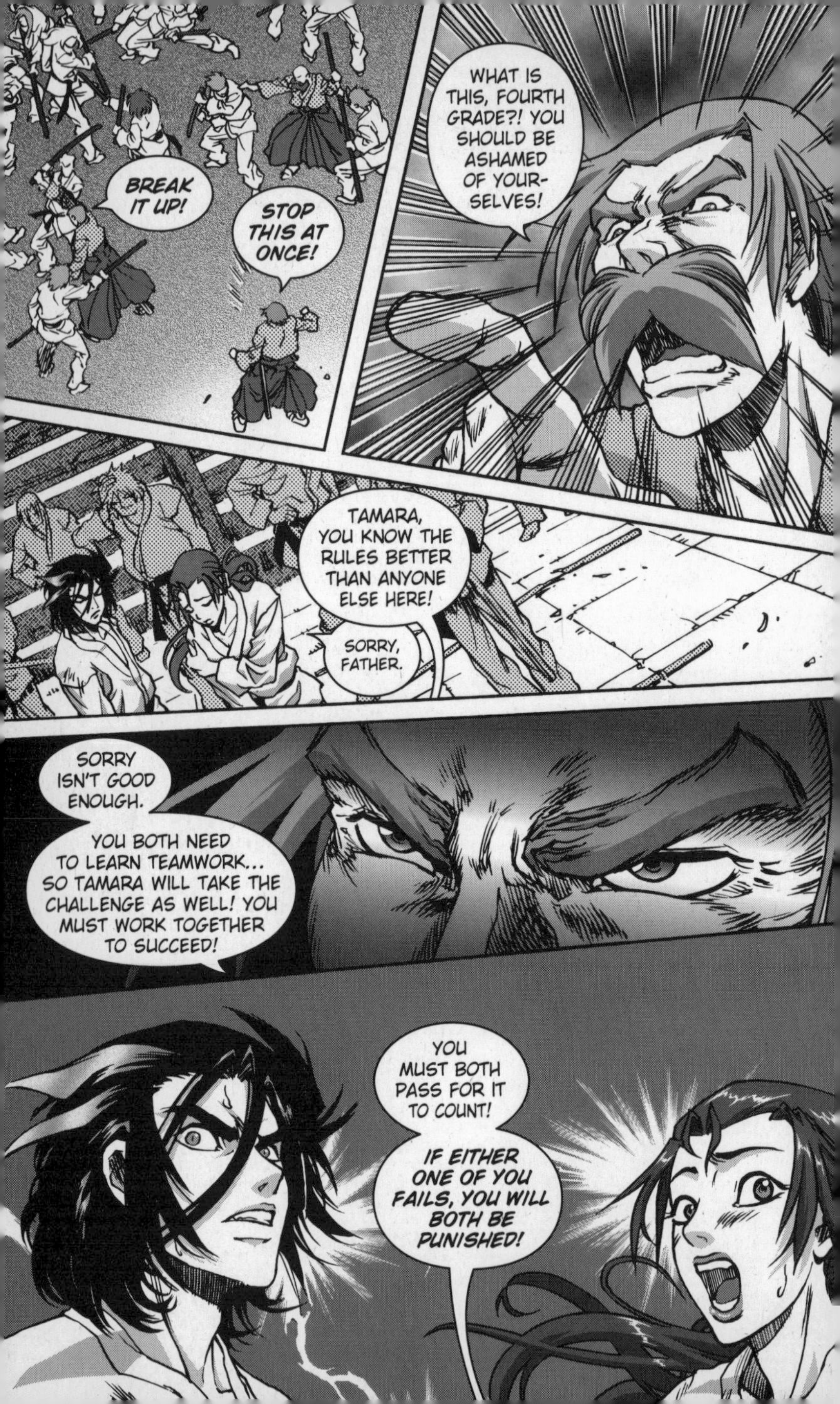
BREAK IT UP!
STOP THIS AT ONCE!
WHAT IS THIS, FOURTH GRADE?! YOU SHOULD BE ASHAMED OF YOUR-SELVES!
TAMARA, YOU KNOW THE RULES BETTER THAN ANYONE ELSE HERE!
SORRY, FATHER.
SORRY ISN'T GOOD ENOUGH.
YOU BOTH NEED TO LEARN TEAMWORK... SO TAMARA WILL TAKE THE CHALLENGE AS WELL! YOU MUST WORK TOGETHER TO SUCCEED!
YOU MUST BOTH PASS FOR IT TO COUNT!
IF EITHER ONE OF YOU FAILS, YOU WILL BOTH BE PUNISHED!

Chapter Four
Wind, Wood and Water

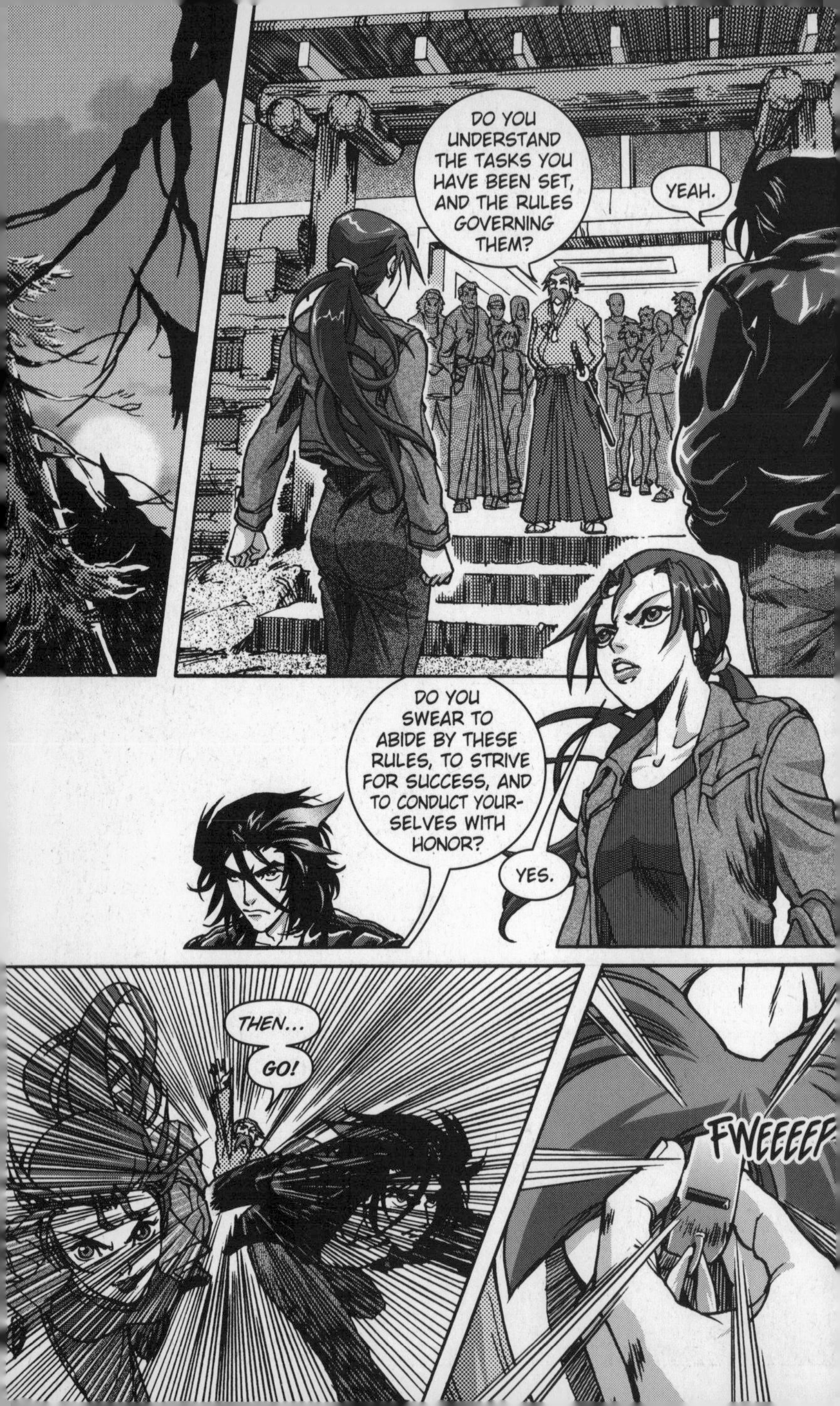
DO YOU UNDERSTAND THE TASKS YOU HAVE BEEN SET, AND THE RULES GOVERNING THEM?
YEAH.
DO YOU SWEAR TO ABIDE BY THESE RULES, TO STRIVE FOR SUCCESS, AND TO CONDUCT YOUR-SELVES WITH HONOR?
YES.
THEN...
GO!
FWEEEEP

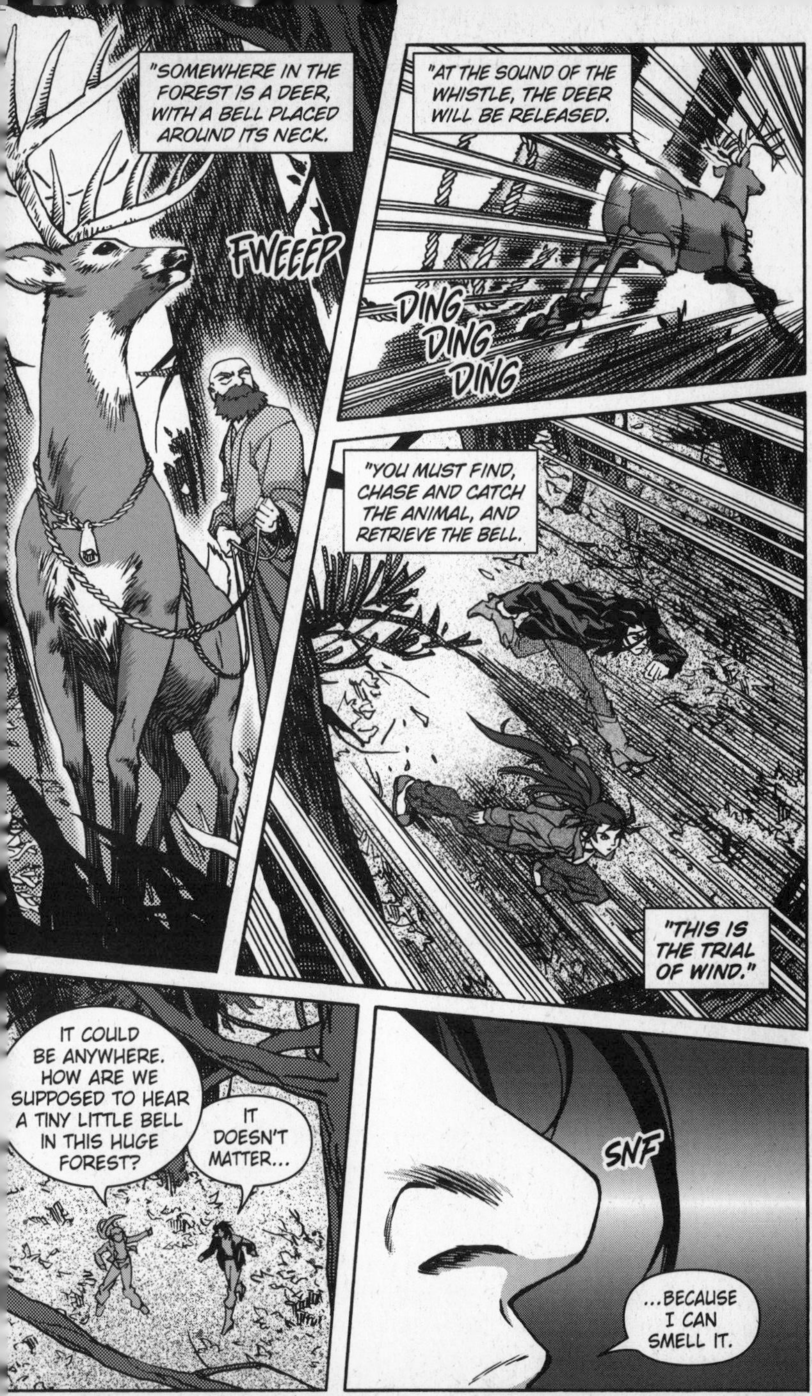

"SOMEWHERE IN THE FOREST IS A DEER, WITH A BELL PLACED AROUND ITS NECK.
FWEEEP
"AT THE SOUND OF THE WHISTLE, THE DEER WILL BE RELEASED.
DING DING DING
"YOU MUST FIND, CHASE AND CATCH THE ANIMAL, AND RETRIEVE THE BELL.
"THIS IS THE TRIAL OF WIND."
IT COULD BE ANYWHERE. HOW ARE WE SUPPOSED TO HEAR A TINY LITTLE BELL IN THIS HUGE FOREST?
IT DOESN'T MATTER...
SNF
...BECAUSE I CAN SMELL IT.

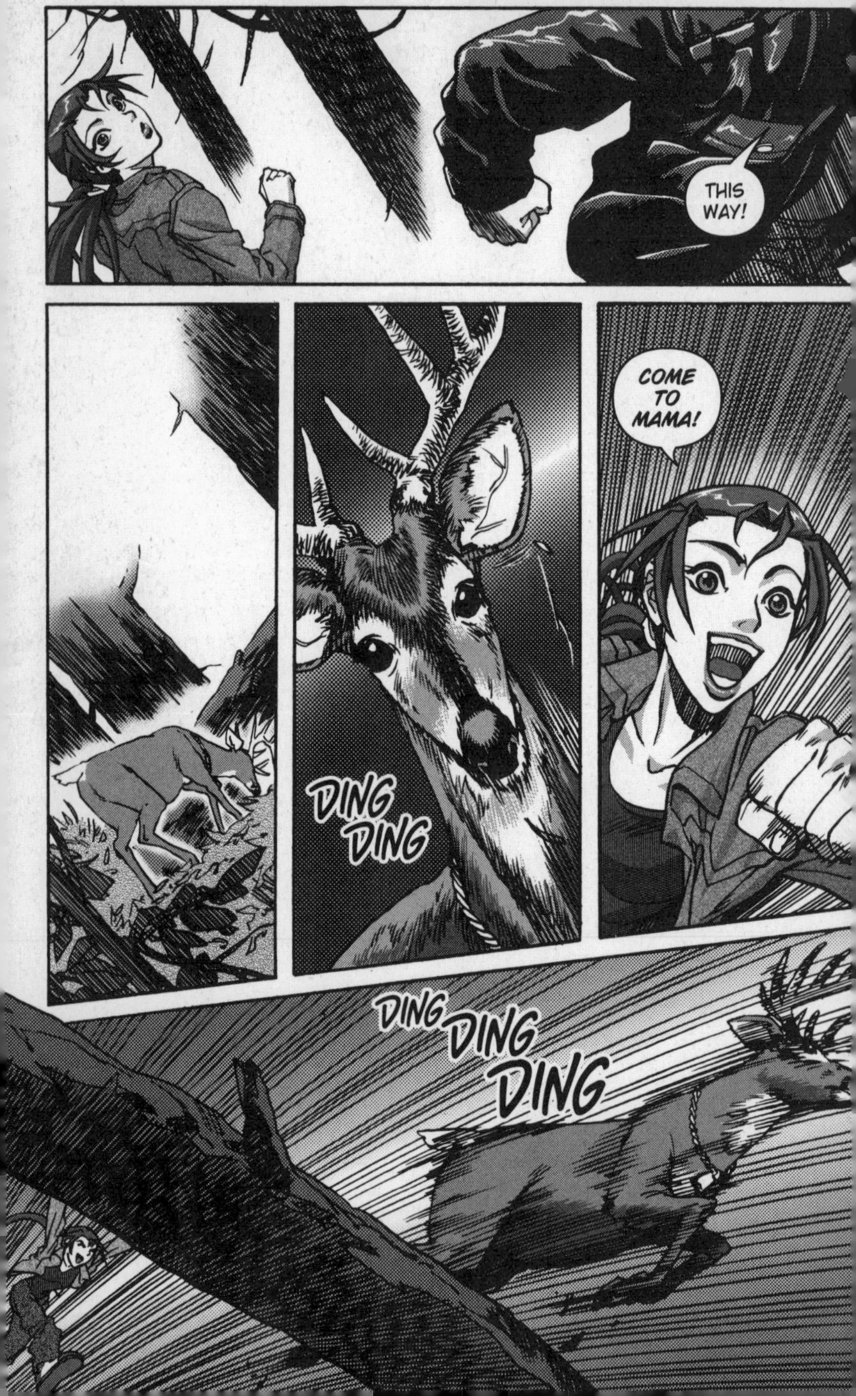
THIS WAY!
COME TO MAMA!
DING DING
DING DING DING

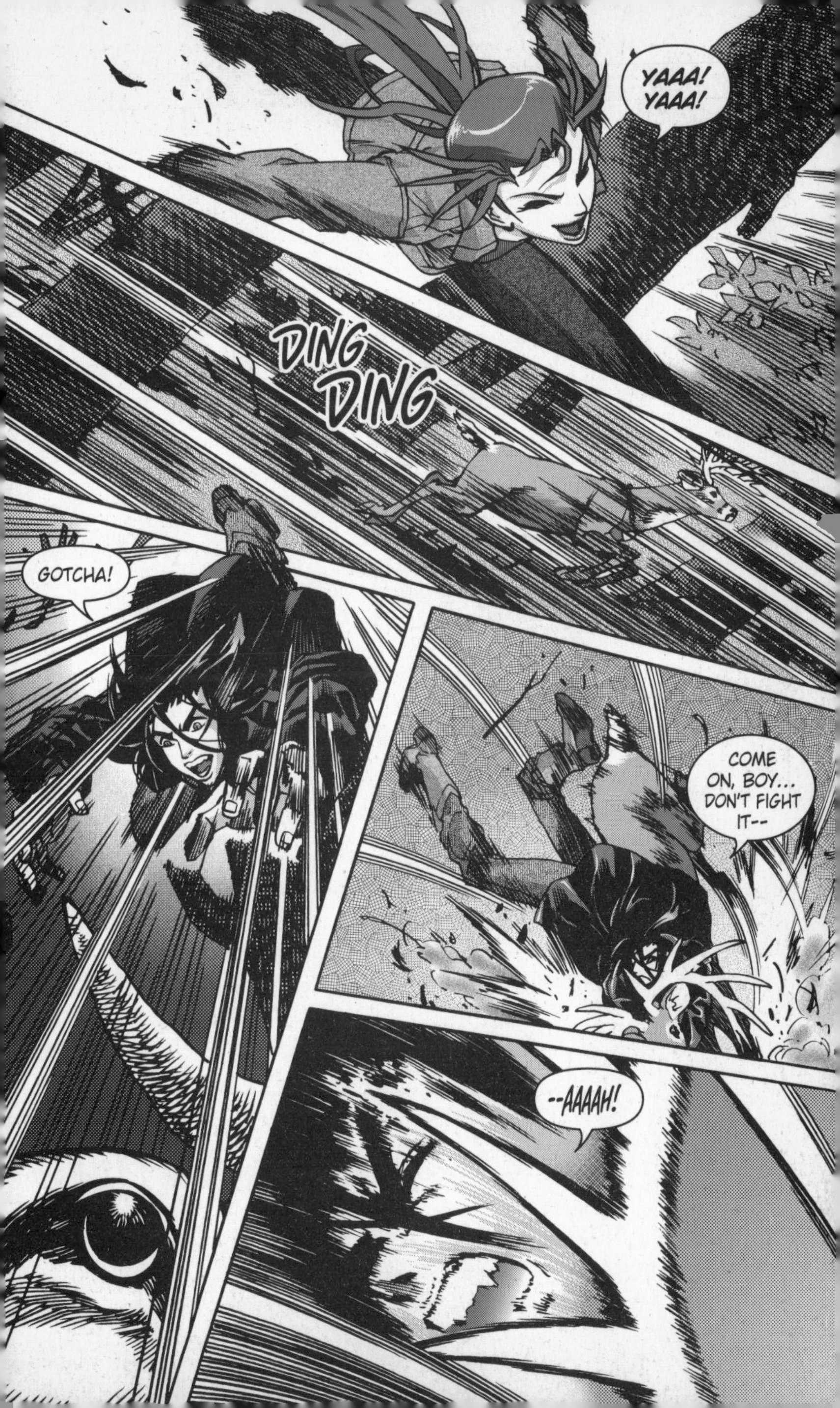
YAAA! YAAA!
DING DING
GOTCHA!
COME ON, BOY... DON'T FIGHT IT--
--AAAAH!

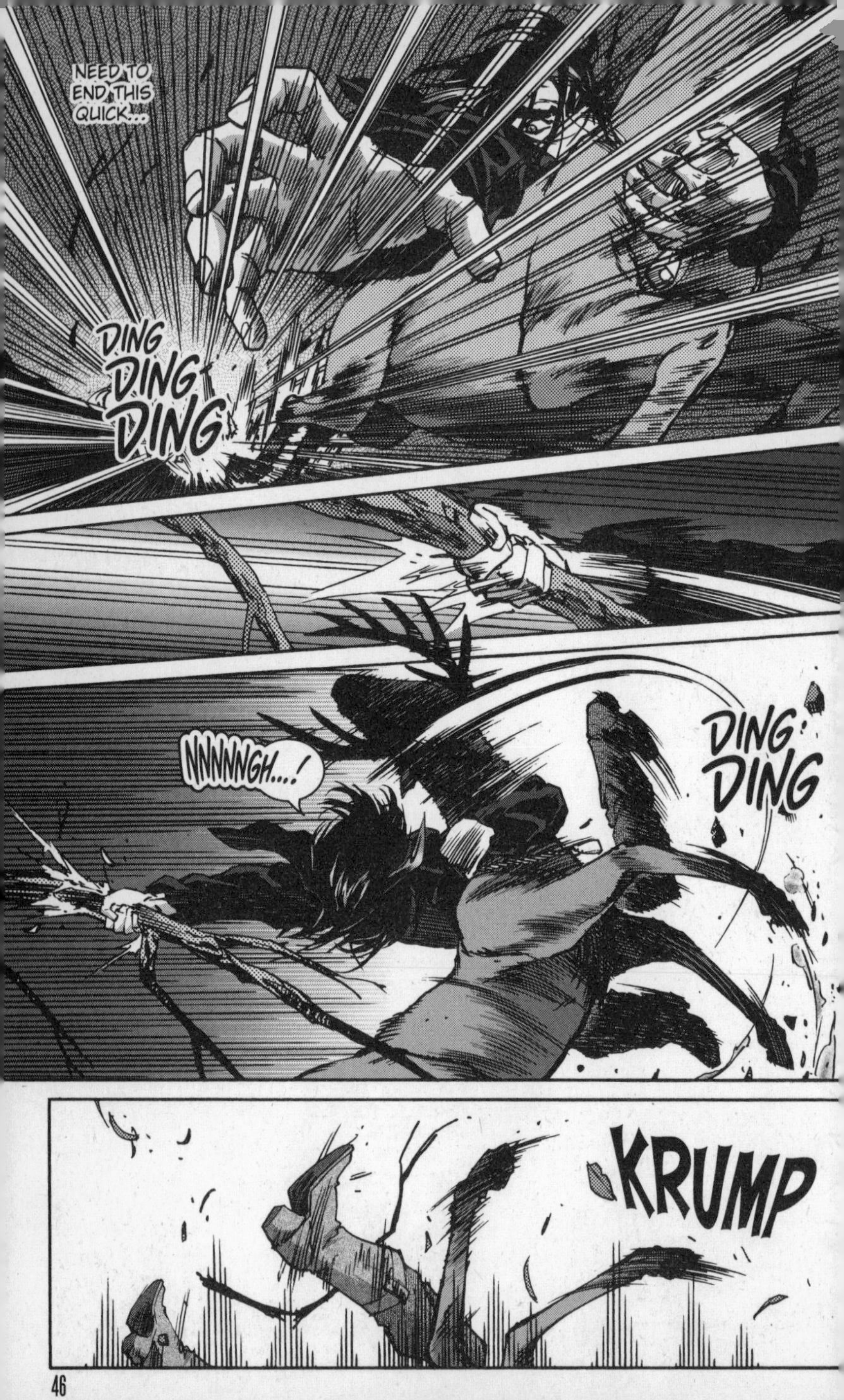
NEED TO END THIS QUICK...
DING DING DING
NNNNNGH...!
DING DING
KRUMP

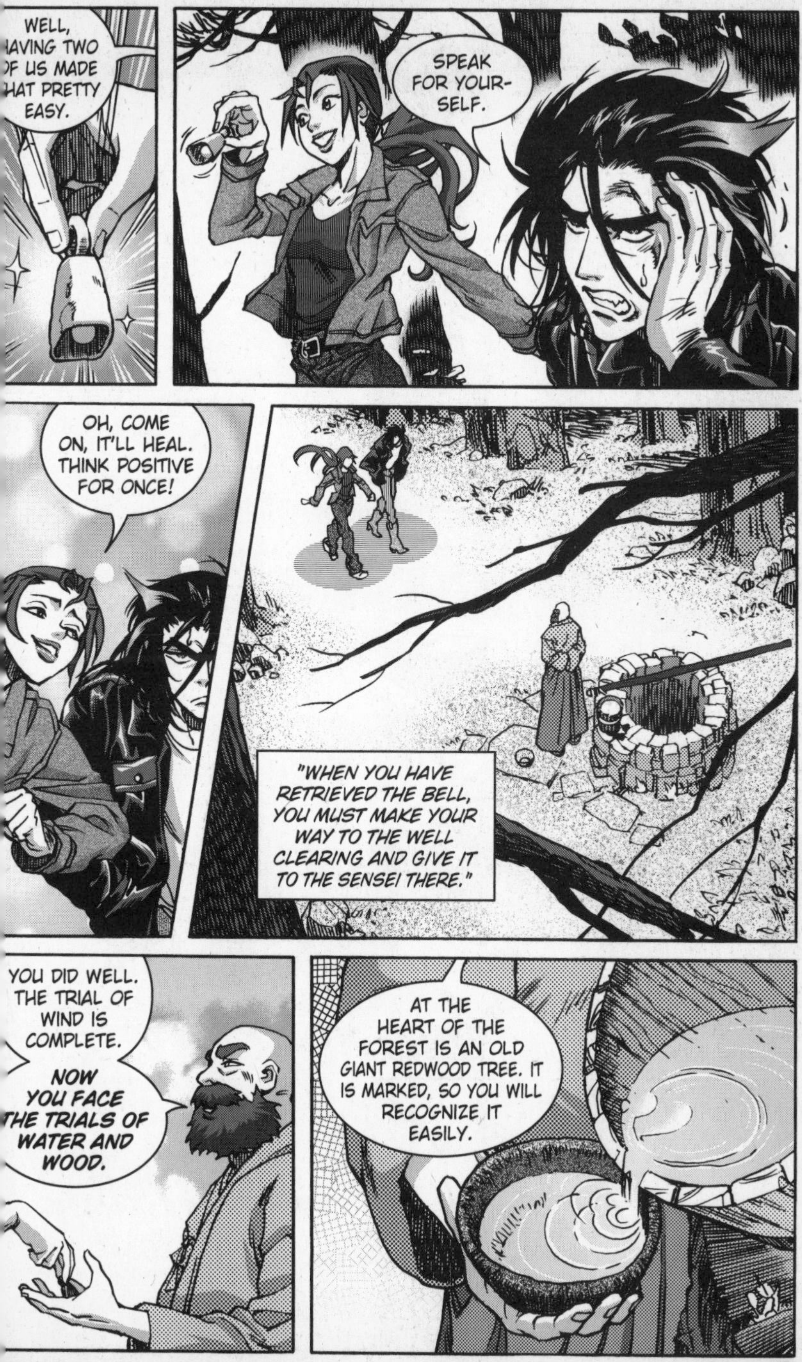

WELL, HAVING TWO OF US MADE THAT PRETTY EASY.
SPEAK FOR YOUR-SELF.
OH, COME ON, IT'LL HEAL. THINK POSITIVE FOR ONCE!
"WHEN YOU HAVE RETRIEVED THE BELL, YOU MUST MAKE YOUR WAY TO THE WELL CLEARING AND GIVE IT TO THE SENSEI THERE."
YOU DID WELL. THE TRIAL OF WIND IS COMPLETE.
NOW YOU FACE THE TRIALS OF WATER AND WOOD.
AT THE HEART OF THE FOREST IS AN OLD GIANT REDWOOD TREE. IT IS MARKED, SO YOU WILL RECOGNIZE IT EASILY.

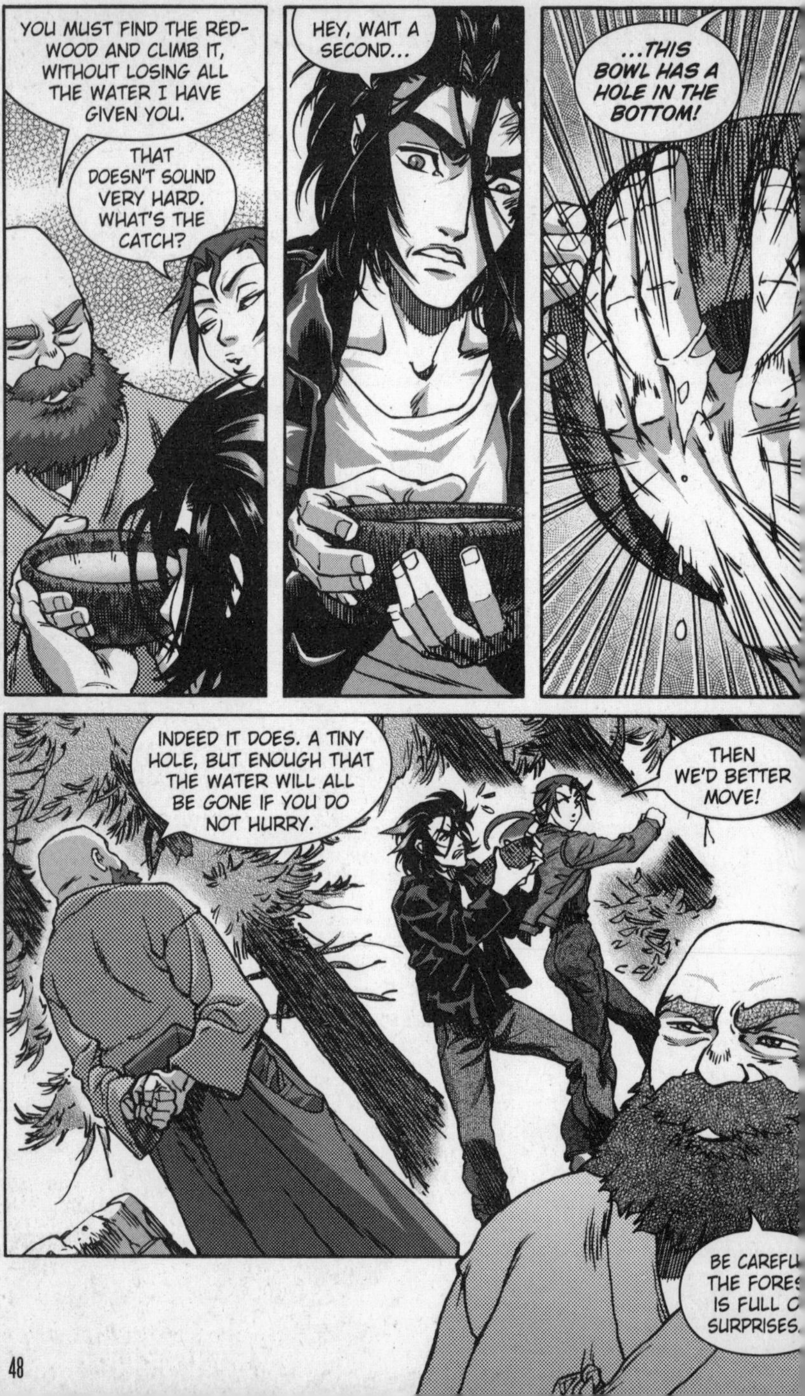

YOU MUST FIND THE RED-WOOD AND CLIMB IT, WITHOUT LOSING ALL THE WATER I HAVE GIVEN YOU.
THAT DOESN'T SOUND VERY HARD. WHAT'S THE CATCH?
HEY, WAIT A SECOND...
...THIS BOWL HAS A HOLE IN THE BOTTOM!
INDEED IT DOES. A TINY HOLE, BUT ENOUGH THAT THE WATER WILL ALL BE GONE IF YOU DO NOT HURRY.
THEN WE'D BETTER MOVE!
BE CAREFU THE FORES IS FULL O SURPRISES.

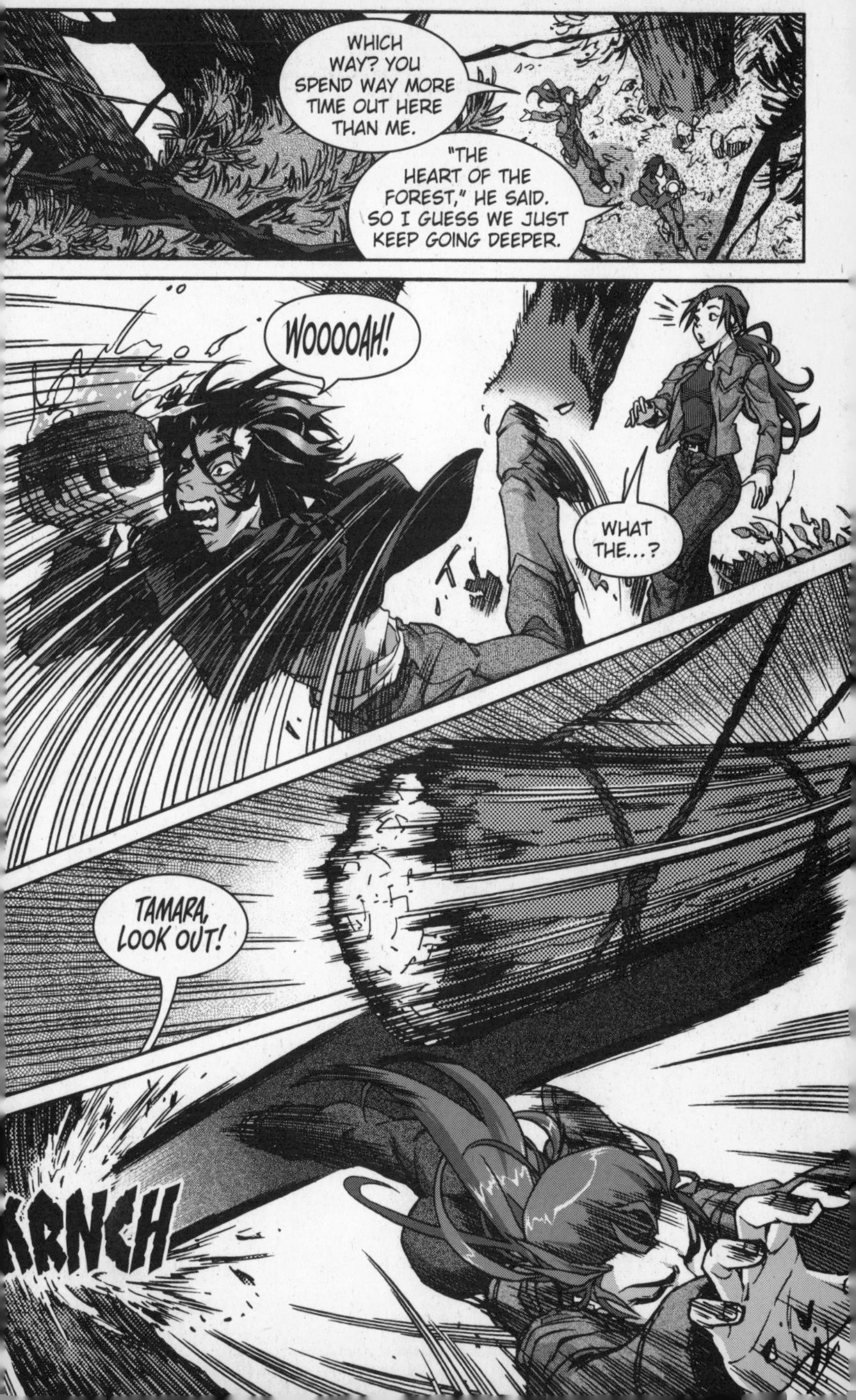
WHICH WAY? YOU SPEND WAY MORE TIME OUT HERE THAN ME.
"THE HEART OF THE FOREST," HE SAID. SO I GUESS WE JUST KEEP GOING DEEPER.
WOOOOAH!
WHAT THE...?
TAMARA, LOOK OUT!
KRNCH

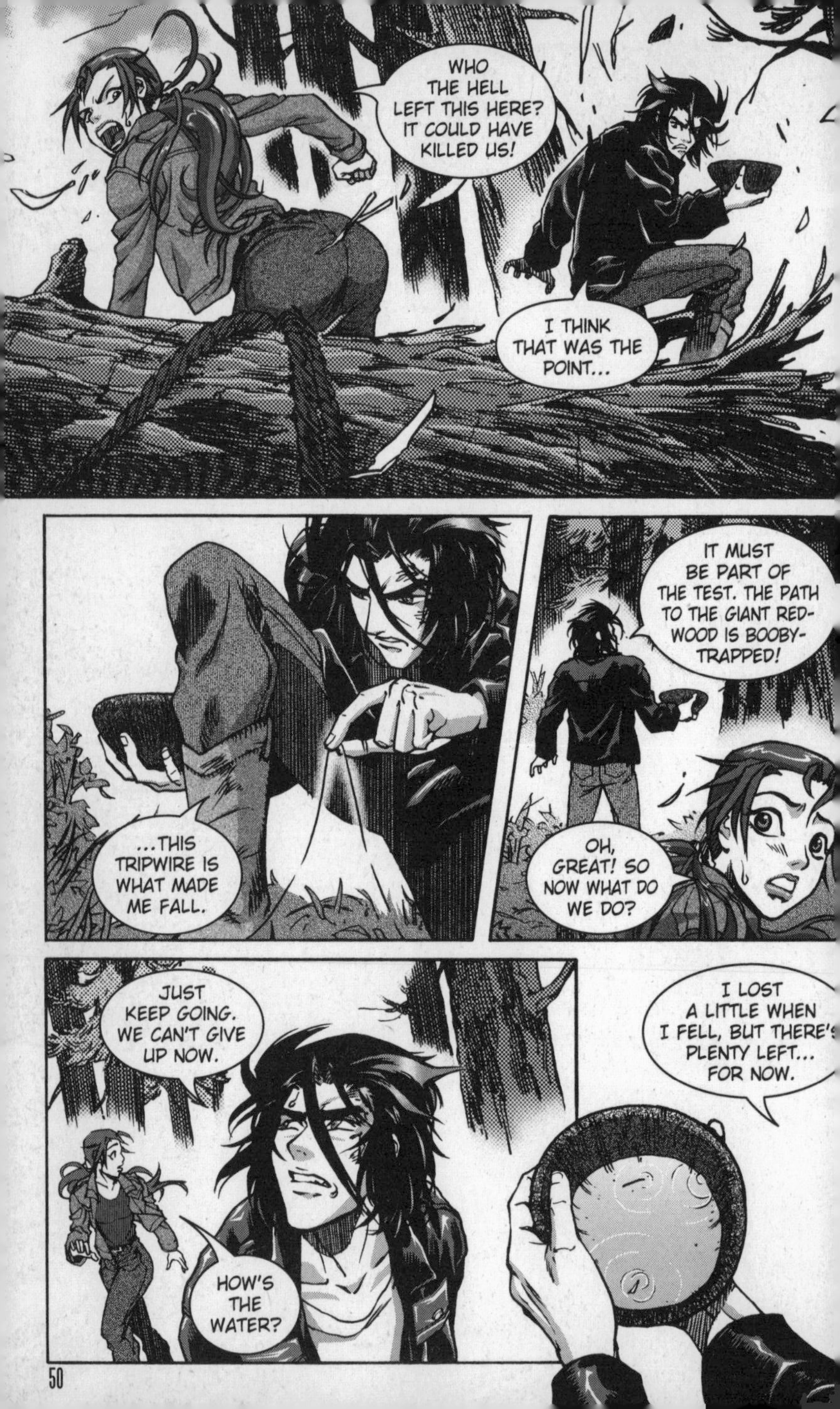
WHO THE HELL LEFT THIS HERE? IT COULD HAVE KILLED US!
I THINK THAT WAS THE POINT...
...THIS TRIPWIRE IS WHAT MADE ME FALL.
IT MUST BE PART OF THE TEST. THE PATH TO THE GIANT RED-WOOD IS BOOBY-TRAPPED!
OH, GREAT! SO NOW WHAT DO WE DO?
JUST KEEP GOING. WE CAN'T GIVE UP NOW.
HOW'S THE WATER?
I LOST A LITTLE WHEN I FELL, BUT THERE'S PLENTY LEFT... FOR NOW.

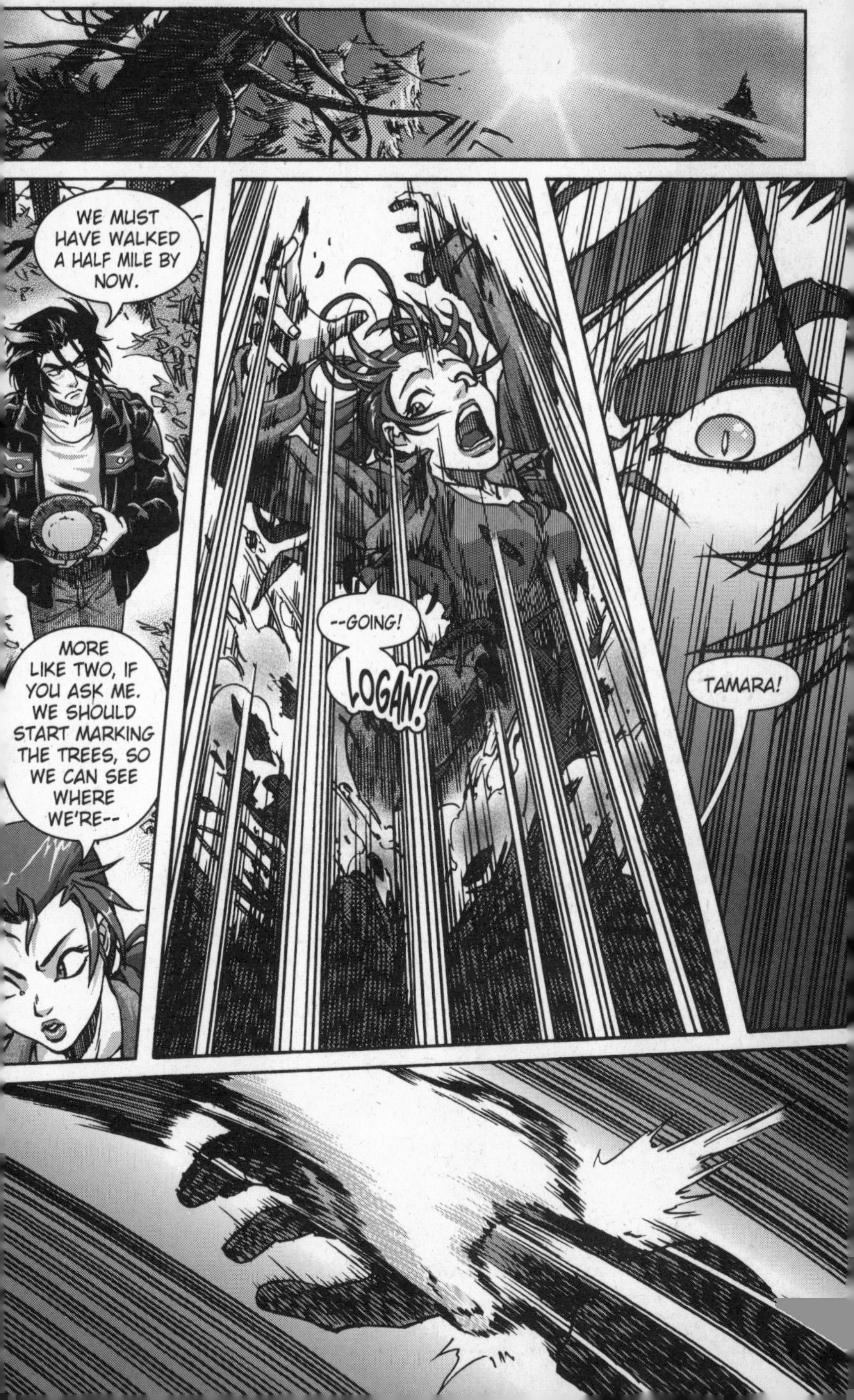
WE MUST HAVE WALKED A HALF MILE BY NOW.
MORE LIKE TWO, IF YOU ASK ME. WE SHOULD START MARKING THE TREES, SO WE CAN SEE WHERE WE'RE--
--GOING!
LOGAN!
TAMARA!

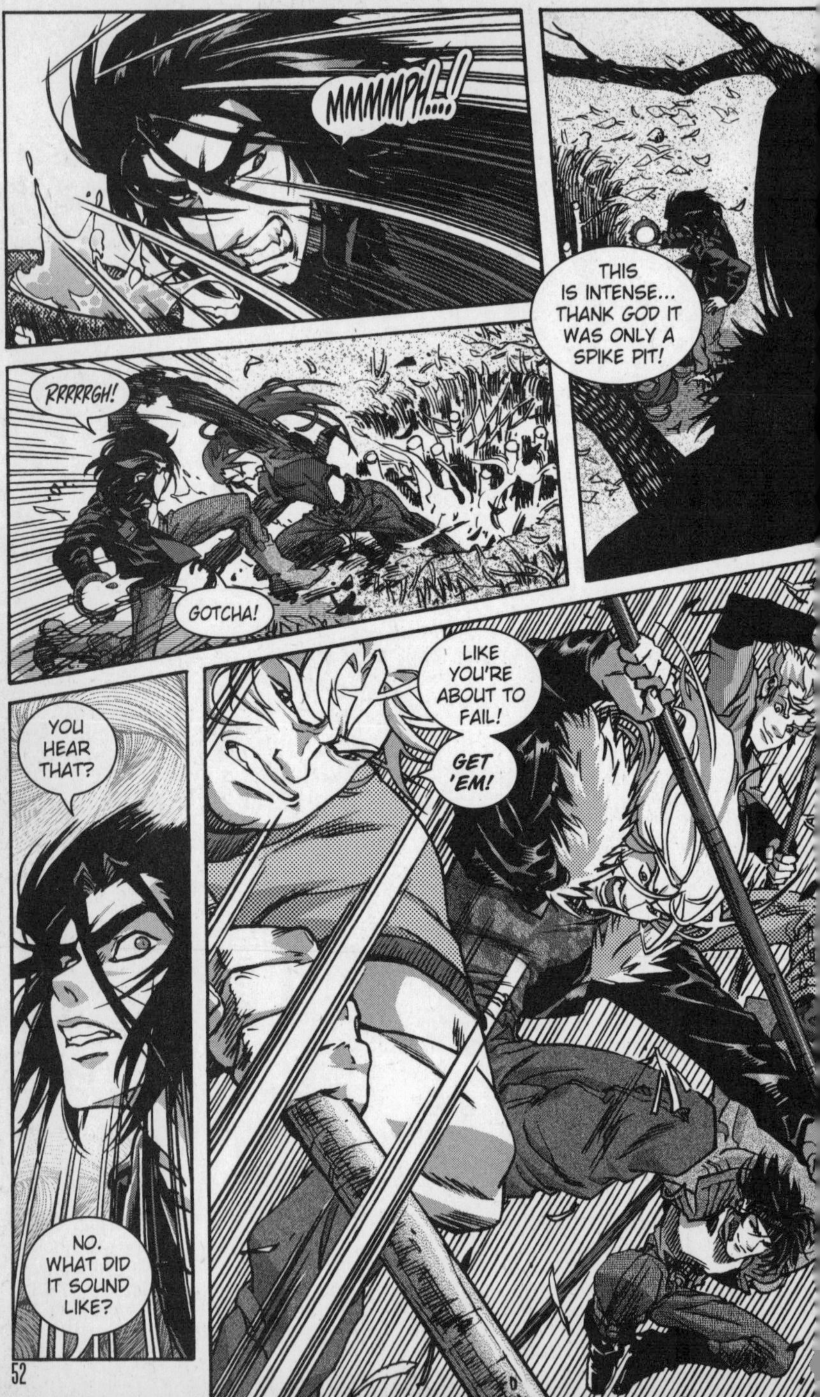
MMMMPH...!
THIS IS INTENSE... THANK GOD IT WAS ONLY A SPIKE PIT!
RRRRRGH!
GOTCHA!
YOU HEAR THAT?
LIKE YOU'RE ABOUT TO FAIL!
GET 'EM!
NO. WHAT DID IT SOUND LIKE?

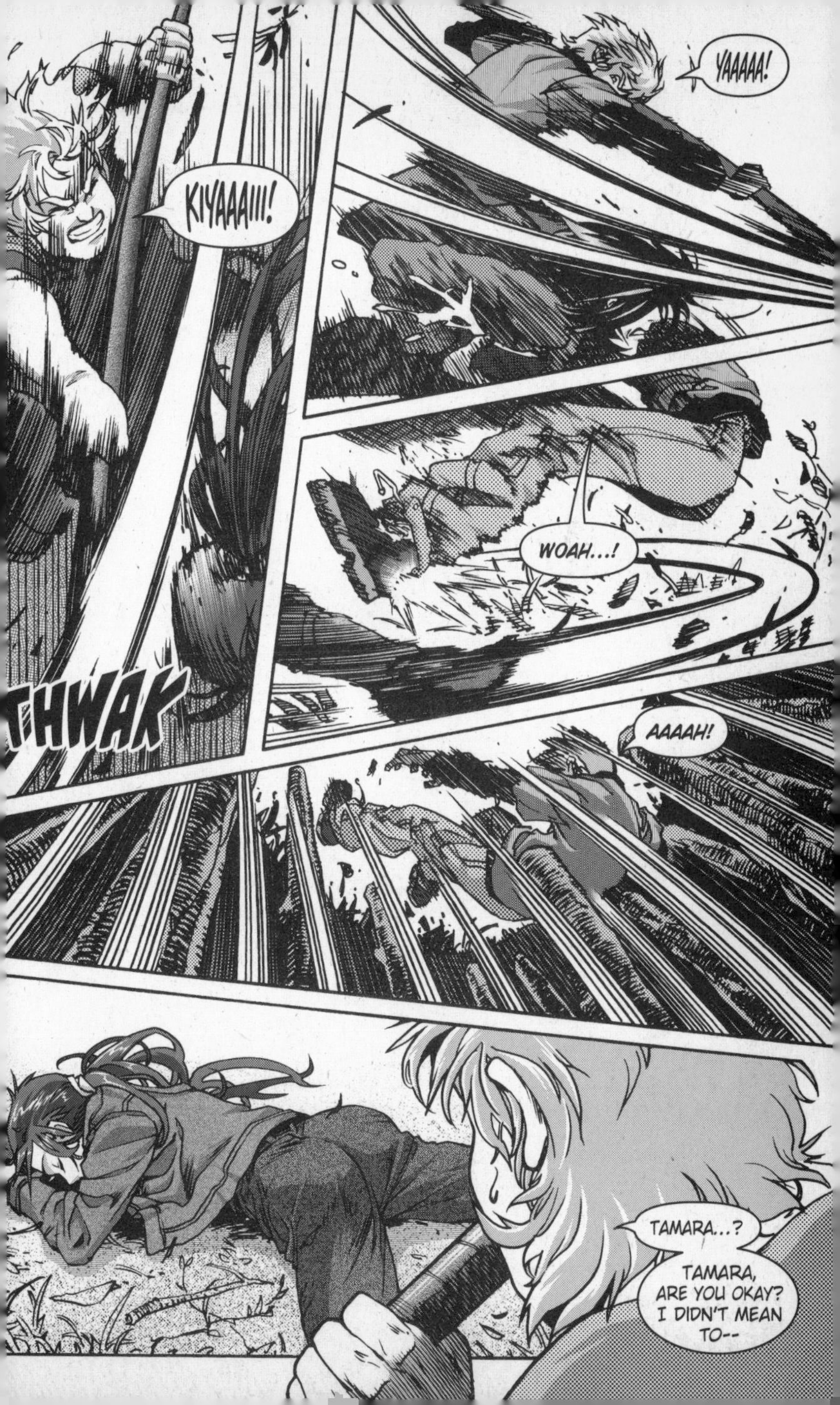
KIYAAAIIII!
THWAK
YAAAAA!
WOAH...!
AAAAH!
TAMARA...?
TAMARA, ARE YOU OKAY? I DIDN'T MEAN TO--

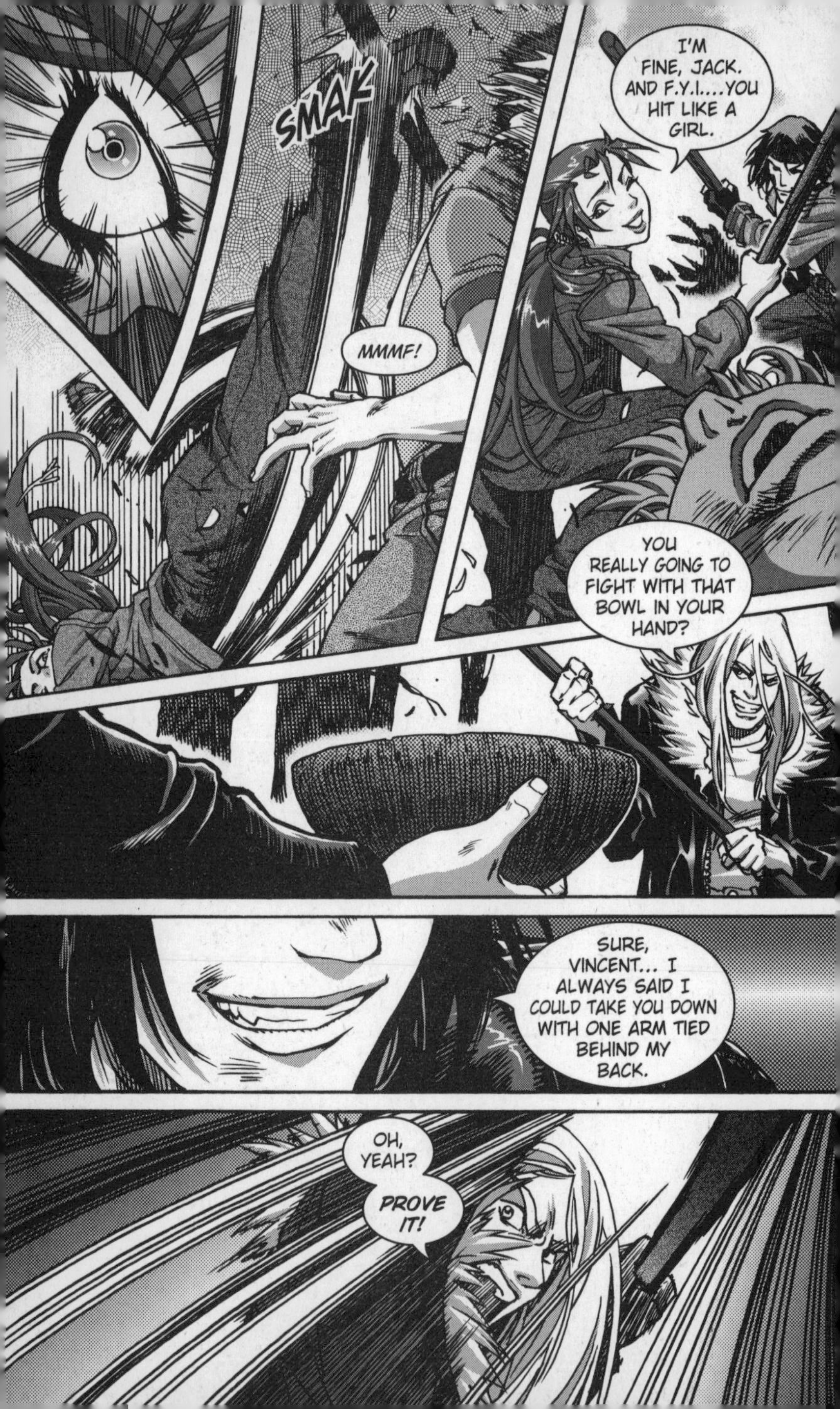
SMAK
MMMF!
I'M FINE, JACK. AND F.Y.I....YOU HIT LIKE A GIRL.
YOU REALLY GOING TO FIGHT WITH THAT BOWL IN YOUR HAND?
SURE, VINCENT... I ALWAYS SAID I COULD TAKE YOU DOWN WITH ONE ARM TIED BEHIND MY BACK.
OH, YEAH?
PROVE IT!

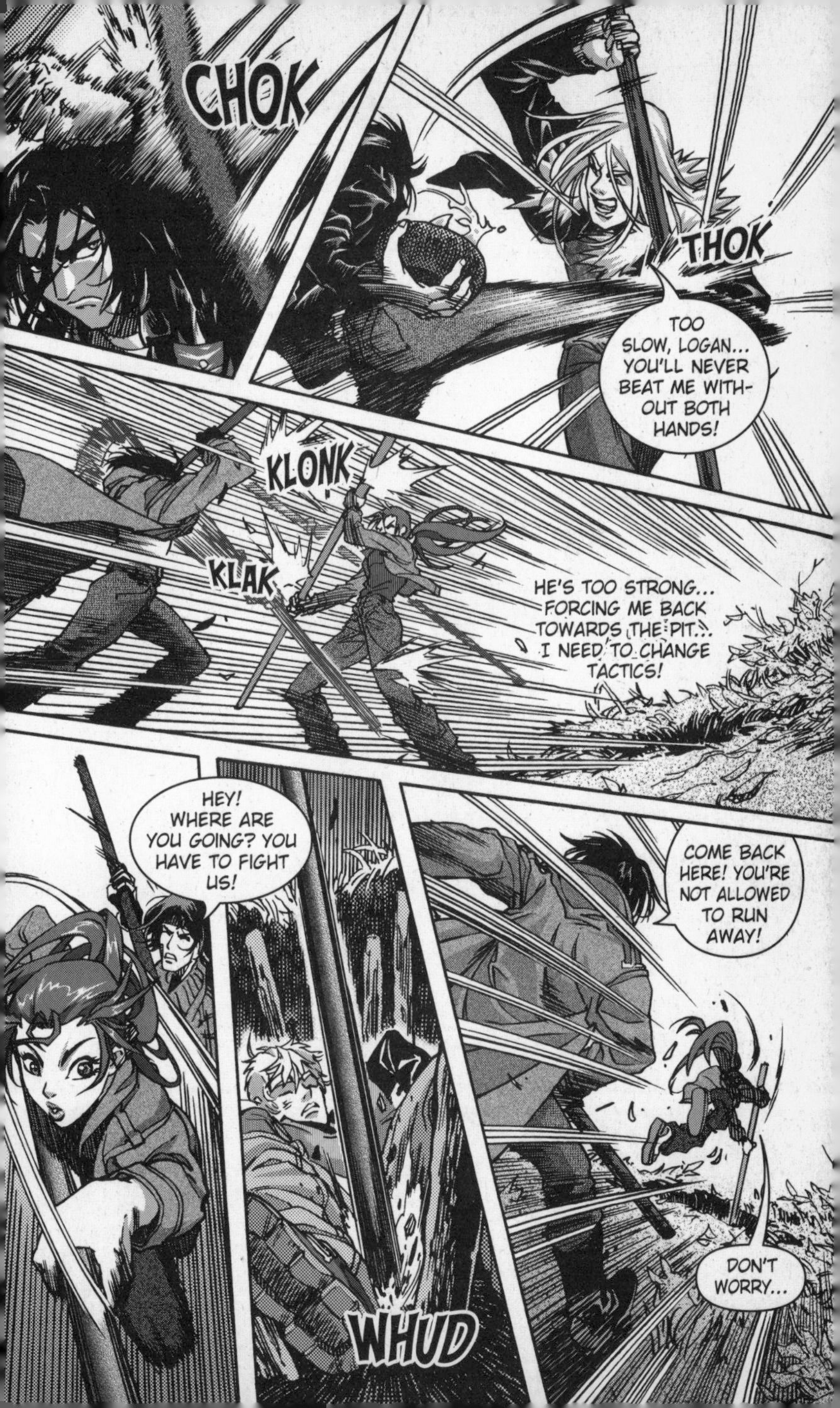

CHOK
THOK
TOO SLOW, LOGAN... YOU'LL NEVER BEAT ME WITHOUT BOTH HANDS!
KLONK
KLAK
HE'S TOO STRONG... FORCING ME BACK TOWARDS THE PIT... I NEED TO CHANGE TACTICS!
HEY! WHERE ARE YOU GOING? YOU HAVE TO FIGHT US!
WHUD
COME BACK HERE! YOU'RE NOT ALLOWED TO RUN AWAY!
DON'T WORRY...

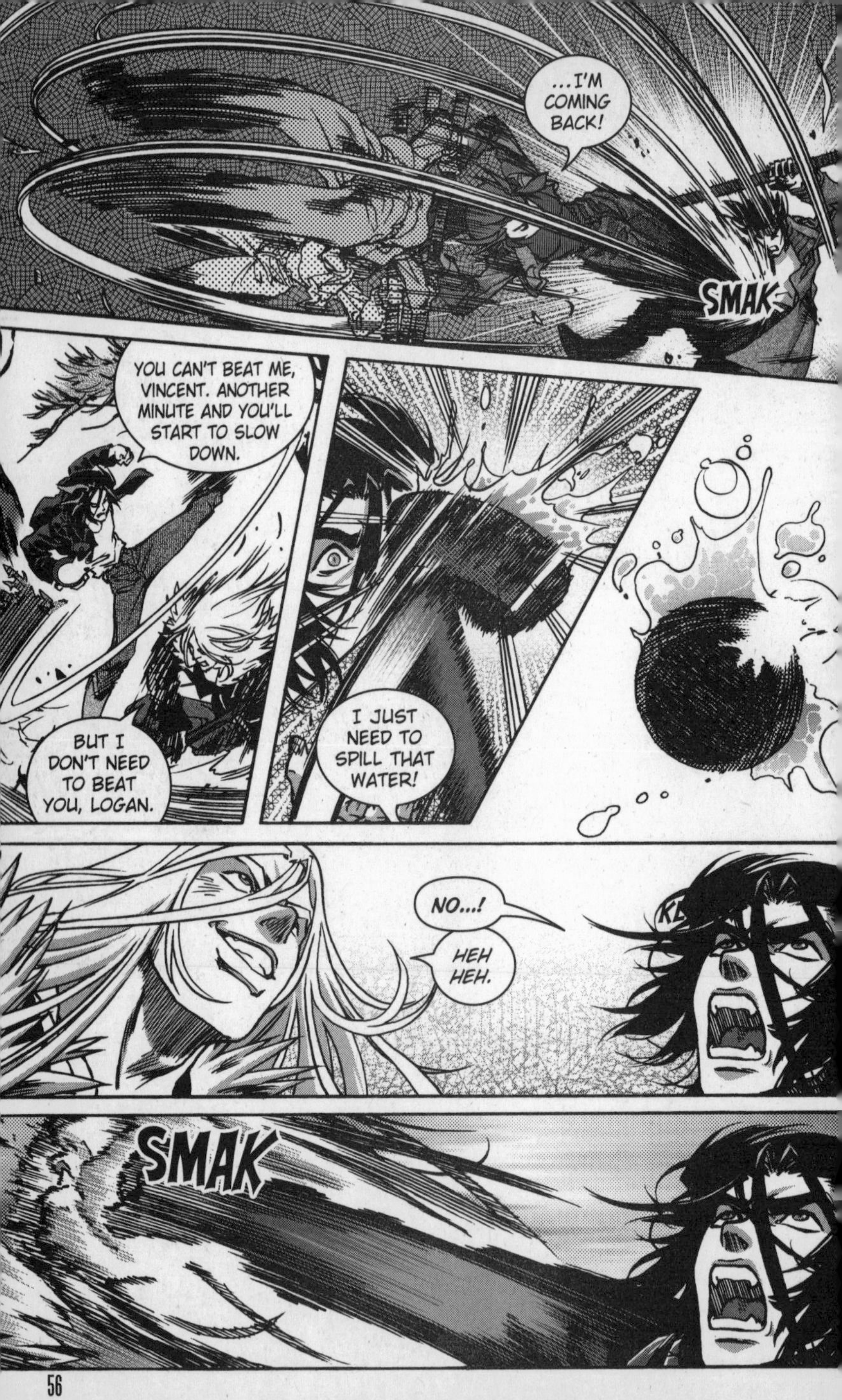
...I'M COMING BACK!
SMAK
YOU CAN'T BEAT ME, VINCENT. ANOTHER MINUTE AND YOU'LL START TO SLOW DOWN.
BUT I DON'T NEED TO BEAT YOU, LOGAN.
I JUST NEED TO SPILL THAT WATER!
NO...!
HEH HEH.
SMAK

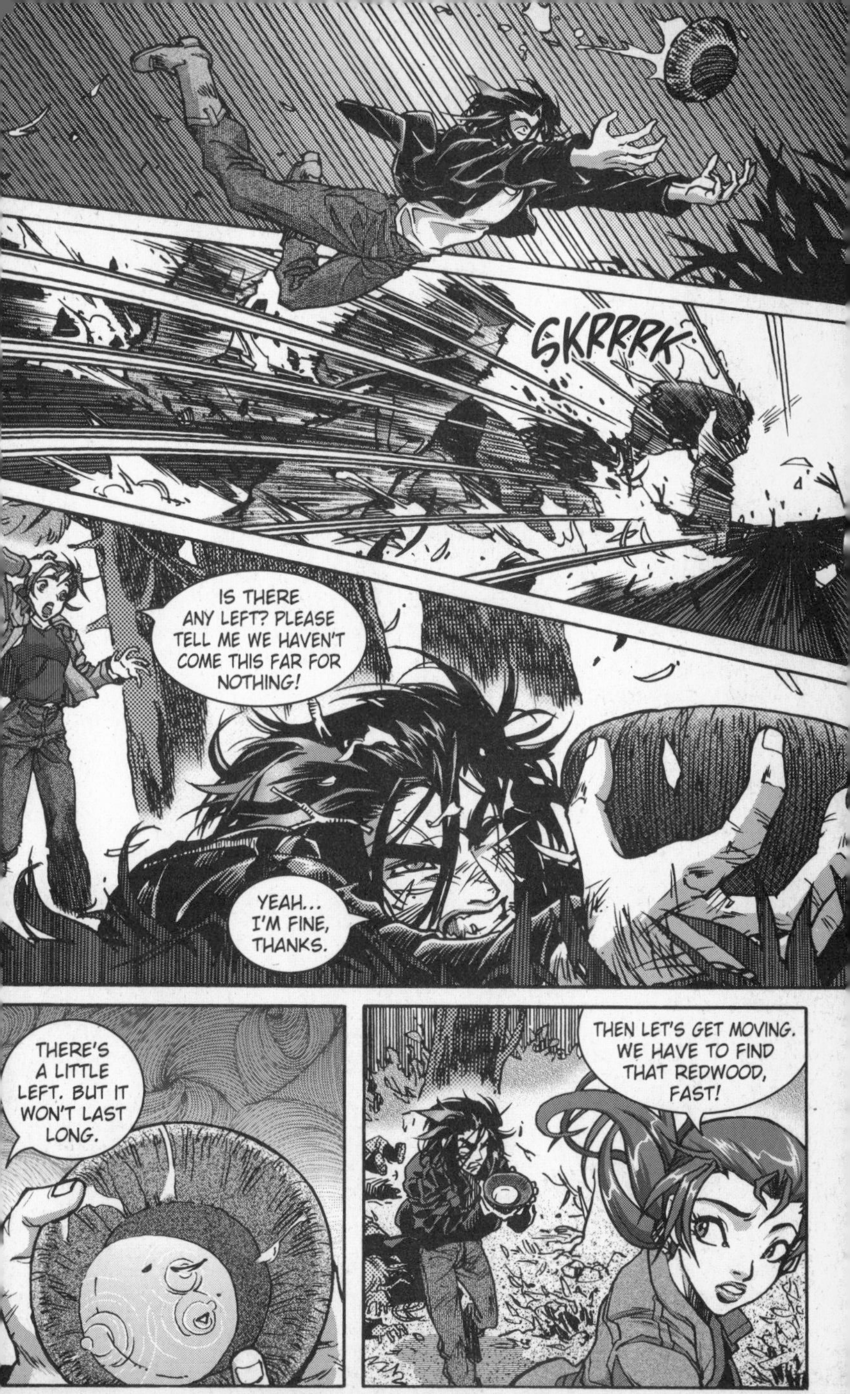
SKRRRK
IS THERE ANY LEFT? PLEASE TELL ME WE HAVEN'T COME THIS FAR FOR NOTHING!
YEAH... I'M FINE, THANKS.
THERE'S A LITTLE LEFT. BUT IT WON'T LAST LONG.
THEN LET'S GET MOVING. WE HAVE TO FIND THAT REDWOOD, FAST!

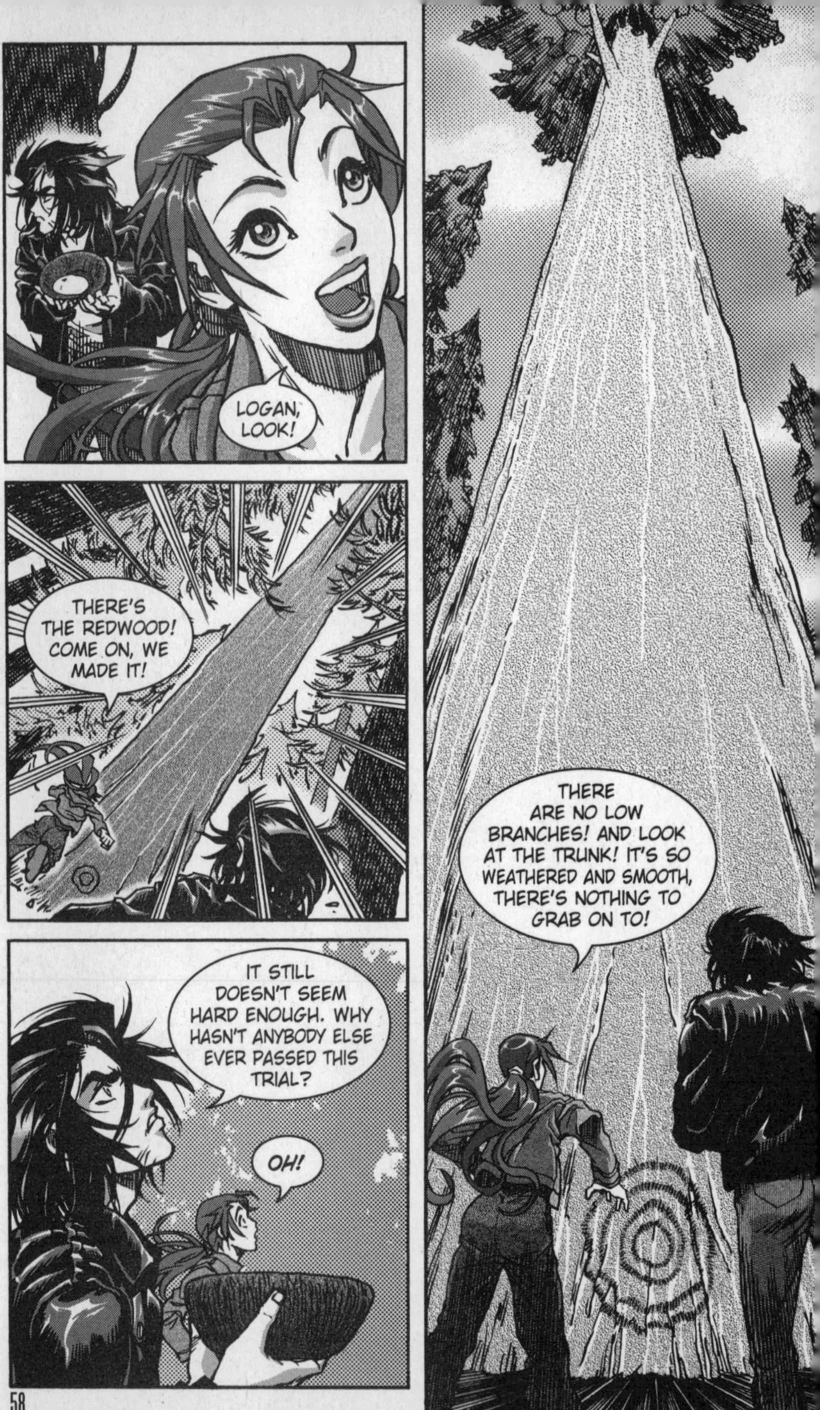
LOGAN, LOOK!
THERE'S THE REDWOOD! COME ON, WE MADE IT!
IT STILL DOESN'T SEEM HARD ENOUGH. WHY HASN'T ANYBODY ELSE EVER PASSED THIS TRIAL?
OH!
THERE ARE NO LOW BRANCHES! AND LOOK AT THE TRUNK! IT'S SO WEATHERED AND SMOOTH, THERE'S NOTHING TO GRAB ON TO!

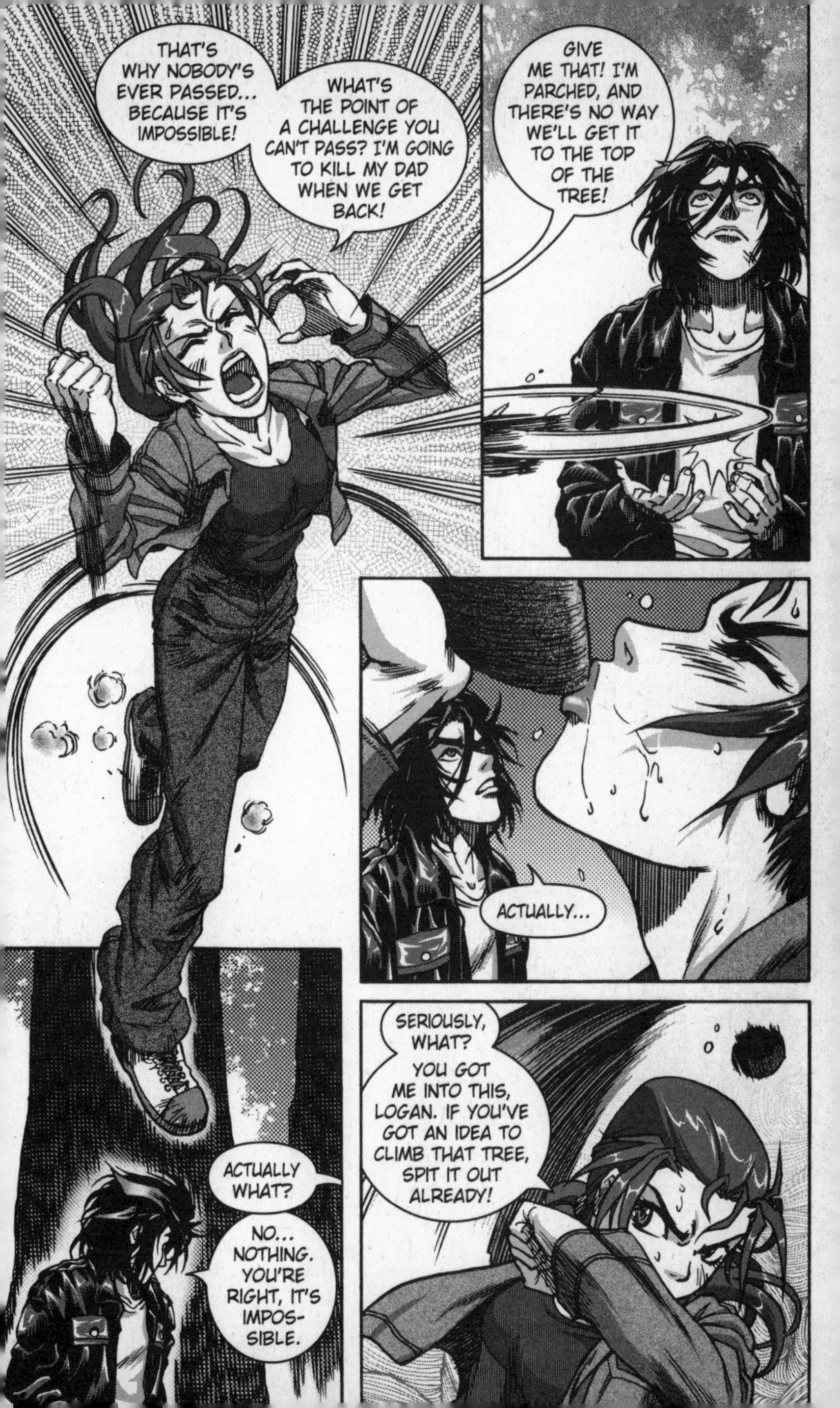
THAT'S WHY NOBODY'S EVER PASSED... BECAUSE IT'S IMPOSSIBLE!
WHAT'S THE POINT OF A CHALLENGE YOU CAN'T PASS? I'M GOING TO KILL MY DAD WHEN WE GET BACK!
GIVE ME THAT! I'M PARCHED, AND THERE'S NO WAY WE'LL GET IT TO THE TOP OF THE TREE!
ACTUALLY...
ACTUALLY WHAT?
NO... NOTHING. YOU'RE RIGHT, IT'S IMPOS-SIBLE.
SERIOUSLY, WHAT?
YOU GOT ME INTO THIS, LOGAN. IF YOU'VE GOT AN IDEA TO CLIMB THAT TREE, SPIT IT OUT ALREADY!

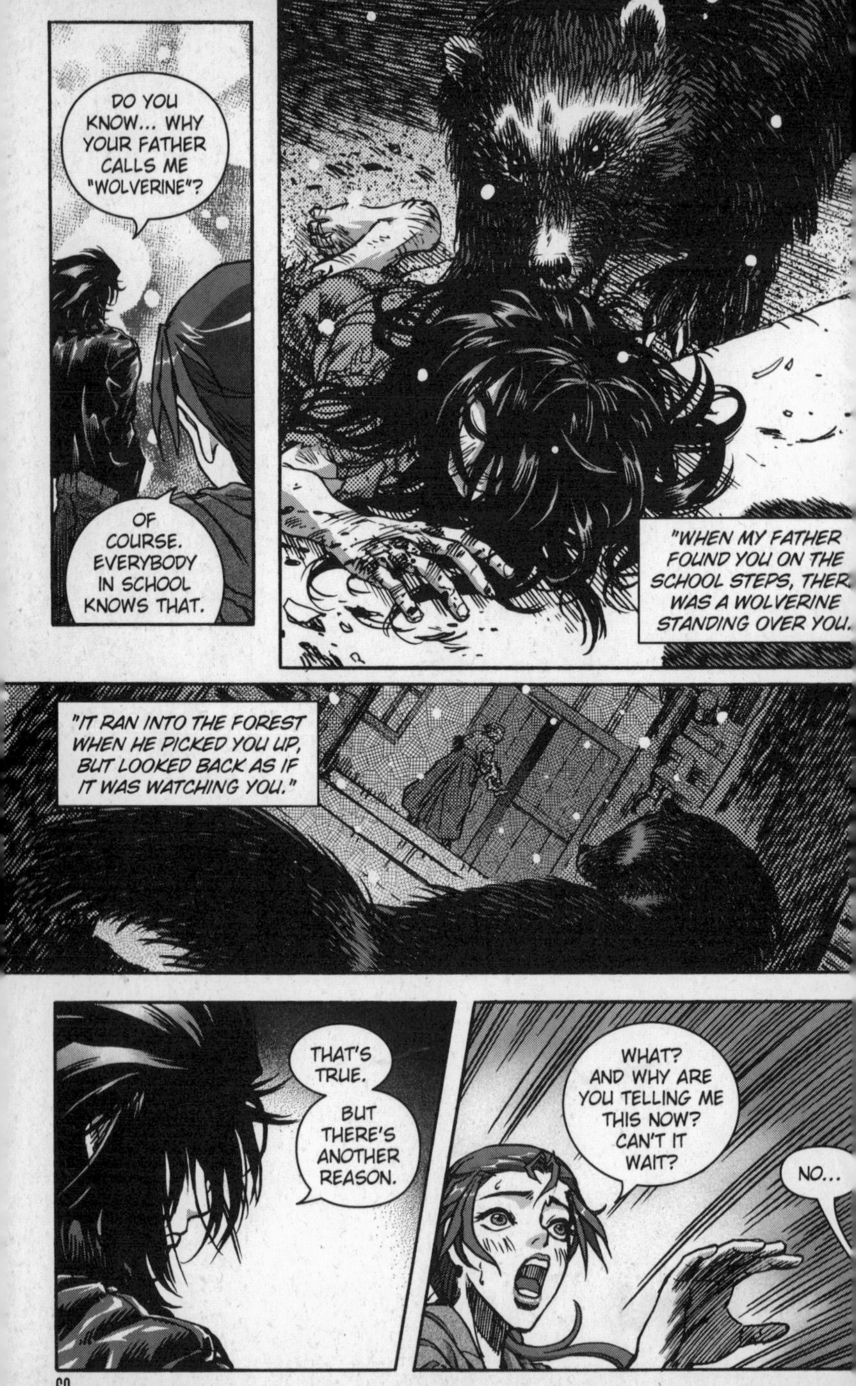
DO YOU KNOW... WHY YOUR FATHER CALLS ME "WOLVERINE"?
OF COURSE. EVERYBODY IN SCHOOL KNOWS THAT.
"WHEN MY FATHER FOUND YOU ON THE SCHOOL STEPS, THERE WAS A WOLVERINE STANDING OVER YOU.
"IT RAN INTO THE FOREST WHEN HE PICKED YOU UP, BUT LOOKED BACK AS IF IT WAS WATCHING YOU."
THAT'S TRUE.
BUT THERE'S ANOTHER REASON.
WHAT? AND WHY ARE YOU TELLING ME THIS NOW? CAN'T IT WAIT?
NO...

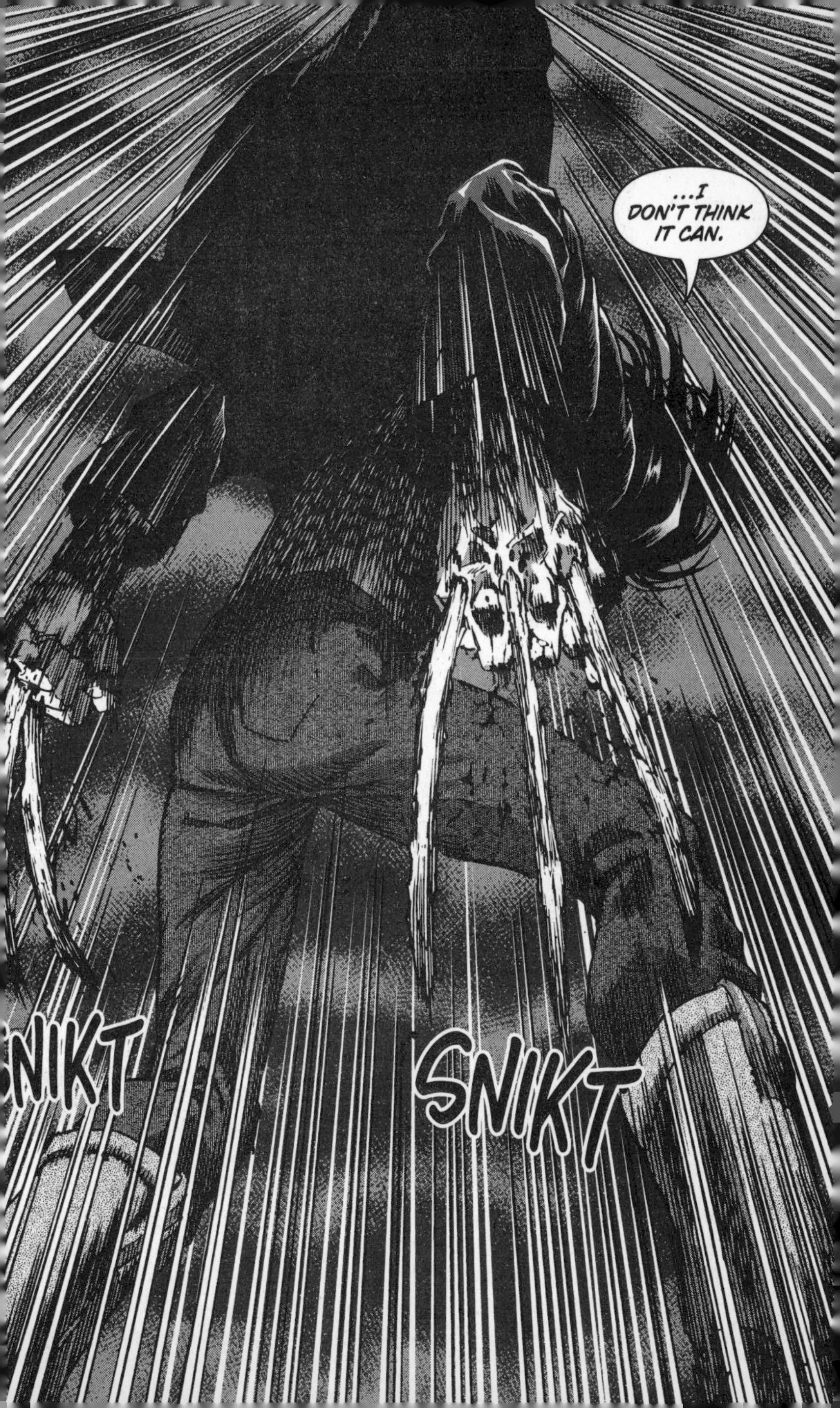
...I DON'T THINK IT CAN.
NIKT
SNIKT

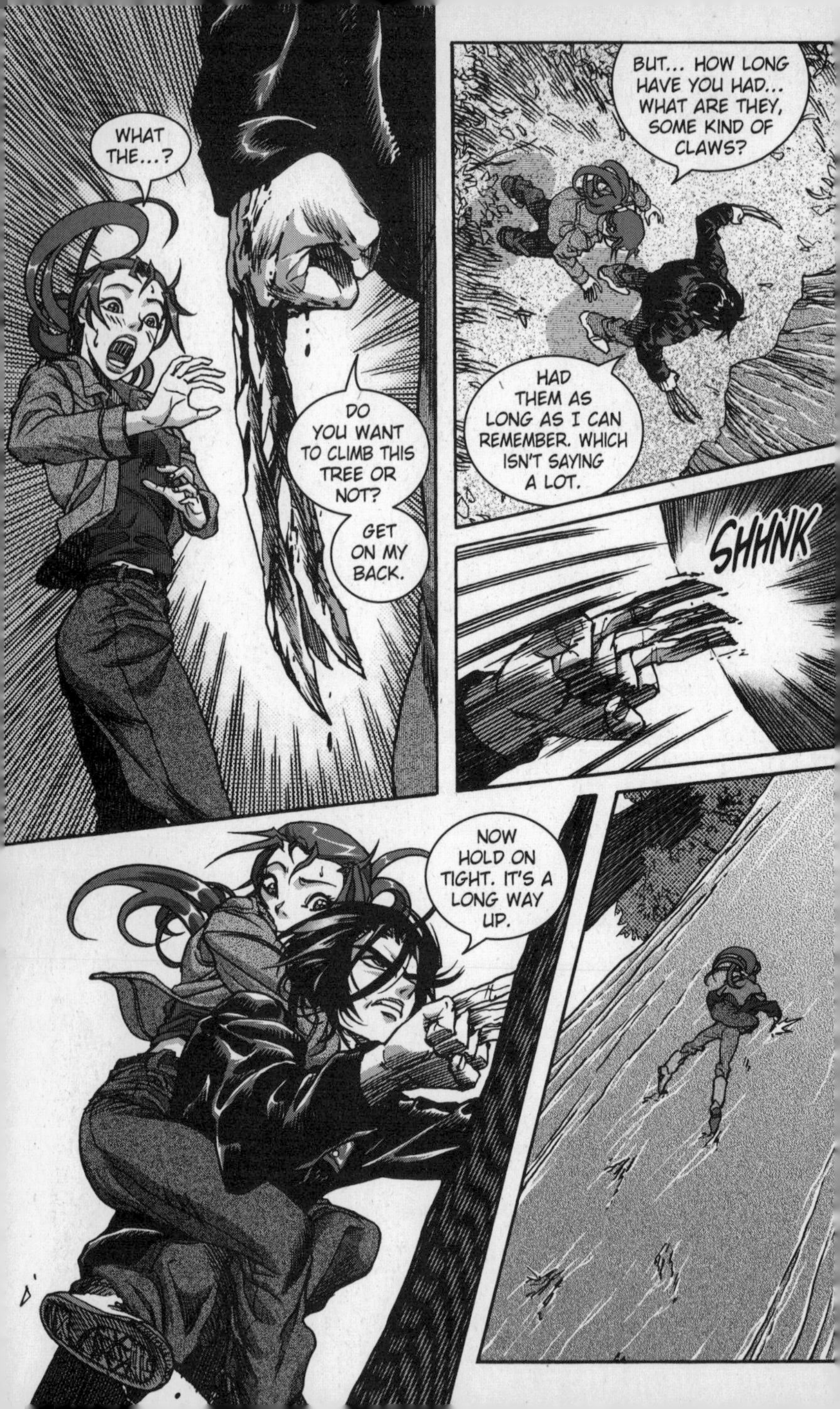
WHAT THE...?
DO YOU WANT TO CLIMB THIS TREE OR NOT?
GET ON MY BACK.
BUT... HOW LONG HAVE YOU HAD... WHAT ARE THEY, SOME KIND OF CLAWS?
HAD THEM AS LONG AS I CAN REMEMBER. WHICH ISN'T SAYING A LOT.
SHHNK
NOW HOLD ON TIGHT. IT'S A LONG WAY UP.

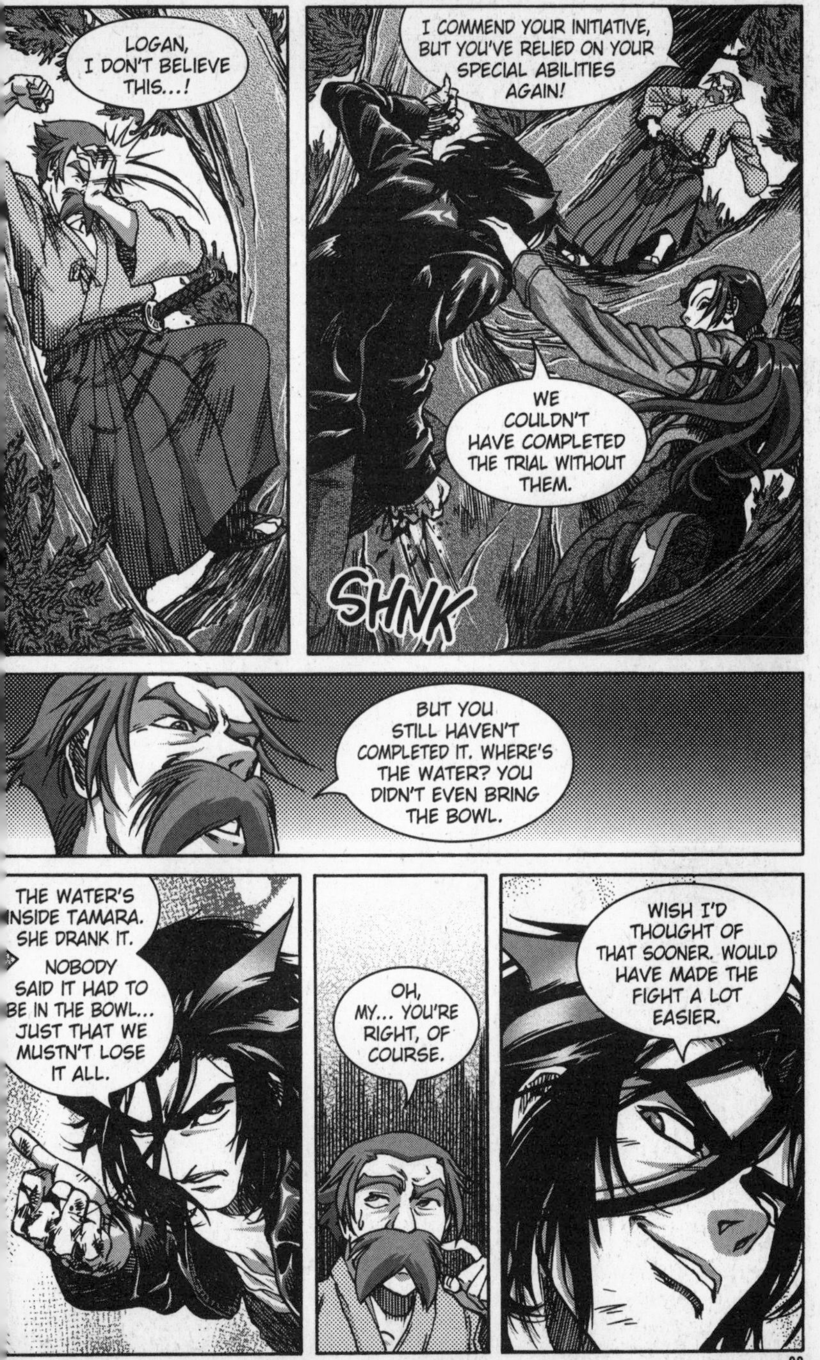
LOGAN, I DON'T BELIEVE THIS...!
I COMMEND YOUR INITIATIVE, BUT YOU'VE RELIED ON YOUR SPECIAL ABILITIES AGAIN!
WE COULDN'T HAVE COMPLETED THE TRIAL WITHOUT THEM.
SHNK
BUT YOU STILL HAVEN'T COMPLETED IT. WHERE'S THE WATER? YOU DIDN'T EVEN BRING THE BOWL.
THE WATER'S INSIDE TAMARA. SHE DRANK IT.
NOBODY SAID IT HAD TO BE IN THE BOWL... JUST THAT WE MUSTN'T LOSE IT ALL.
OH, MY... YOU'RE RIGHT, OF COURSE.
WISH I'D THOUGHT OF THAT SOONER. WOULD HAVE MADE THE FIGHT A LOT EASIER.

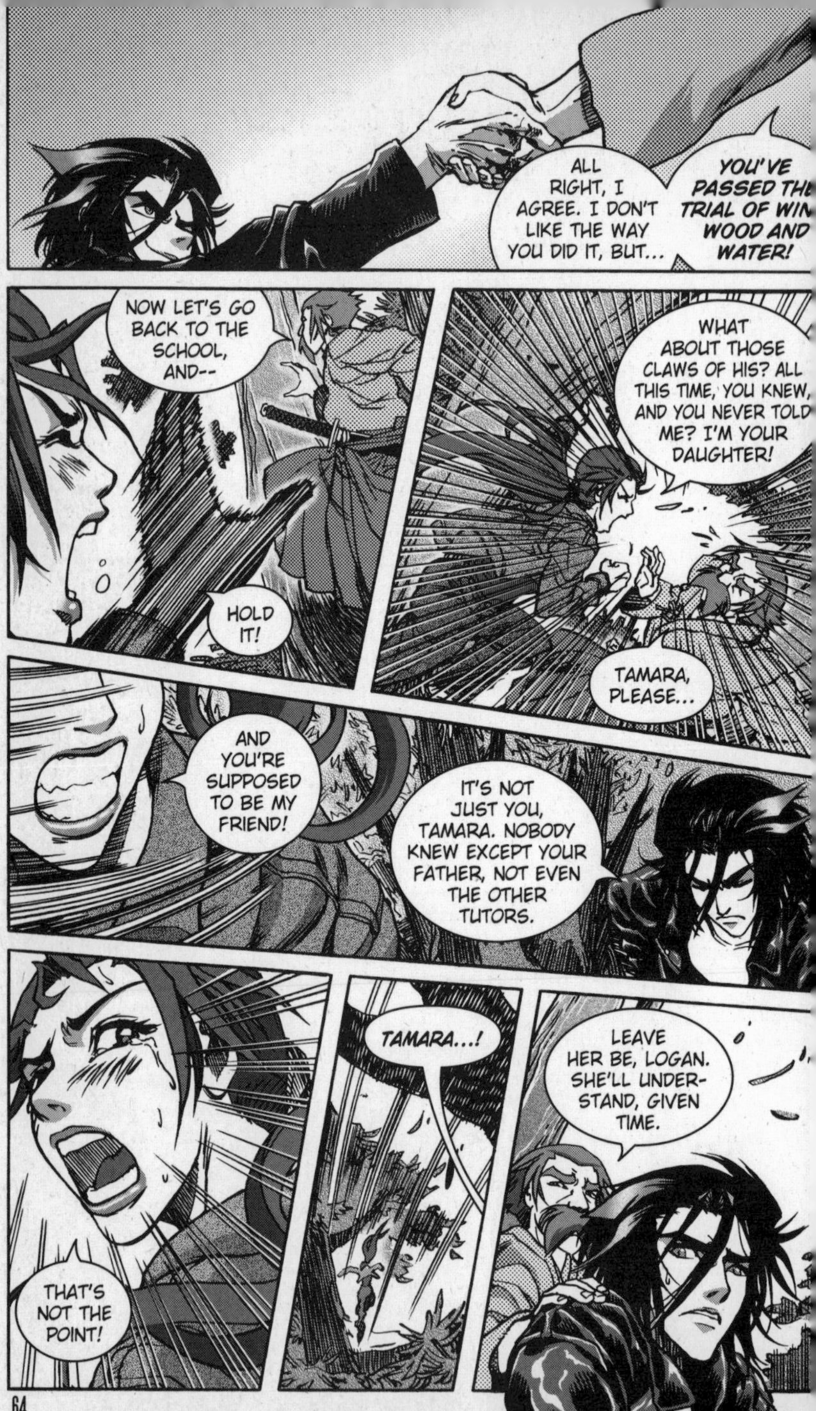
ALL RIGHT, I AGREE. I DON'T LIKE THE WAY YOU DID IT, BUT...
YOU'VE PASSED THE TRIAL OF WIN WOOD AND WATER!
NOW LET'S GO BACK TO THE SCHOOL, AND--
HOLD IT!
WHAT ABOUT THOSE CLAWS OF HIS? ALL THIS TIME, YOU KNEW, AND YOU NEVER TOLD ME? I'M YOUR DAUGHTER!
TAMARA, PLEASE...
AND YOU'RE SUPPOSED TO BE MY FRIEND!
IT'S NOT JUST YOU, TAMARA. NOBODY KNEW EXCEPT YOUR FATHER, NOT EVEN THE OTHER TUTORS.
THAT'S NOT THE POINT!
TAMARA...!
LEAVE HER BE, LOGAN. SHE'LL UNDER-STAND, GIVEN TIME.

Chapter Five
Mean Streets

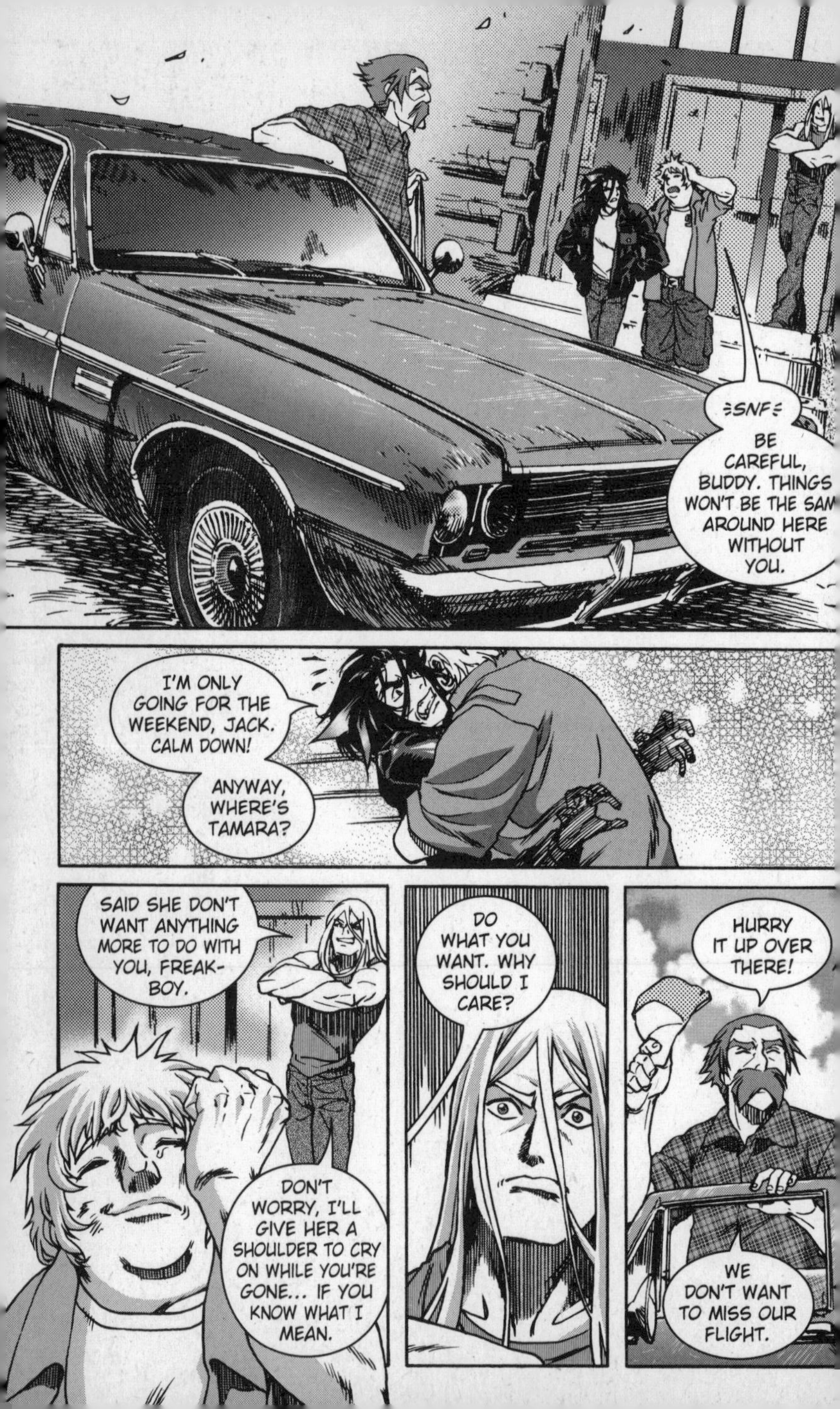

SNF
BE CAREFUL, BUDDY. THINGS WON'T BE THE SAM AROUND HERE WITHOUT YOU.
I'M ONLY GOING FOR THE WEEKEND, JACK. CALM DOWN!
ANYWAY, WHERE'S TAMARA?
SAID SHE DON'T WANT ANYTHING MORE TO DO WITH YOU, FREAK-BOY.
DON'T WORRY, I'LL GIVE HER A SHOULDER TO CRY ON WHILE YOU'RE GONE... IF YOU KNOW WHAT I MEAN.
DO WHAT YOU WANT. WHY SHOULD I CARE?
HURRY IT UP OVER THERE!
WE DON'T WANT TO MISS OUR FLIGHT.

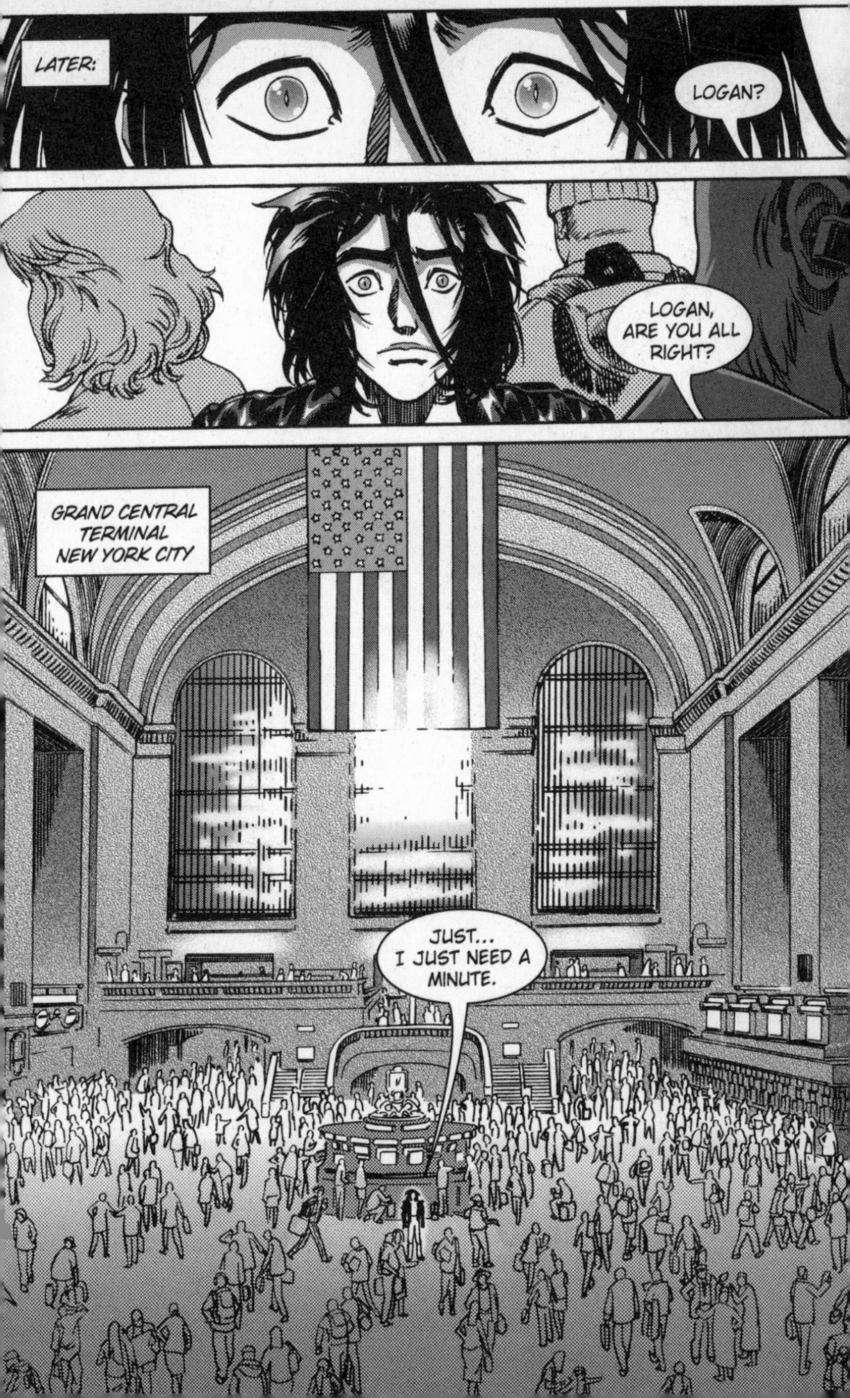
LATER:
LOGAN?
LOGAN, ARE YOU ALL RIGHT?
GRAND CENTRAL TERMINAL NEW YORK CITY
JUST... I JUST NEED A MINUTE.

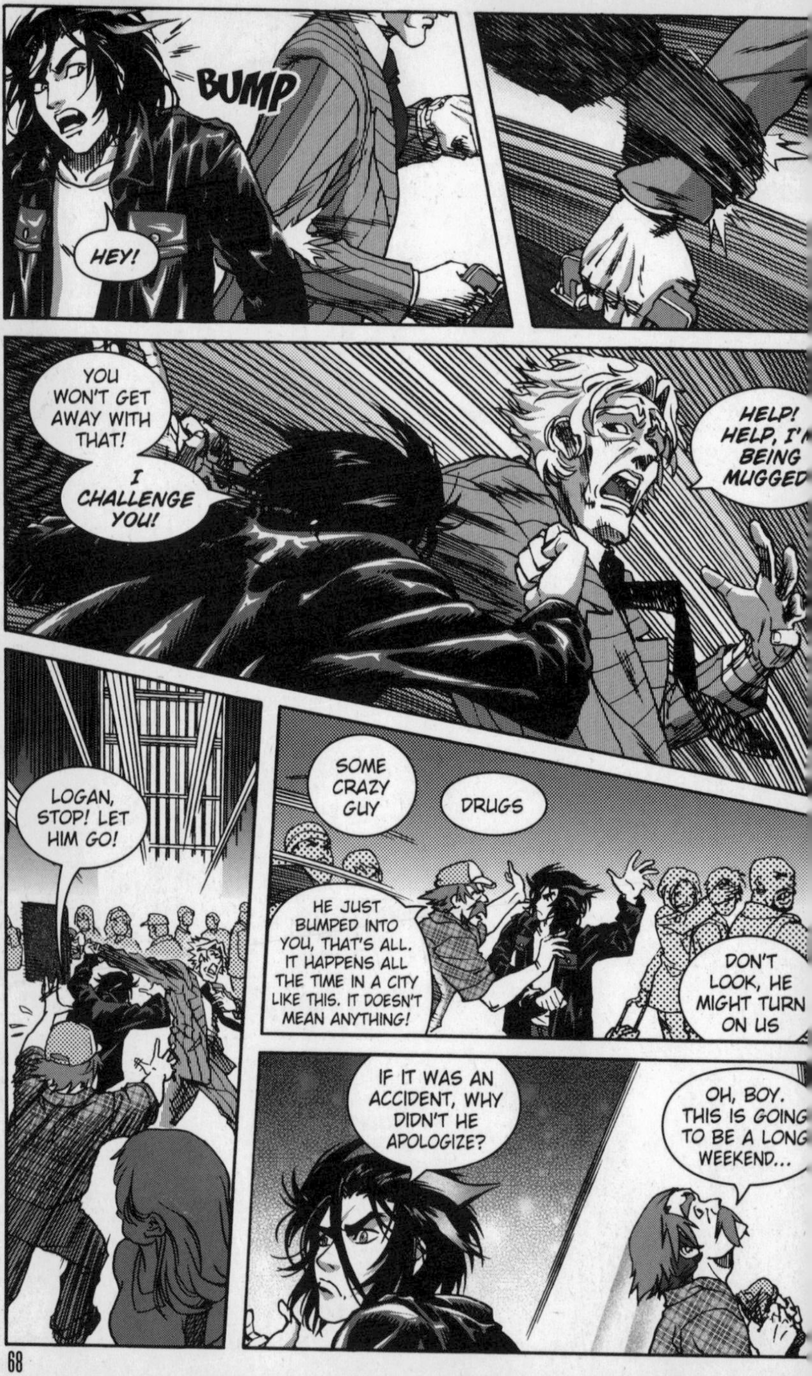
BUMP
HEY!
YOU WON'T GET AWAY WITH THAT!
I CHALLENGE YOU!
HELP! HELP, I'M BEING MUGGED
LOGAN, STOP! LET HIM GO!
SOME CRAZY GUY
DRUGS
HE JUST BUMPED INTO YOU, THAT'S ALL. IT HAPPENS ALL THE TIME IN A CITY LIKE THIS. IT DOESN'T MEAN ANYTHING!
DON'T LOOK, HE MIGHT TURN ON US
IF IT WAS AN ACCIDENT, WHY DIDN'T HE APOLOGIZE?
OH, BOY. THIS IS GOING TO BE A LONG WEEKEND...

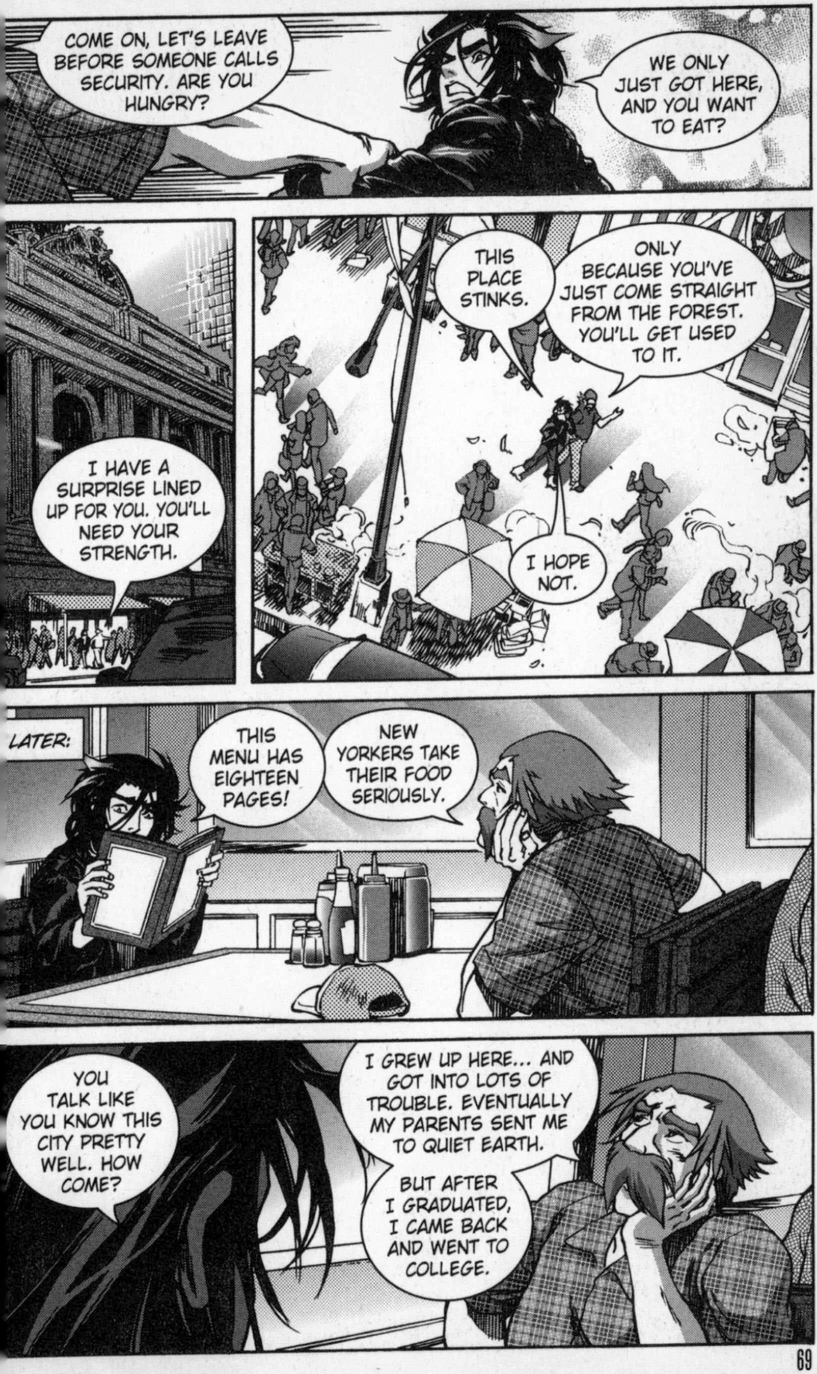

COME ON, LET'S LEAVE BEFORE SOMEONE CALLS SECURITY. ARE YOU HUNGRY?
WE ONLY JUST GOT HERE, AND YOU WANT TO EAT?
I HAVE A SURPRISE LINED UP FOR YOU. YOU'LL NEED YOUR STRENGTH.
THIS PLACE STINKS.
ONLY BECAUSE YOU'VE JUST COME STRAIGHT FROM THE FOREST. YOU'LL GET USED TO IT.
I HOPE NOT.
LATER:
THIS MENU HAS EIGHTEEN PAGES!
NEW YORKERS TAKE THEIR FOOD SERIOUSLY.
YOU TALK LIKE YOU KNOW THIS CITY PRETTY WELL. HOW COME?
I GREW UP HERE... AND GOT INTO LOTS OF TROUBLE. EVENTUALLY MY PARENTS SENT ME TO QUIET EARTH.
BUT AFTER I GRADUATED, I CAME BACK AND WENT TO COLLEGE.

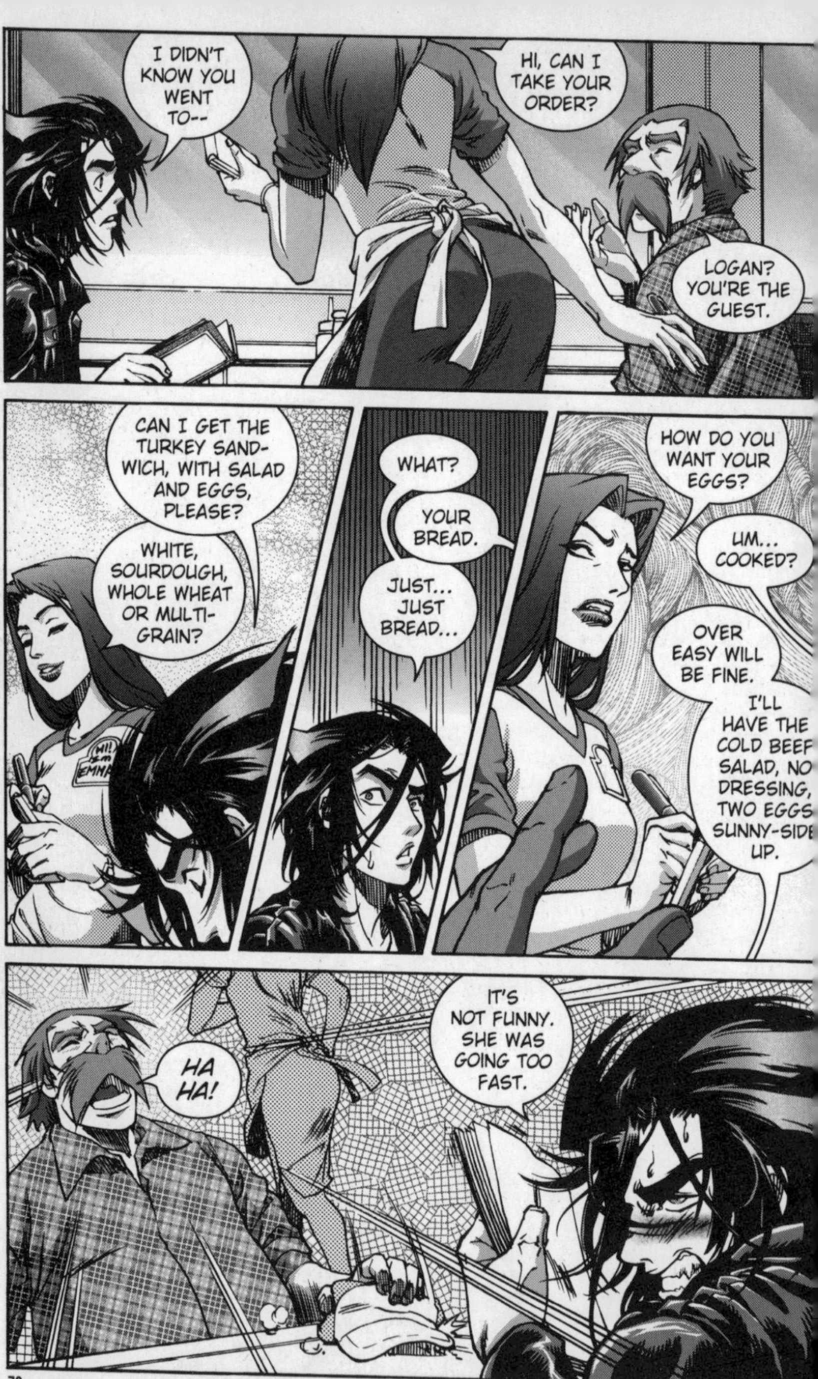

I DIDN'T KNOW YOU WENT TO--
HI, CAN I TAKE YOUR ORDER?
LOGAN? YOU'RE THE GUEST.
CAN I GET THE TURKEY SAND-WICH, WITH SALAD AND EGGS, PLEASE?
WHITE, SOURDOUGH, WHOLE WHEAT OR MULTI-GRAIN?
WHAT?
YOUR BREAD.
JUST... JUST BREAD...
HOW DO YOU WANT YOUR EGGS?
UM... COOKED?
OVER EASY WILL BE FINE.
I'LL HAVE THE COLD BEEF SALAD, NO DRESSING, TWO EGGS SUNNY-SIDE UP.
HA HA!
IT'S NOT FUNNY. SHE WAS GOING TOO FAST.

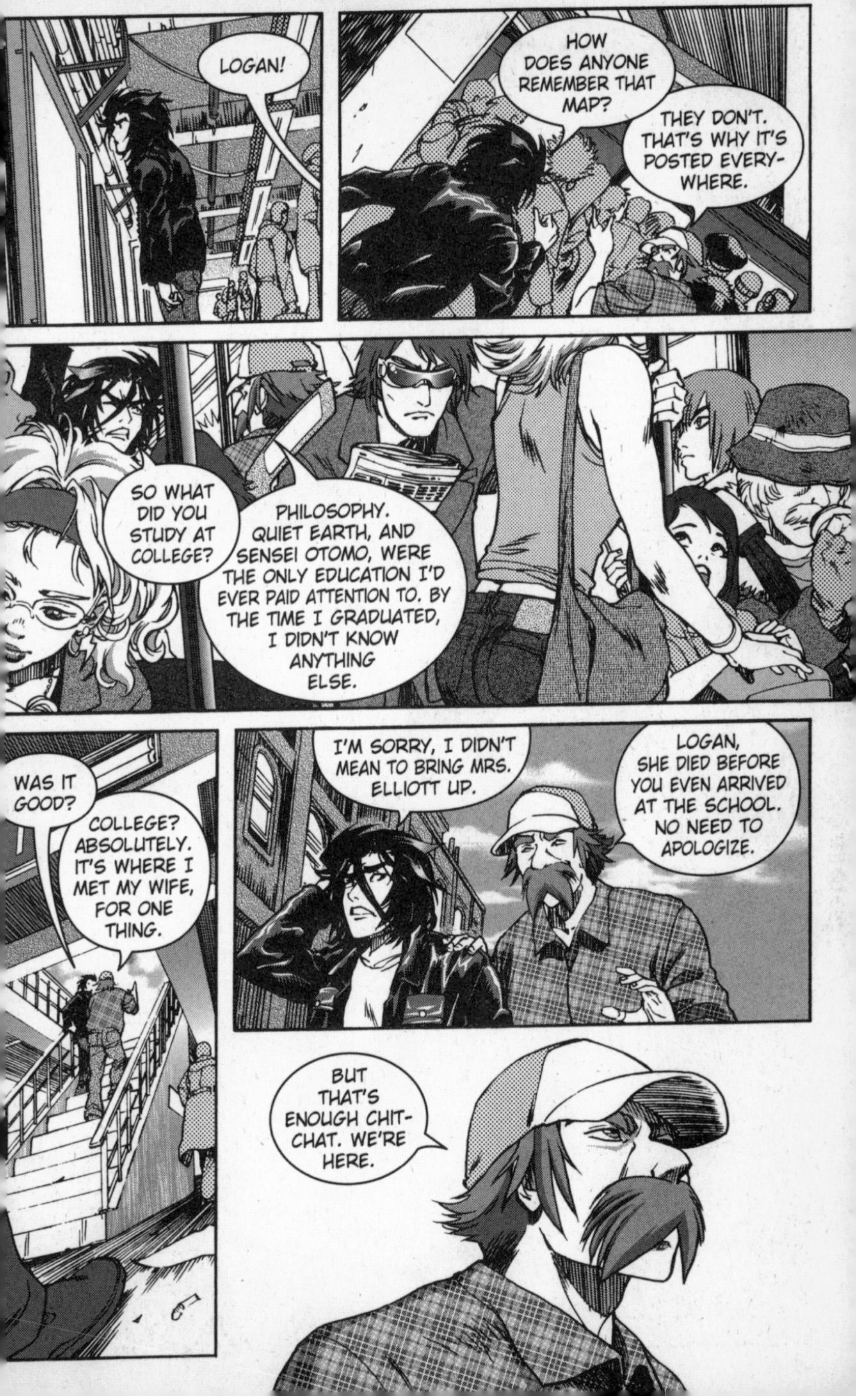
LOGAN!
HOW DOES ANYONE REMEMBER THAT MAP?
THEY DON'T. THAT'S WHY IT'S POSTED EVERY-WHERE.
SO WHAT DID YOU STUDY AT COLLEGE?
PHILOSOPHY. QUIET EARTH, AND SENSEI OTOMO, WERE THE ONLY EDUCATION I'D EVER PAID ATTENTION TO. BY THE TIME I GRADUATED, I DIDN'T KNOW ANYTHING ELSE.
WAS IT GOOD?
COLLEGE? ABSOLUTELY. IT'S WHERE I MET MY WIFE, FOR ONE THING.
I'M SORRY, I DIDN'T MEAN TO BRING MRS. ELLIOTT UP.
LOGAN, SHE DIED BEFORE YOU EVEN ARRIVED AT THE SCHOOL. NO NEED TO APOLOGIZE.
BUT THAT'S ENOUGH CHIT-CHAT. WE'RE HERE.

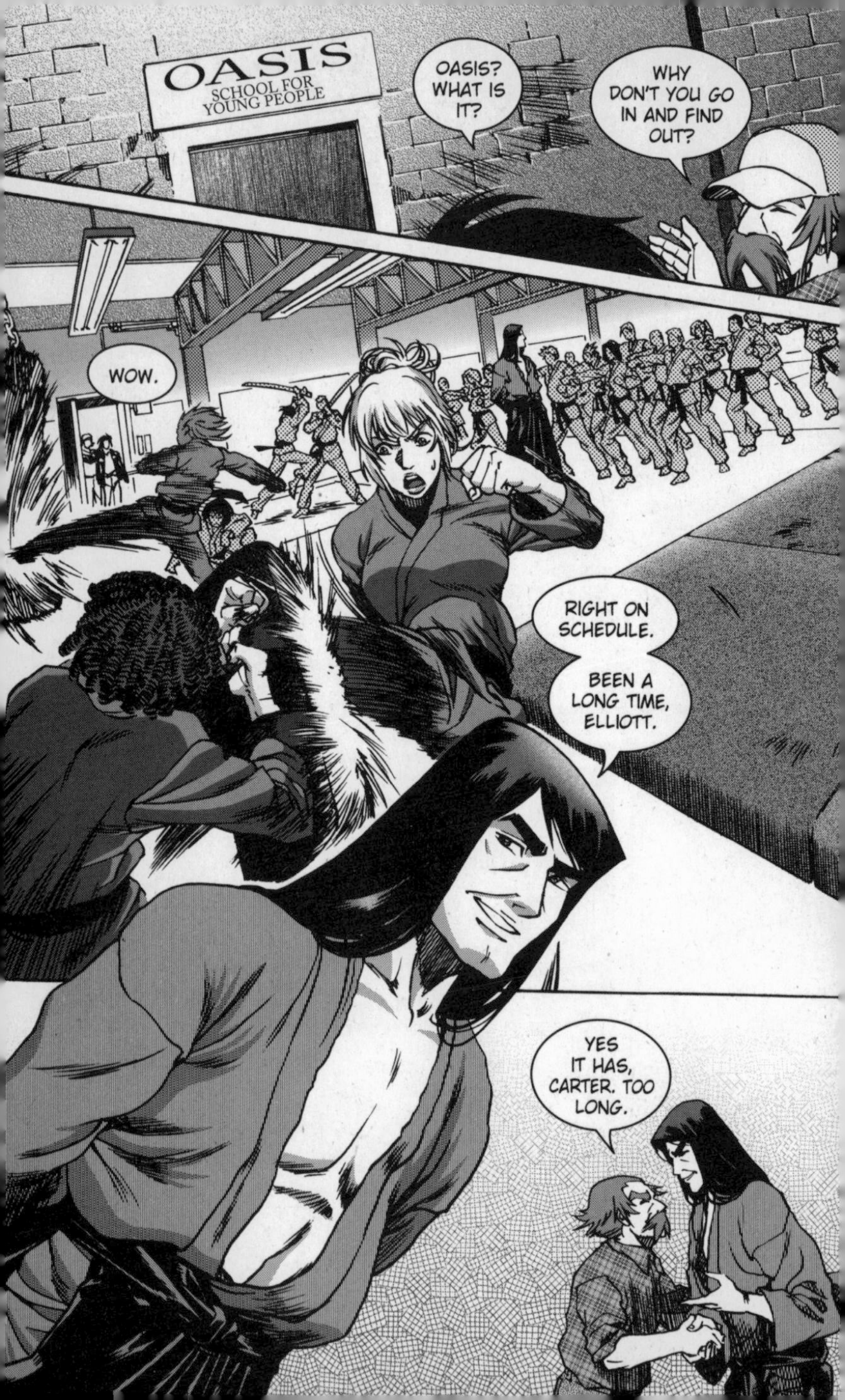
OASIS
SCHOOL FOR YOUNG PEOPLE
OASIS? WHAT IS IT?
WHY DON'T YOU GO IN AND FIND OUT?
WOW.
RIGHT ON SCHEDULE.
BEEN A LONG TIME, ELLIOTT.
YES IT HAS, CARTER. TOO LONG.

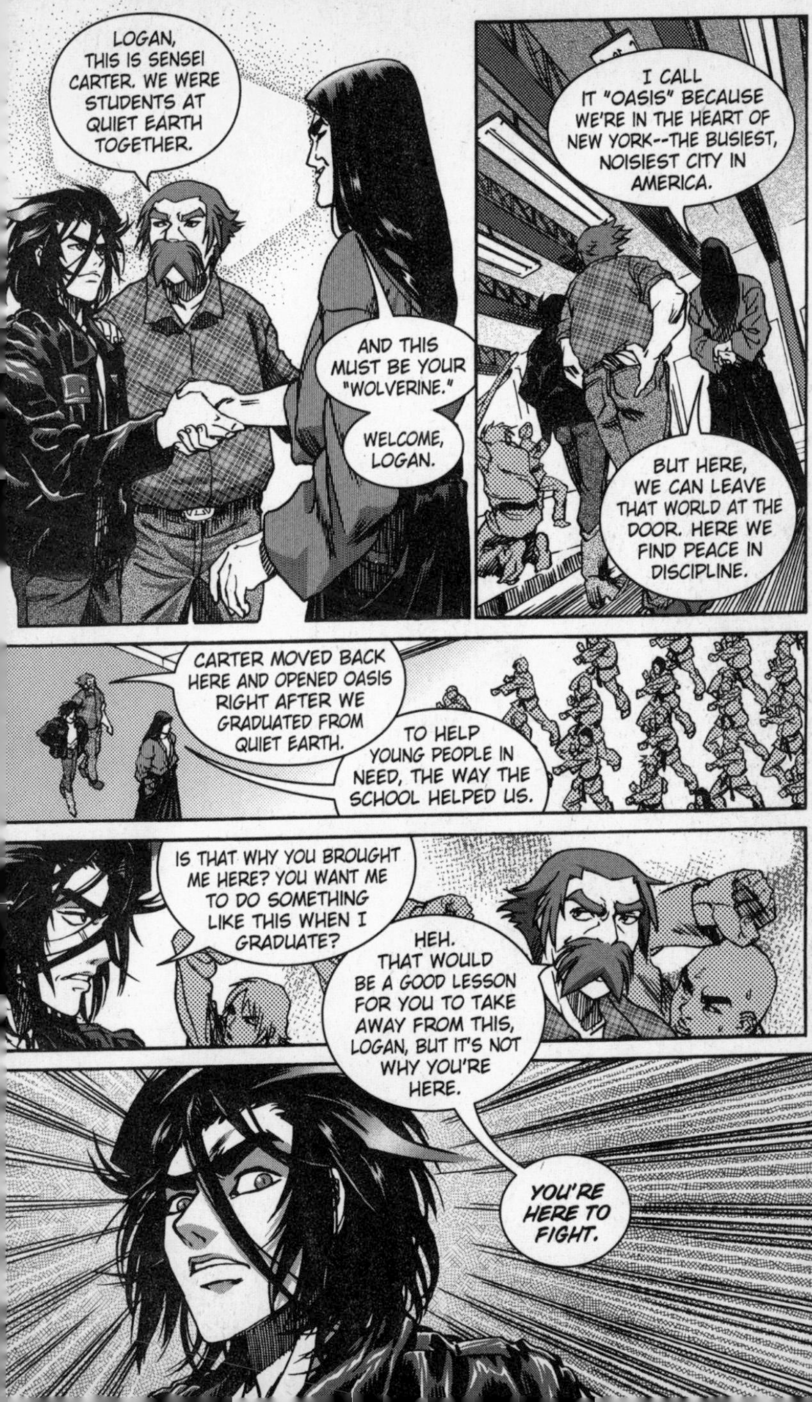
LOGAN, THIS IS SENSEI CARTER. WE WERE STUDENTS AT QUIET EARTH TOGETHER.
AND THIS MUST BE YOUR "WOLVERINE."
WELCOME, LOGAN.
I CALL IT "OASIS" BECAUSE WE'RE IN THE HEART OF NEW YORK--THE BUSIEST, NOISIEST CITY IN AMERICA.
BUT HERE, WE CAN LEAVE THAT WORLD AT THE DOOR. HERE WE FIND PEACE IN DISCIPLINE.
CARTER MOVED BACK HERE AND OPENED OASIS RIGHT AFTER WE GRADUATED FROM QUIET EARTH.
TO HELP YOUNG PEOPLE IN NEED, THE WAY THE SCHOOL HELPED US.
IS THAT WHY YOU BROUGHT ME HERE? YOU WANT ME TO DO SOMETHING LIKE THIS WHEN I GRADUATE?
HEH. THAT WOULD BE A GOOD LESSON FOR YOU TO TAKE AWAY FROM THIS, LOGAN, BUT IT'S NOT WHY YOU'RE HERE.
YOU'RE HERE TO FIGHT.

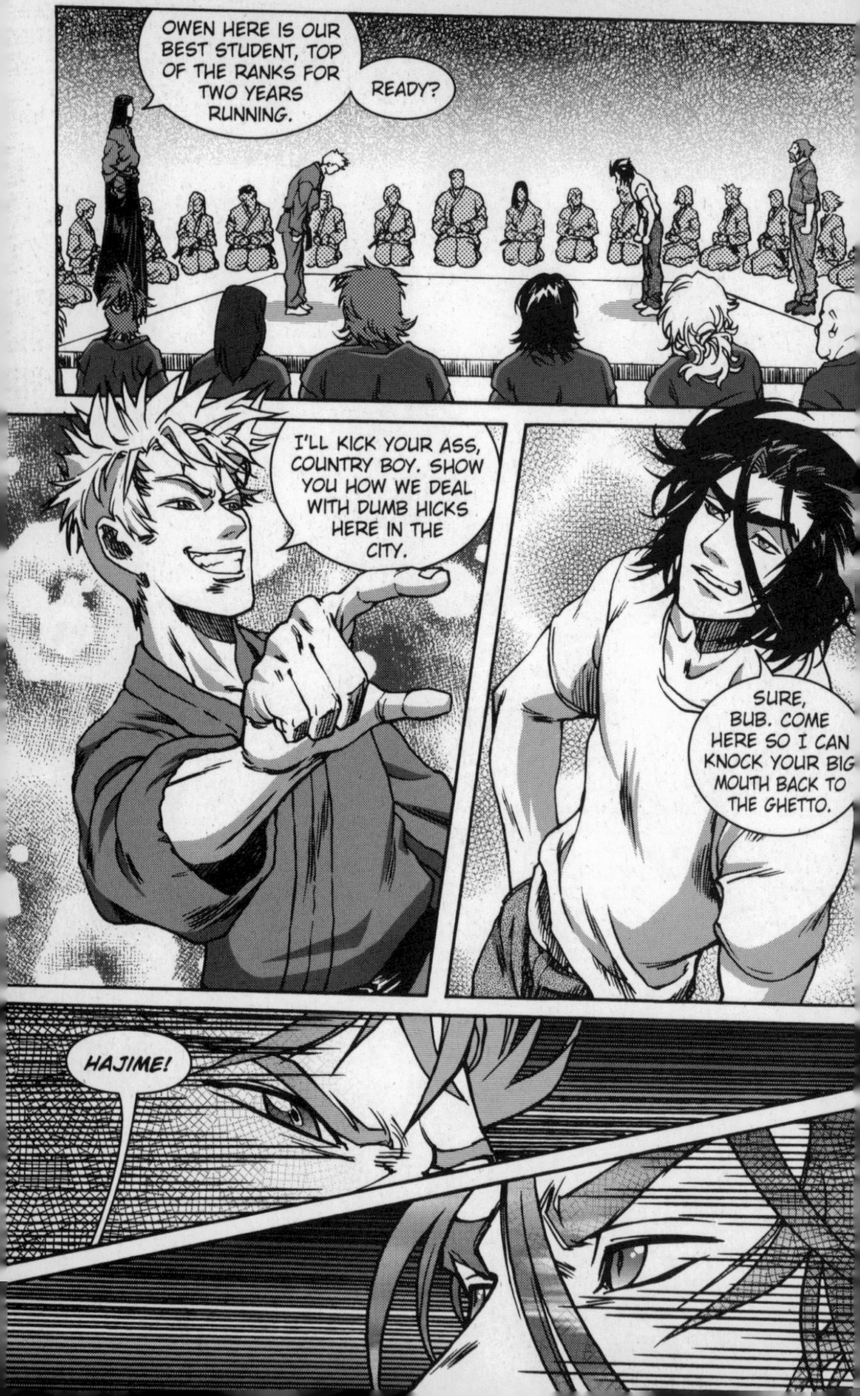
OWEN HERE IS OUR BEST STUDENT, TOP OF THE RANKS FOR TWO YEARS RUNNING.
READY?
I'LL KICK YOUR ASS, COUNTRY BOY. SHOW YOU HOW WE DEAL WITH DUMB HICKS HERE IN THE CITY.
SURE, BUB. COME HERE SO I CAN KNOCK YOUR BIG MOUTH BACK TO THE GHETTO.
HAJIME!

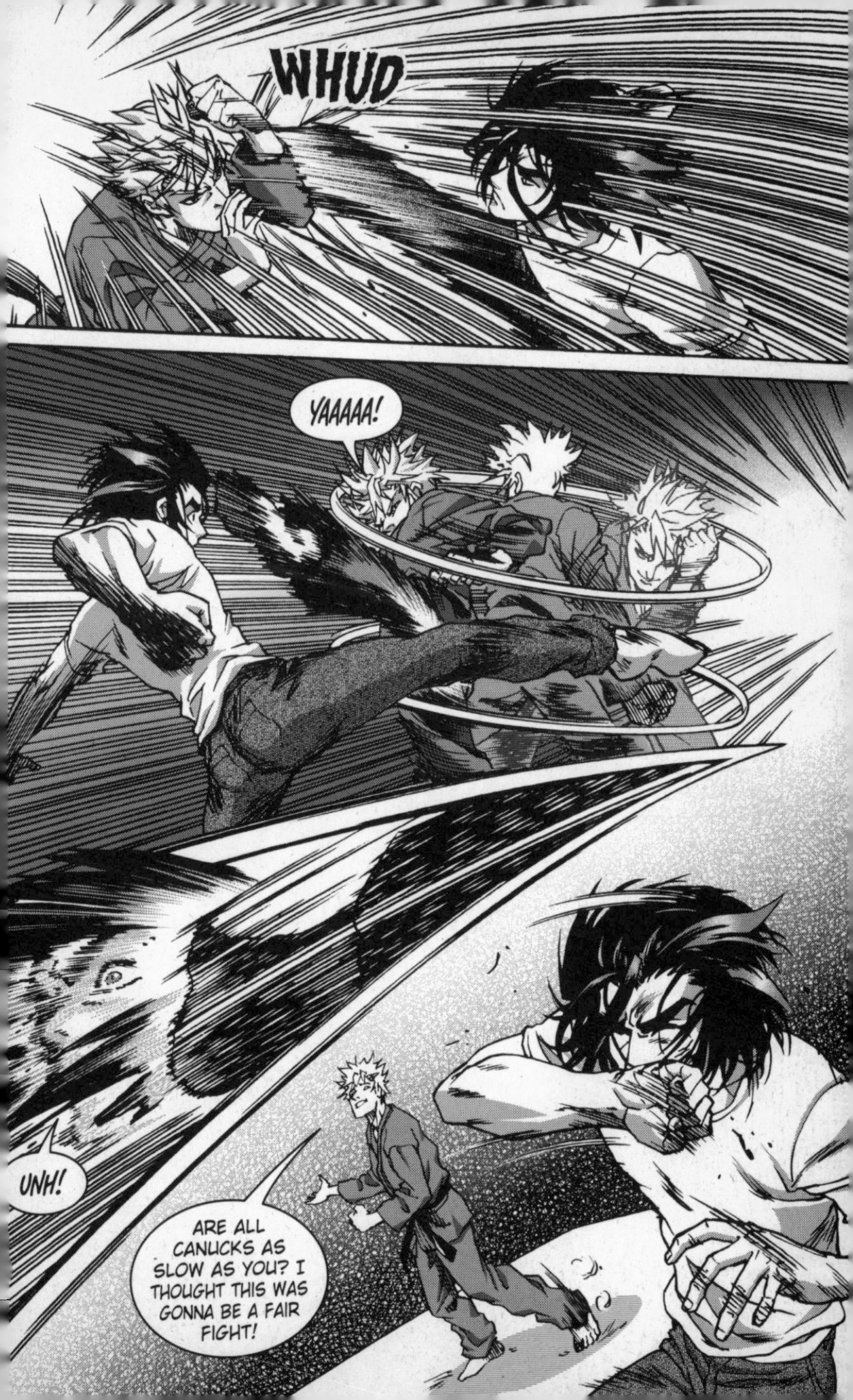
WHUD
YAAAAA!
UNH!
ARE ALL CANUCKS AS SLOW AS YOU? I THOUGHT THIS WAS GONNA BE A FAIR FIGHT!

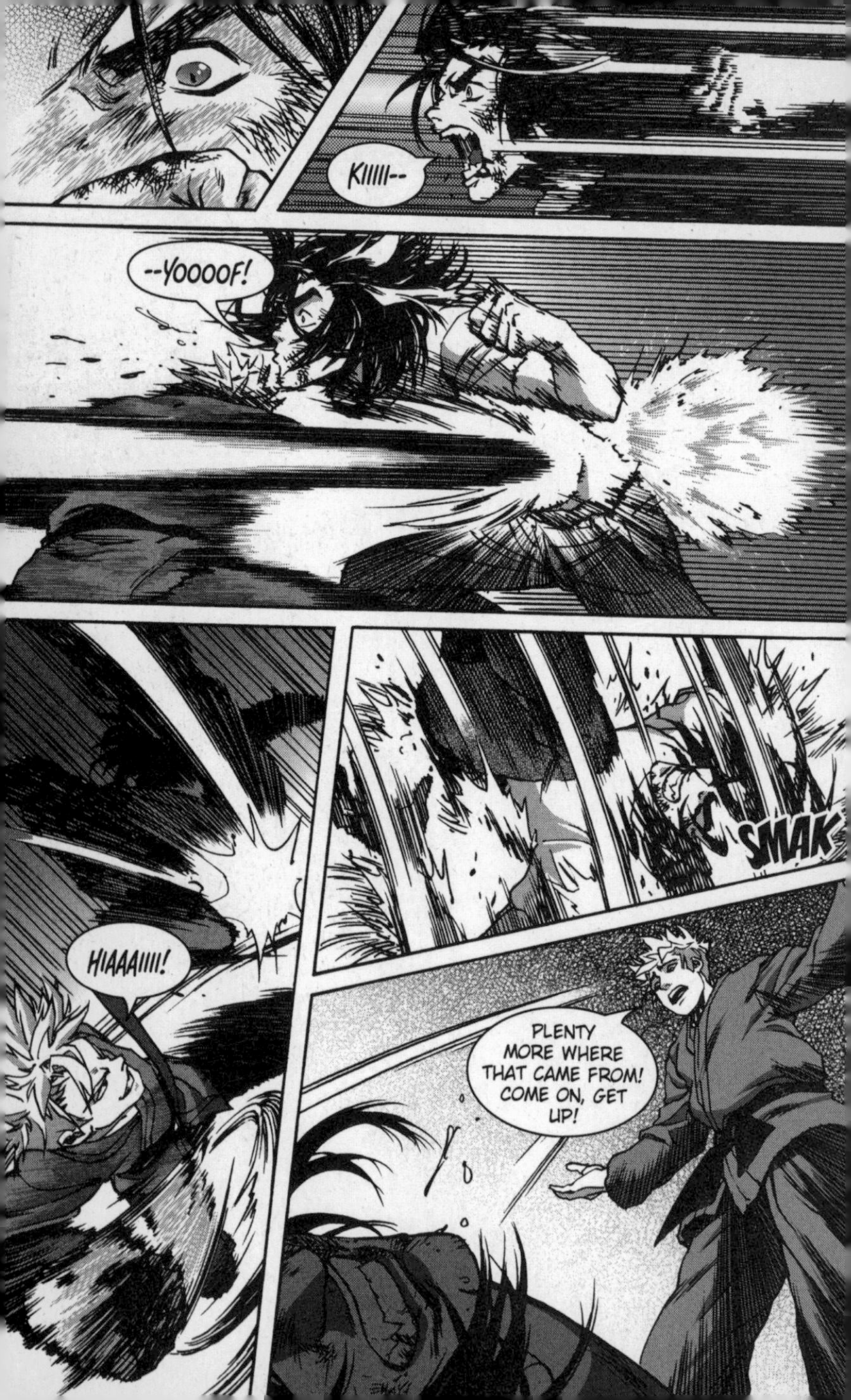
KIIIII--
--YOOOOF!
SMAK
HIAAAIIII!
PLENTY MORE WHERE THAT CAME FROM! COME ON, GET UP!

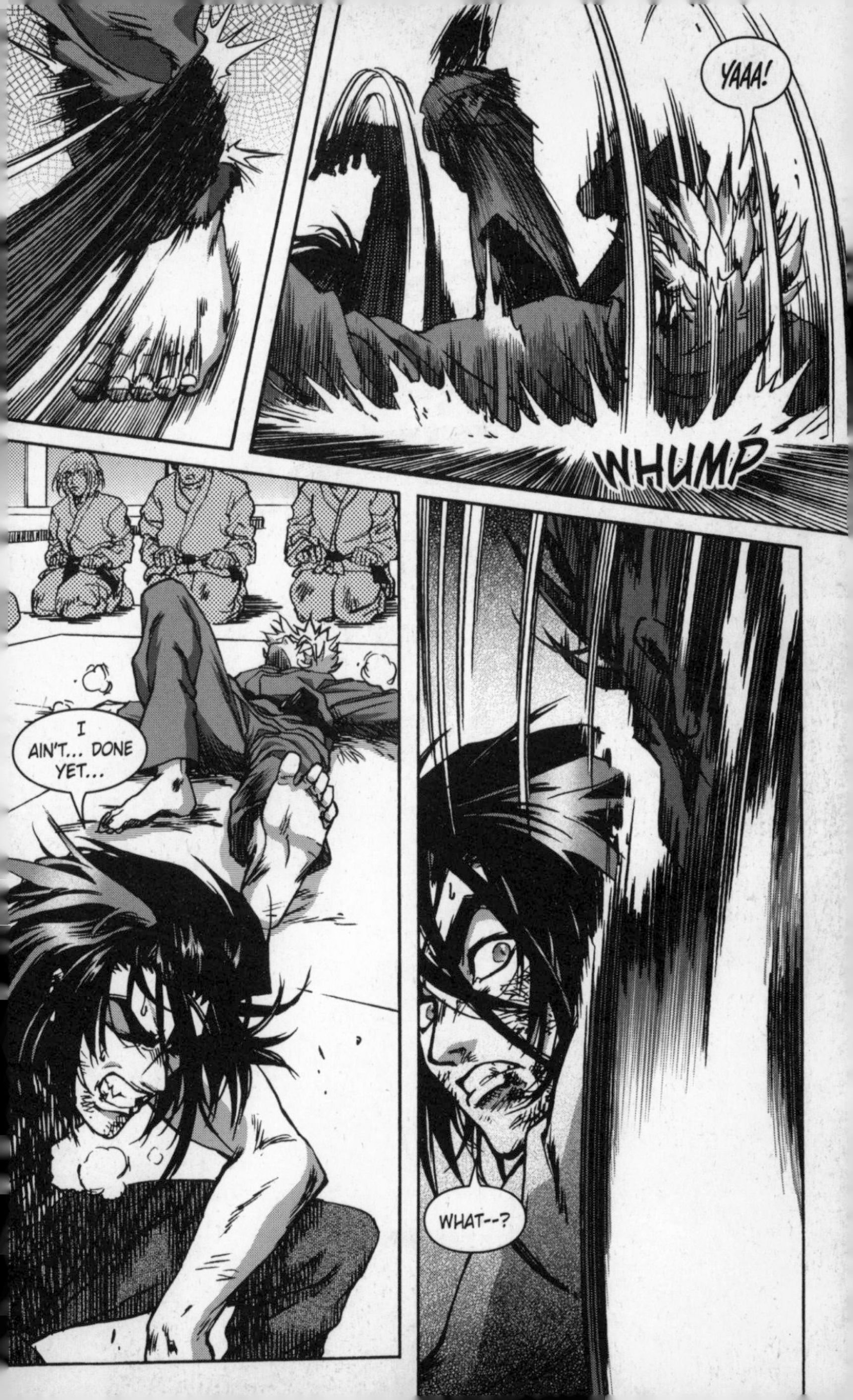
YAAA!
WHUMP
I AIN'T... DONE YET...
WHAT--?

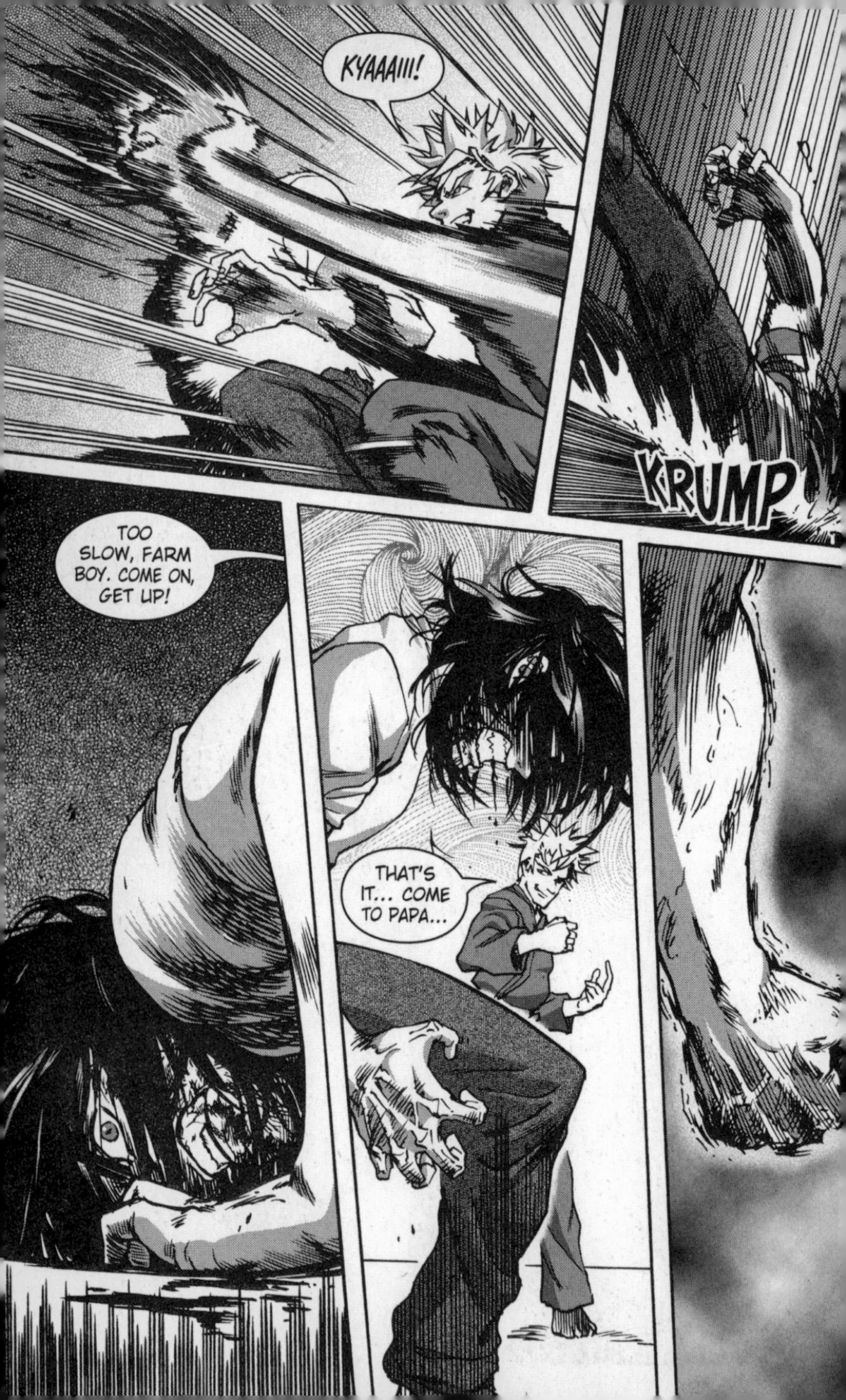
KYAAAIII!
KRUMP
TOO SLOW, FARM BOY. COME ON, GET UP!
THAT'S IT... COME TO PAPA...

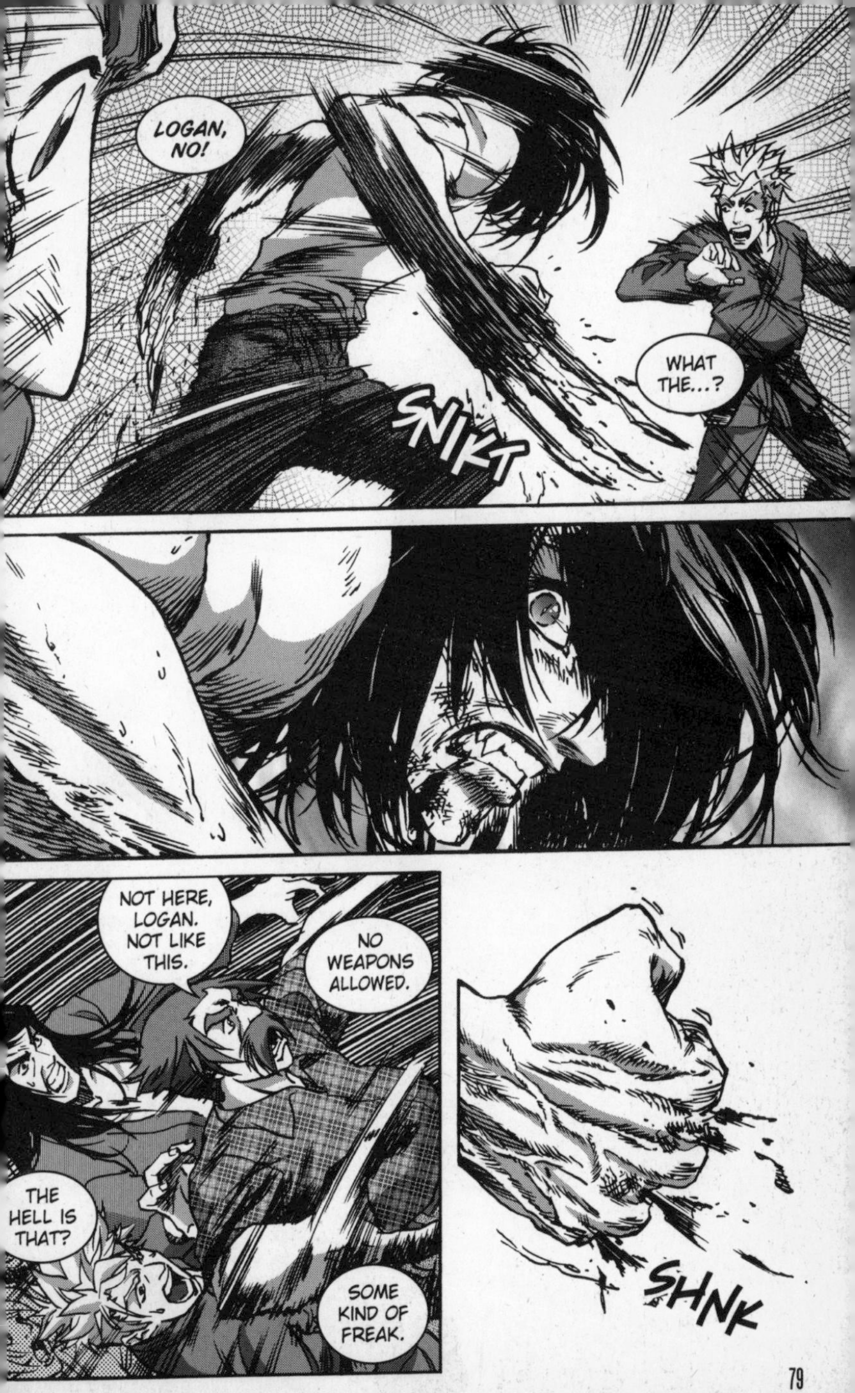
LOGAN, NO!
SNIKT
WHAT THE...?
NOT HERE, LOGAN. NOT LIKE THIS.
NO WEAPONS ALLOWED.
THE HELL IS THAT?
SOME KIND OF FREAK.
SHNK

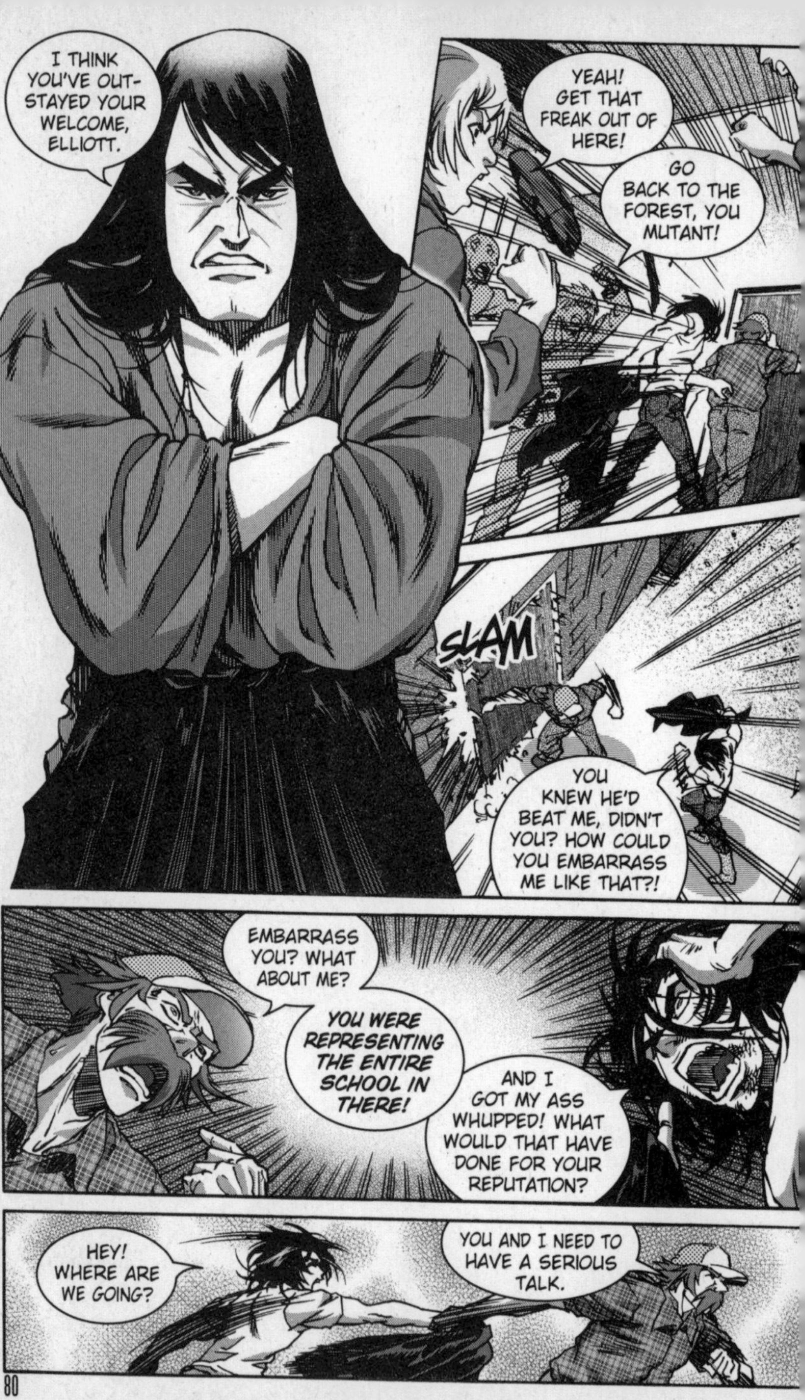
I THINK YOU'VE OUT-STAYED YOUR WELCOME, ELLIOTT.
YEAH! GET THAT FREAK OUT OF HERE!
GO BACK TO THE FOREST, YOU MUTANT!
SLAM
YOU KNEW HE'D BEAT ME, DIDN'T YOU? HOW COULD YOU EMBARRASS ME LIKE THAT?!
EMBARRASS YOU? WHAT ABOUT ME?
YOU WERE REPRESENTING THE ENTIRE SCHOOL IN THERE!
AND I GOT MY ASS WHUPPED! WHAT WOULD THAT HAVE DONE FOR YOUR REPUTATION?
HEY! WHERE ARE WE GOING?
YOU AND I NEED TO HAVE A SERIOUS TALK.

Chapter Six
The Sound of Silence

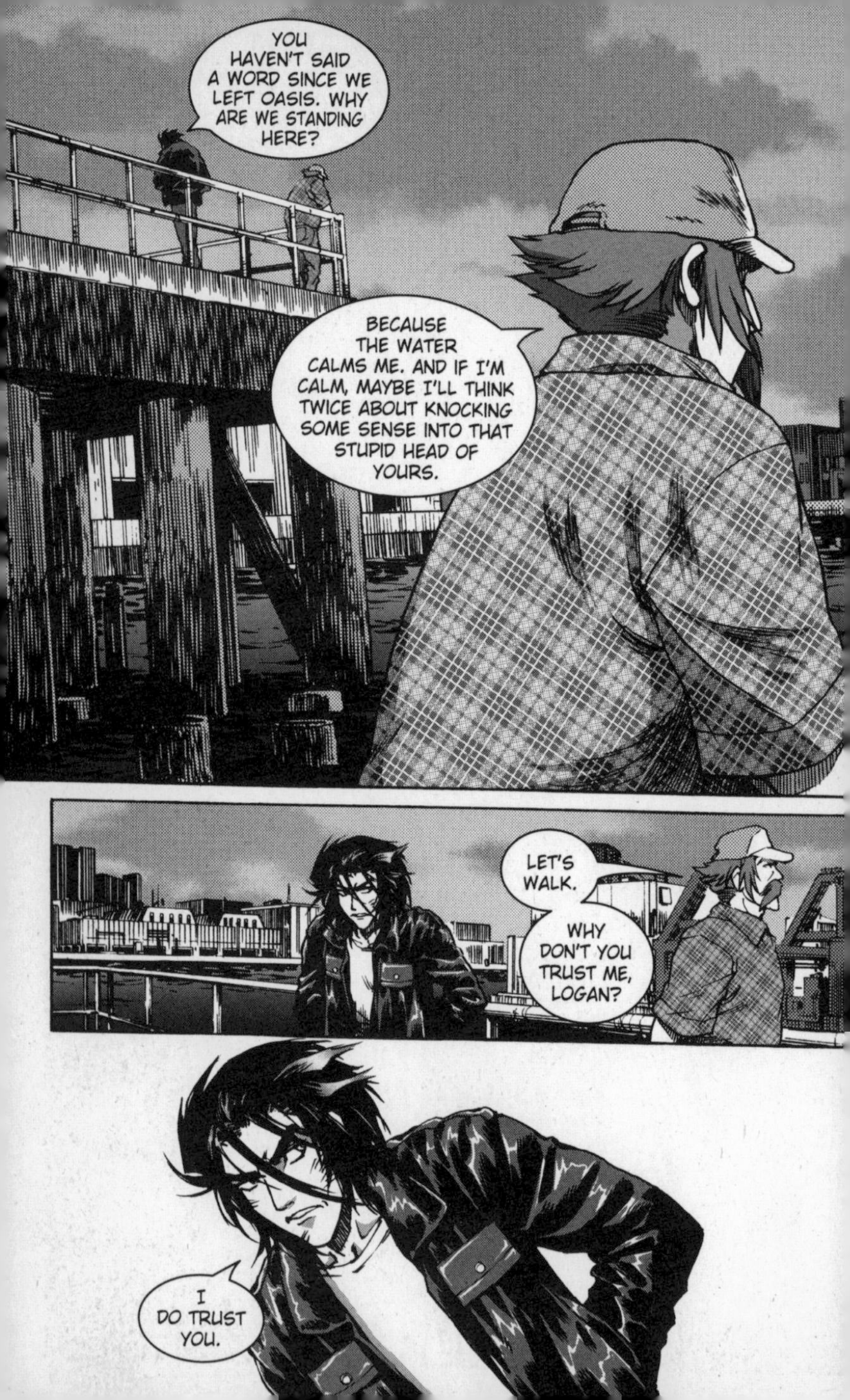
YOU HAVEN'T SAID A WORD SINCE WE LEFT OASIS. WHY ARE WE STANDING HERE?
BECAUSE THE WATER CALMS ME. AND IF I'M CALM, MAYBE I'LL THINK TWICE ABOUT KNOCKING SOME SENSE INTO THAT STUPID HEAD OF YOURS.
LET'S WALK.
WHY DON'T YOU TRUST ME, LOGAN?
I DO TRUST YOU.

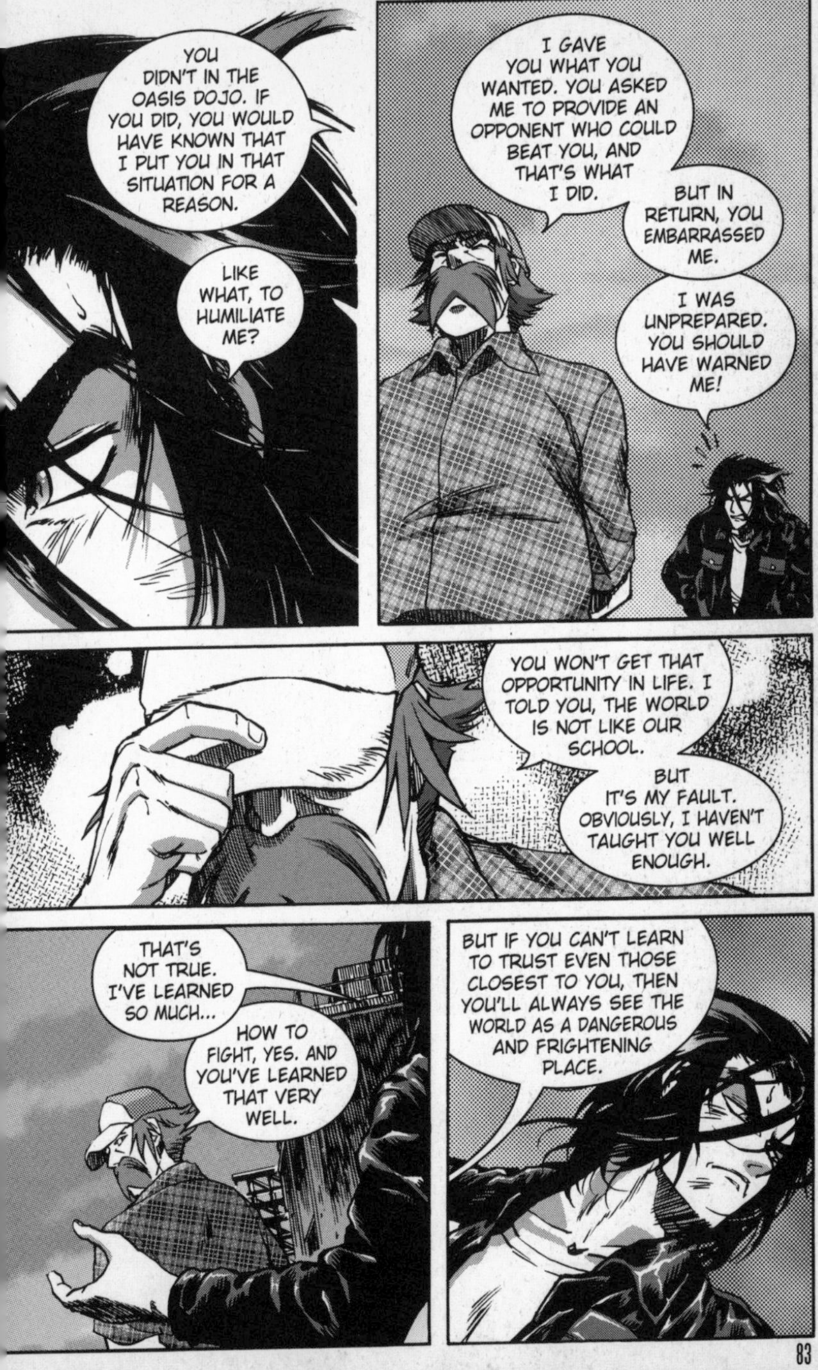
YOU DIDN'T IN THE OASIS DOJO. IF YOU DID, YOU WOULD HAVE KNOWN THAT I PUT YOU IN THAT SITUATION FOR A REASON.
LIKE WHAT, TO HUMILIATE ME?
I GAVE YOU WHAT YOU WANTED. YOU ASKED ME TO PROVIDE AN OPPONENT WHO COULD BEAT YOU, AND THAT'S WHAT I DID.
BUT IN RETURN, YOU EMBARRASSED ME.
I WAS UNPREPARED. YOU SHOULD HAVE WARNED ME!
YOU WON'T GET THAT OPPORTUNITY IN LIFE. I TOLD YOU, THE WORLD IS NOT LIKE OUR SCHOOL.
BUT IT'S MY FAULT. OBVIOUSLY, I HAVEN'T TAUGHT YOU WELL ENOUGH.
THAT'S NOT TRUE. I'VE LEARNED SO MUCH...
HOW TO FIGHT, YES. AND YOU'VE LEARNED THAT VERY WELL.
BUT IF YOU CAN'T LEARN TO TRUST EVEN THOSE CLOSEST TO YOU, THEN YOU'LL ALWAYS SEE THE WORLD AS A DANGEROUS AND FRIGHTENING PLACE.

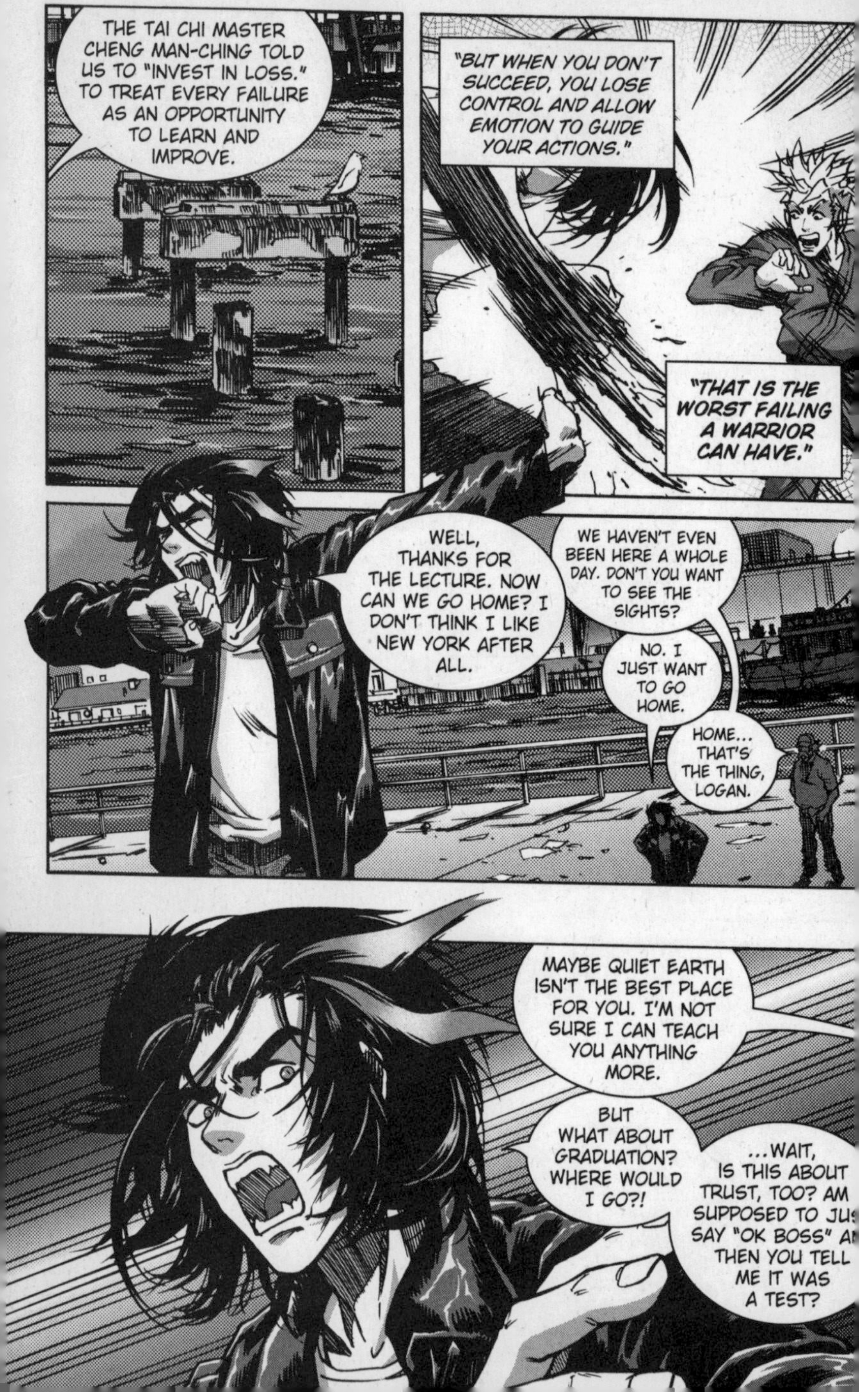
THE TAI CHI MASTER CHENG MAN-CHING TOLD US TO "INVEST IN LOSS." TO TREAT EVERY FAILURE AS AN OPPORTUNITY TO LEARN AND IMPROVE.
"BUT WHEN YOU DON'T SUCCEED, YOU LOSE CONTROL AND ALLOW EMOTION TO GUIDE YOUR ACTIONS."
"THAT IS THE WORST FAILING A WARRIOR CAN HAVE."
WELL, THANKS FOR THE LECTURE. NOW CAN WE GO HOME? I DON'T THINK I LIKE NEW YORK AFTER ALL.
WE HAVEN'T EVEN BEEN HERE A WHOLE DAY. DON'T YOU WANT TO SEE THE SIGHTS?
NO. I JUST WANT TO GO HOME.
HOME... THAT'S THE THING, LOGAN.
MAYBE QUIET EARTH ISN'T THE BEST PLACE FOR YOU. I'M NOT SURE I CAN TEACH YOU ANYTHING MORE.
BUT WHAT ABOUT GRADUATION? WHERE WOULD I GO?!
...WAIT, IS THIS ABOUT TRUST, TOO? AM SUPPOSED TO JU SAY "OK BOSS" A THEN YOU TELL ME IT WAS A TEST?

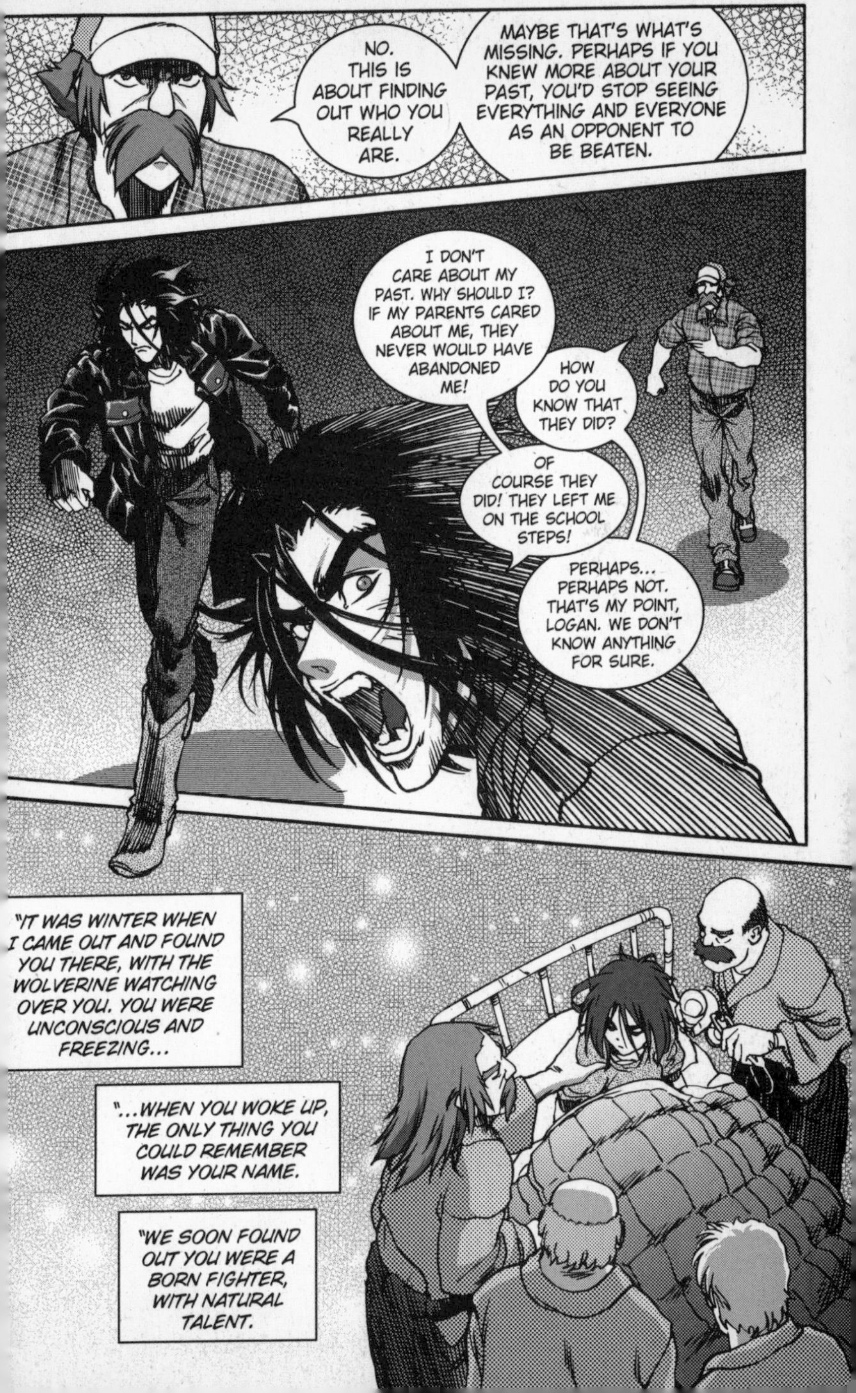
NO. THIS IS ABOUT FINDING OUT WHO YOU REALLY ARE.
MAYBE THAT'S WHAT'S MISSING. PERHAPS IF YOU KNEW MORE ABOUT YOUR PAST, YOU'D STOP SEEING EVERYTHING AND EVERYONE AS AN OPPONENT TO BE BEATEN.
I DON'T CARE ABOUT MY PAST. WHY SHOULD I? IF MY PARENTS CARED ABOUT ME, THEY NEVER WOULD HAVE ABANDONED ME!
HOW DO YOU KNOW THAT THEY DID?
OF COURSE THEY DID! THEY LEFT ME ON THE SCHOOL STEPS!
PERHAPS... PERHAPS NOT. THAT'S MY POINT, LOGAN. WE DON'T KNOW ANYTHING FOR SURE.
"IT WAS WINTER WHEN I CAME OUT AND FOUND YOU THERE, WITH THE WOLVERINE WATCHING OVER YOU. YOU WERE UNCONSCIOUS AND FREEZING...
"...WHEN YOU WOKE UP, THE ONLY THING YOU COULD REMEMBER WAS YOUR NAME.
"WE SOON FOUND OUT YOU WERE A BORN FIGHTER, WITH NATURAL TALENT.

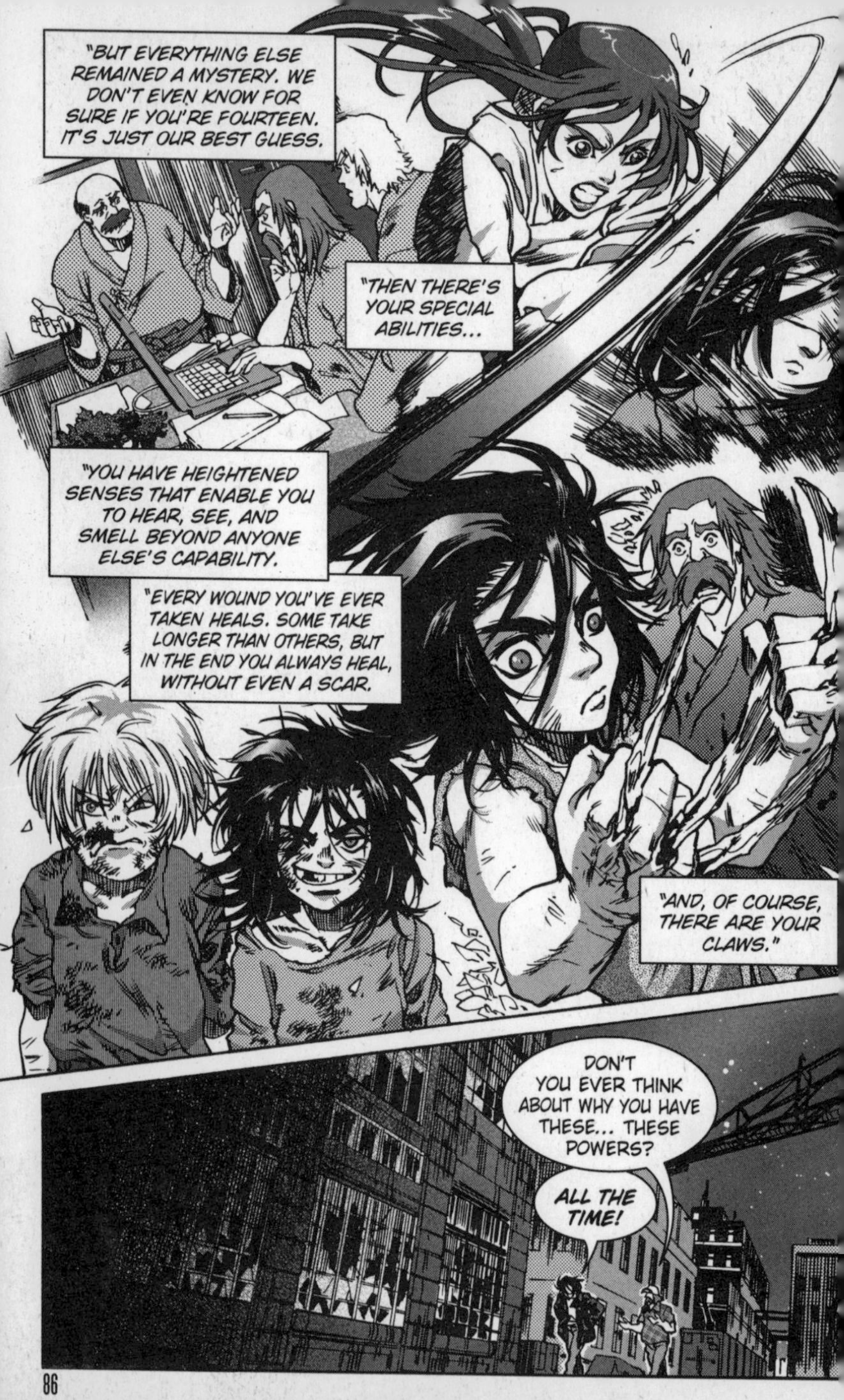
"BUT EVERYTHING ELSE REMAINED A MYSTERY. WE DON'T EVEN KNOW FOR SURE IF YOU'RE FOURTEEN. IT'S JUST OUR BEST GUESS.
"THEN THERE'S YOUR SPECIAL ABILITIES...
"YOU HAVE HEIGHTENED SENSES THAT ENABLE YOU TO HEAR, SEE, AND SMELL BEYOND ANYONE ELSE'S CAPABILITY.
"EVERY WOUND YOU'VE EVER TAKEN HEALS. SOME TAKE LONGER THAN OTHERS, BUT IN THE END YOU ALWAYS HEAL, WITHOUT EVEN A SCAR.
"AND, OF COURSE, THERE ARE YOUR CLAWS."
DON'T YOU EVER THINK ABOUT WHY YOU HAVE THESE... THESE POWERS?
ALL THE TIME!

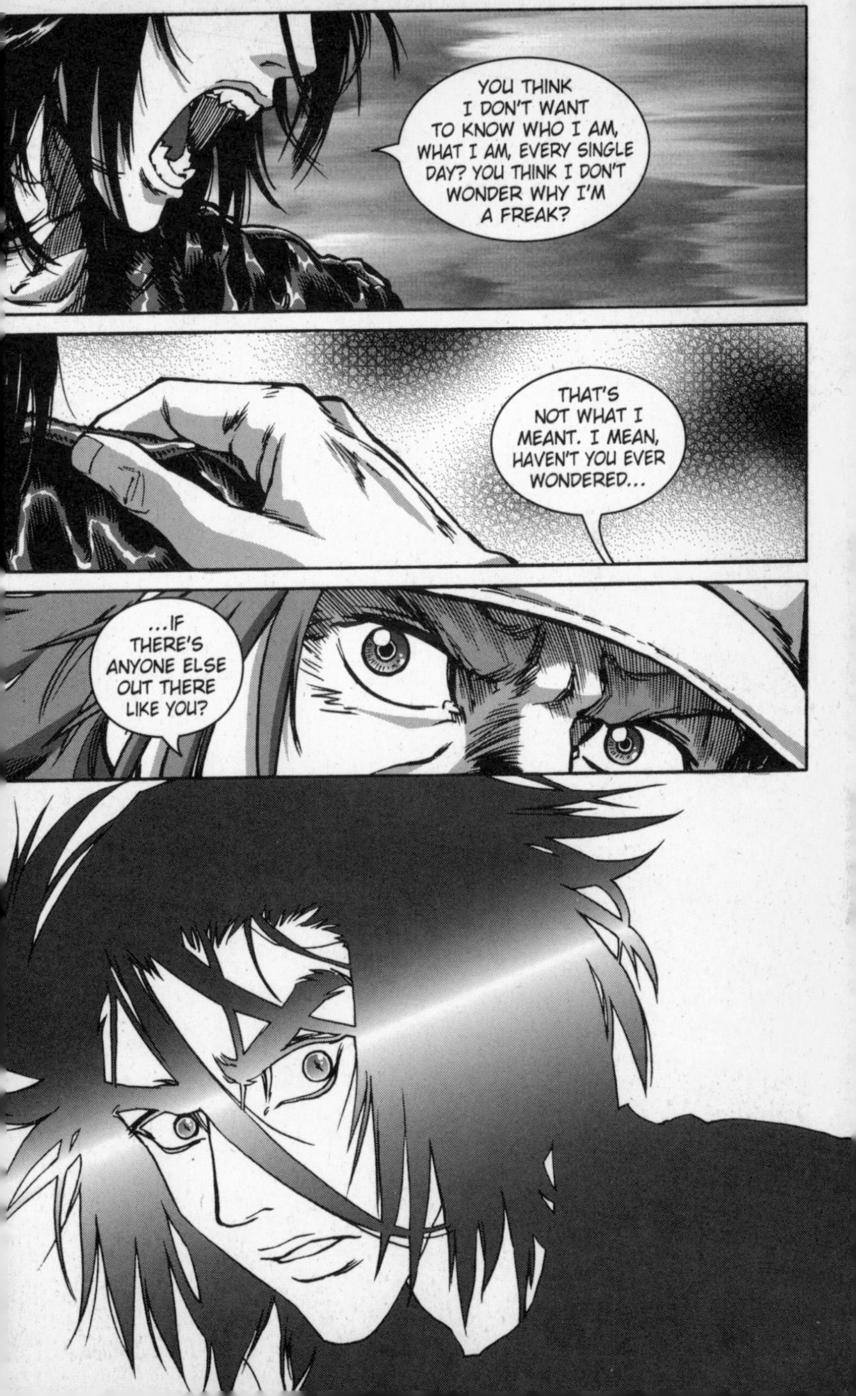
YOU THINK I DON'T WANT TO KNOW WHO I AM, WHAT I AM, EVERY SINGLE DAY? YOU THINK I DON'T WONDER WHY I'M A FREAK?
THAT'S NOT WHAT I MEANT. I MEAN, HAVEN'T YOU EVER WONDERED...
...IF THERE'S ANYONE ELSE OUT THERE LIKE YOU?

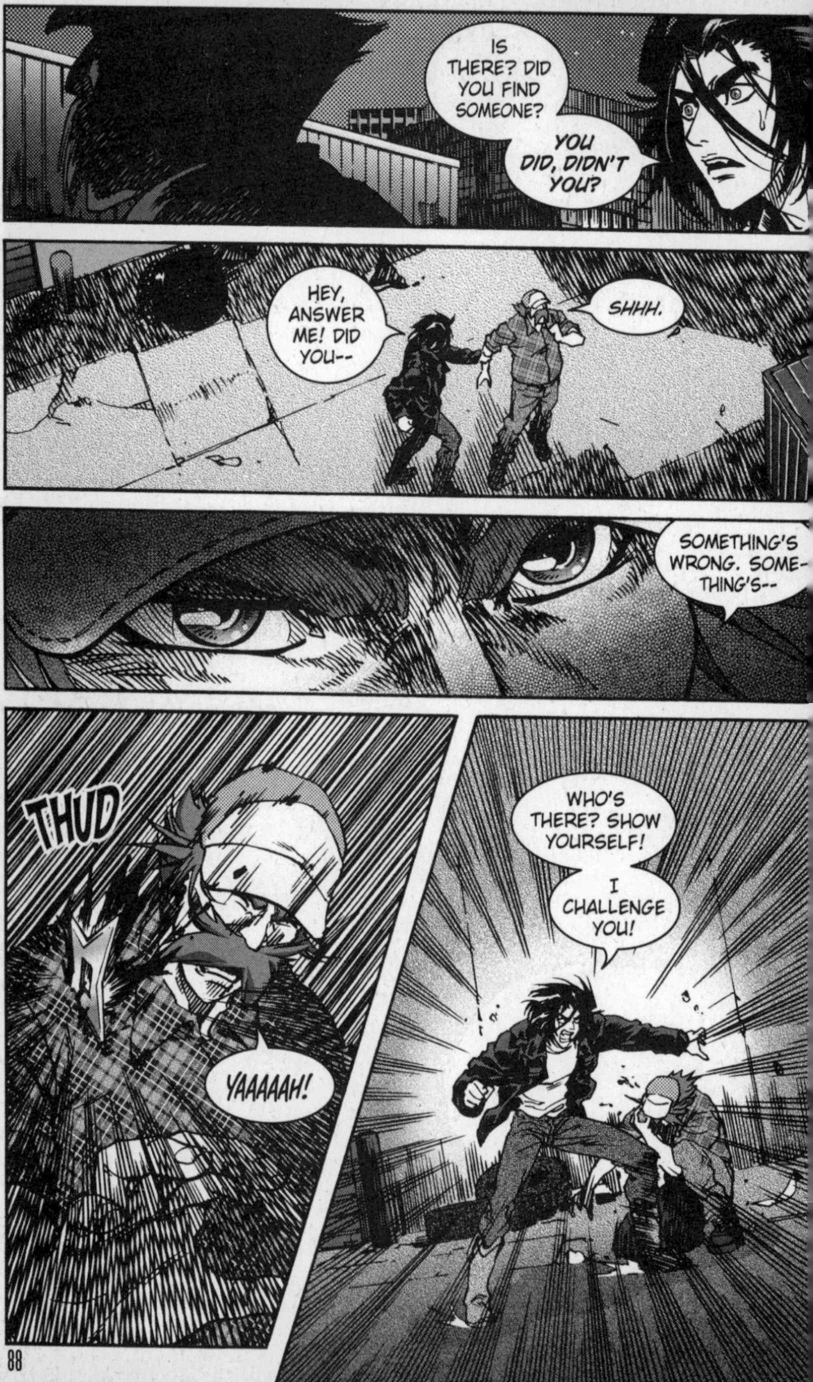
IS THERE? DID YOU FIND SOMEONE?
YOU DID, DIDN'T YOU?
HEY, ANSWER ME! DID YOU--
SHHH.
SOMETHING'S WRONG. SOMETHING'S--
THUD
YAAAAAH!
WHO'S THERE? SHOW YOURSELF!
I CHALLENGE YOU!

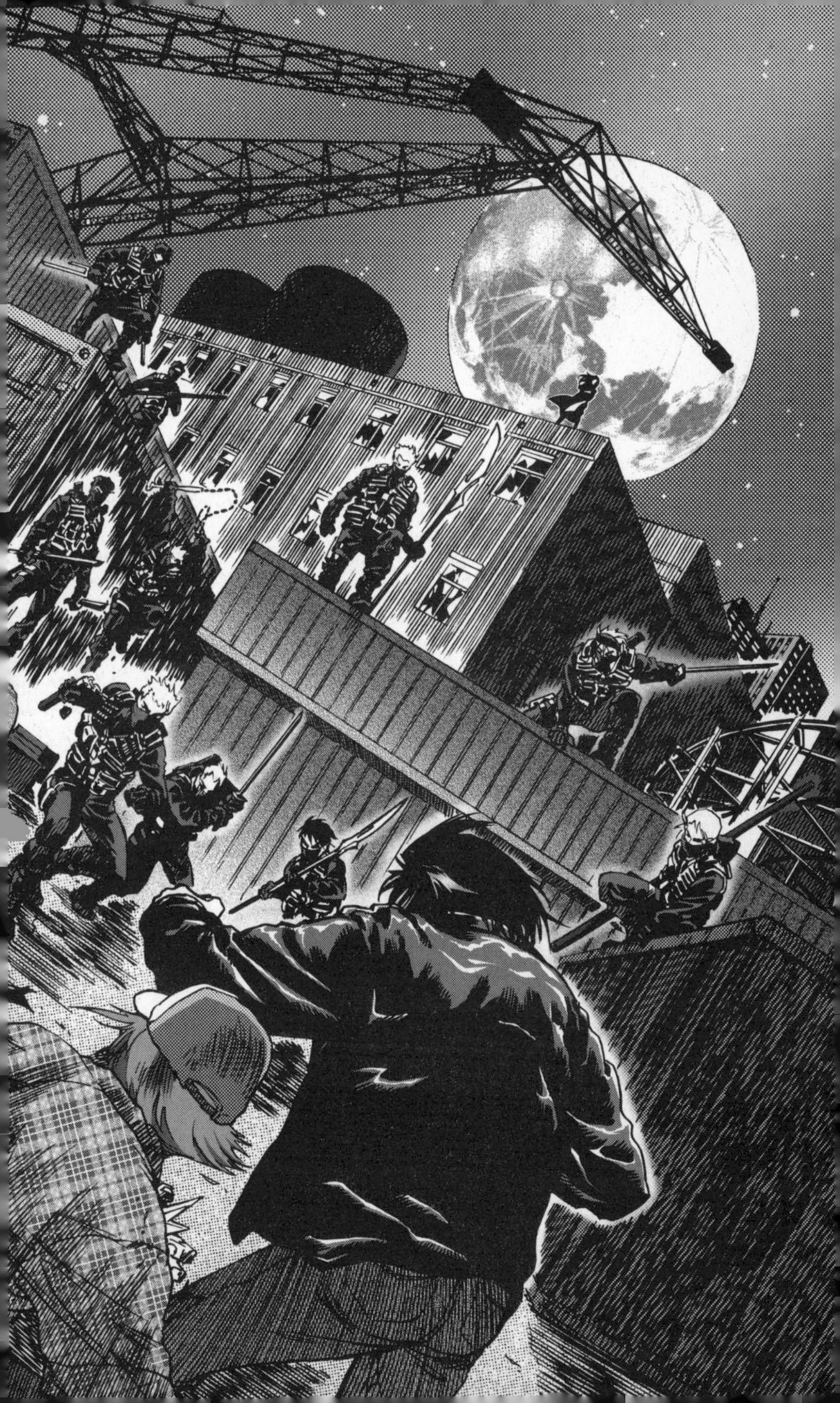

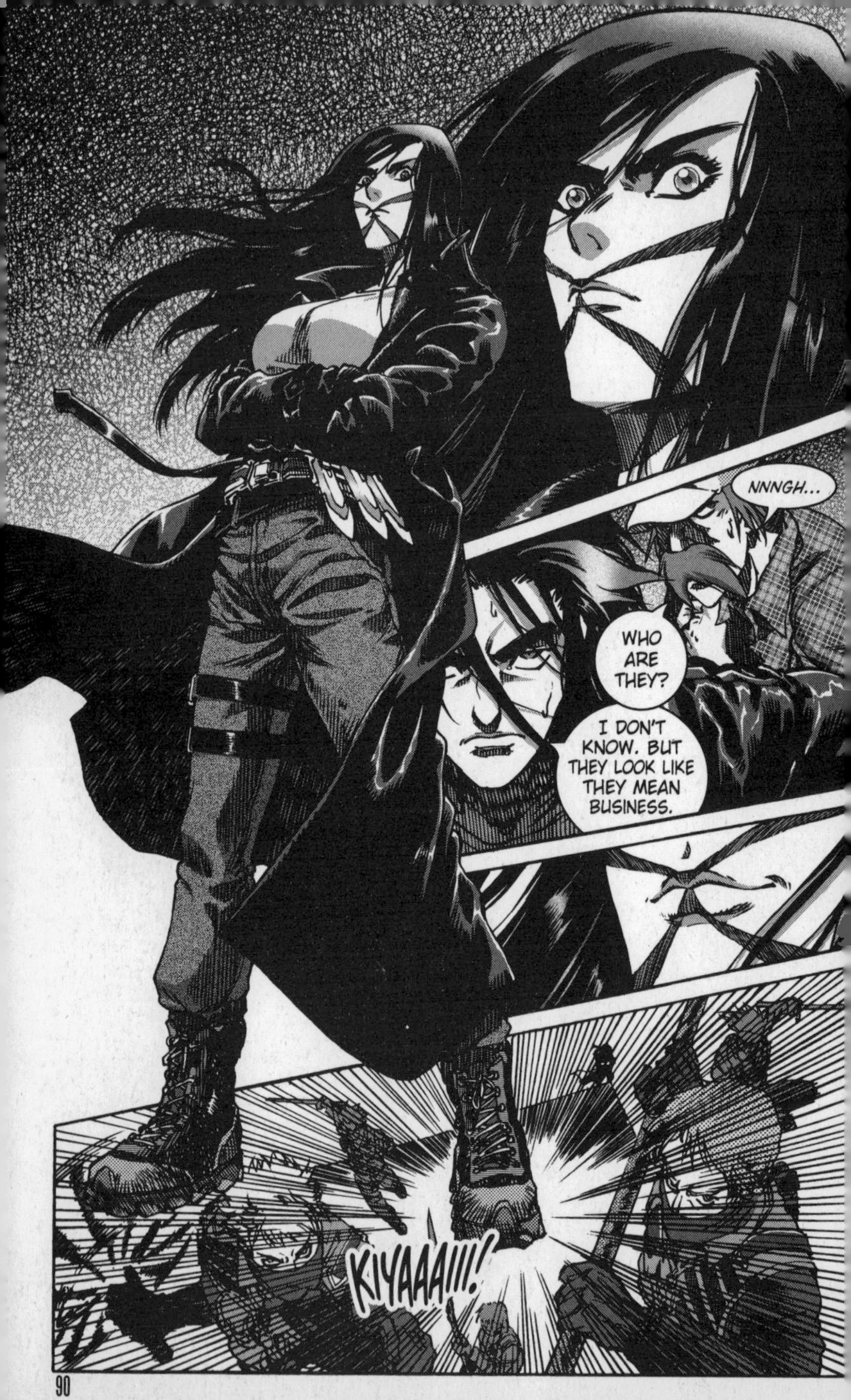
NNNGH...
WHO ARE THEY?
I DON'T KNOW. BUT THEY LOOK LIKE THEY MEAN BUSINESS.
KIYAAA!!!!

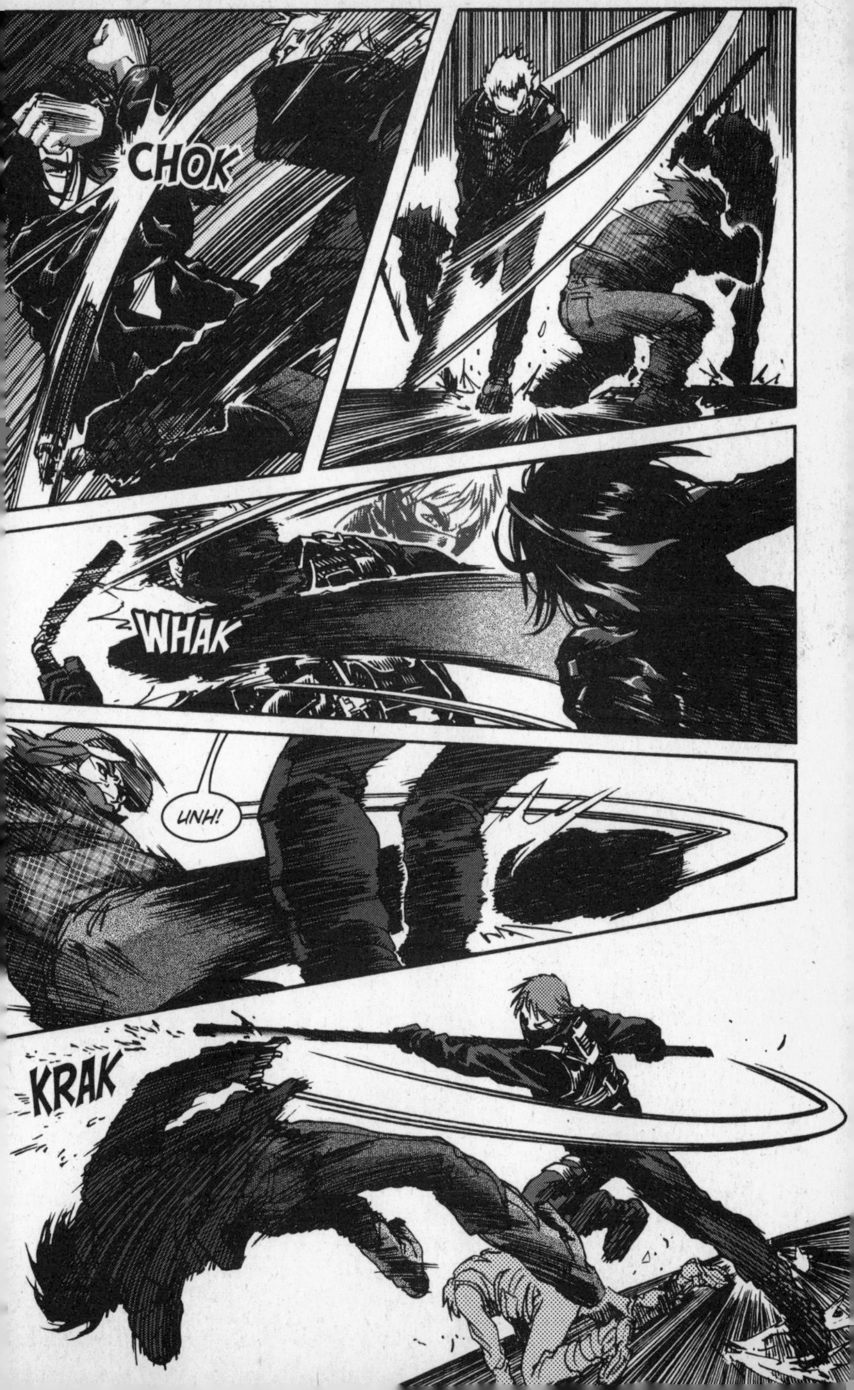
CHOK
WHAK
UNH!
KRAK

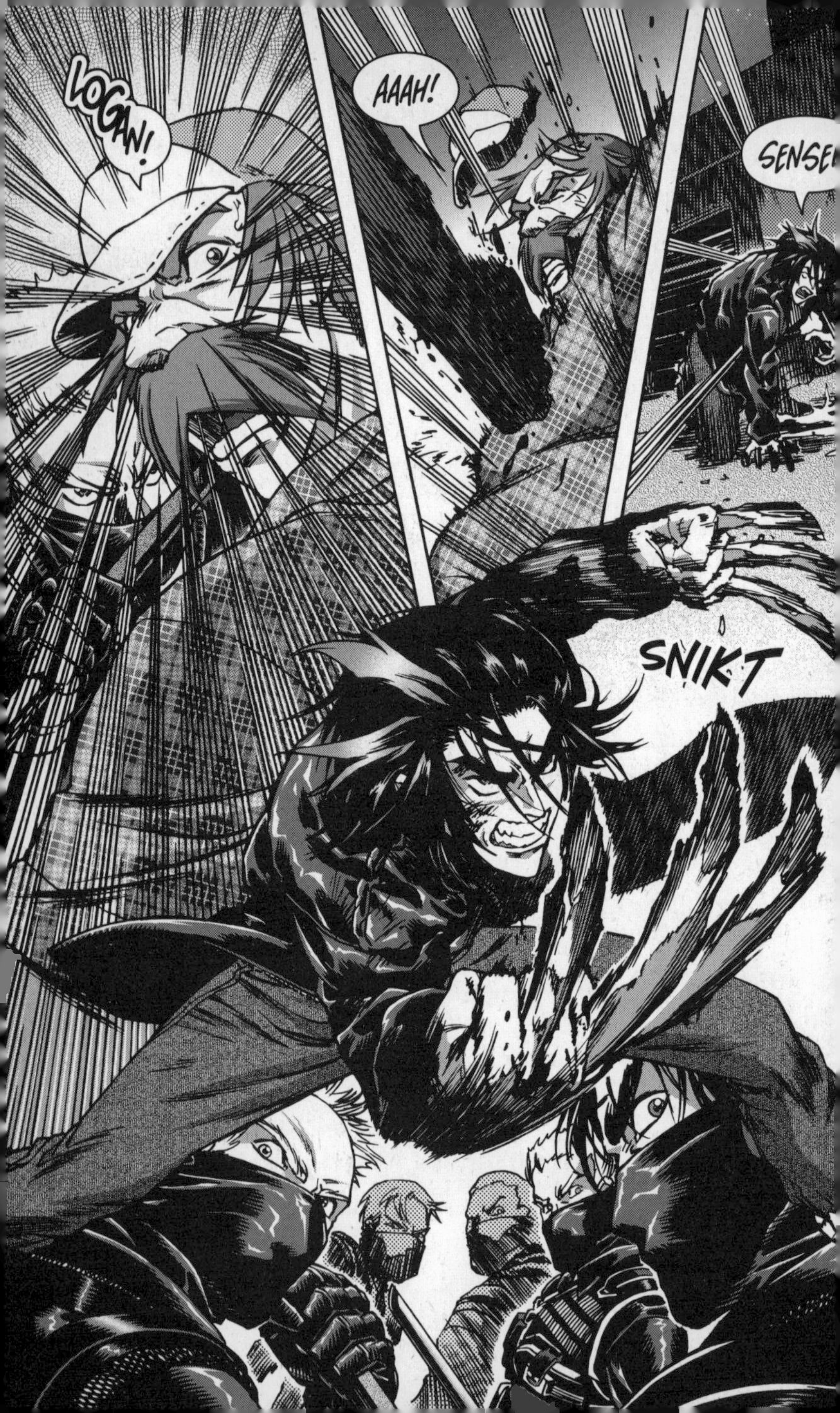
LOGAN!
AAAH!
SENSEI
SNIKT

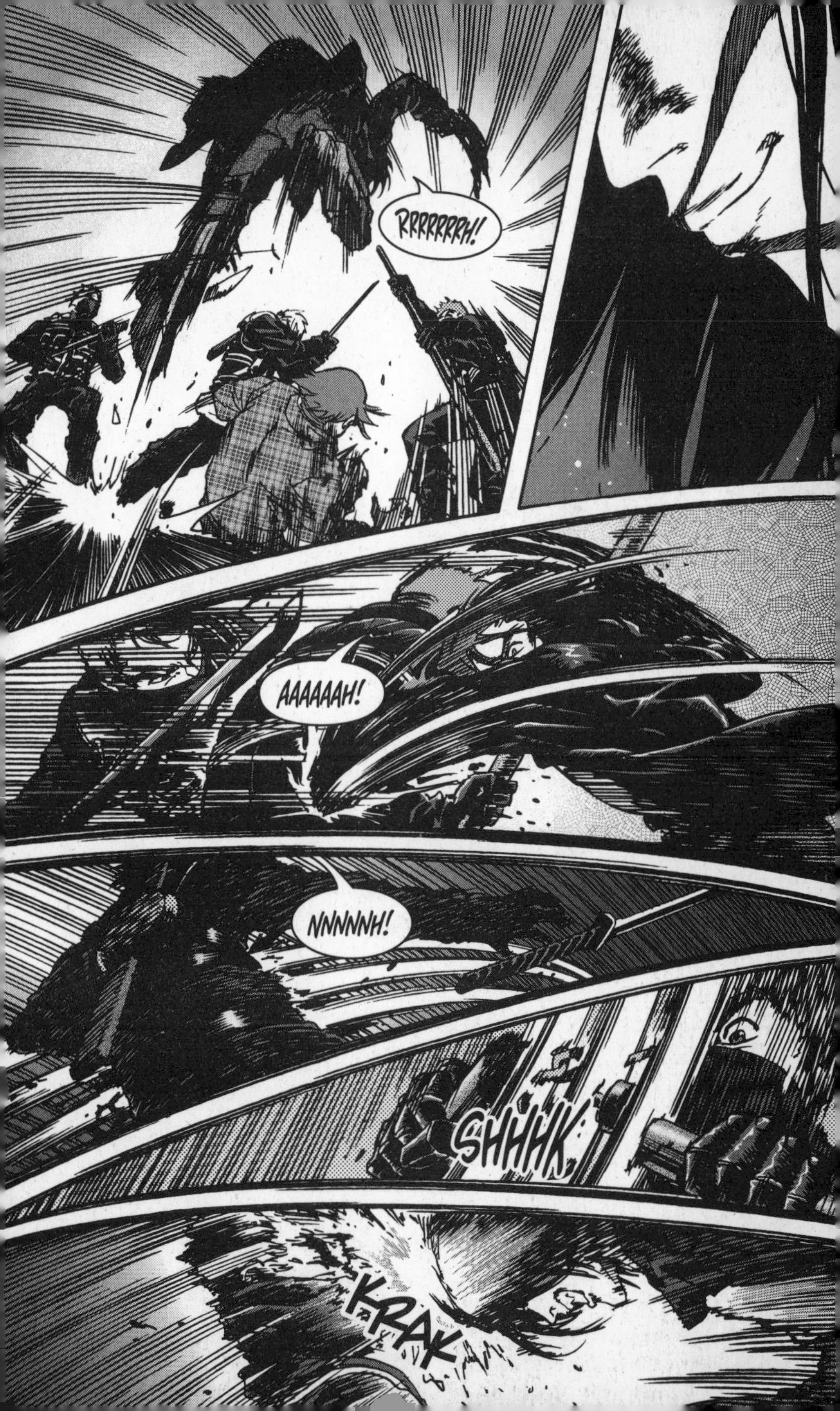
RRRRRRRH!
AAAAAAH!
NNNNNH!
SHHHK
KRAK

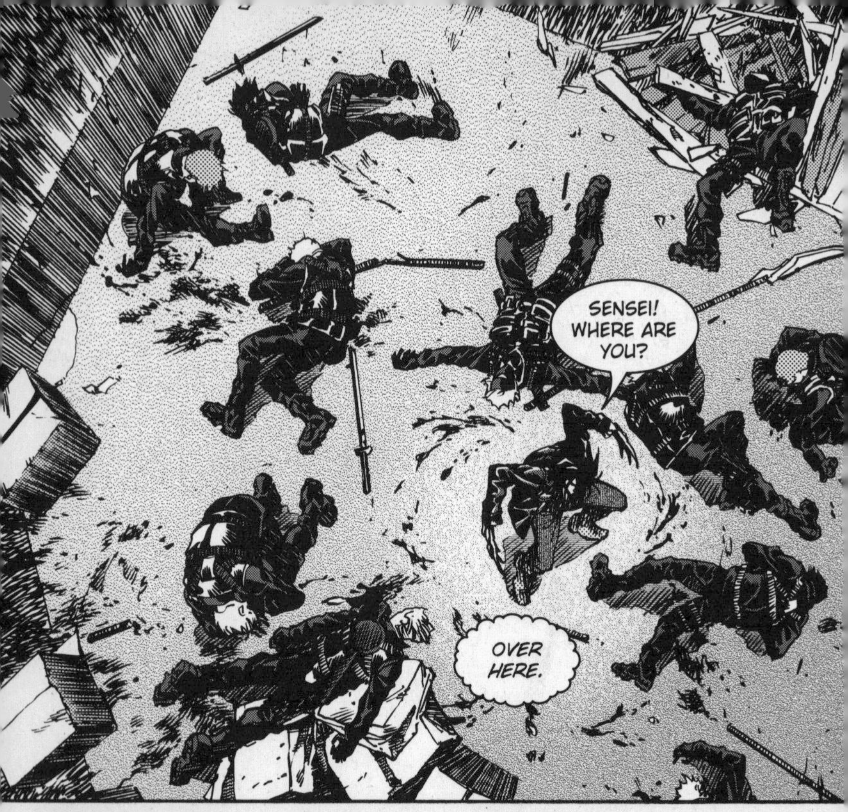
SENSEI! WHERE ARE YOU?
OVER HERE.
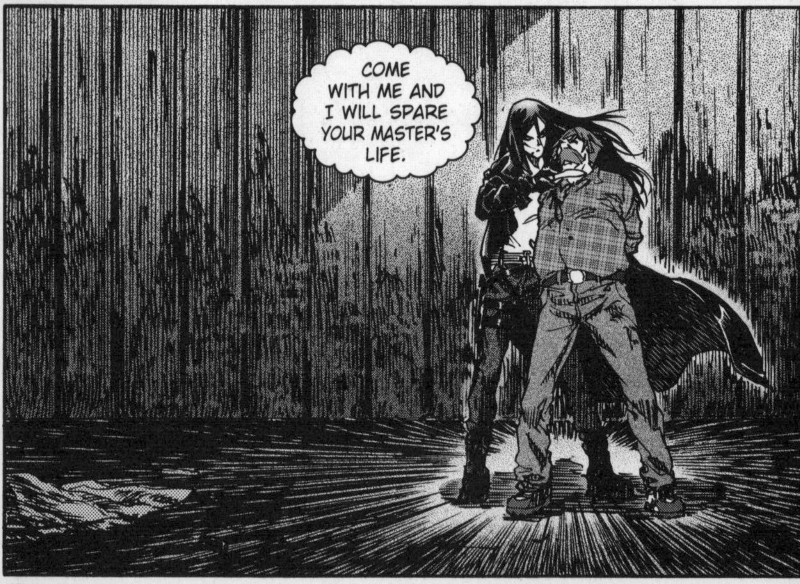
COME WITH ME AND I WILL SPARE YOUR MASTER'S LIFE.

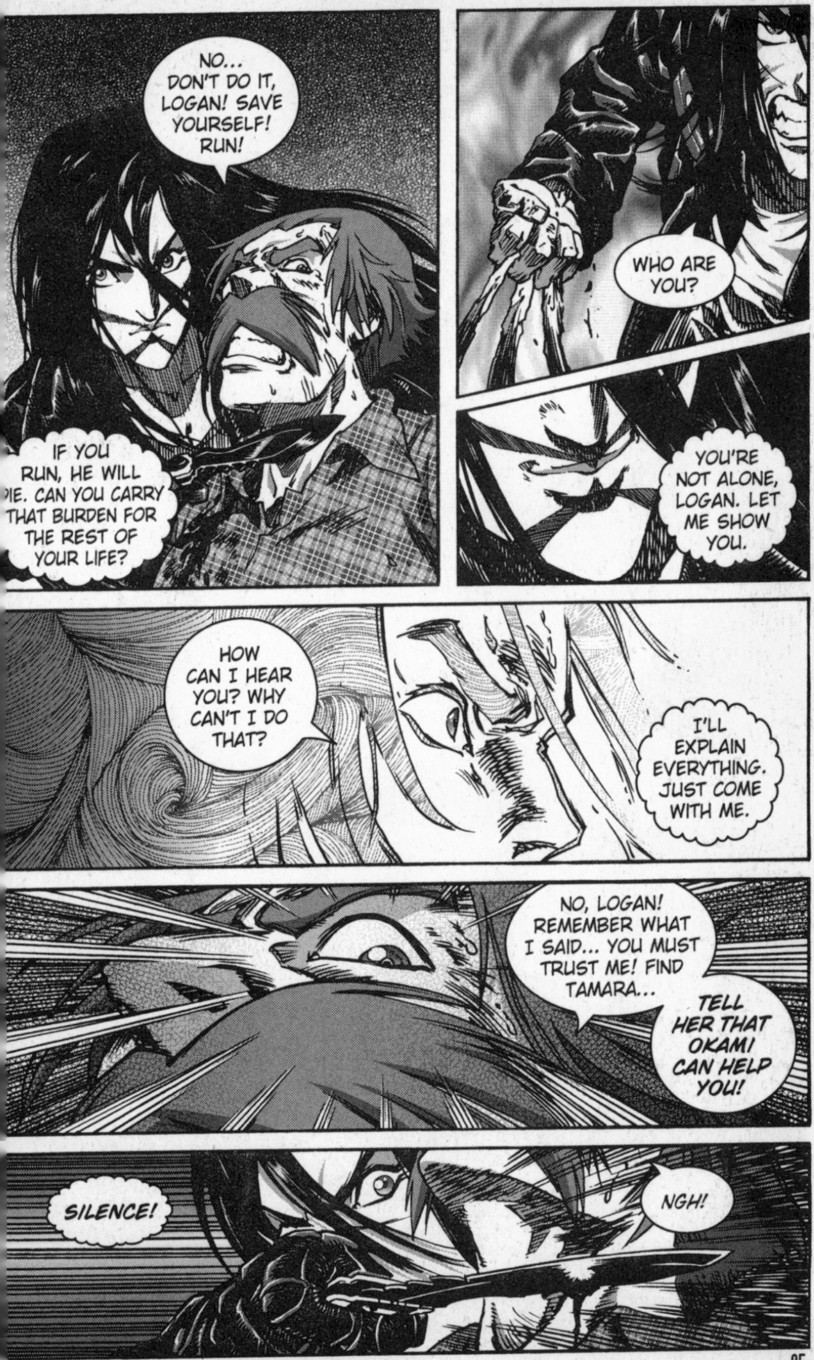
NO... DON'T DO IT, LOGAN! SAVE YOURSELF! RUN!
IF YOU RUN, HE WILL DIE. CAN YOU CARRY THAT BURDEN FOR THE REST OF YOUR LIFE?
WHO ARE YOU?
YOU'RE NOT ALONE, LOGAN. LET ME SHOW YOU.
HOW CAN I HEAR YOU? WHY CAN'T I DO THAT?
I'LL EXPLAIN EVERYTHING. JUST COME WITH ME.
NO, LOGAN! REMEMBER WHAT I SAID... YOU MUST TRUST ME! FIND TAMARA...
TELL HER THAT OKAMI CAN HELP YOU!
SILENCE!
NGH!

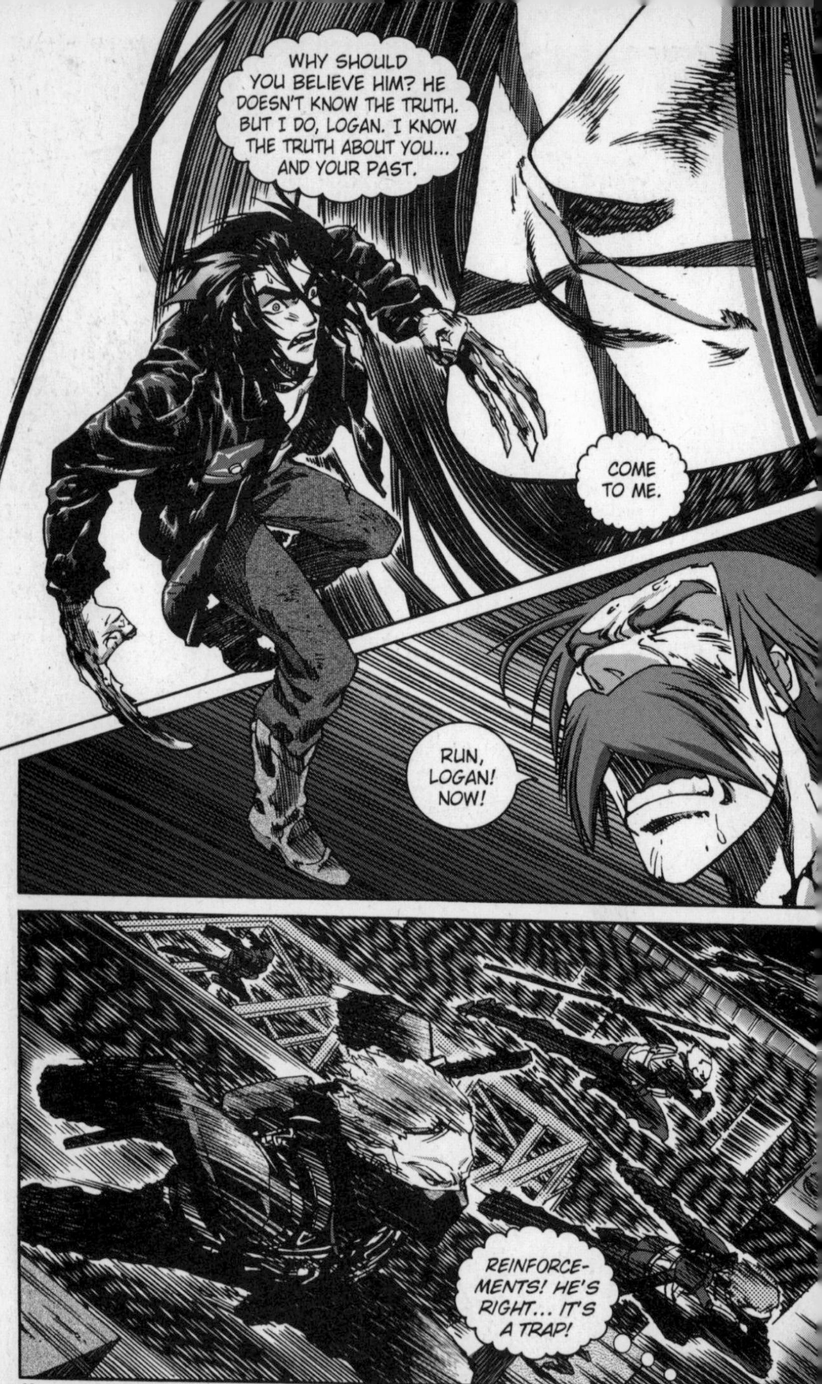
WHY SHOULD YOU BELIEVE HIM? HE DOESN'T KNOW THE TRUTH. BUT I DO, LOGAN. I KNOW THE TRUTH ABOUT YOU... AND YOUR PAST.
COME TO ME.
RUN, LOGAN! NOW!
REINFORCE-MENTS! HE'S RIGHT... IT'S A TRAP!

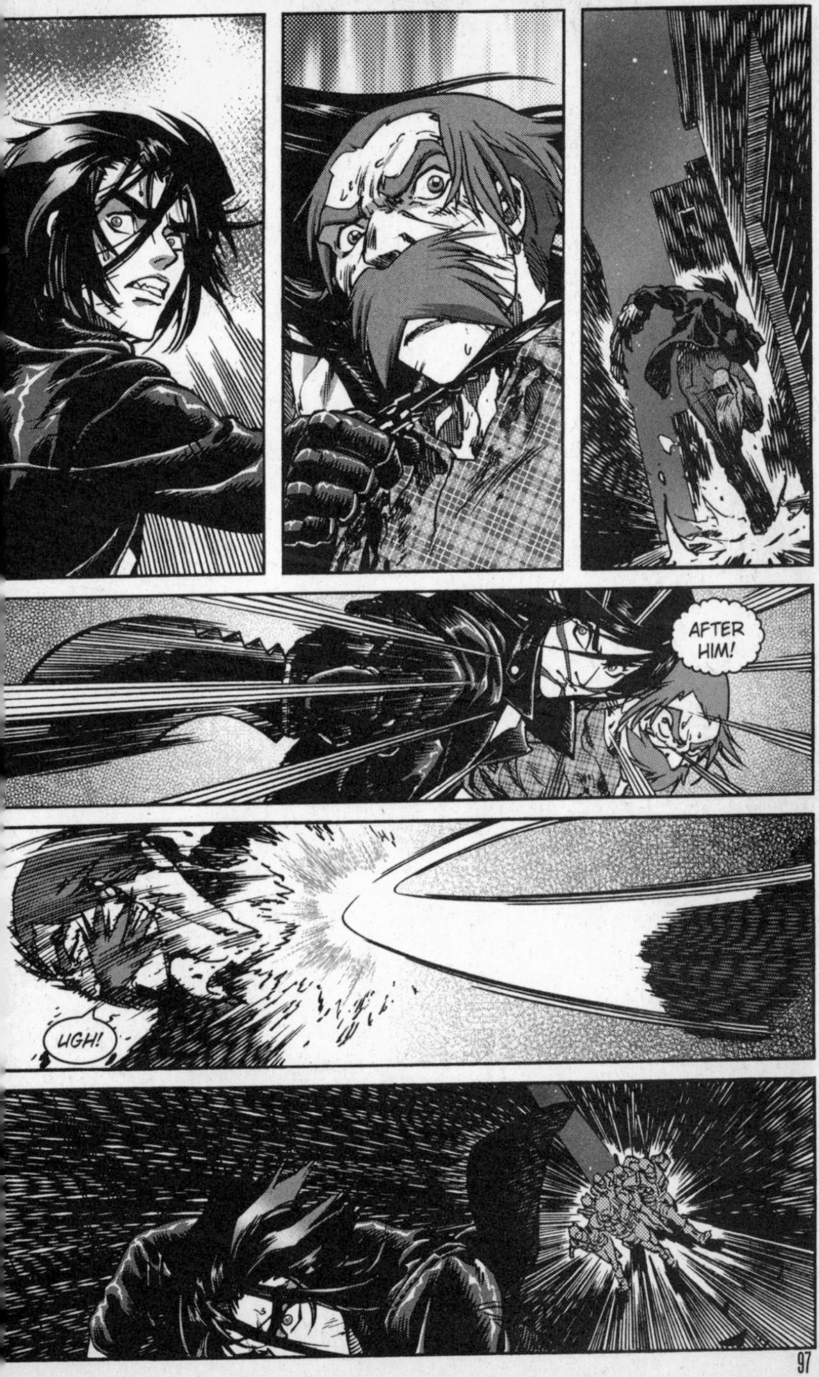
AFTER HIM!
UGH!

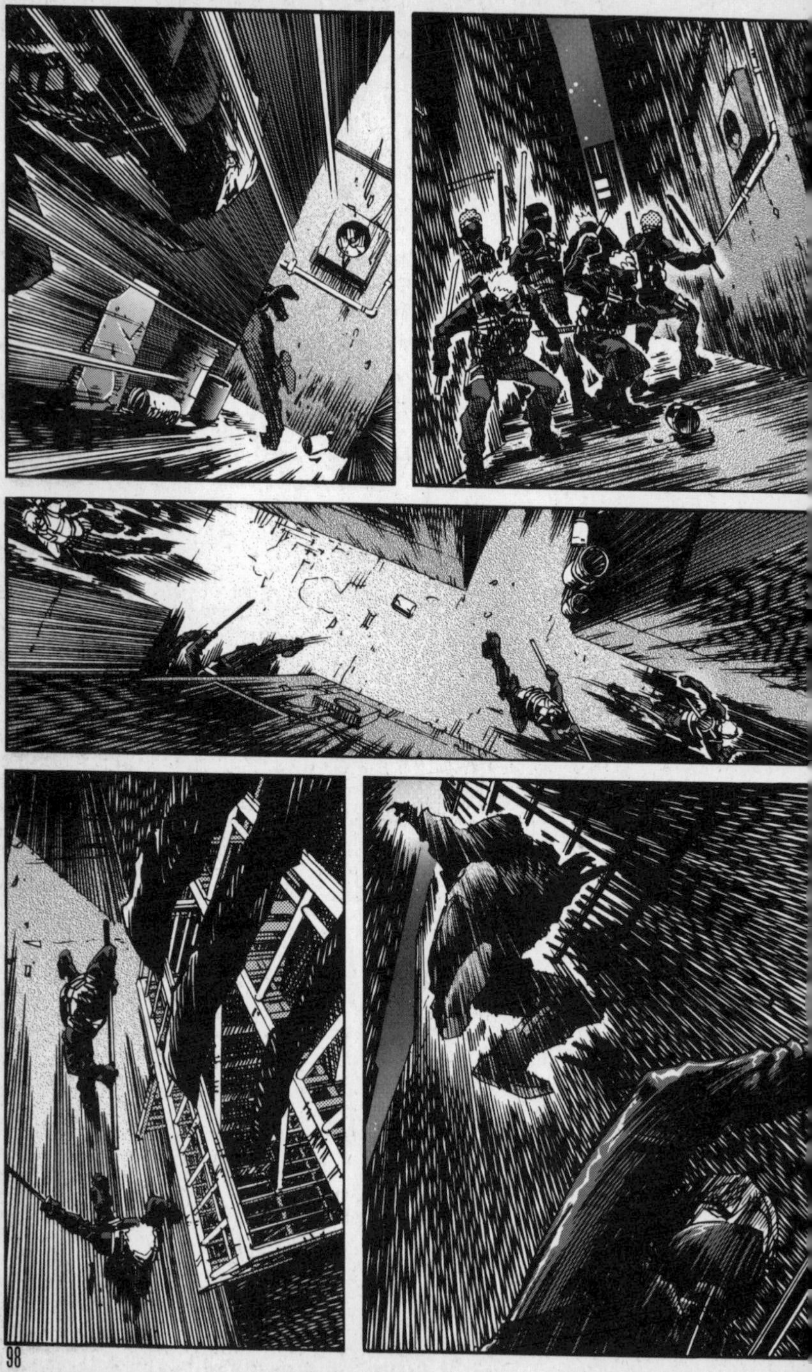

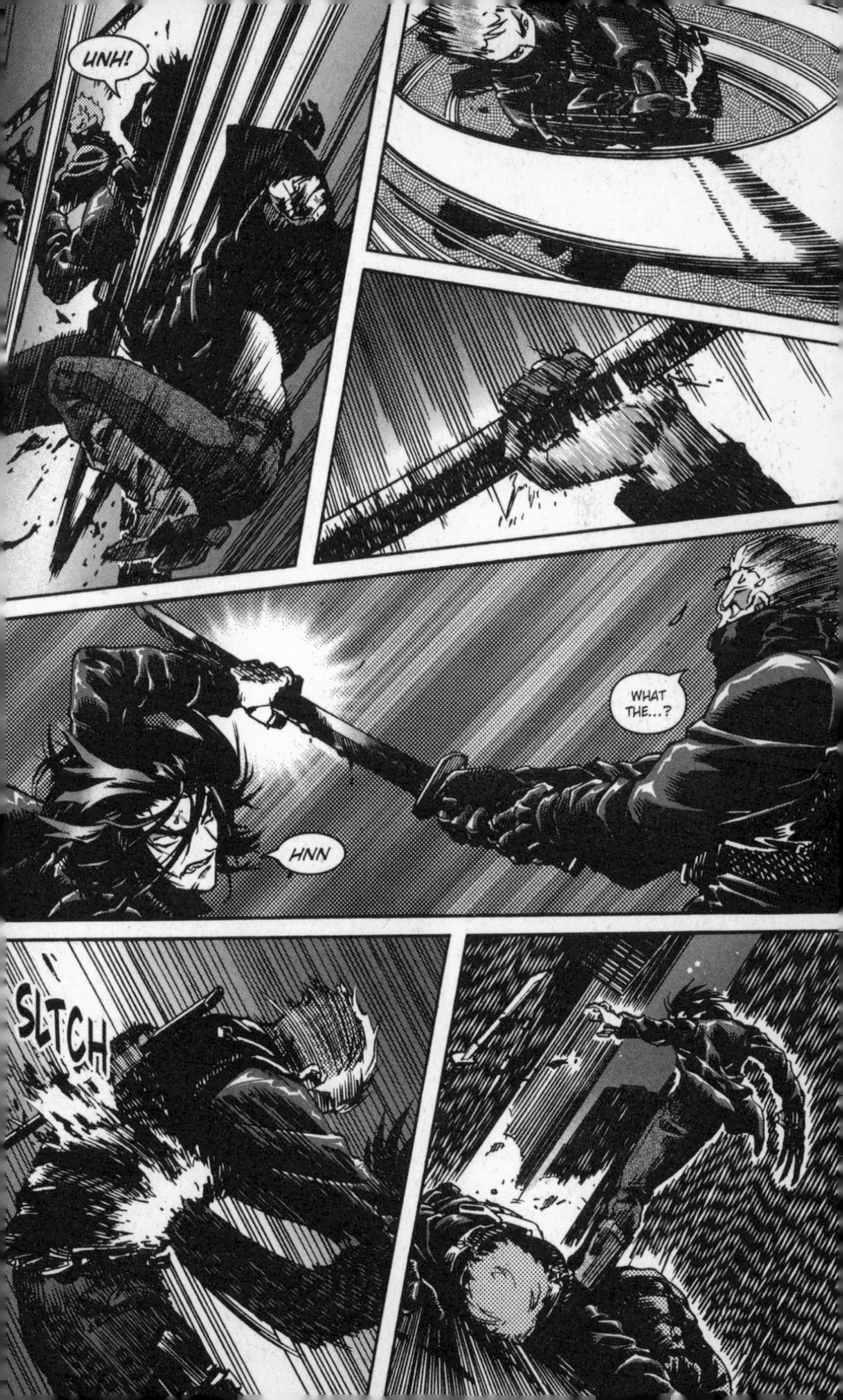
UNH!
WHAT THE...?
HNN
SLTCH

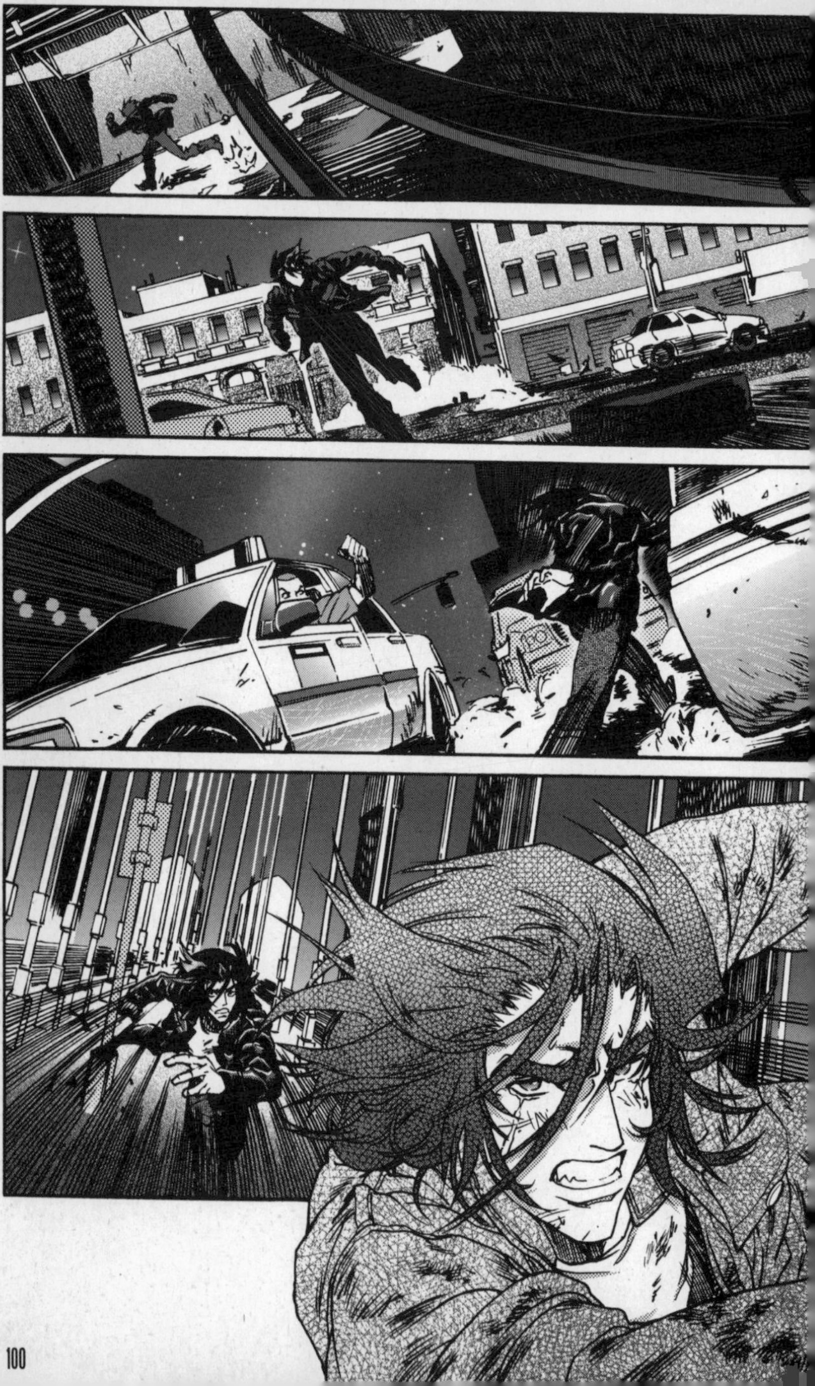

Chapter Seven
Silent Running

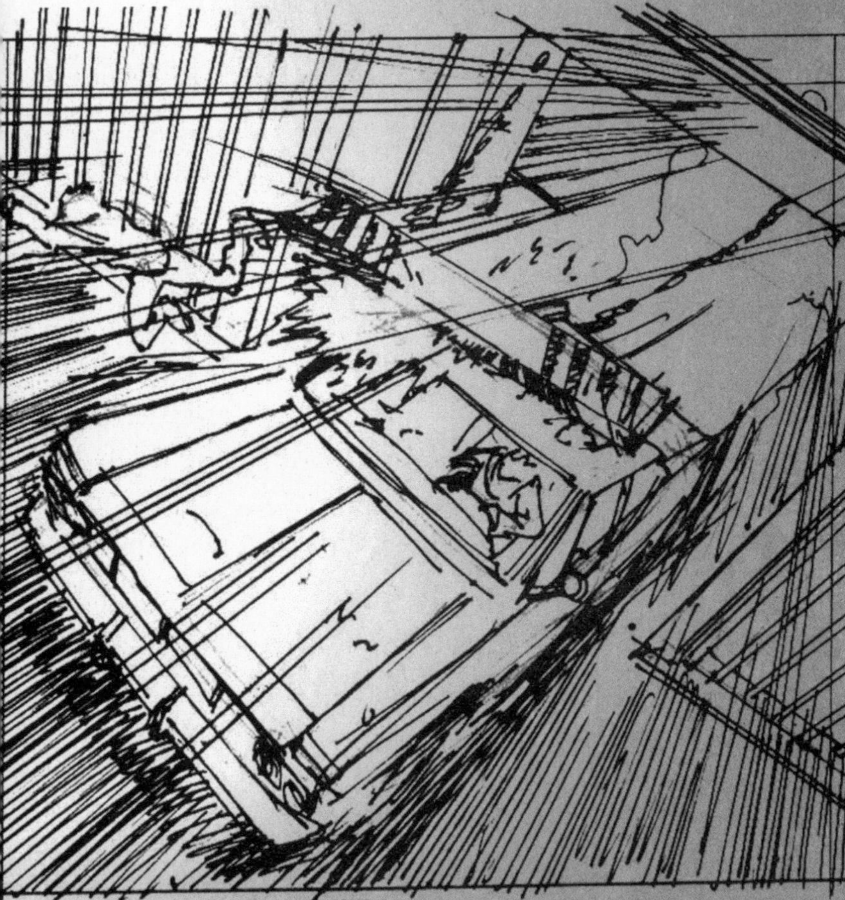

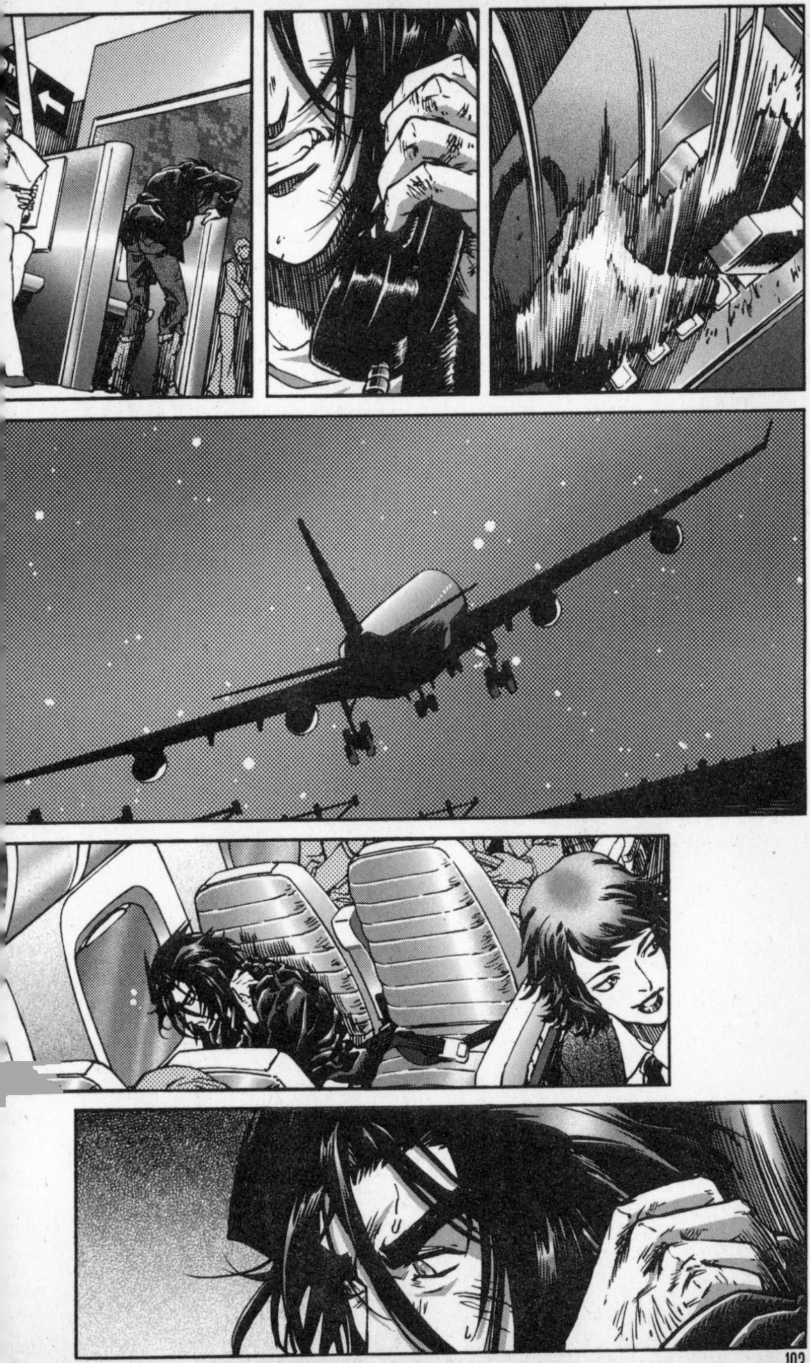

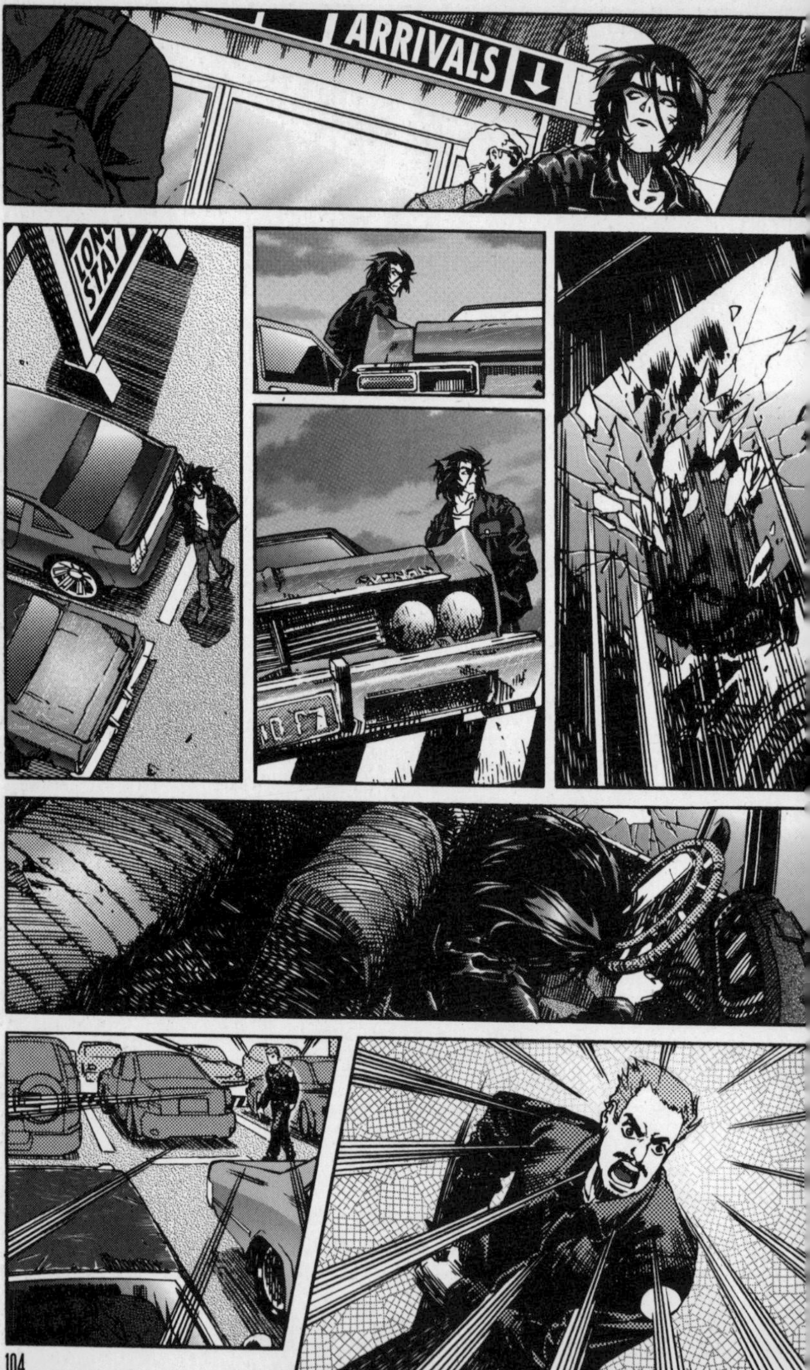
ARRIVALS

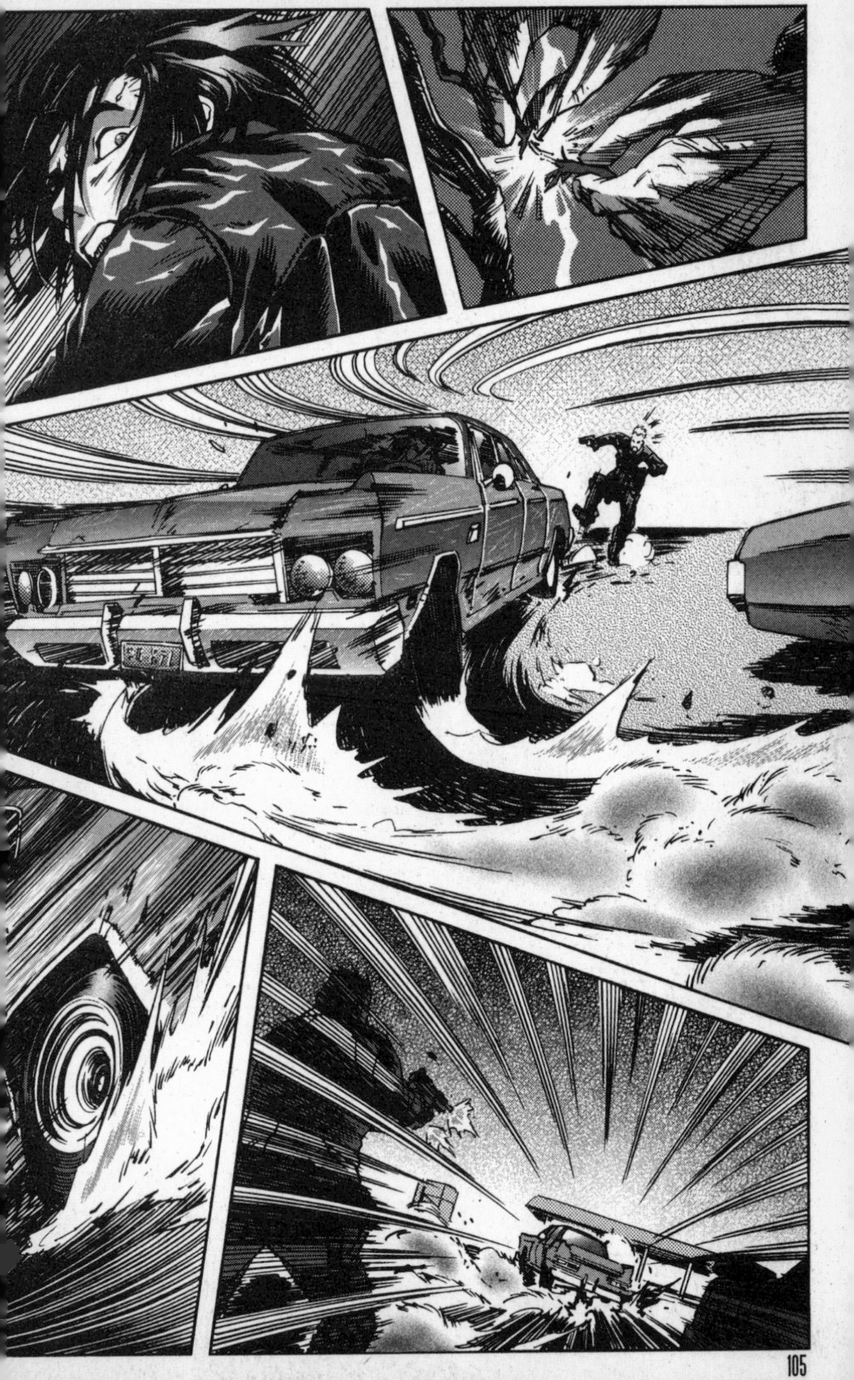

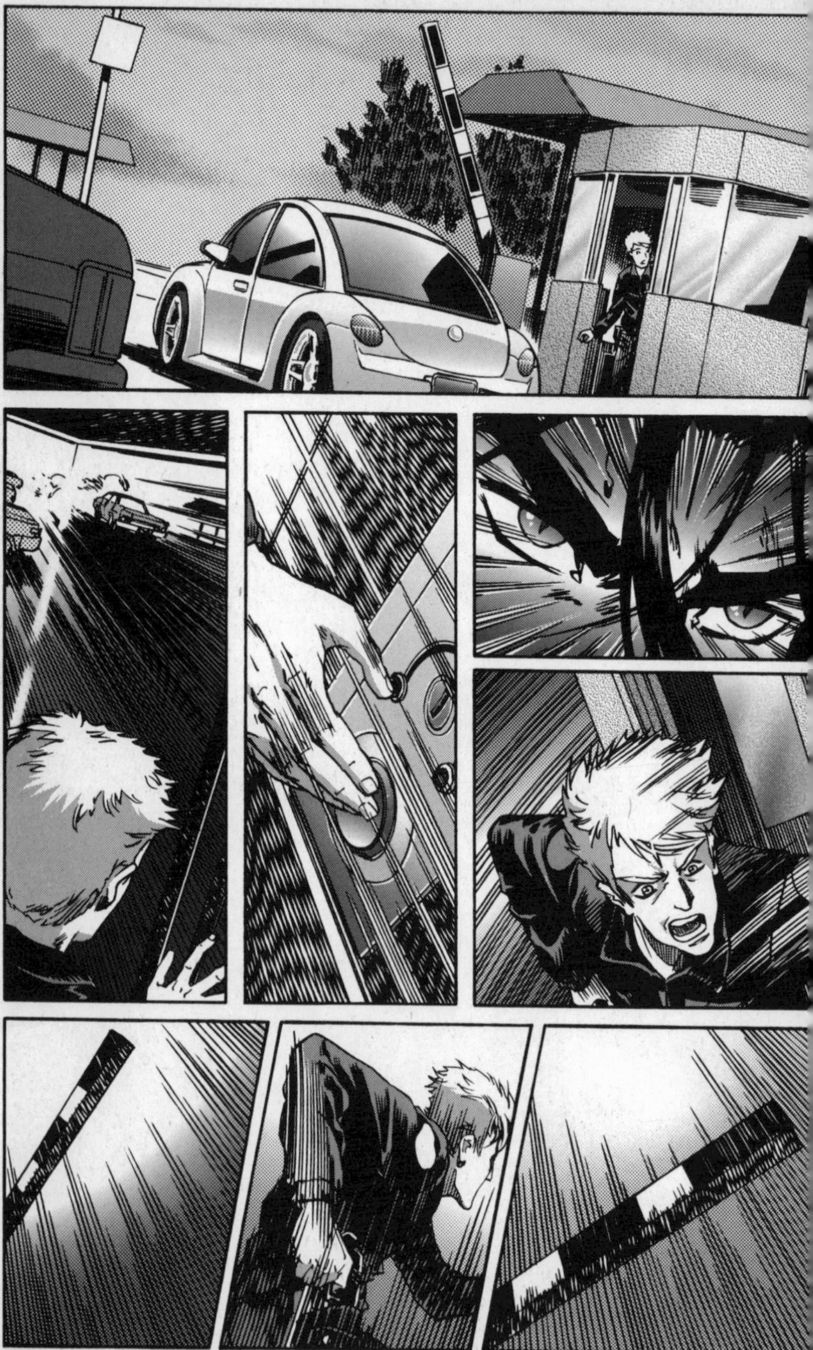

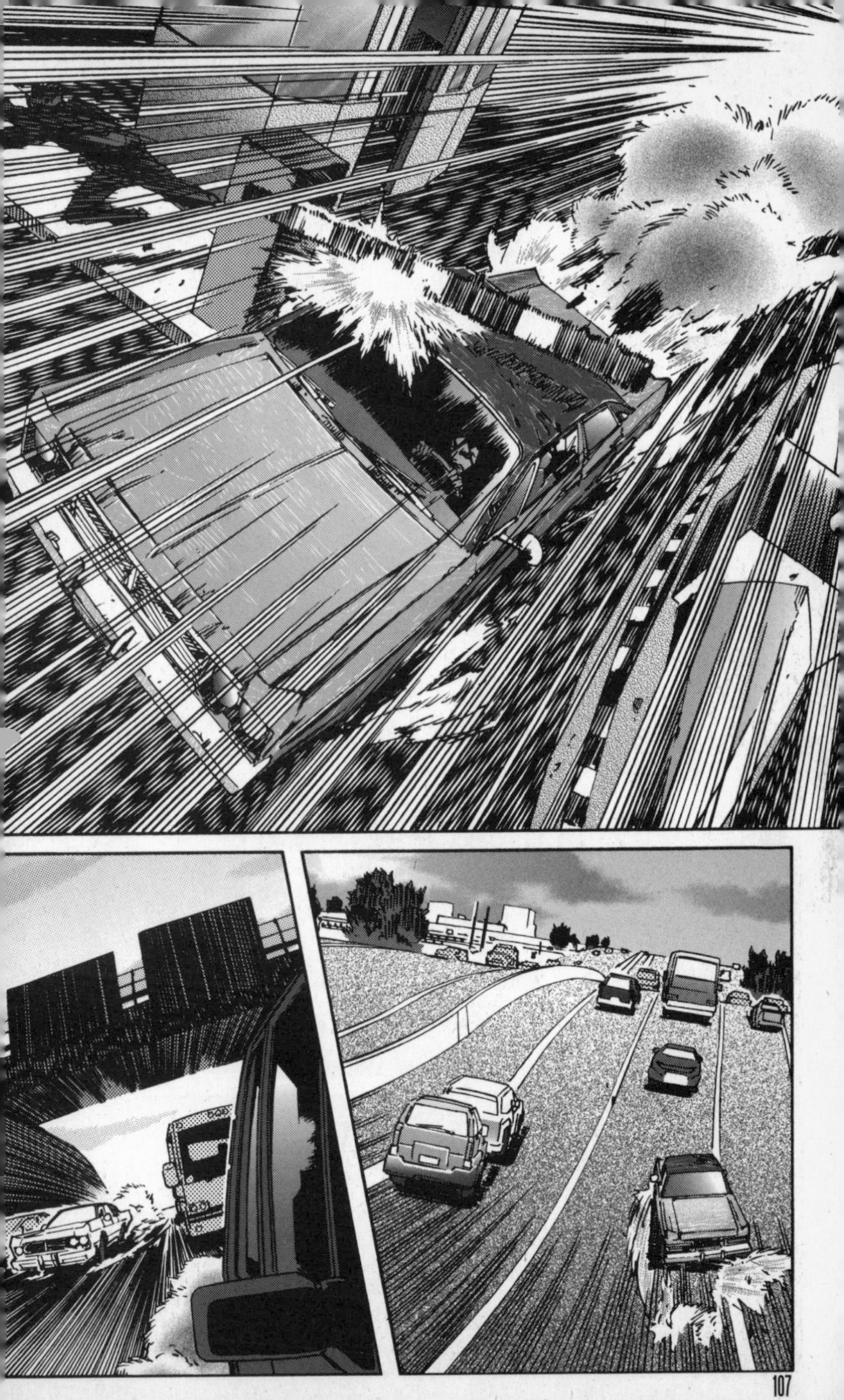

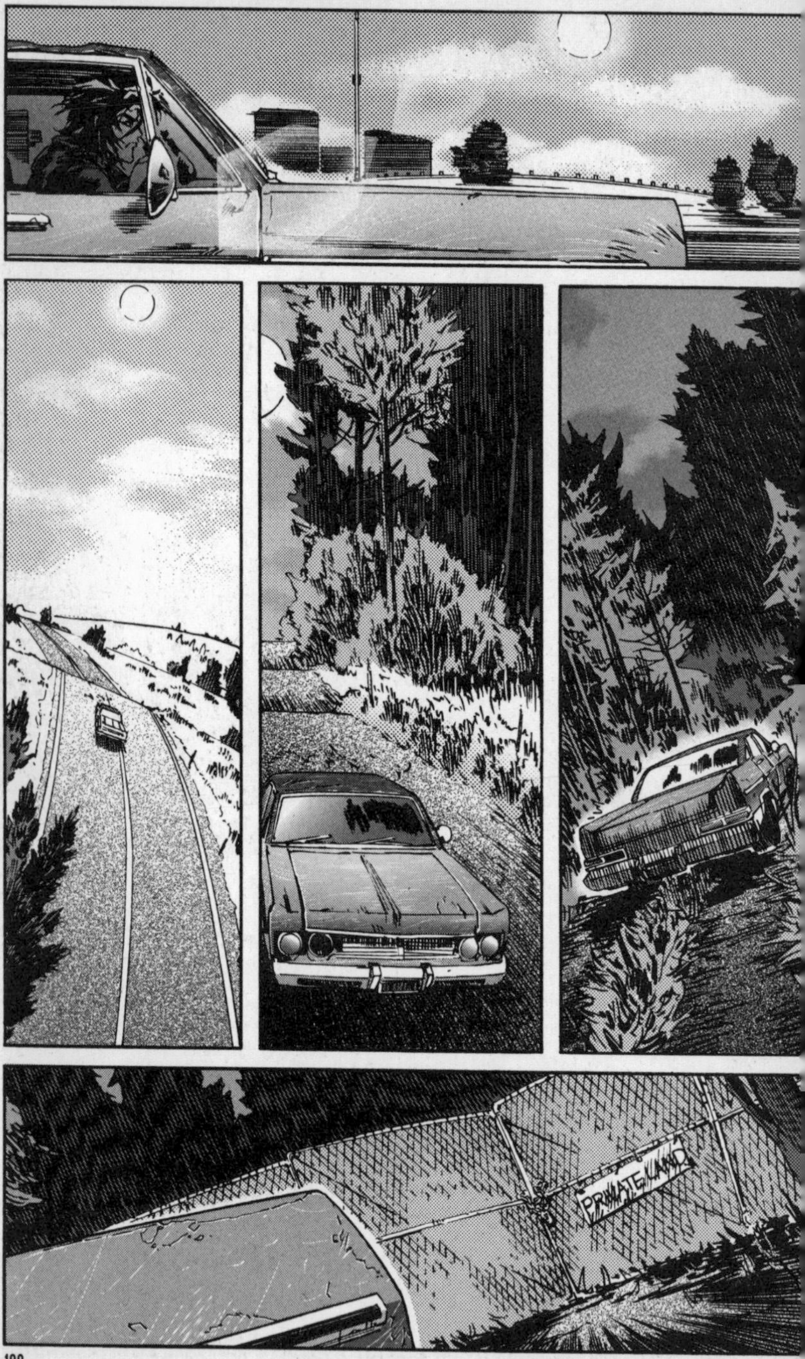
PRIVATE LAND

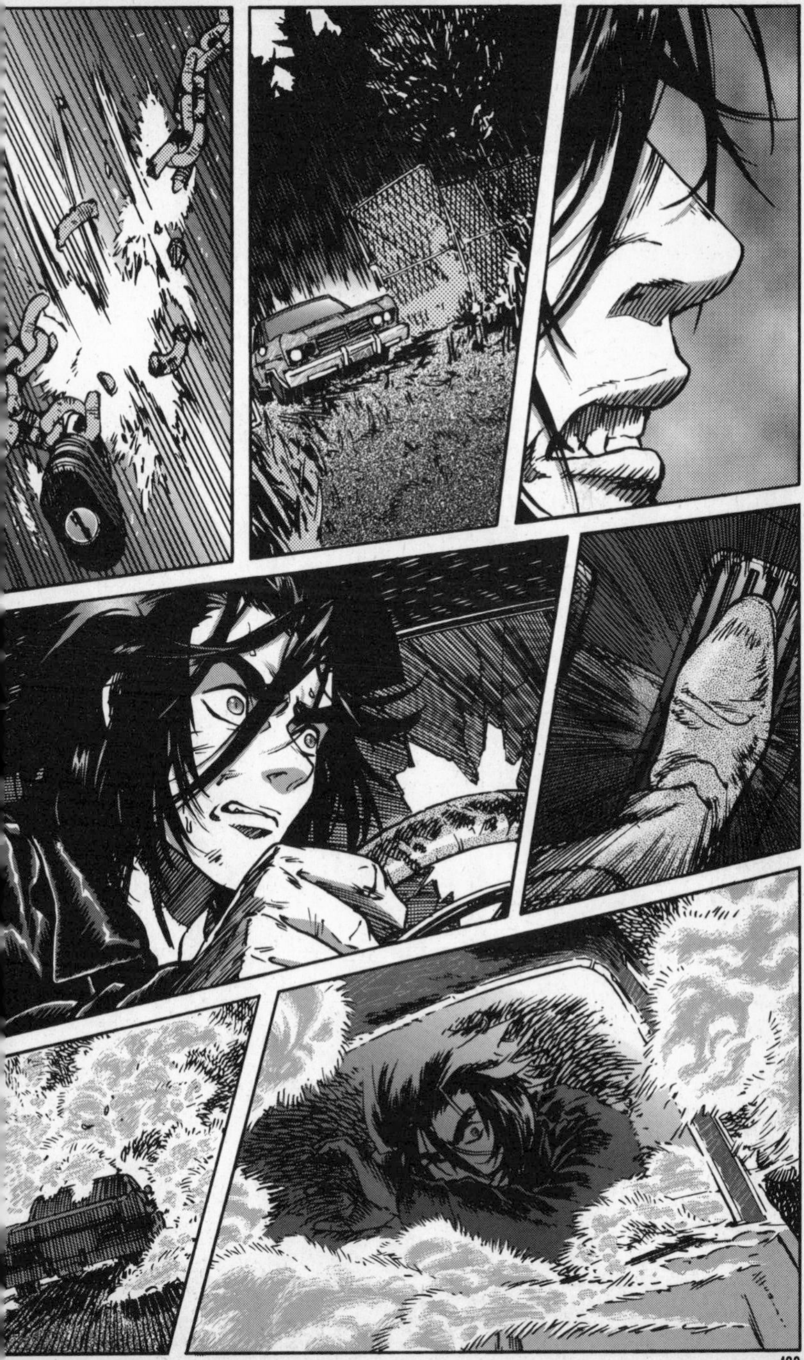

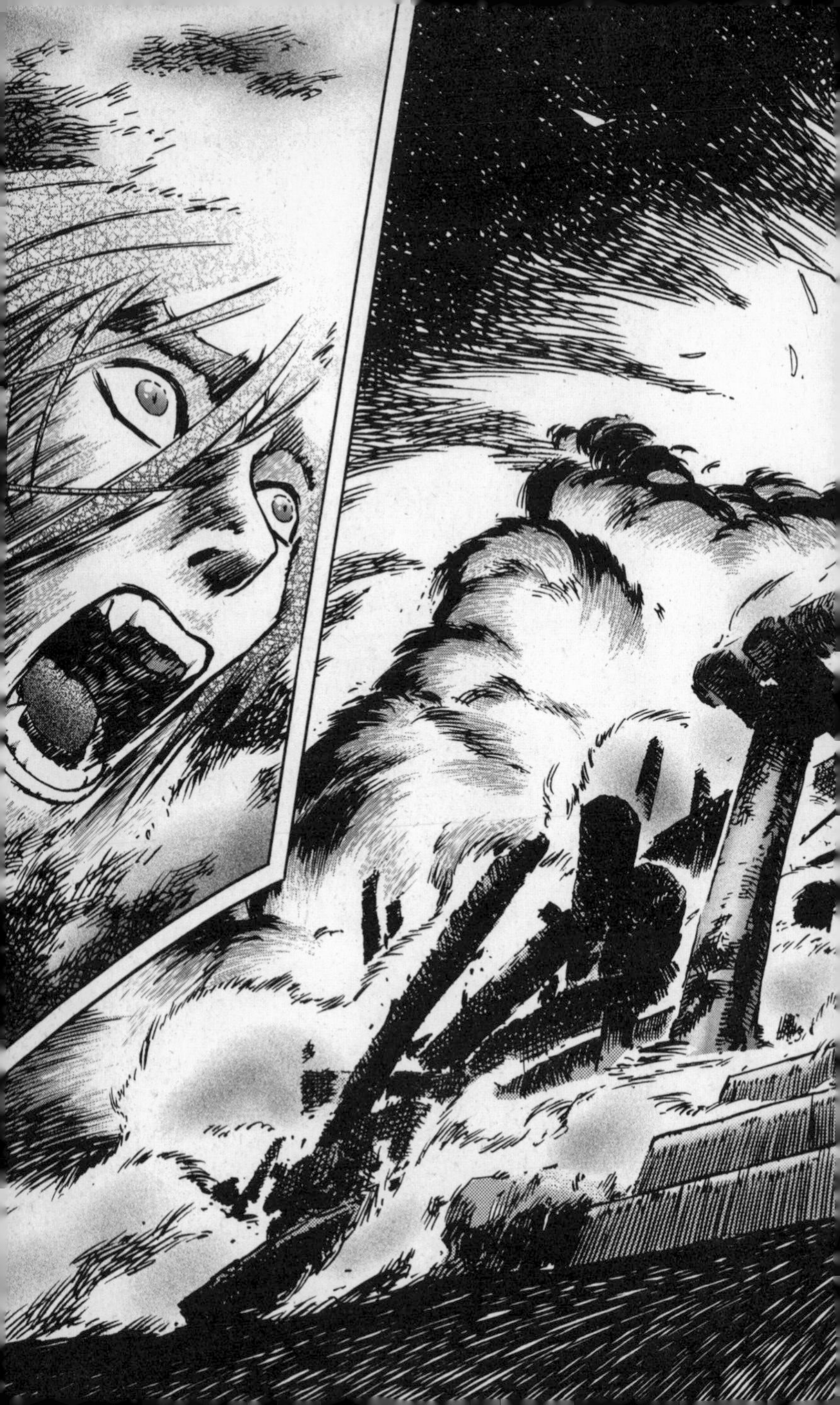

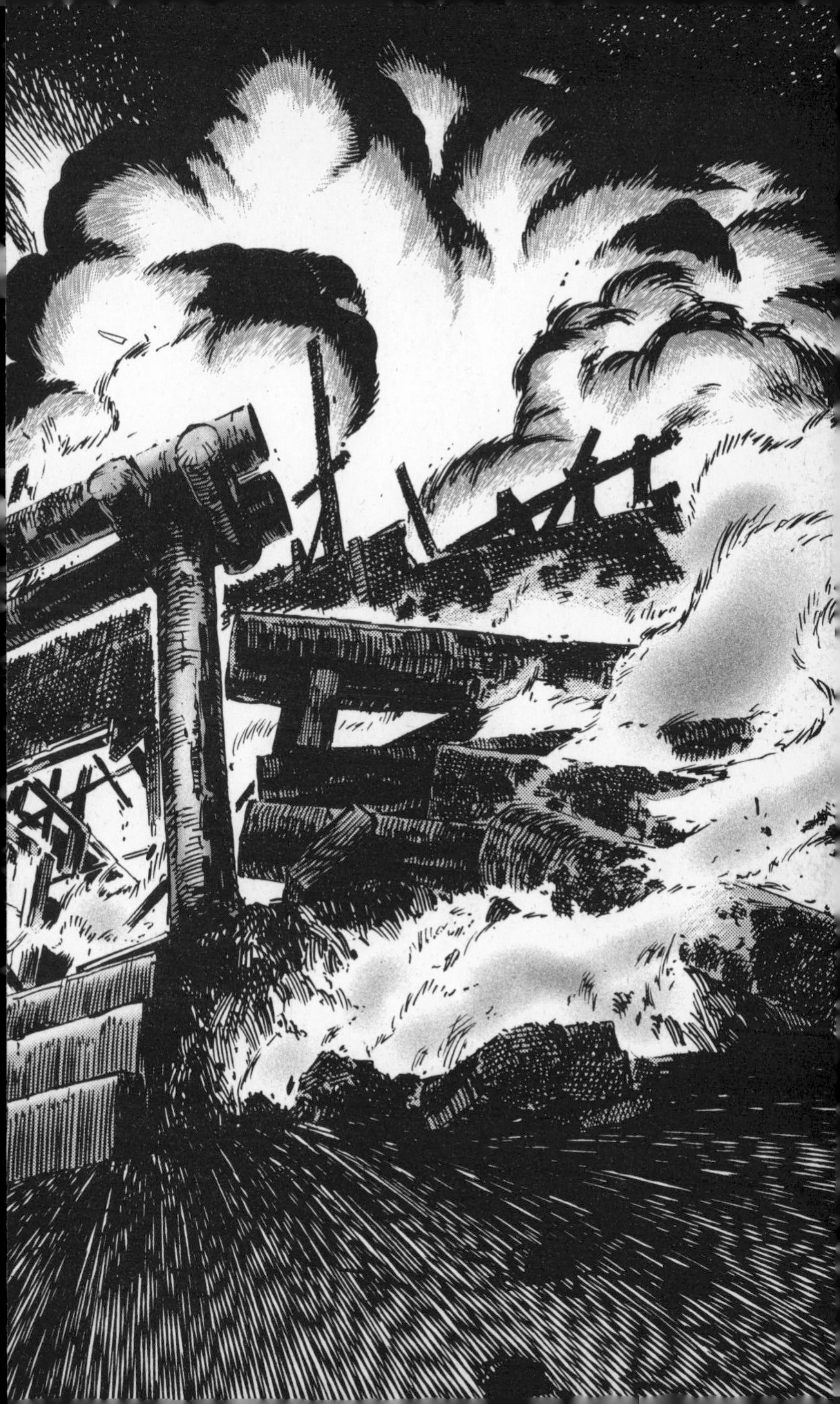

Chapter Eight
The End of the Beginning

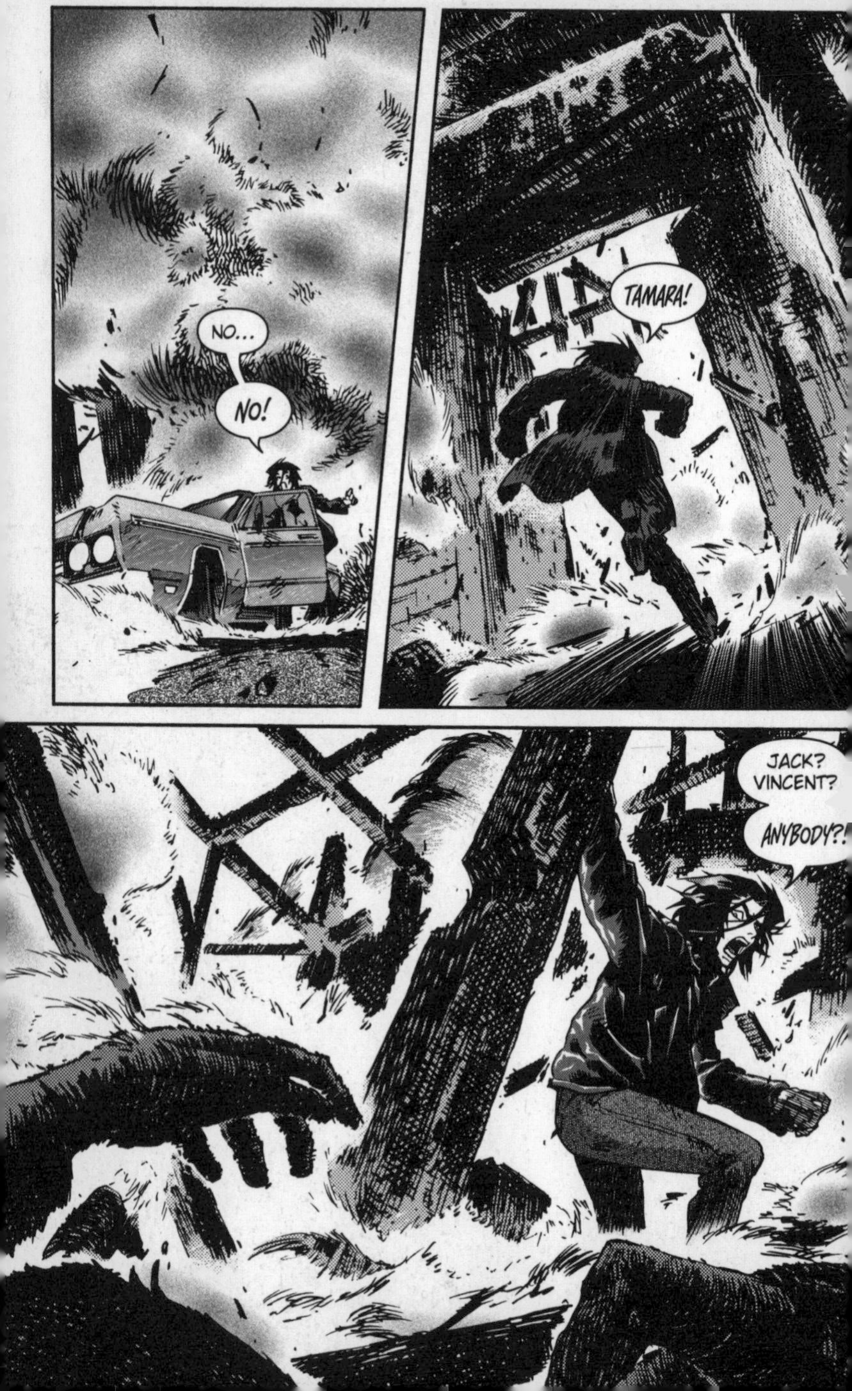
NO...
NO!
TAMARA!
JACK? VINCENT?
ANYBODY?!

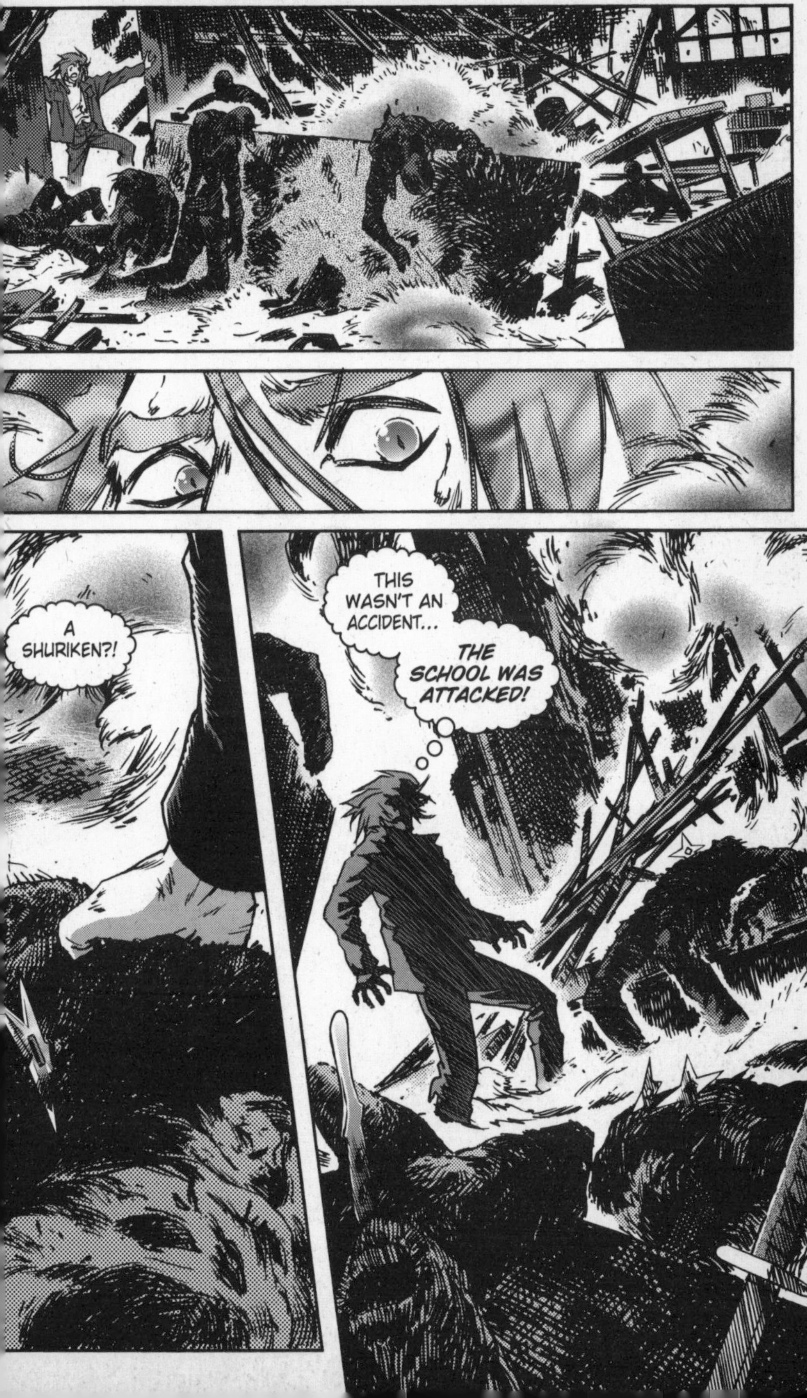
A SHURIKEN?!
THIS WASN'T AN ACCIDENT...
THE SCHOOL WAS ATTACKED!

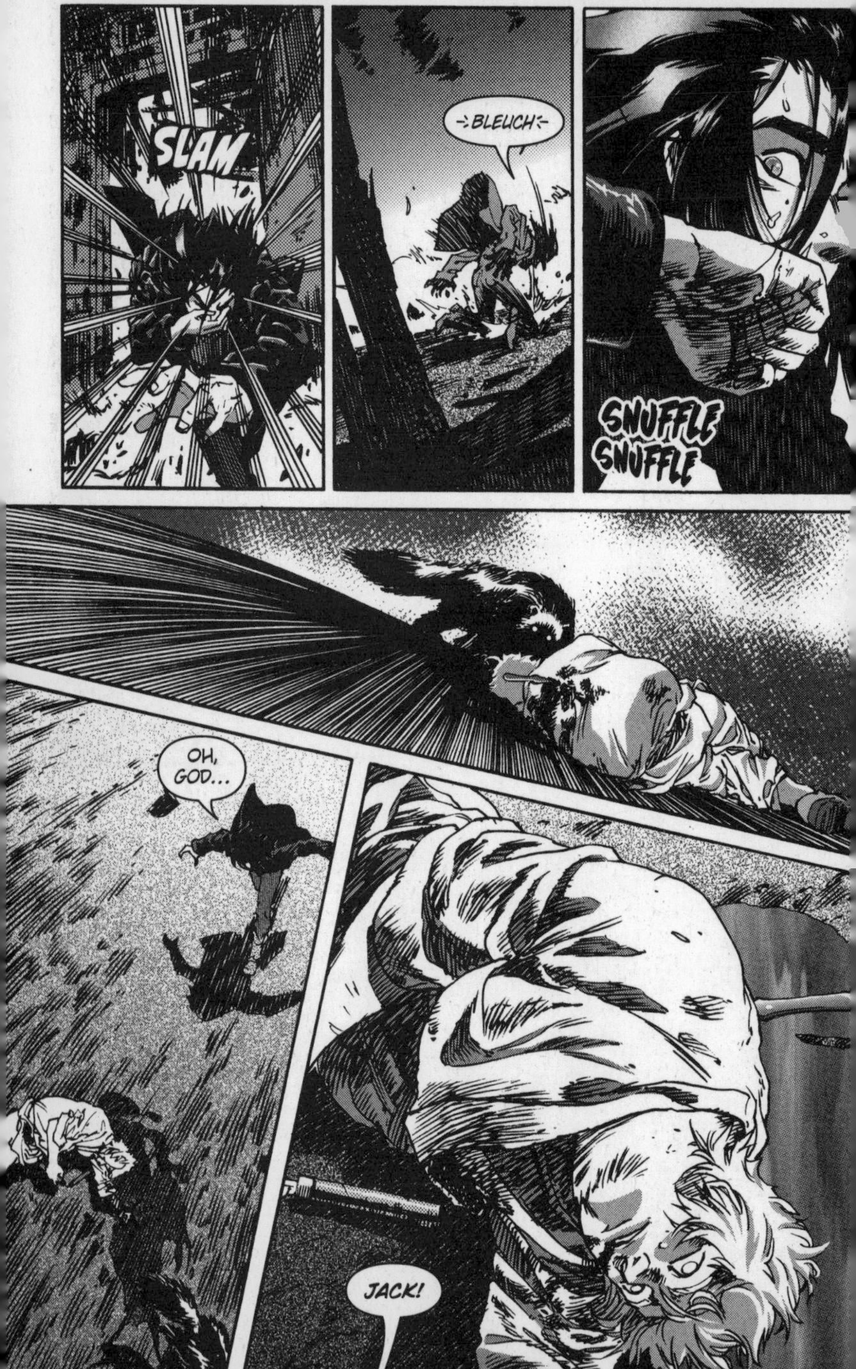
SLAM
-BLEUCH-
SNUFFLE SNUFFLE
OH, GOD...
JACK!

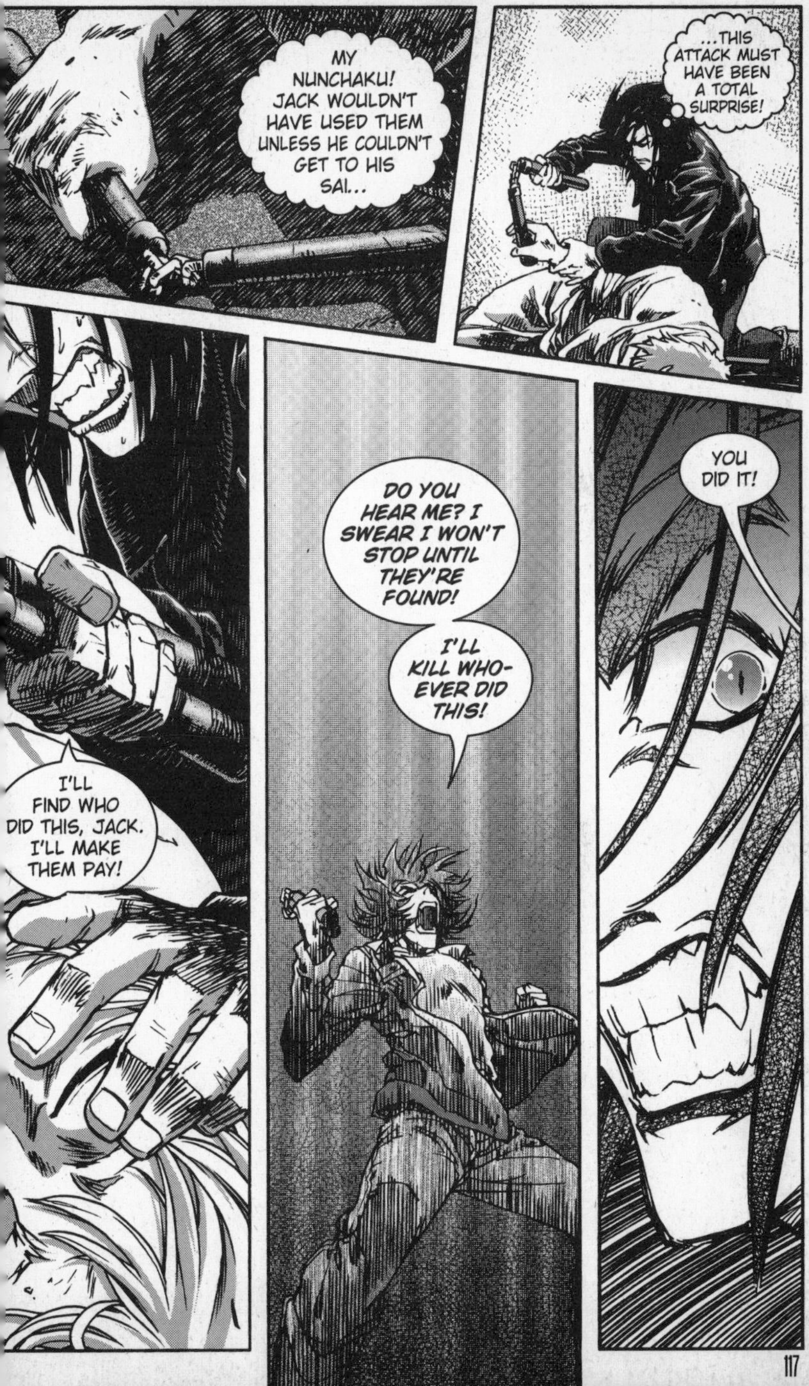
MY NUNCHAKU! JACK WOULDN'T HAVE USED THEM UNLESS HE COULDN'T GET TO HIS SAI...
...THIS ATTACK MUST HAVE BEEN A TOTAL SURPRISE!
I'LL FIND WHO DID THIS, JACK. I'LL MAKE THEM PAY!
DO YOU HEAR ME? I SWEAR I WON'T STOP UNTIL THEY'RE FOUND!
I'LL KILL WHO-EVER DID THIS!
YOU DID IT!

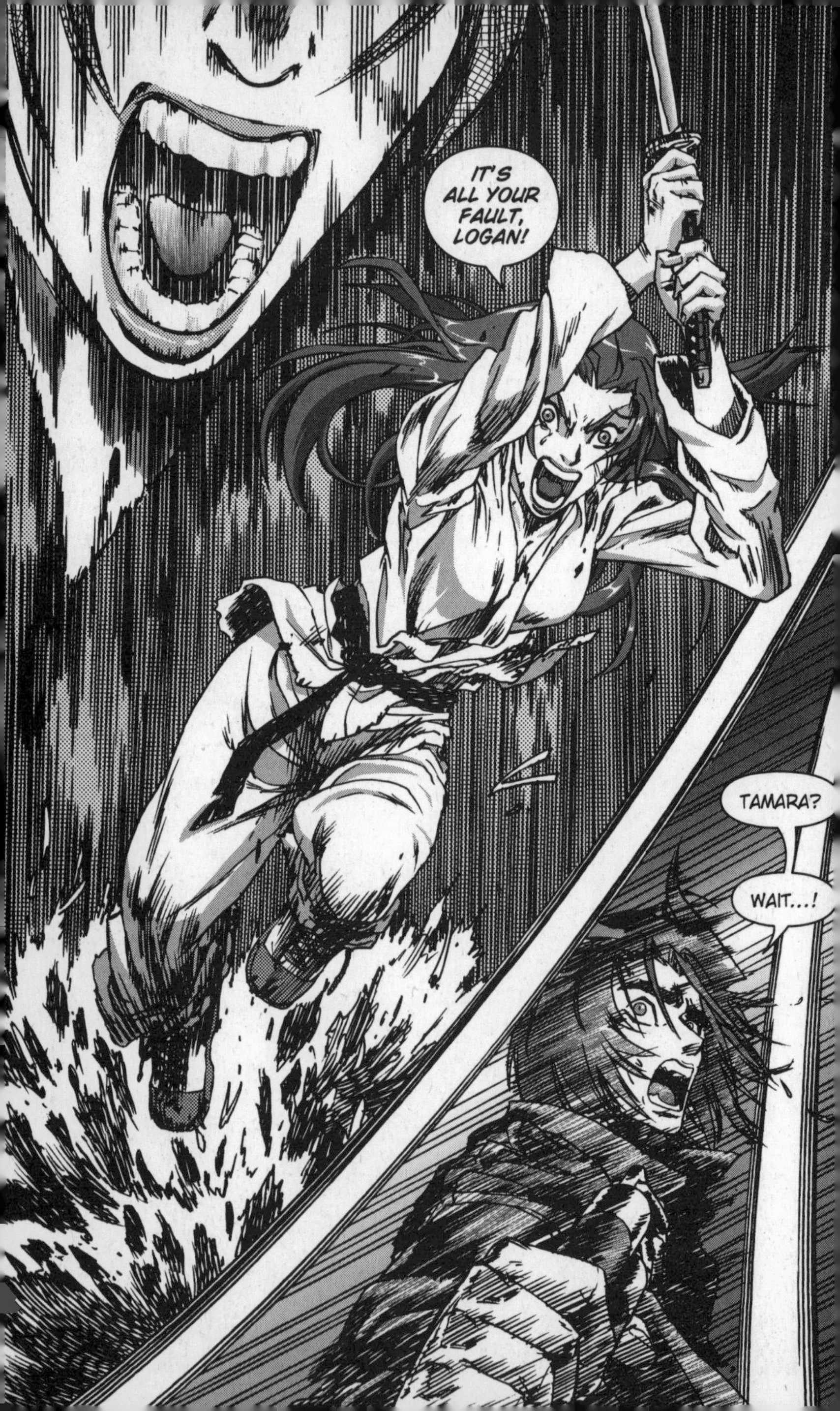
IT'S ALL YOUR FAULT, LOGAN!
TAMARA?
WAIT...!

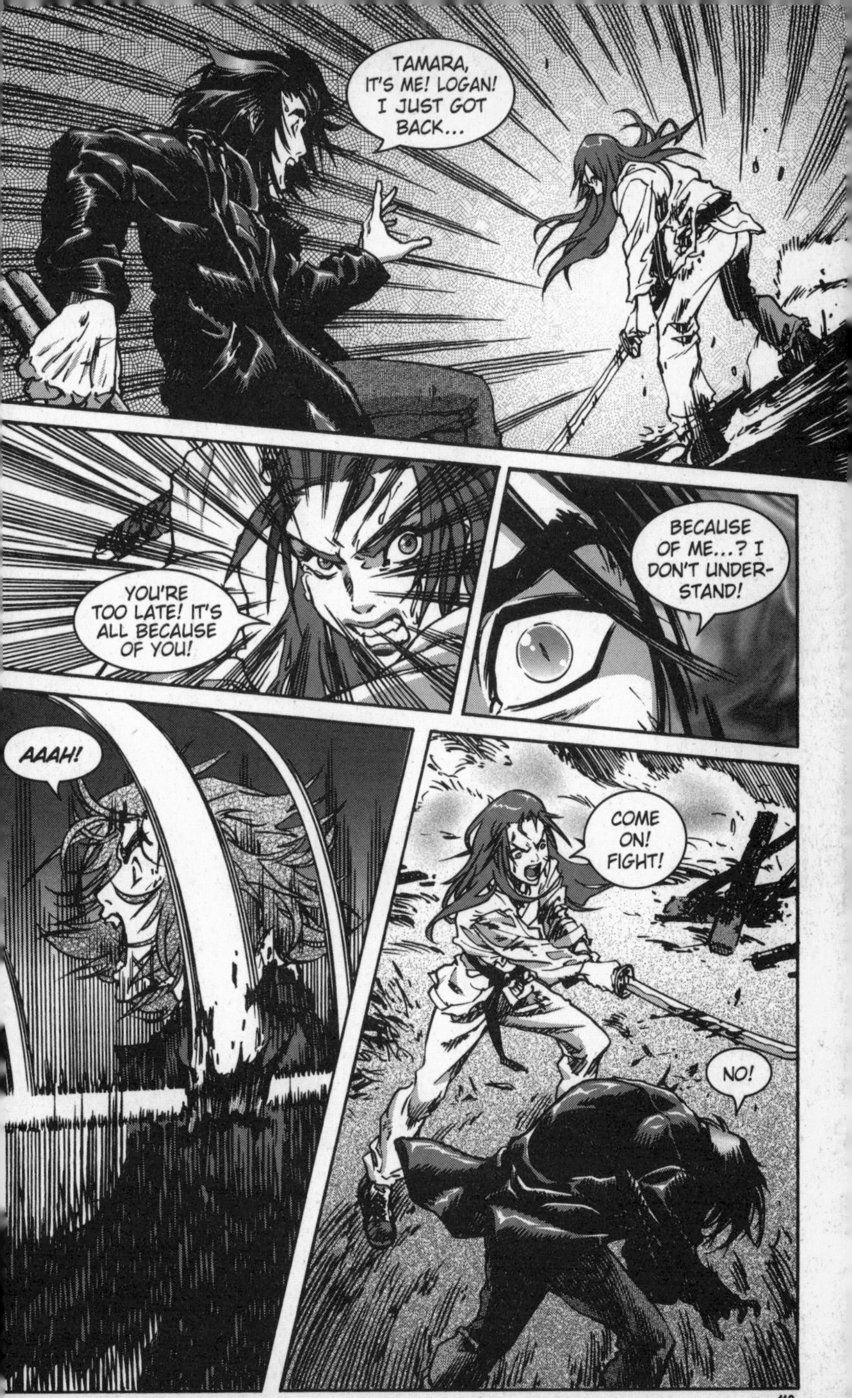
TAMARA, IT'S ME! LOGAN! I JUST GOT BACK...
YOU'RE TOO LATE! IT'S ALL BECAUSE OF YOU!
BECAUSE OF ME...? I DON'T UNDER-STAND!
AAAH!
COME ON! FIGHT!
NO!

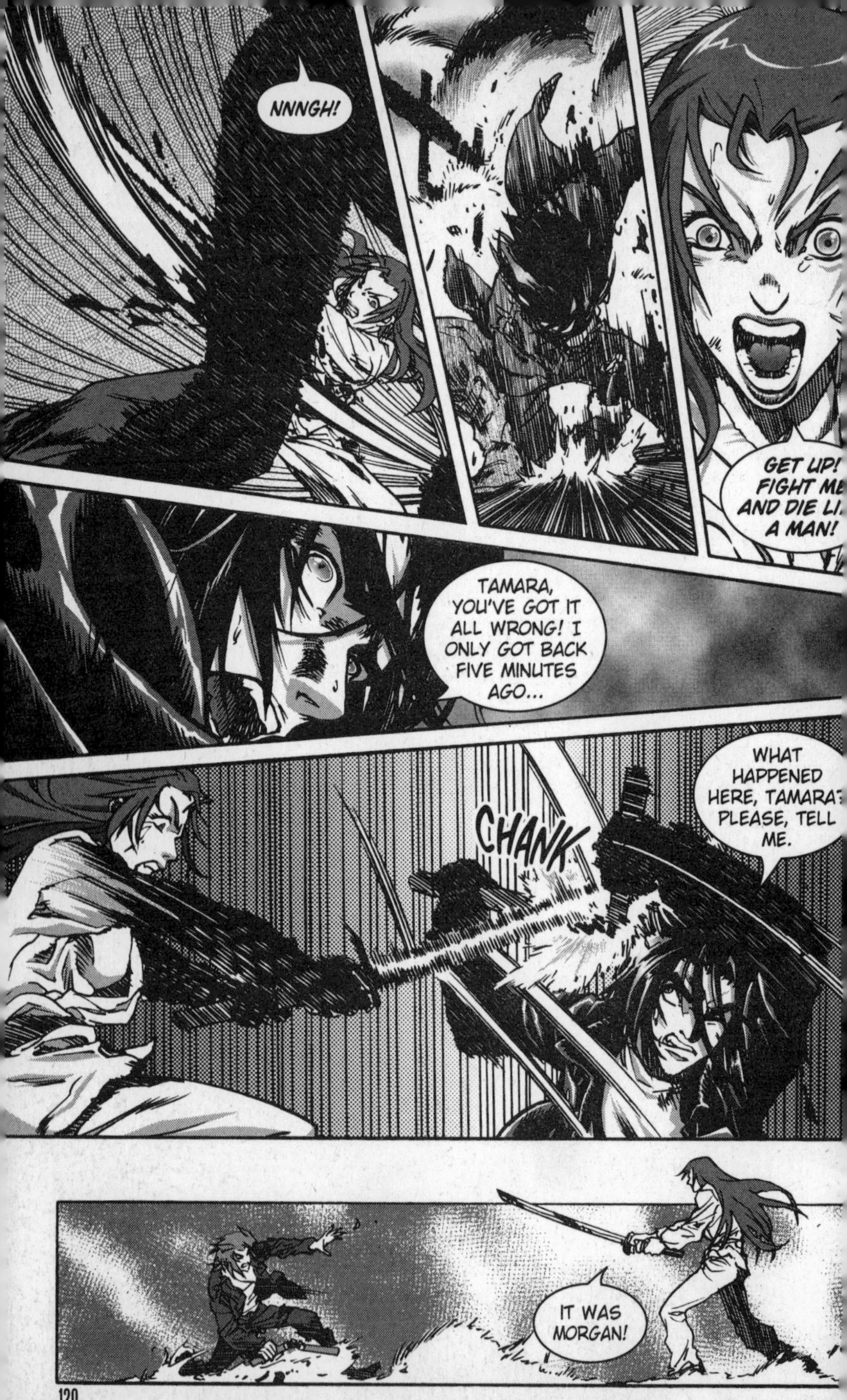
NNNGH!
GET UP! FIGHT ME AND DIE LI A MAN!
TAMARA, YOU'VE GOT IT ALL WRONG! I ONLY GOT BACK FIVE MINUTES AGO...
CHANK
WHAT HAPPENED HERE, TAMARA? PLEASE, TELL ME.
IT WAS MORGAN!

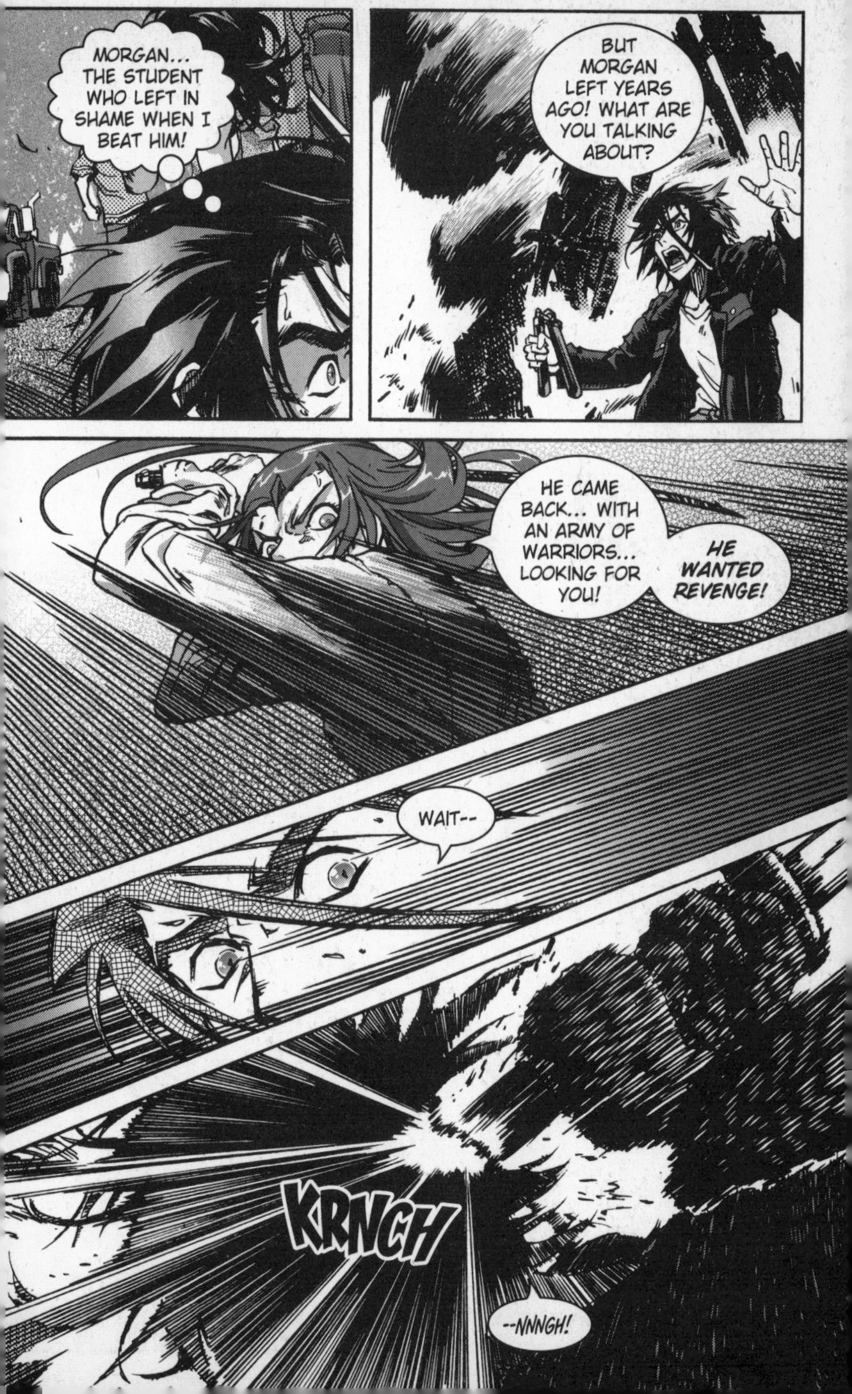
MORGAN... THE STUDENT WHO LEFT IN SHAME WHEN I BEAT HIM!
BUT MORGAN LEFT YEARS AGO! WHAT ARE YOU TALKING ABOUT?
HE CAME BACK... WITH AN ARMY OF WARRIORS... LOOKING FOR YOU!
HE WANTED REVENGE!
WAIT--
KRNCH
--NNNGH!

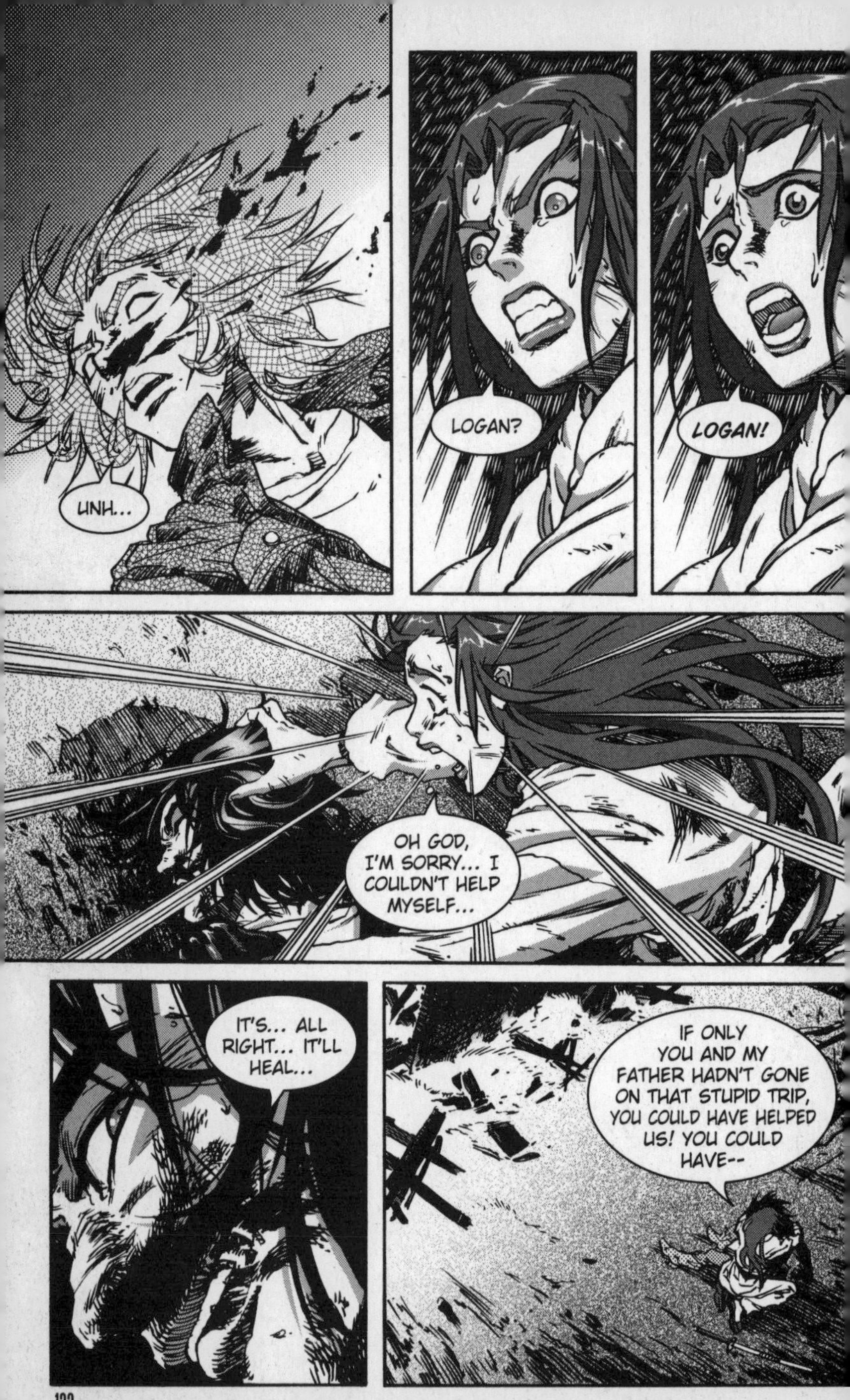
UNH...
LOGAN?
LOGAN!
OH GOD, I'M SORRY... I COULDN'T HELP MYSELF...
IT'S... ALL RIGHT... IT'LL HEAL...
IF ONLY YOU AND MY FATHER HADN'T GONE ON THAT STUPID TRIP, YOU COULD HAVE HELPED US! YOU COULD HAVE--

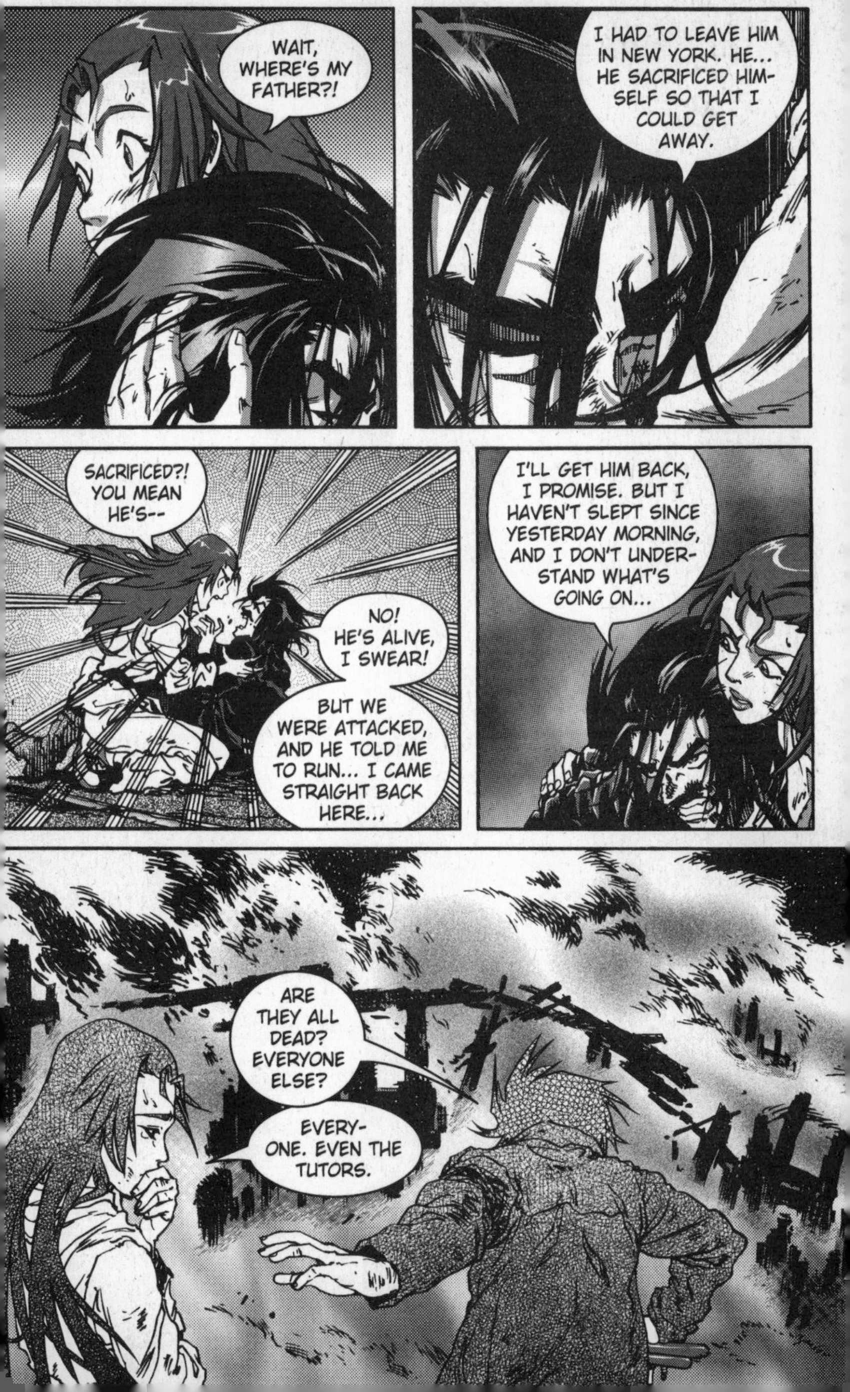
WAIT, WHERE'S MY FATHER?!
I HAD TO LEAVE HIM IN NEW YORK. HE... HE SACRIFICED HIM-SELF SO THAT I COULD GET AWAY.
SACRIFICED?! YOU MEAN HE'S--
NO! HE'S ALIVE, I SWEAR!
BUT WE WERE ATTACKED, AND HE TOLD ME TO RUN... I CAME STRAIGHT BACK HERE...
I'LL GET HIM BACK, I PROMISE. BUT I HAVEN'T SLEPT SINCE YESTERDAY MORNING, AND I DON'T UNDER-STAND WHAT'S GOING ON...
ARE THEY ALL DEAD? EVERYONE ELSE?
EVERY-ONE. EVEN THE TUTORS.

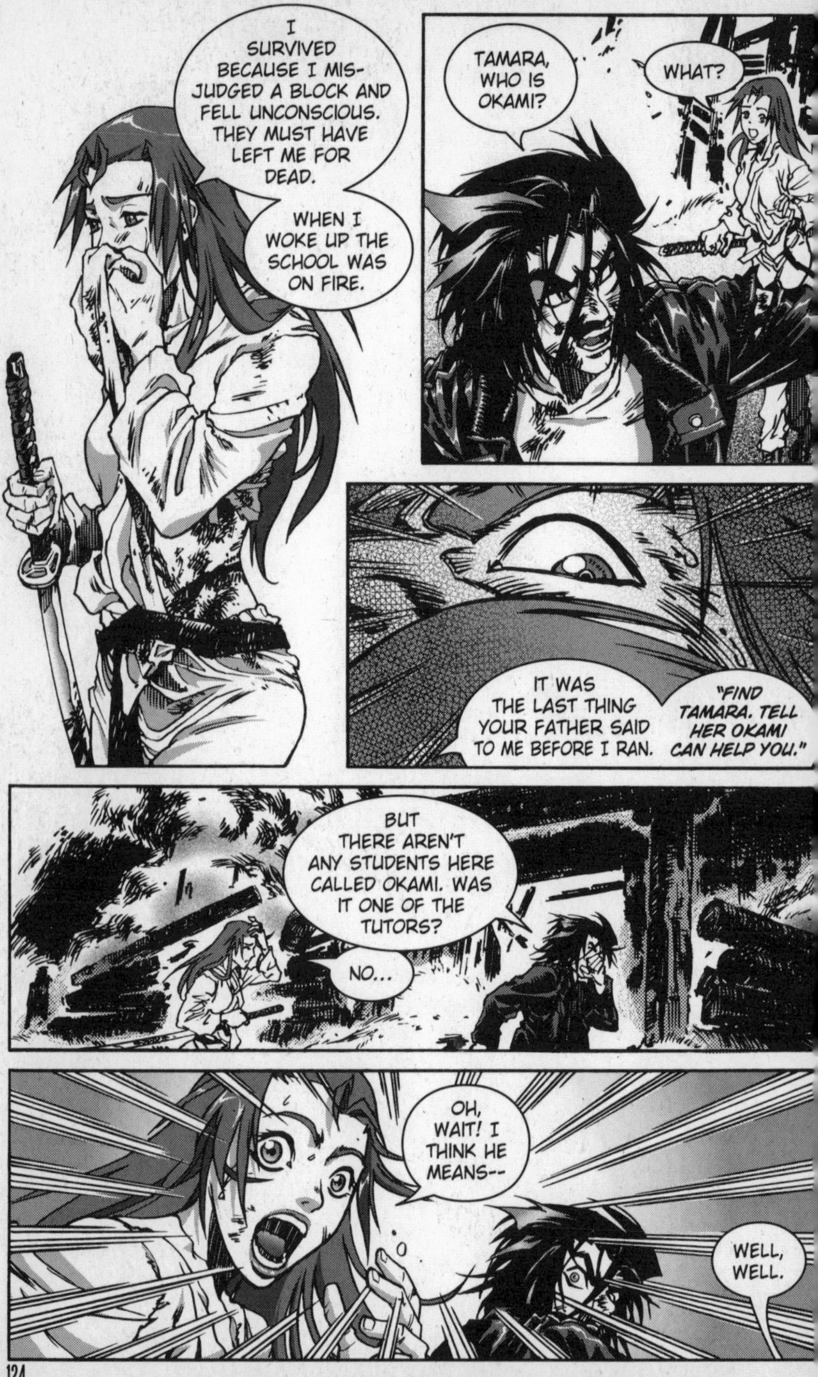
I SURVIVED BECAUSE I MIS-JUDGED A BLOCK AND FELL UNCONSCIOUS. THEY MUST HAVE LEFT ME FOR DEAD.
WHEN I WOKE UP THE SCHOOL WAS ON FIRE.
TAMARA, WHO IS OKAMI?
WHAT?
IT WAS THE LAST THING YOUR FATHER SAID TO ME BEFORE I RAN.
"FIND TAMARA. TELL HER OKAMI CAN HELP YOU."
BUT THERE AREN'T ANY STUDENTS HERE CALLED OKAMI. WAS IT ONE OF THE TUTORS?
NO...
OH, WAIT! I THINK HE MEANS--
WELL, WELL.

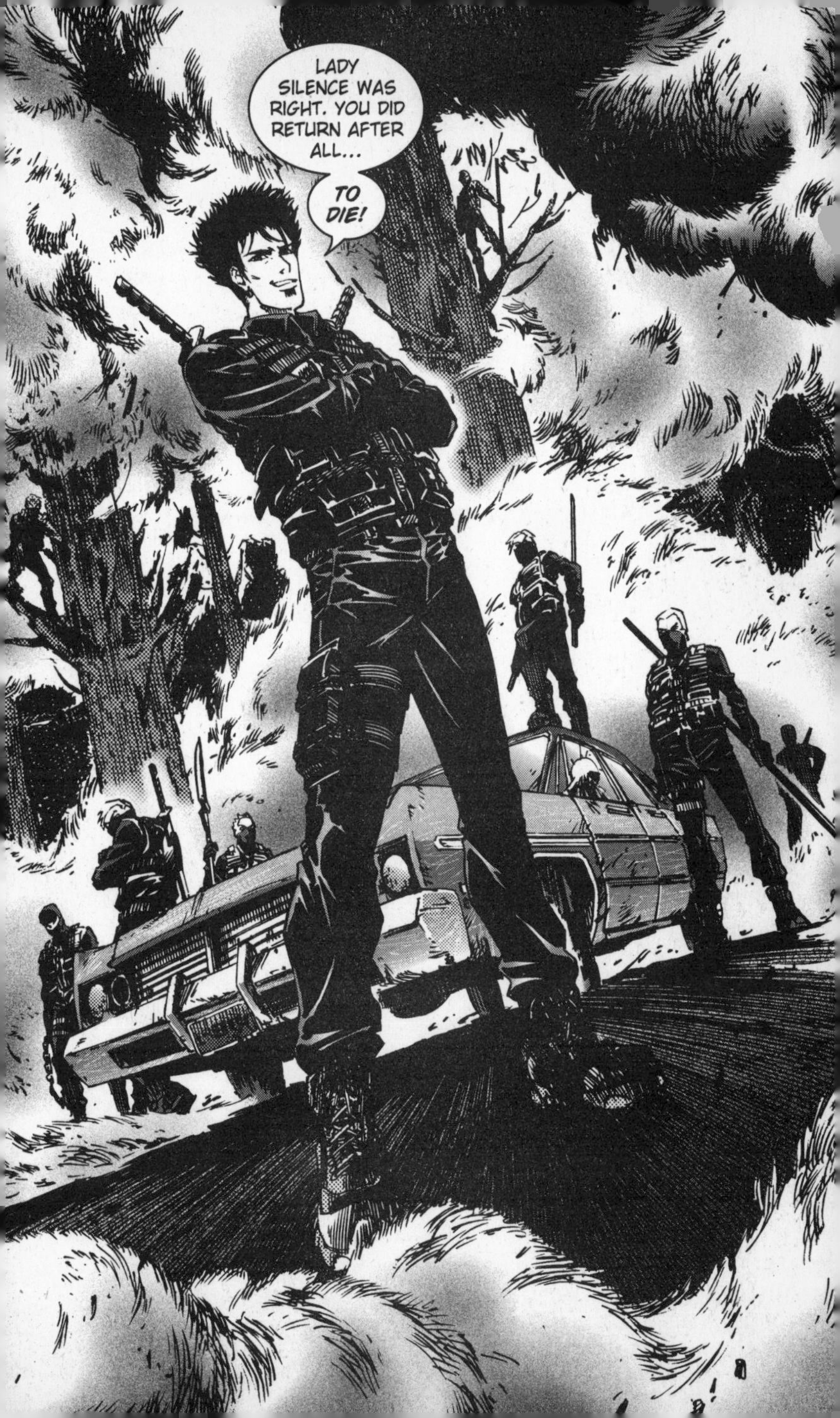
LADY SILENCE WAS RIGHT. YOU DID RETURN AFTER ALL...
TO DIE!

Chapter Nine
The Truth Will Set You Free

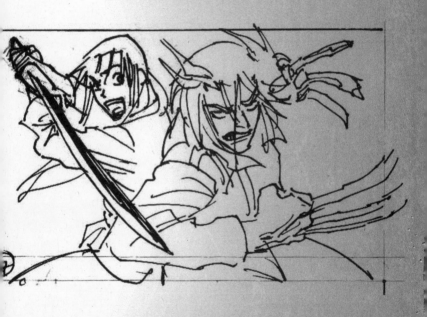

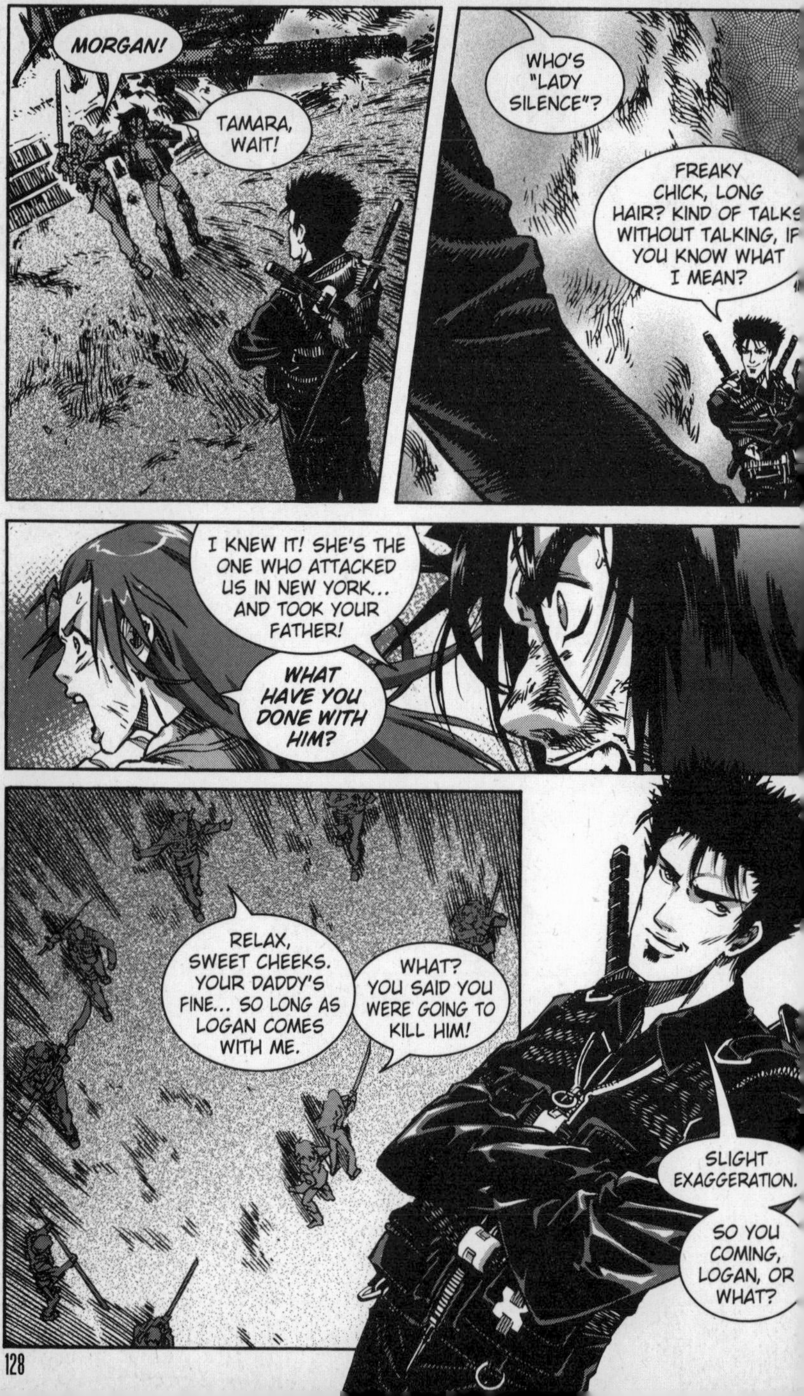
MORGAN!
TAMARA, WAIT!
WHO'S "LADY SILENCE"?
FREAKY CHICK, LONG HAIR? KIND OF TALKS WITHOUT TALKING, IF YOU KNOW WHAT I MEAN?
I KNEW IT! SHE'S THE ONE WHO ATTACKED US IN NEW YORK... AND TOOK YOUR FATHER!
WHAT HAVE YOU DONE WITH HIM?
RELAX, SWEET CHEEKS. YOUR DADDY'S FINE... SO LONG AS LOGAN COMES WITH ME.
WHAT? YOU SAID YOU WERE GOING TO KILL HIM!
SLIGHT EXAGGERATION.
SO YOU COMING, LOGAN, OR WHAT?

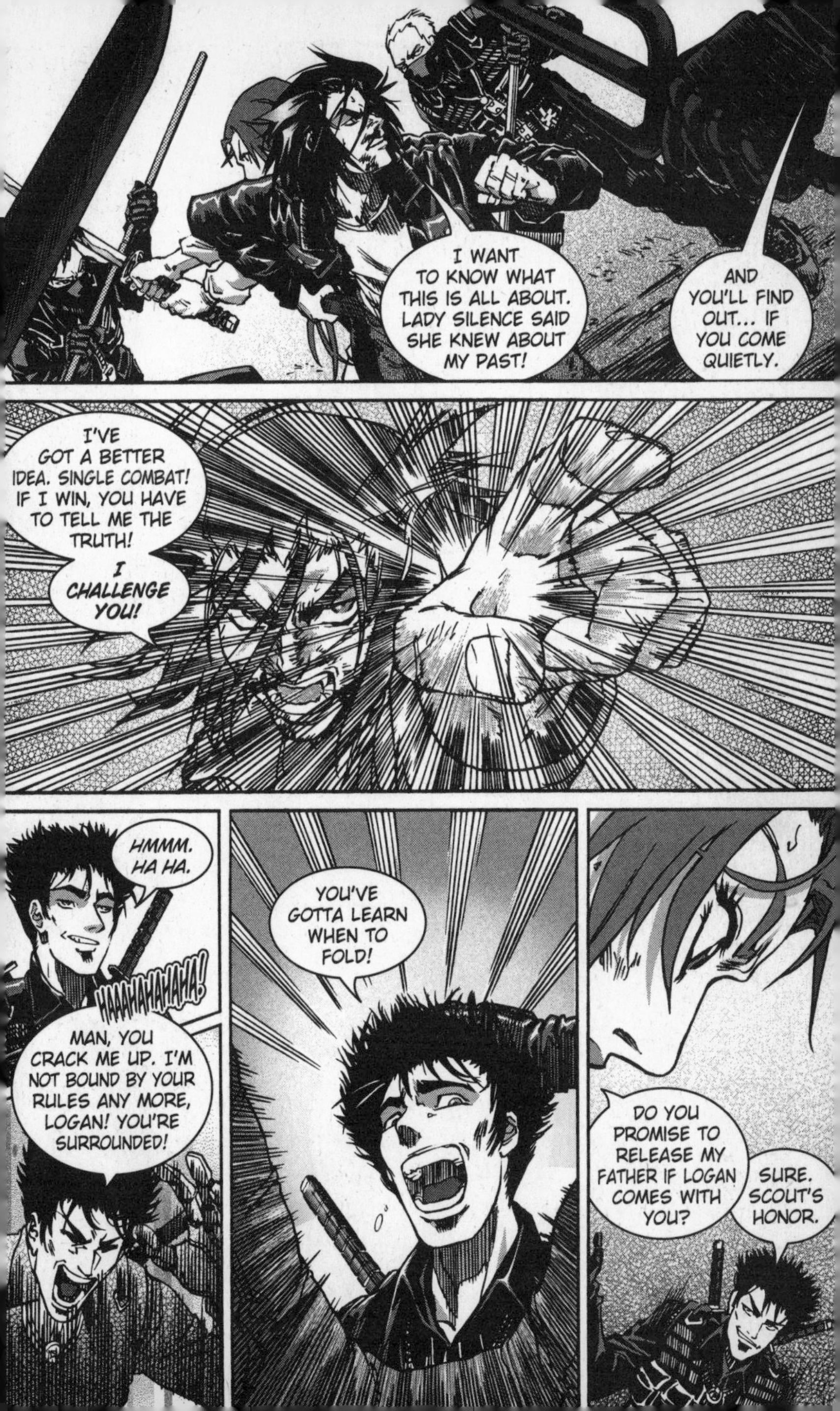
I WANT TO KNOW WHAT THIS IS ALL ABOUT. LADY SILENCE SAID SHE KNEW ABOUT MY PAST!
AND YOU'LL FIND OUT... IF YOU COME QUIETLY.
I'VE GOT A BETTER IDEA. SINGLE COMBAT! IF I WIN, YOU HAVE TO TELL ME THE TRUTH!
I CHALLENGE YOU!
HMMM. HA HA.
HAAAHAHAHAHA!
MAN, YOU CRACK ME UP. I'M NOT BOUND BY YOUR RULES ANY MORE, LOGAN! YOU'RE SURROUNDED!
YOU'VE GOTTA LEARN WHEN TO FOLD!
DO YOU PROMISE TO RELEASE MY FATHER IF LOGAN COMES WITH YOU?
SURE. SCOUT'S HONOR.

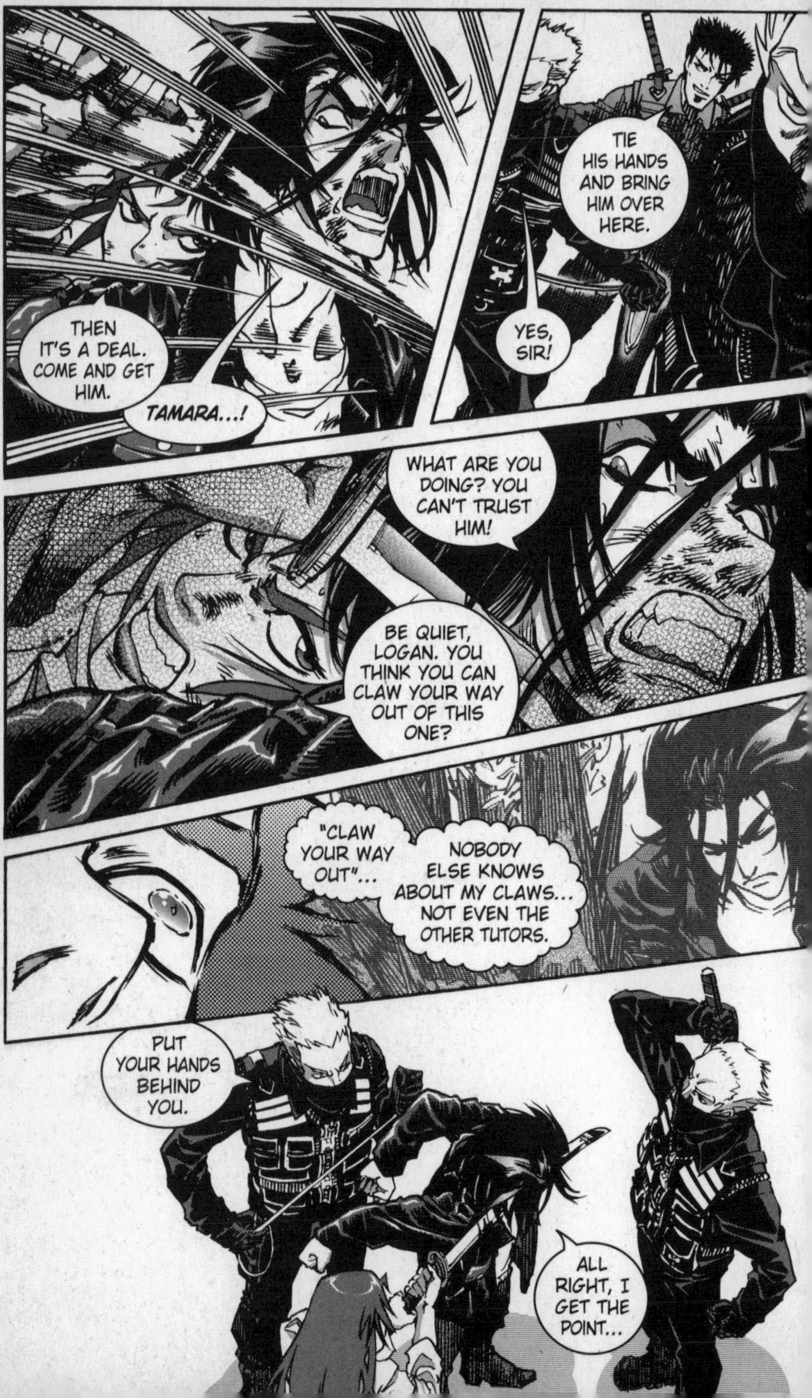
THEN IT'S A DEAL. COME AND GET HIM.
TAMARA...!
TIE HIS HANDS AND BRING HIM OVER HERE.
YES, SIR!
WHAT ARE YOU DOING? YOU CAN'T TRUST HIM!
BE QUIET, LOGAN. YOU THINK YOU CAN CLAW YOUR WAY OUT OF THIS ONE?
"CLAW YOUR WAY OUT"...
NOBODY ELSE KNOWS ABOUT MY CLAWS... NOT EVEN THE OTHER TUTORS.
PUT YOUR HANDS BEHIND YOU.
ALL RIGHT, I GET THE POINT...

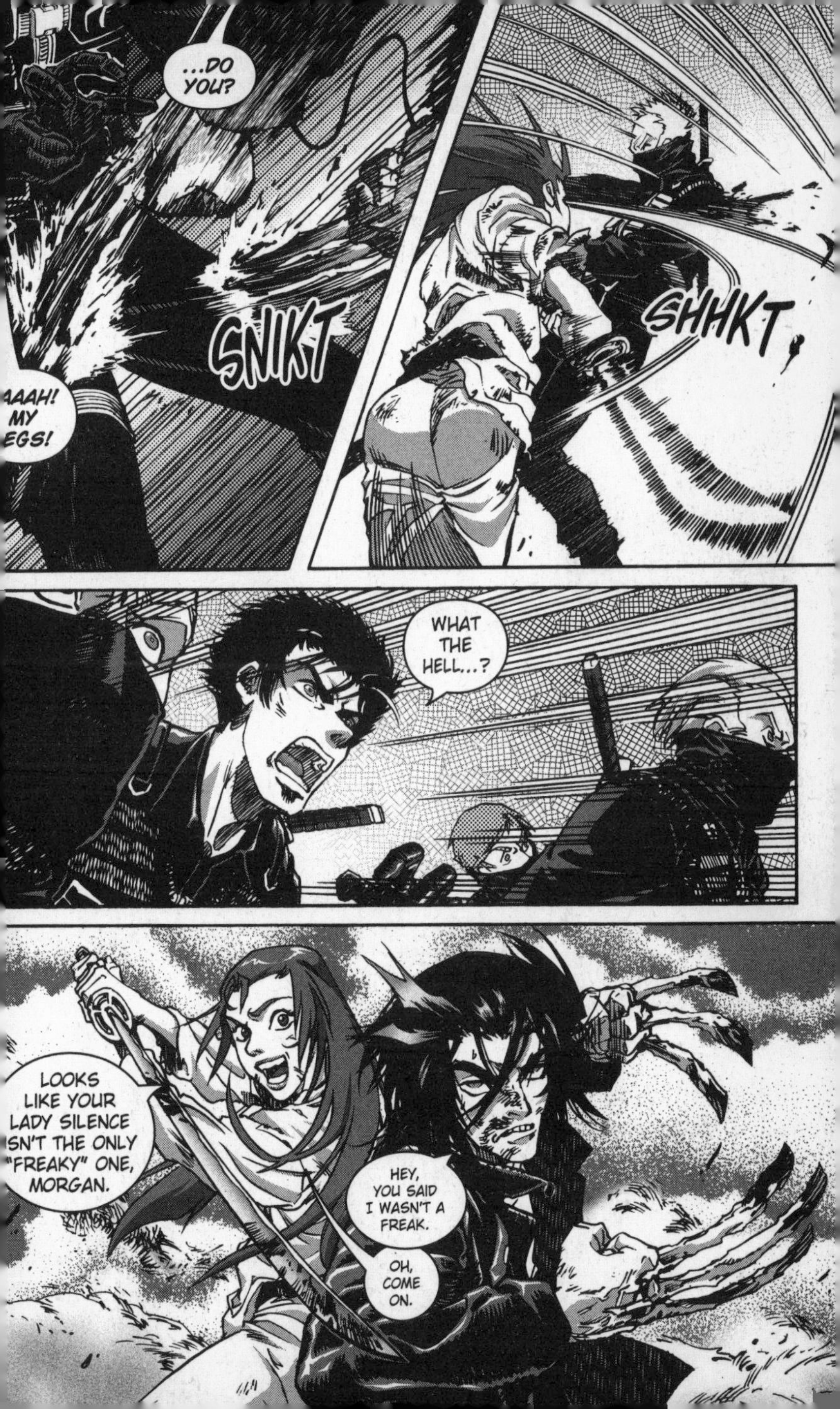
...DO YOU?
SNIKT
AAAH! MY EGS!
SHHKT
WHAT THE HELL...?
LOOKS LIKE YOUR LADY SILENCE SN'T THE ONLY "FREAKY" ONE, MORGAN.
HEY, YOU SAID I WASN'T A FREAK.
OH, COME ON.

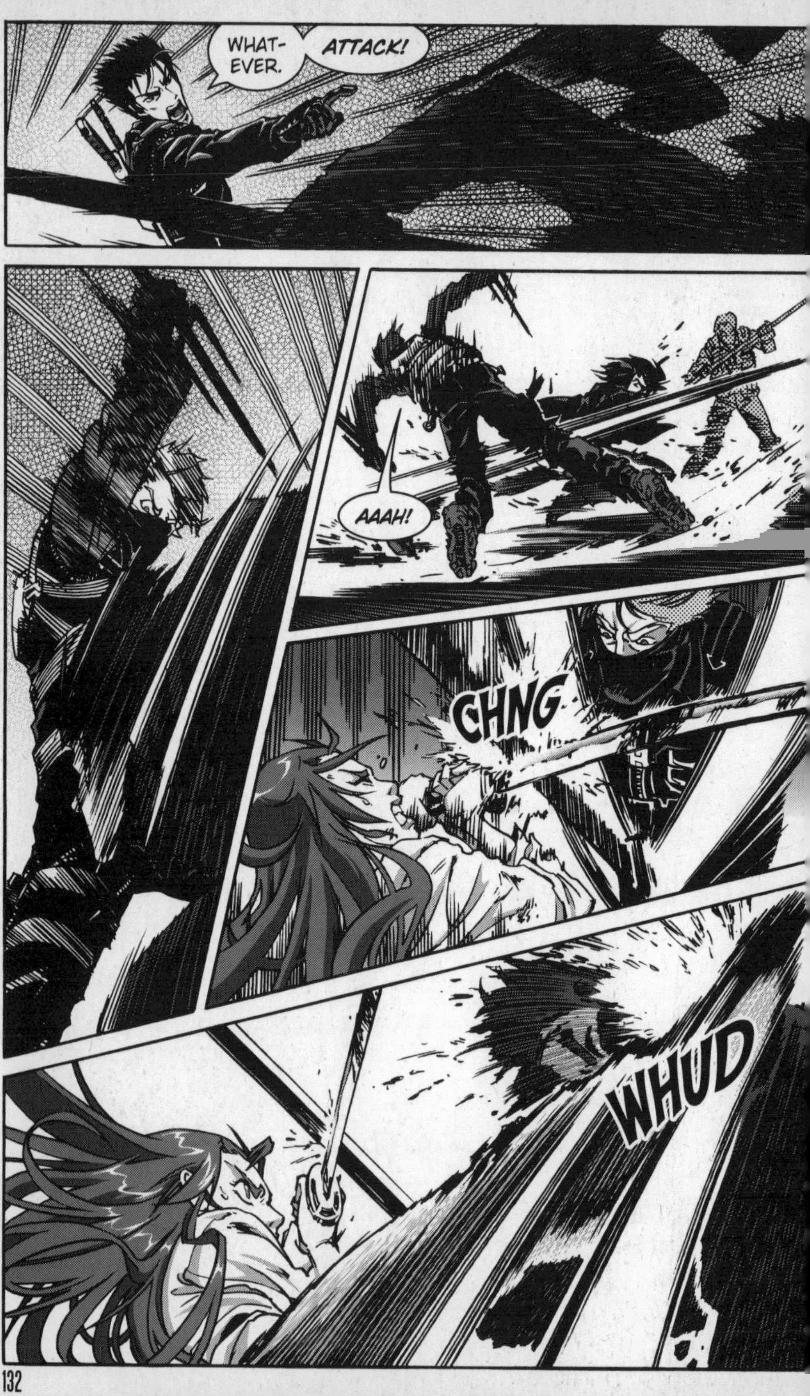
WHAT-EVER.
ATTACK!
AAAH!
CHNG
WHUD

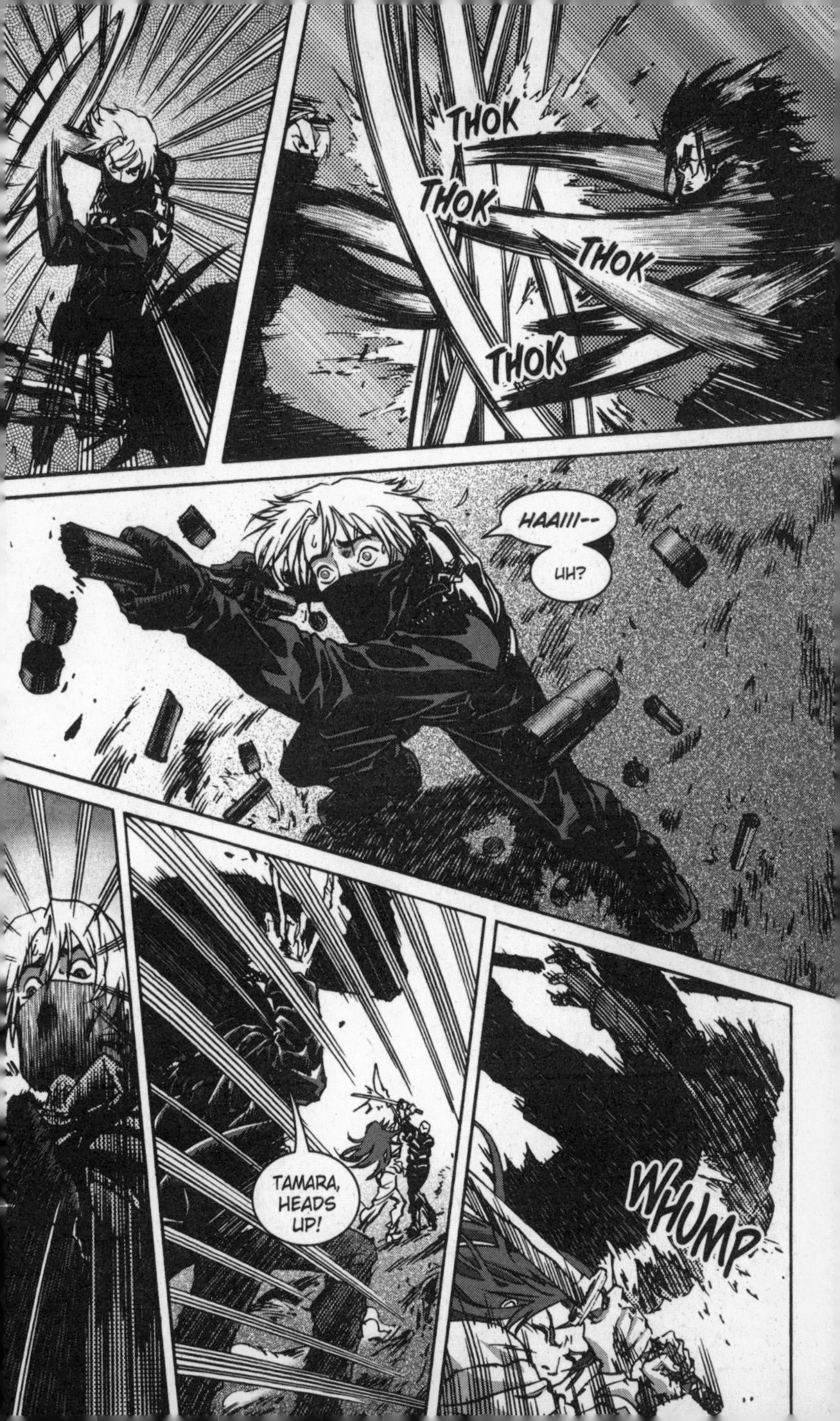
THOK
THOK
THOK
THOK
HAAIII--
UH?
TAMARA, HEADS UP!
WHUMP

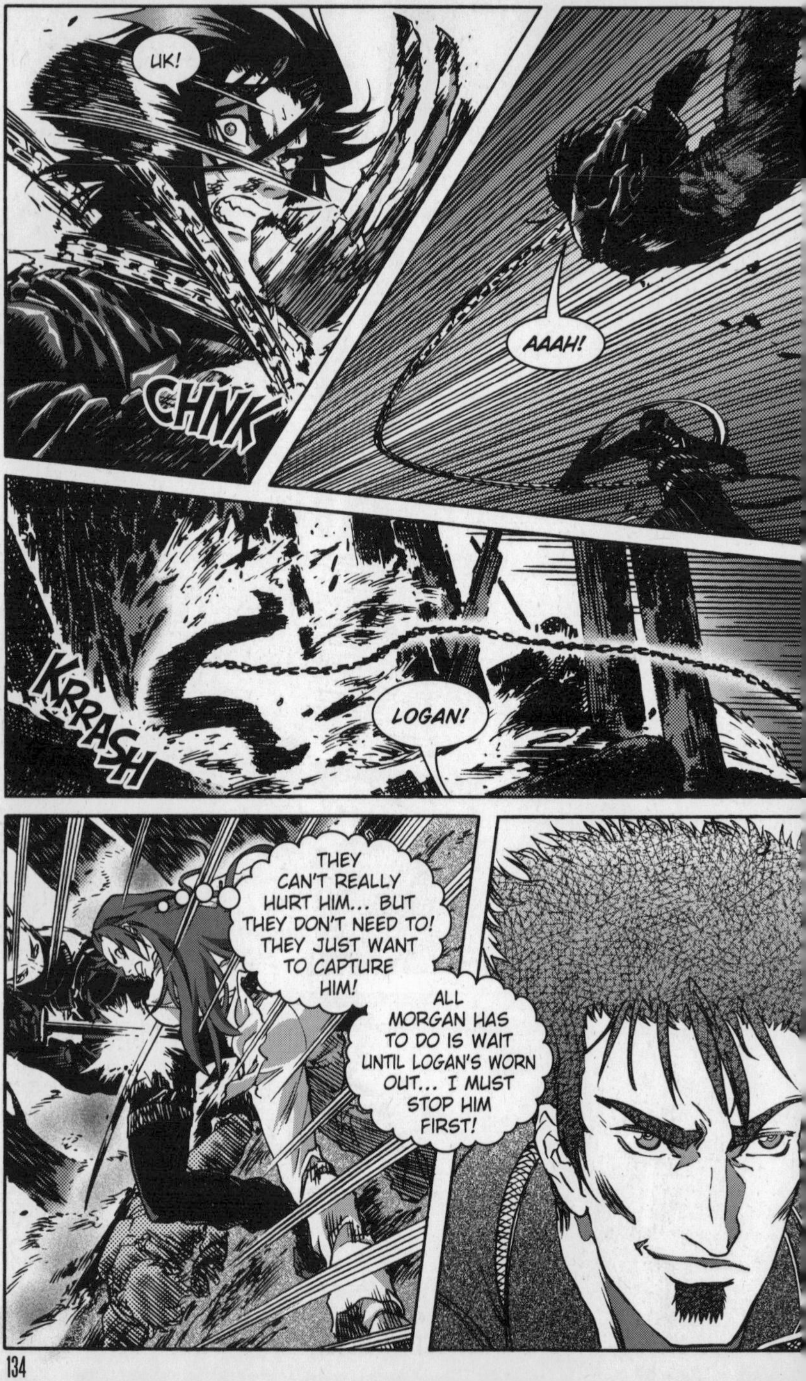
UK!
CHNK
AAAH!
KRRASH
LOGAN!
THEY CAN'T REALLY HURT HIM... BUT THEY DON'T NEED TO! THEY JUST WANT TO CAPTURE HIM!
ALL MORGAN HAS TO DO IS WAIT UNTIL LOGAN'S WORN OUT... I MUST STOP HIM FIRST!

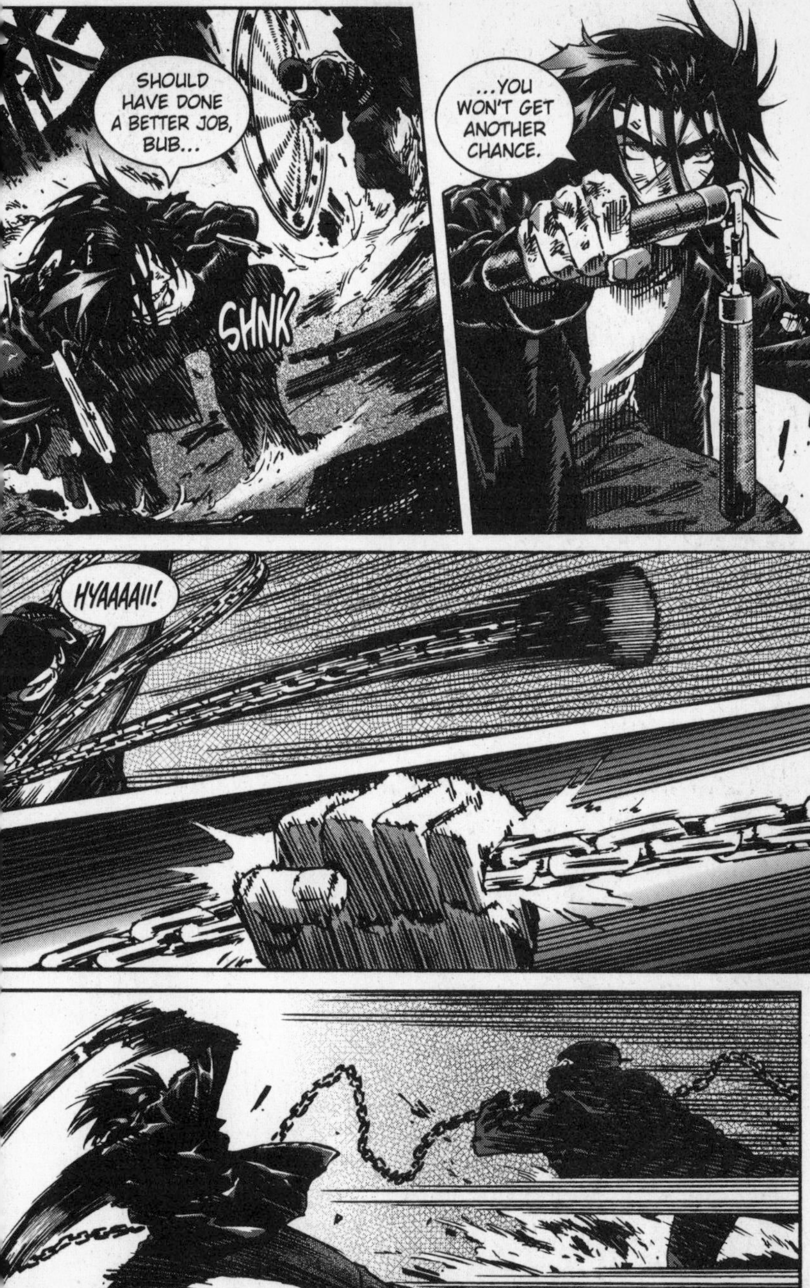
SHOULD HAVE DONE A BETTER JOB, BUB...
SHNK
...YOU WON'T GET ANOTHER CHANCE.
HYAAAA!!!

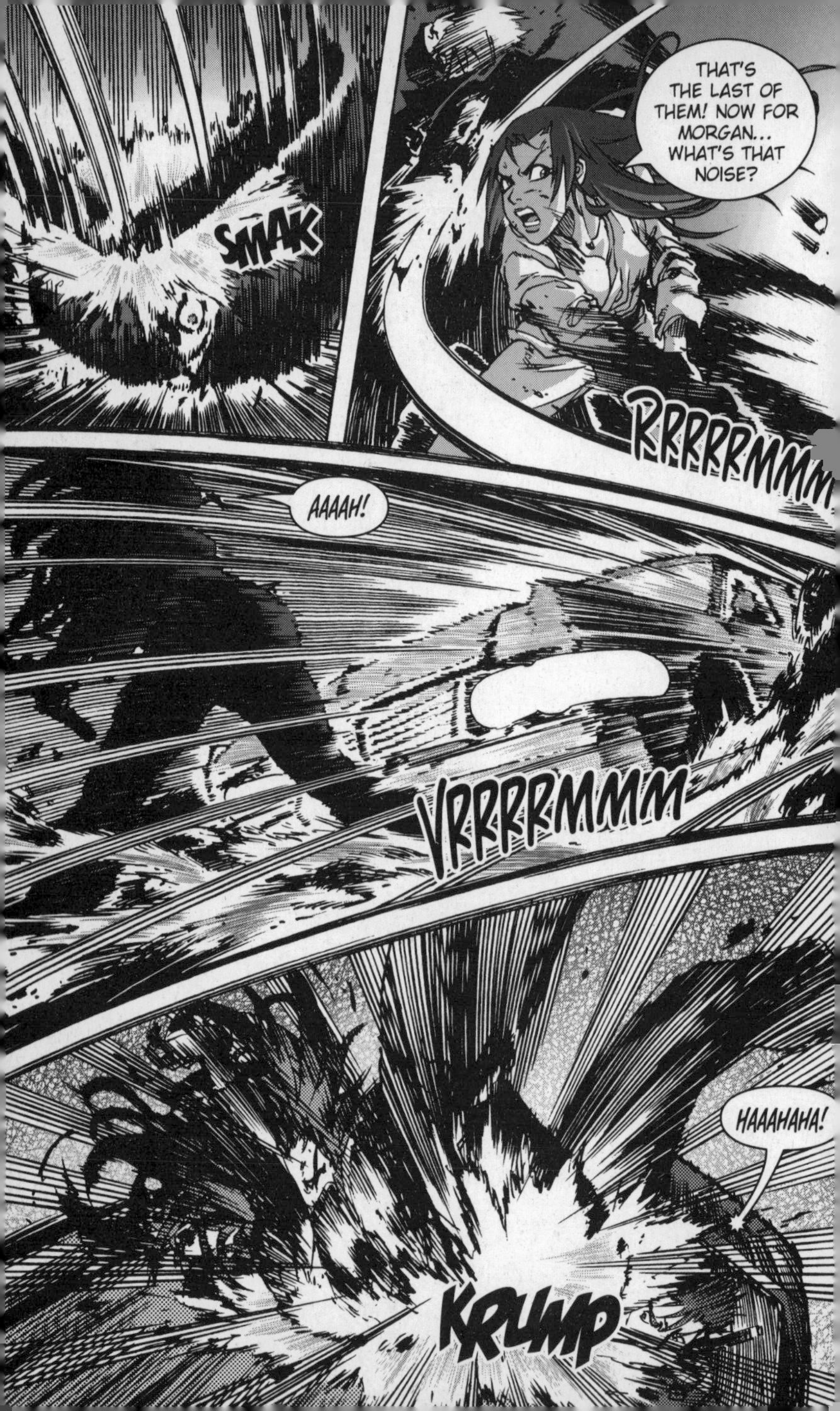
SMAK
THAT'S THE LAST OF THEM! NOW FOR MORGAN... WHAT'S THAT NOISE?
RRRRRMMM
AAAAH!
VRRRRMMM
HAAAHAHA!
KRUMP

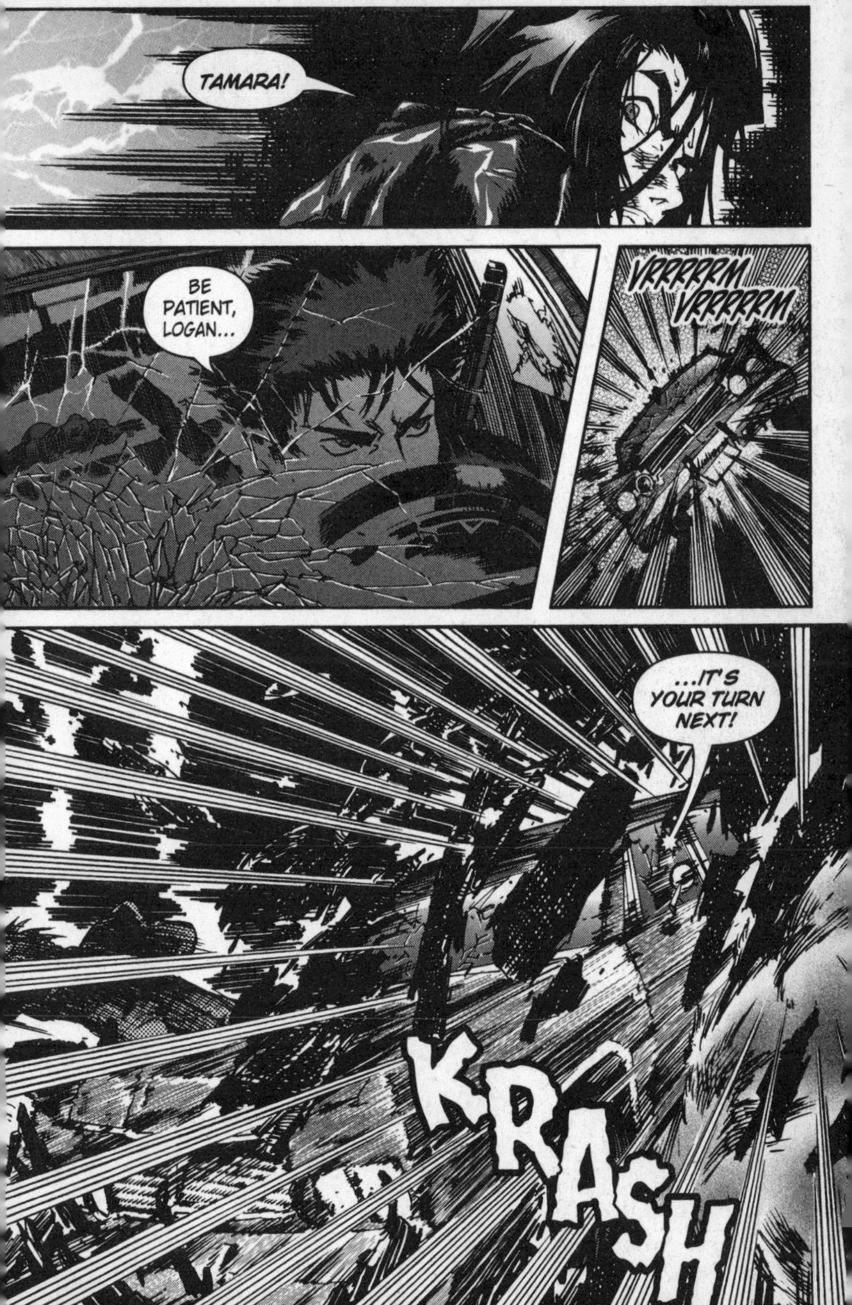
TAMARA!
BE PATIENT, LOGAN...
VRRRRRM VRRRRRM
...IT'S YOUR TURN NEXT!
KRASH

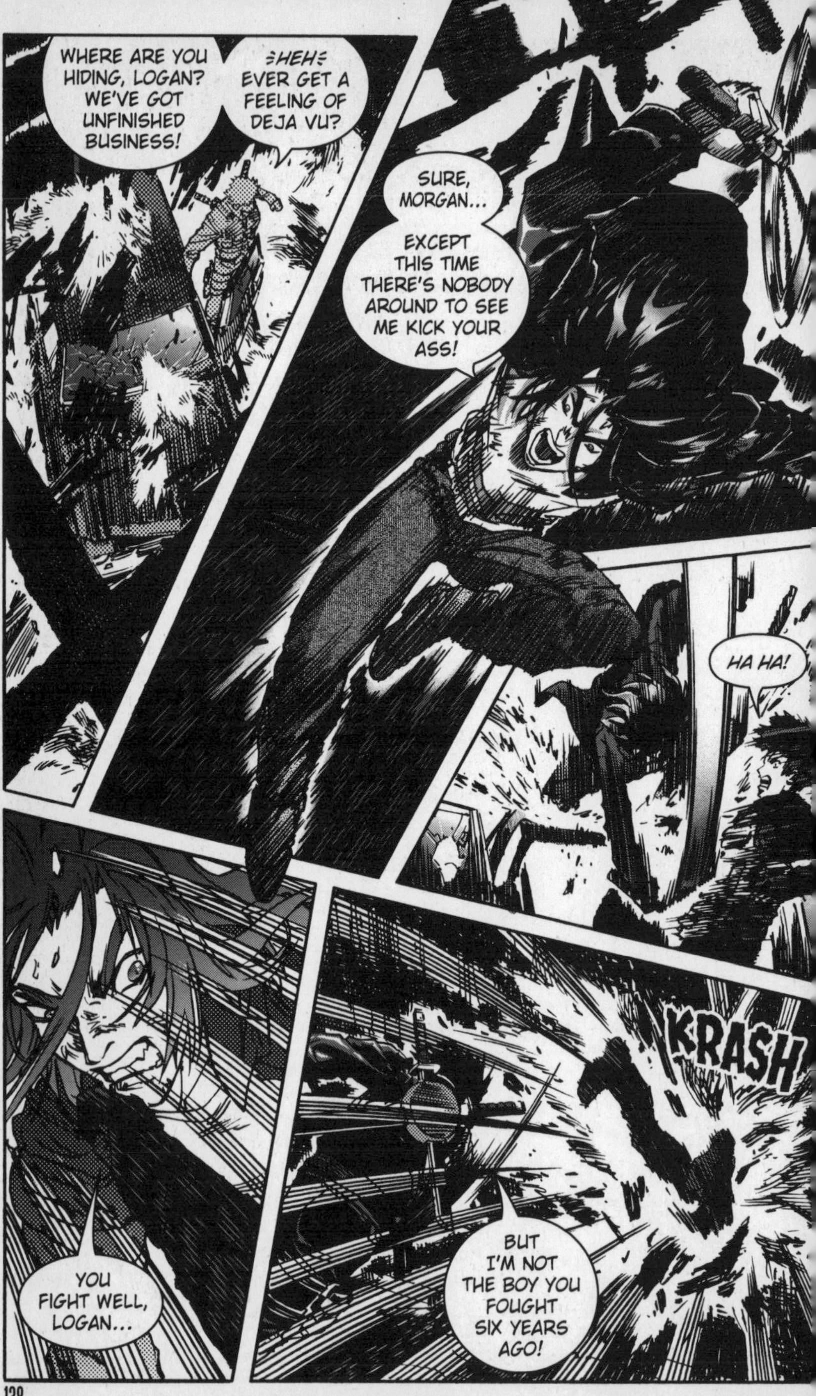
WHERE ARE YOU HIDING, LOGAN? WE'VE GOT UNFINISHED BUSINESS!
HEH EVER GET A FEELING OF DEJA VU?
SURE, MORGAN...
EXCEPT THIS TIME THERE'S NOBODY AROUND TO SEE ME KICK YOUR ASS!
HA HA!
YOU FIGHT WELL, LOGAN...
BUT I'M NOT THE BOY YOU FOUGHT SIX YEARS AGO!
KRASH

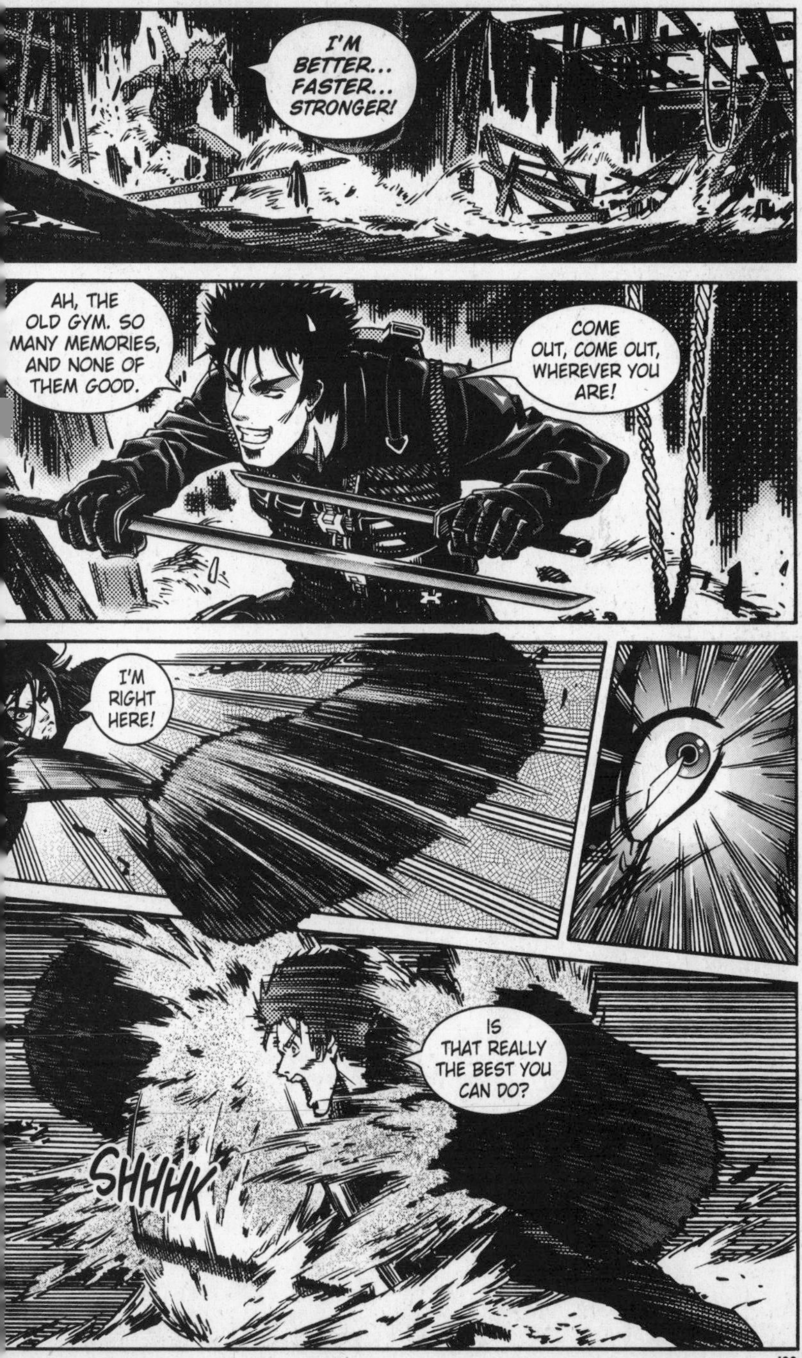
I'M BETTER... FASTER... STRONGER!
AH, THE OLD GYM. SO MANY MEMORIES, AND NONE OF THEM GOOD.
COME OUT, COME OUT, WHEREVER YOU ARE!
I'M RIGHT HERE!
IS THAT REALLY THE BEST YOU CAN DO?
SHHHK

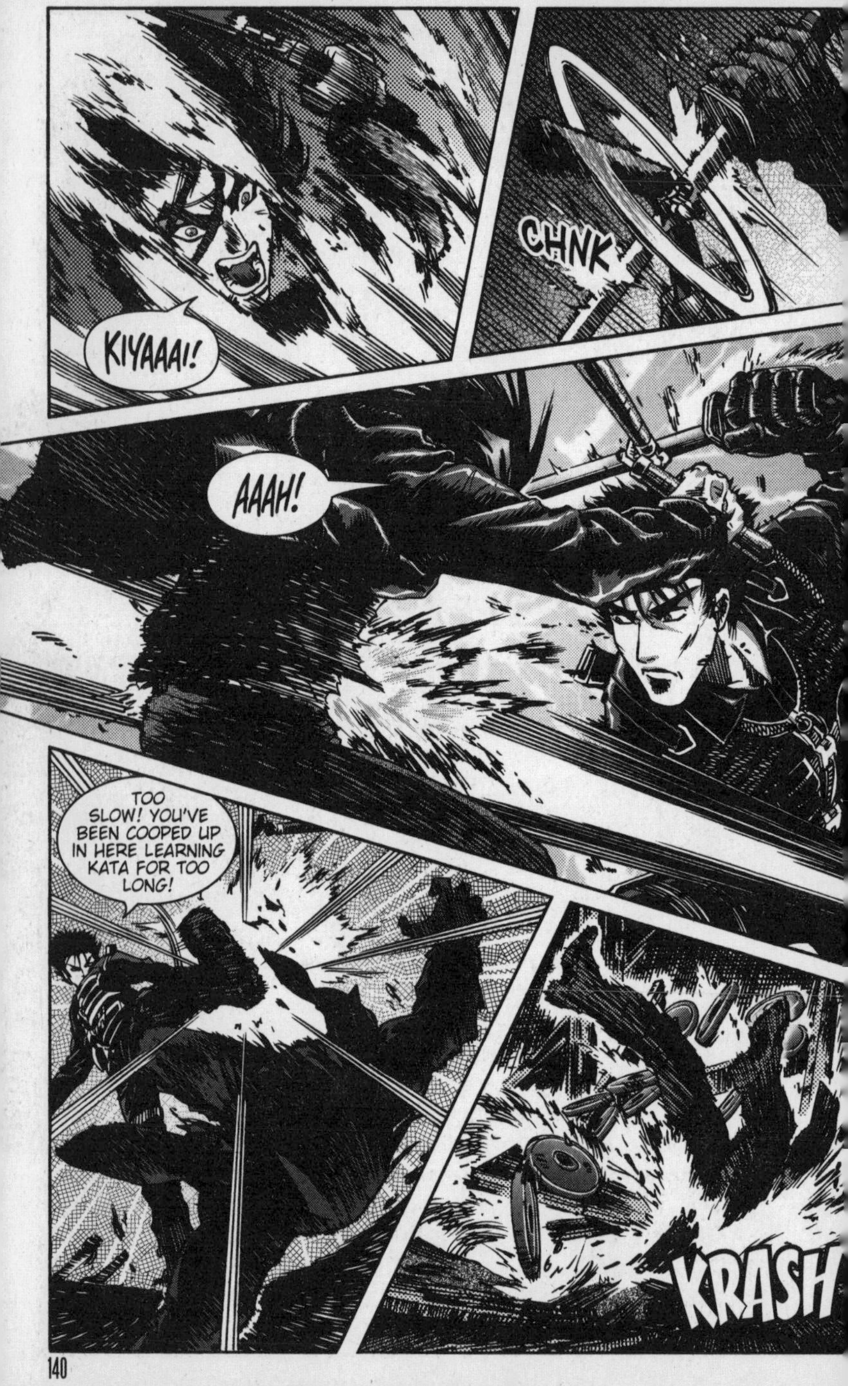
KIYAAAI!
CHNK
AAAH!
TOO SLOW! YOU'VE BEEN COOPED UP IN HERE LEARNING KATA FOR TOO LONG!
KRASH

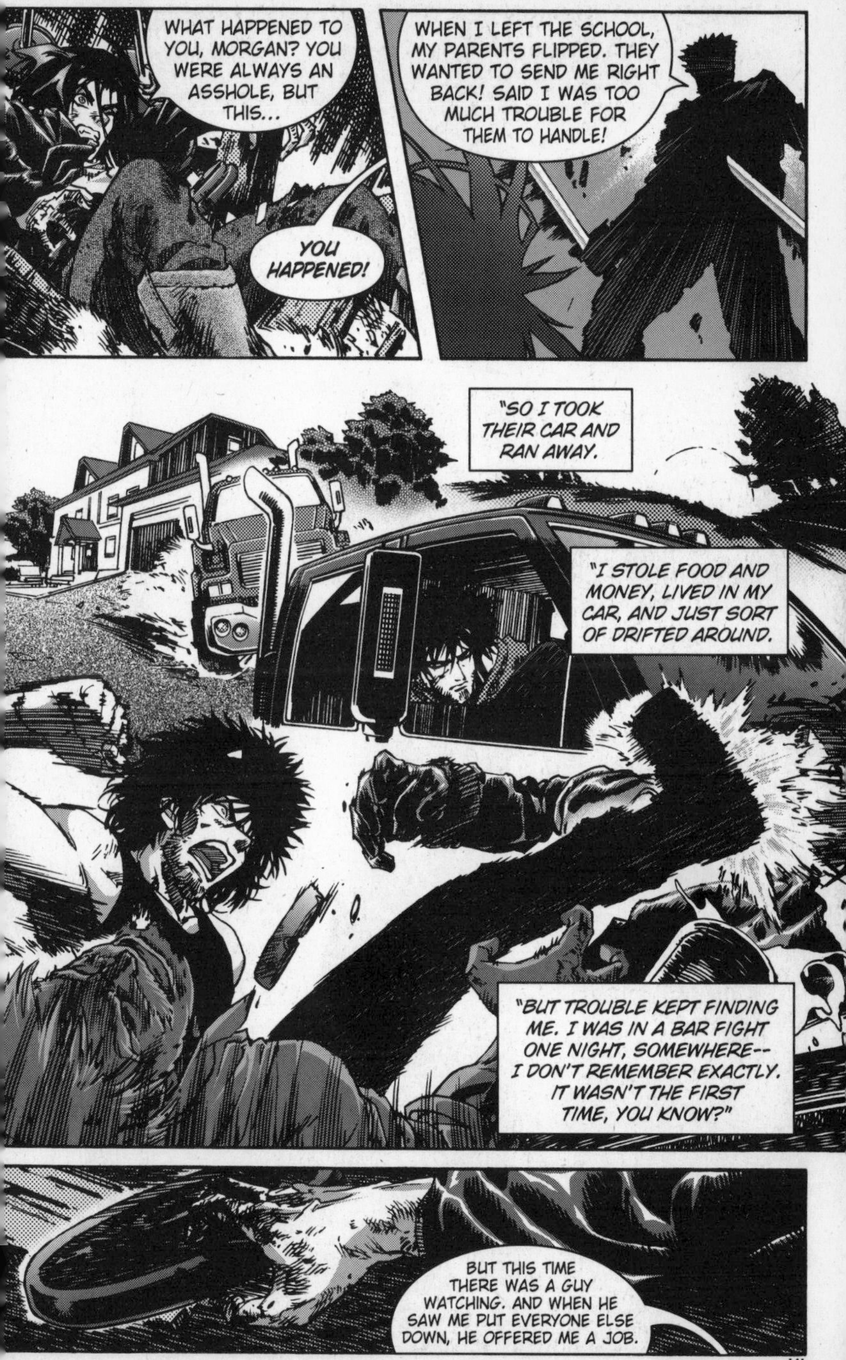
WHAT HAPPENED TO YOU, MORGAN? YOU WERE ALWAYS AN ASSHOLE, BUT THIS...
YOU HAPPENED!
WHEN I LEFT THE SCHOOL, MY PARENTS FLIPPED. THEY WANTED TO SEND ME RIGHT BACK! SAID I WAS TOO MUCH TROUBLE FOR THEM TO HANDLE!
"SO I TOOK THEIR CAR AND RAN AWAY.
"I STOLE FOOD AND MONEY, LIVED IN MY CAR, AND JUST SORT OF DRIFTED AROUND.
"BUT TROUBLE KEPT FINDING ME. I WAS IN A BAR FIGHT ONE NIGHT, SOMEWHERE-- I DON'T REMEMBER EXACTLY. IT WASN'T THE FIRST TIME, YOU KNOW?"
BUT THIS TIME THERE WAS A GUY WATCHING. AND WHEN HE SAW ME PUT EVERYONE ELSE DOWN, HE OFFERED ME A JOB.

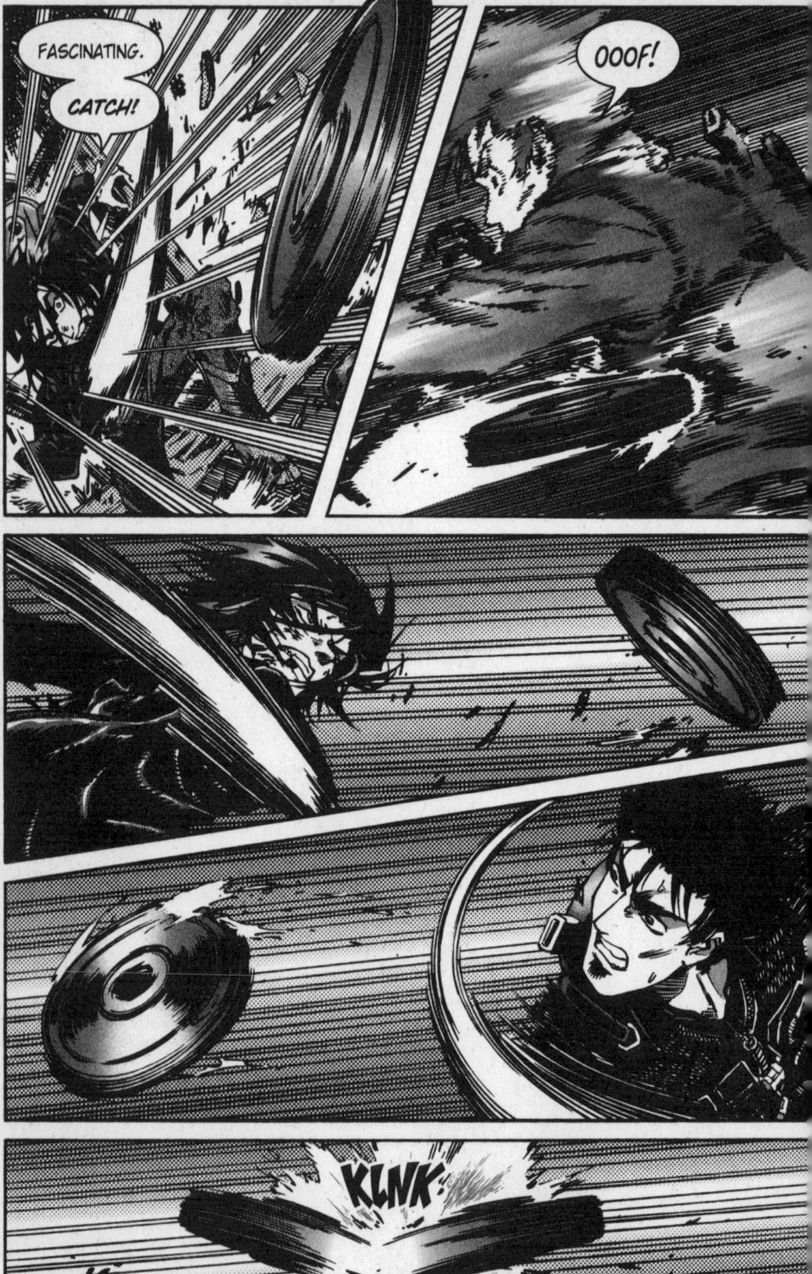
FASCINATING.
CATCH!
OOOF!
KLNK

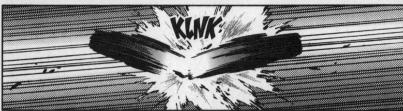

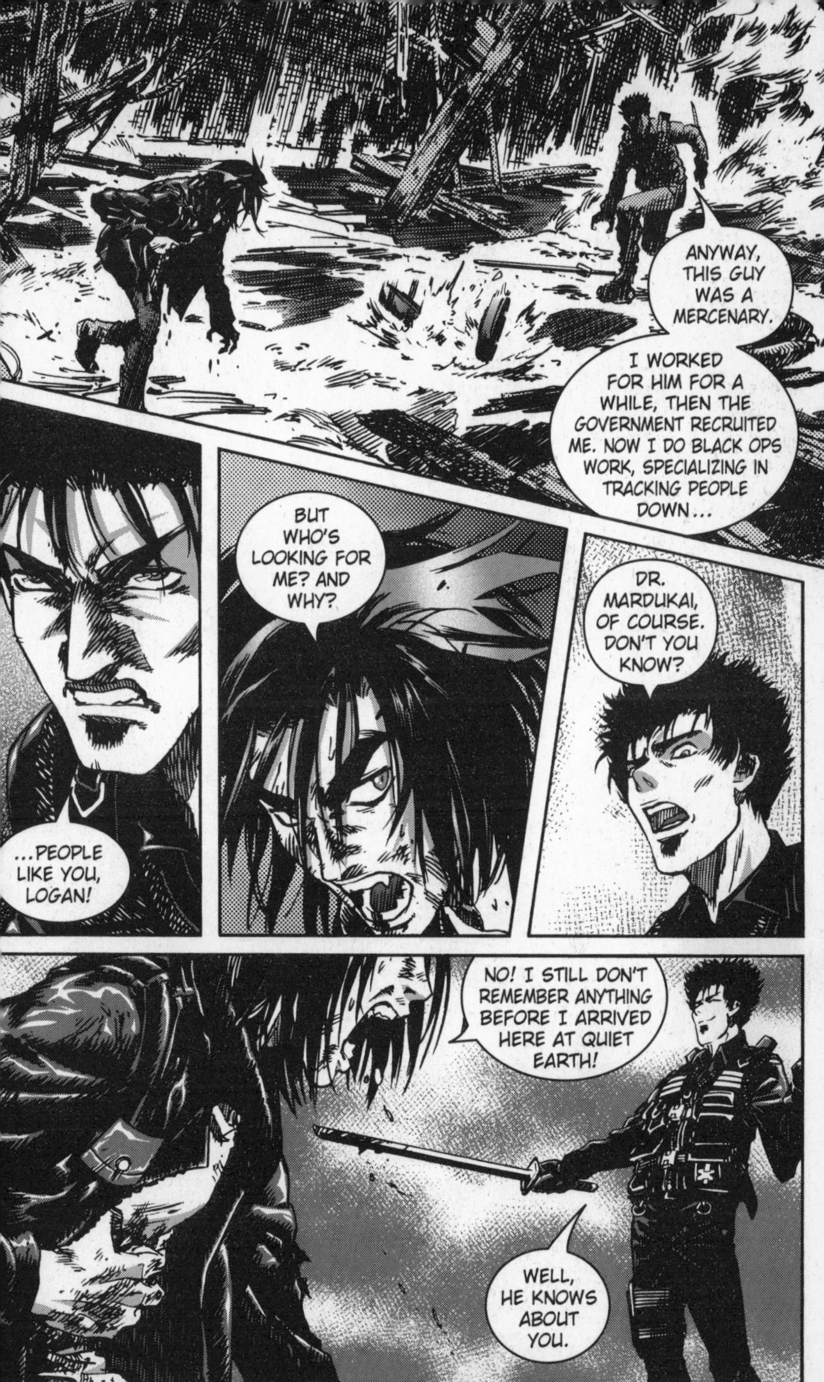
ANYWAY, THIS GUY WAS A MERCENARY.
I WORKED FOR HIM FOR A WHILE, THEN THE GOVERNMENT RECRUITED ME. NOW I DO BLACK OPS WORK, SPECIALIZING IN TRACKING PEOPLE DOWN...
...PEOPLE LIKE YOU, LOGAN!
BUT WHO'S LOOKING FOR ME? AND WHY?
DR. MARDUKAI, OF COURSE. DON'T YOU KNOW?
NO! I STILL DON'T REMEMBER ANYTHING BEFORE I ARRIVED HERE AT QUIET EARTH!
WELL, HE KNOWS ABOUT YOU.

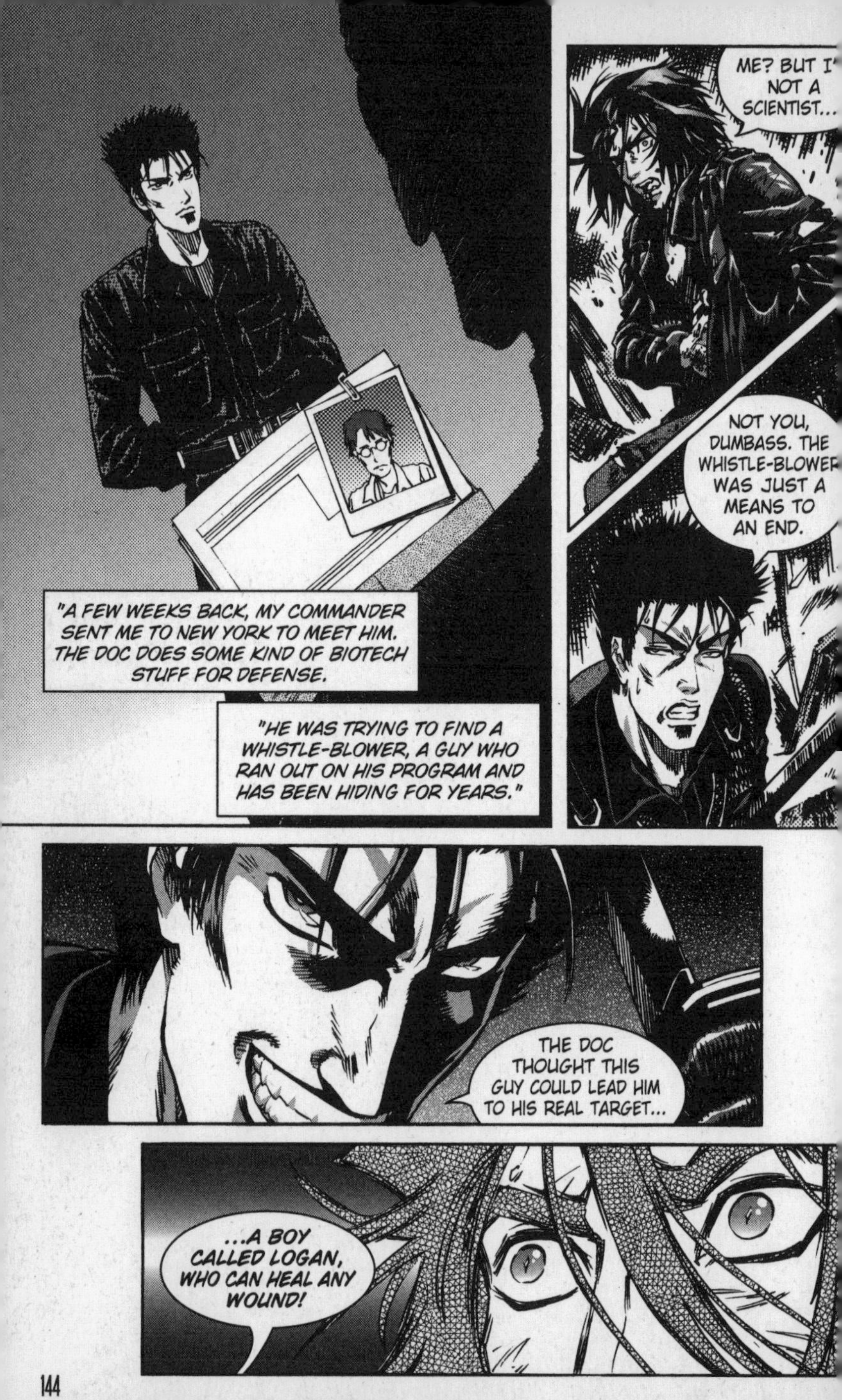
"A FEW WEEKS BACK, MY COMMANDER SENT ME TO NEW YORK TO MEET HIM. THE DOC DOES SOME KIND OF BIOTECH STUFF FOR DEFENSE.
"HE WAS TRYING TO FIND A WHISTLE-BLOWER, A GUY WHO RAN OUT ON HIS PROGRAM AND HAS BEEN HIDING FOR YEARS."
ME? BUT I' NOT A SCIENTIST...
NOT YOU, DUMBASS. THE WHISTLE-BLOWER WAS JUST A MEANS TO AN END.
THE DOC THOUGHT THIS GUY COULD LEAD HIM TO HIS REAL TARGET...
...A BOY CALLED LOGAN, WHO CAN HEAL ANY WOUND!

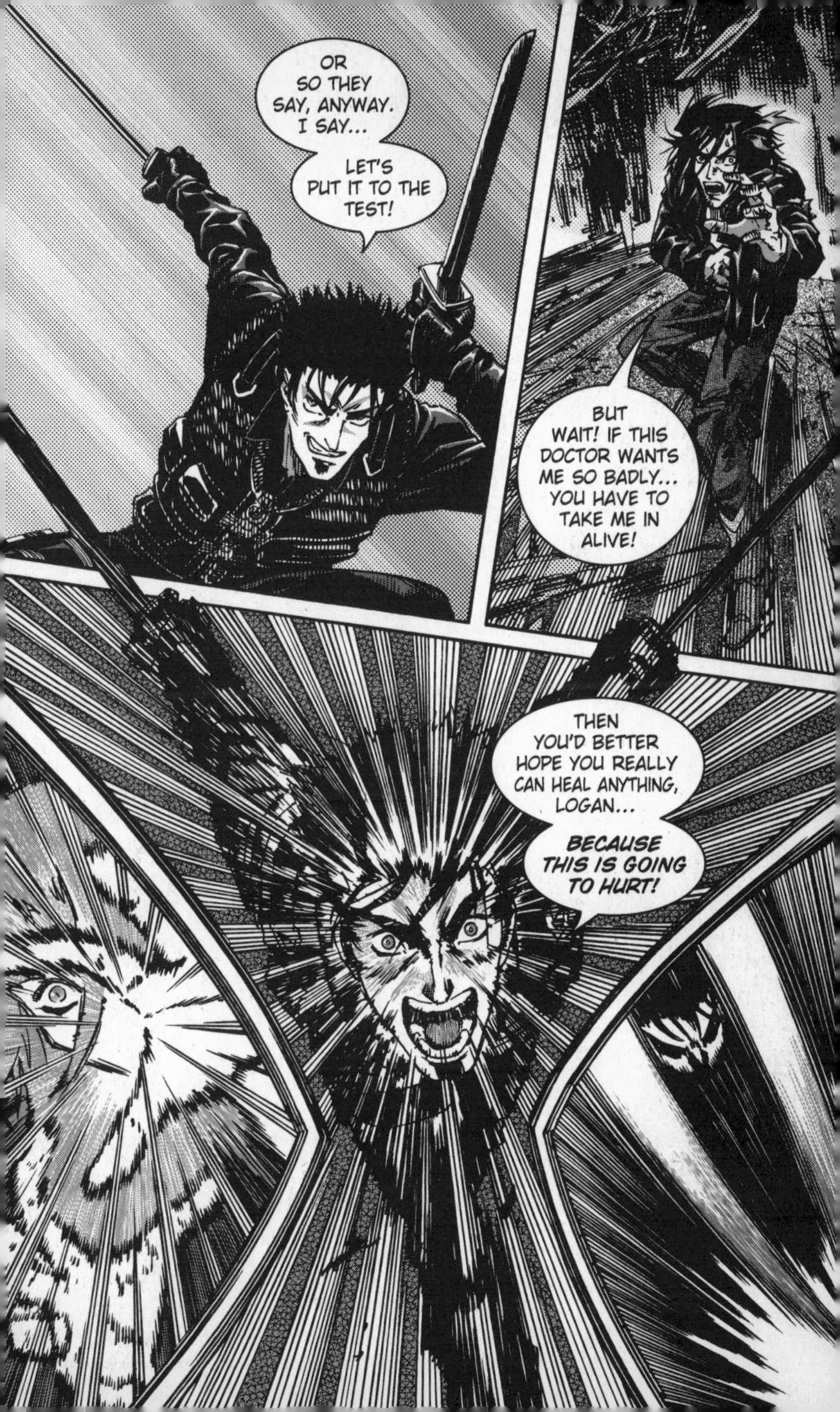
OR SO THEY SAY, ANYWAY. I SAY...
LET'S PUT IT TO THE TEST!
BUT WAIT! IF THIS DOCTOR WANTS ME SO BADLY... YOU HAVE TO TAKE ME IN ALIVE!
THEN YOU'D BETTER HOPE YOU REALLY CAN HEAL ANYTHING, LOGAN...
BECAUSE THIS IS GOING TO HURT!

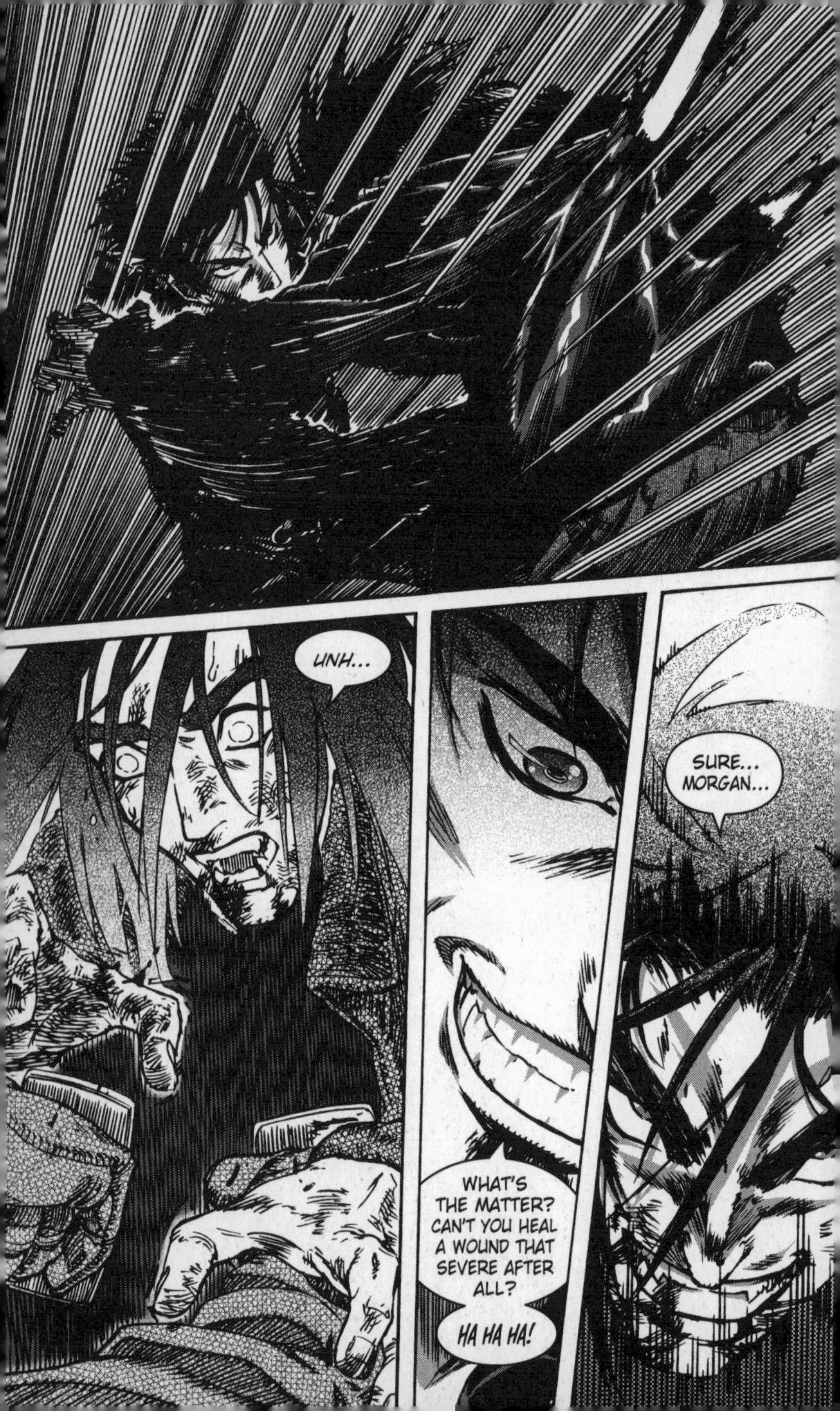
UNH...
WHAT'S THE MATTER? CAN'T YOU HEAL A WOUND THAT SEVERE AFTER ALL?
HA HA HA!
SURE... MORGAN...

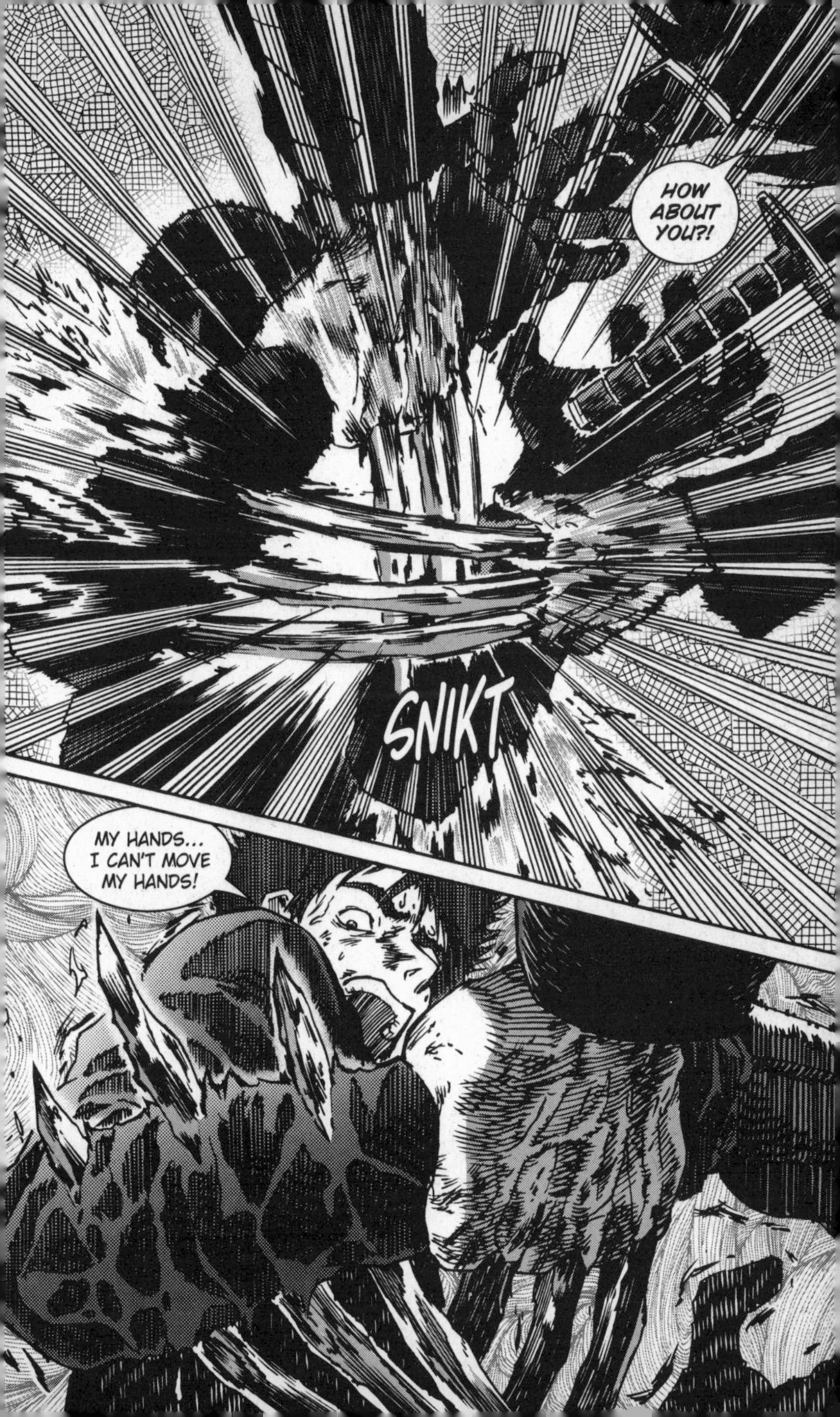
HOW ABOUT YOU?!
SNIKT
MY HANDS... I CAN'T MOVE MY HANDS!

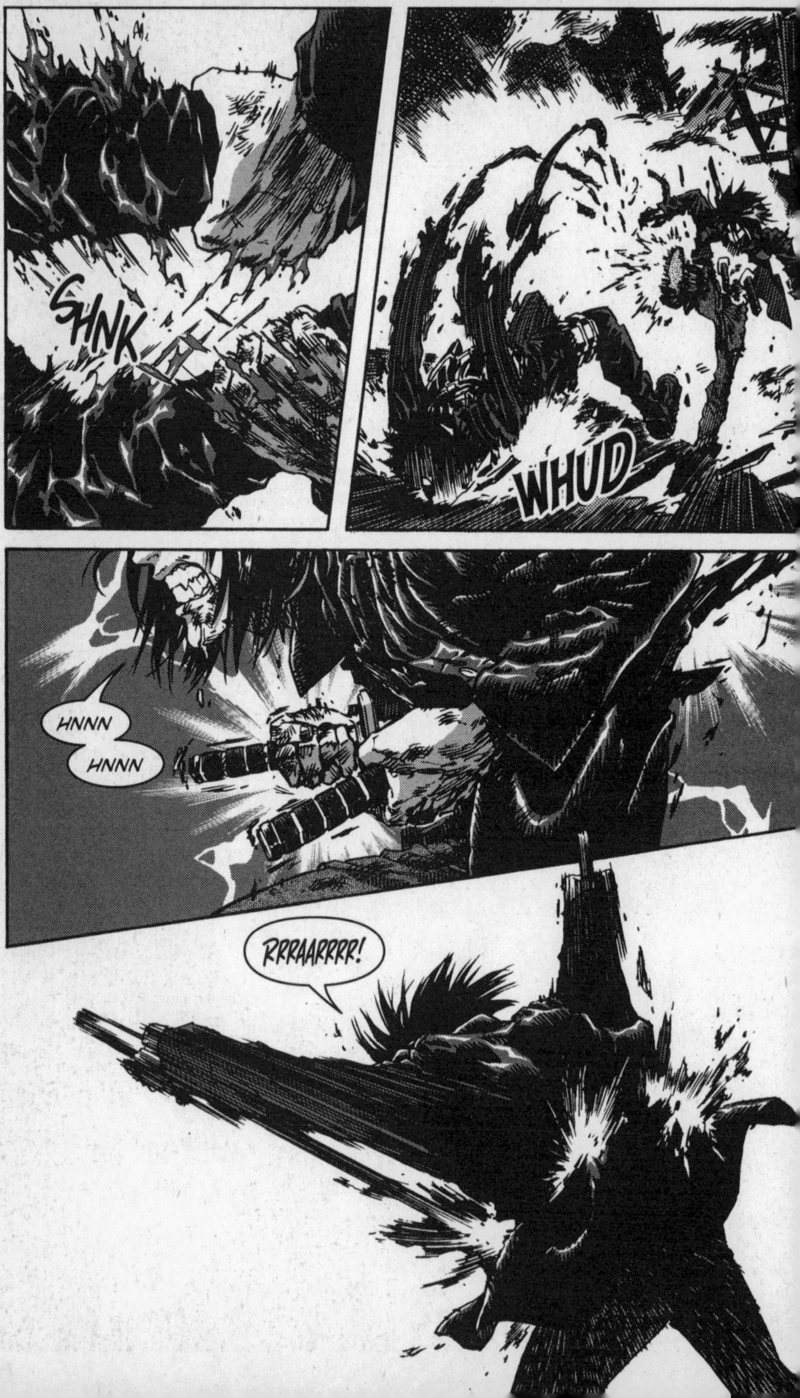
SHNK
WHUD
HNNN
HNNN
RRRAARRRR!

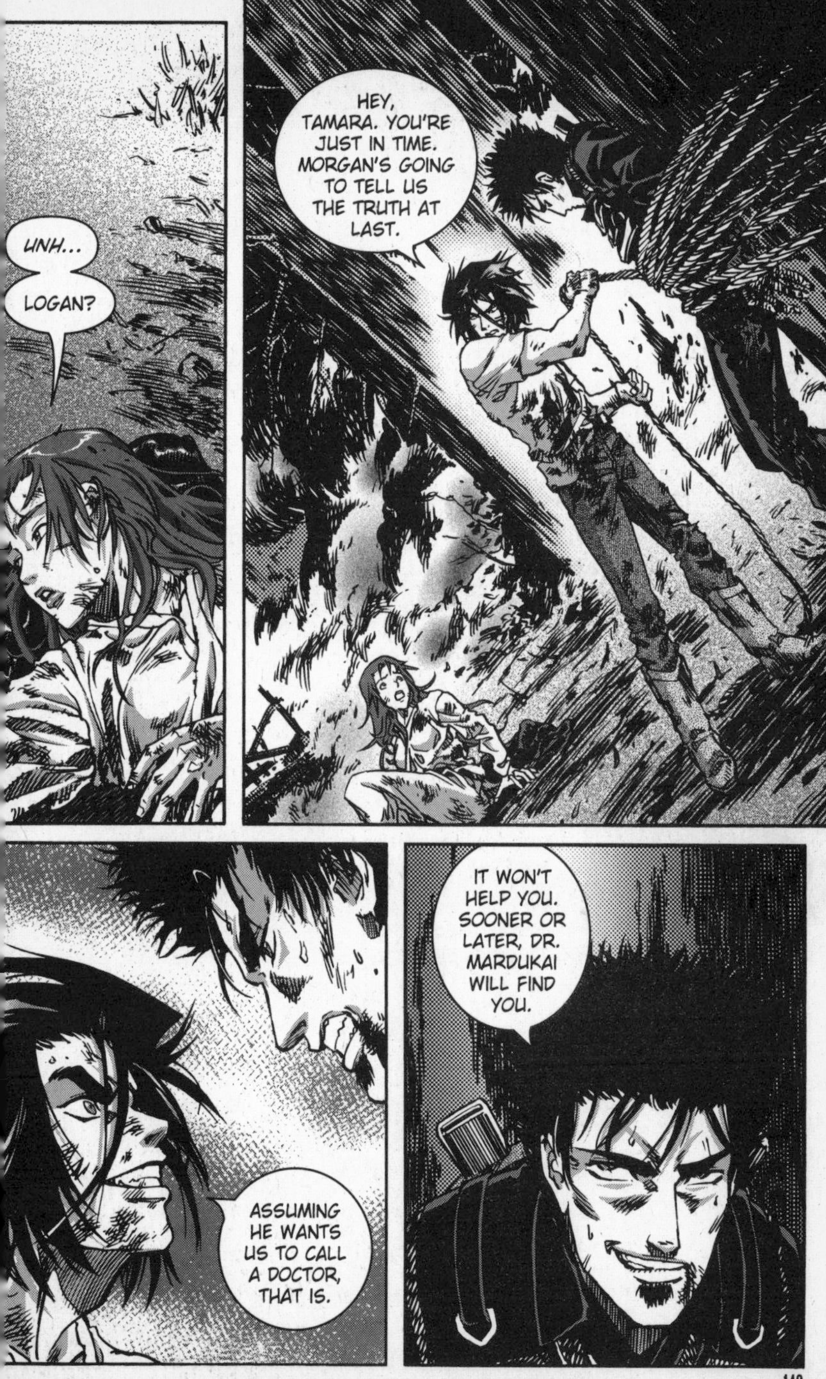
UNH...
LOGAN?
HEY, TAMARA. YOU'RE JUST IN TIME. MORGAN'S GOING TO TELL US THE TRUTH AT LAST.
ASSUMING HE WANTS US TO CALL A DOCTOR, THAT IS.
IT WON'T HELP YOU. SOONER OR LATER, DR. MARDUKAI WILL FIND YOU.

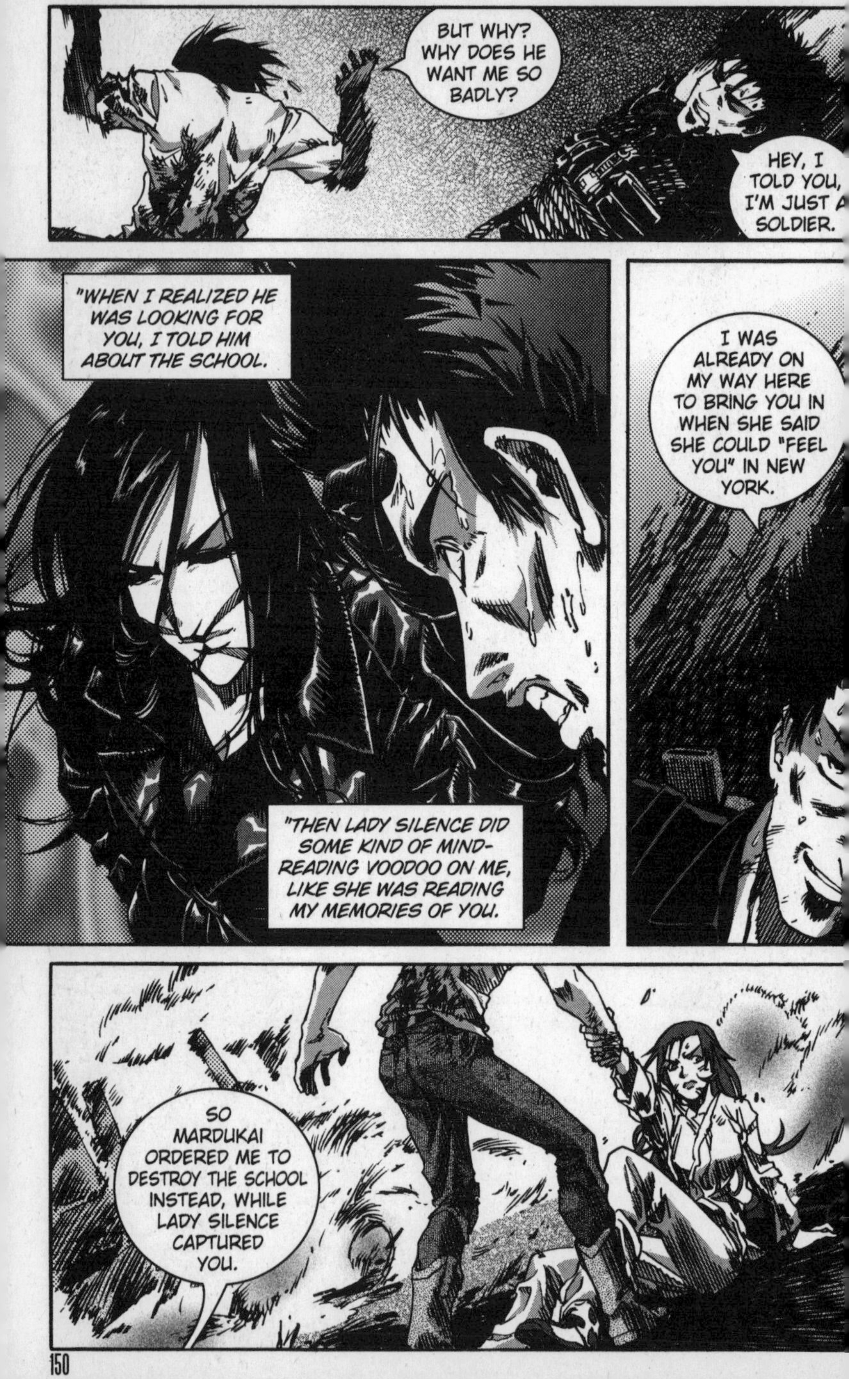
BUT WHY? WHY DOES HE WANT ME SO BADLY?
HEY, I TOLD YOU, I'M JUST A SOLDIER.
"WHEN I REALIZED HE WAS LOOKING FOR YOU, I TOLD HIM ABOUT THE SCHOOL.
"THEN LADY SILENCE DID SOME KIND OF MIND-READING VOODOO ON ME, LIKE SHE WAS READING MY MEMORIES OF YOU.
I WAS ALREADY ON MY WAY HERE TO BRING YOU IN WHEN SHE SAID SHE COULD "FEEL YOU" IN NEW YORK.
SO MARDUKAI ORDERED ME TO DESTROY THE SCHOOL INSTEAD, WHILE LADY SILENCE CAPTURED YOU.

BUT HOW COULD YOU DO IT? WE WERE YOUR FRIENDS, YOUR TUTORS...

DON'T GIVE ME THAT CRAP!

FROM THE SECOND HE ARRIVED IT WAS LOGAN THIS AND LOGAN THAT! LOGAN THE MYSTERY BOY, HE'S SOOOO AMAZING!

I WAS THE TOP STUDENT HERE! BUT WHEN "WOLVERINE" BOY CAME ALONG, ALL ANY-ONE CARED ABOUT WAS SEEING IF HE COULD BEAT ME!

AND I DID. SO NOTHING'S CHANGED.

WHATEVER. THAT'S WHY I LEFT, LOGAN. BECAUSE THEY THREW ME ON THE SCRAP HEAP.

SO DON'T TELL ME THESE LOSERS CARED ABOUT ME!

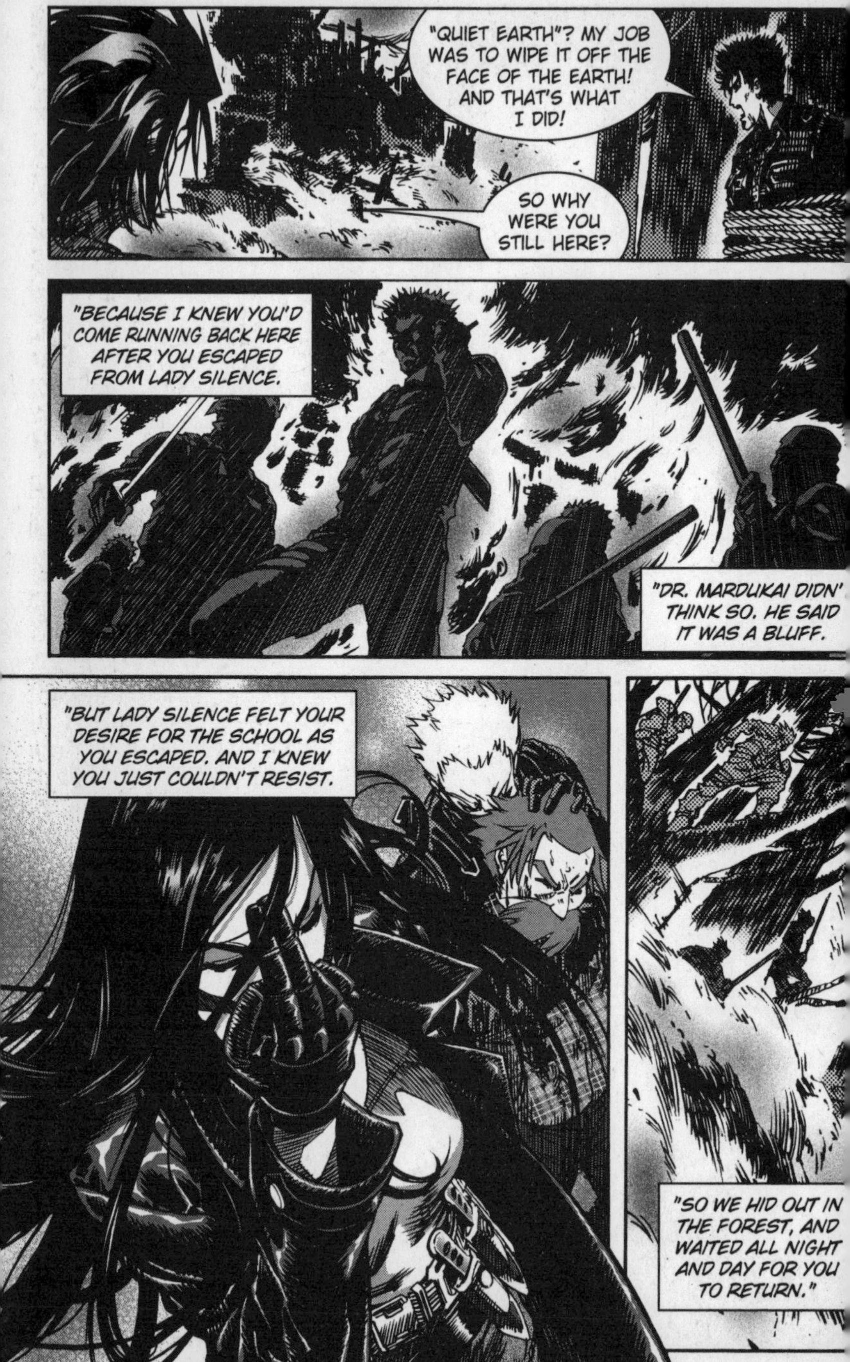
"QUIET EARTH"? MY JOB WAS TO WIPE IT OFF THE FACE OF THE EARTH! AND THAT'S WHAT I DID!
SO WHY WERE YOU STILL HERE?
"BECAUSE I KNEW YOU'D COME RUNNING BACK HERE AFTER YOU ESCAPED FROM LADY SILENCE.
"DR. MARDUKAI DIDN' THINK SO. HE SAID IT WAS A BLUFF.
"BUT LADY SILENCE FELT YOUR DESIRE FOR THE SCHOOL AS YOU ESCAPED. AND I KNEW YOU JUST COULDN'T RESIST.
"SO WE HID OUT IN THE FOREST, AND WAITED ALL NIGHT AND DAY FOR YOU TO RETURN."

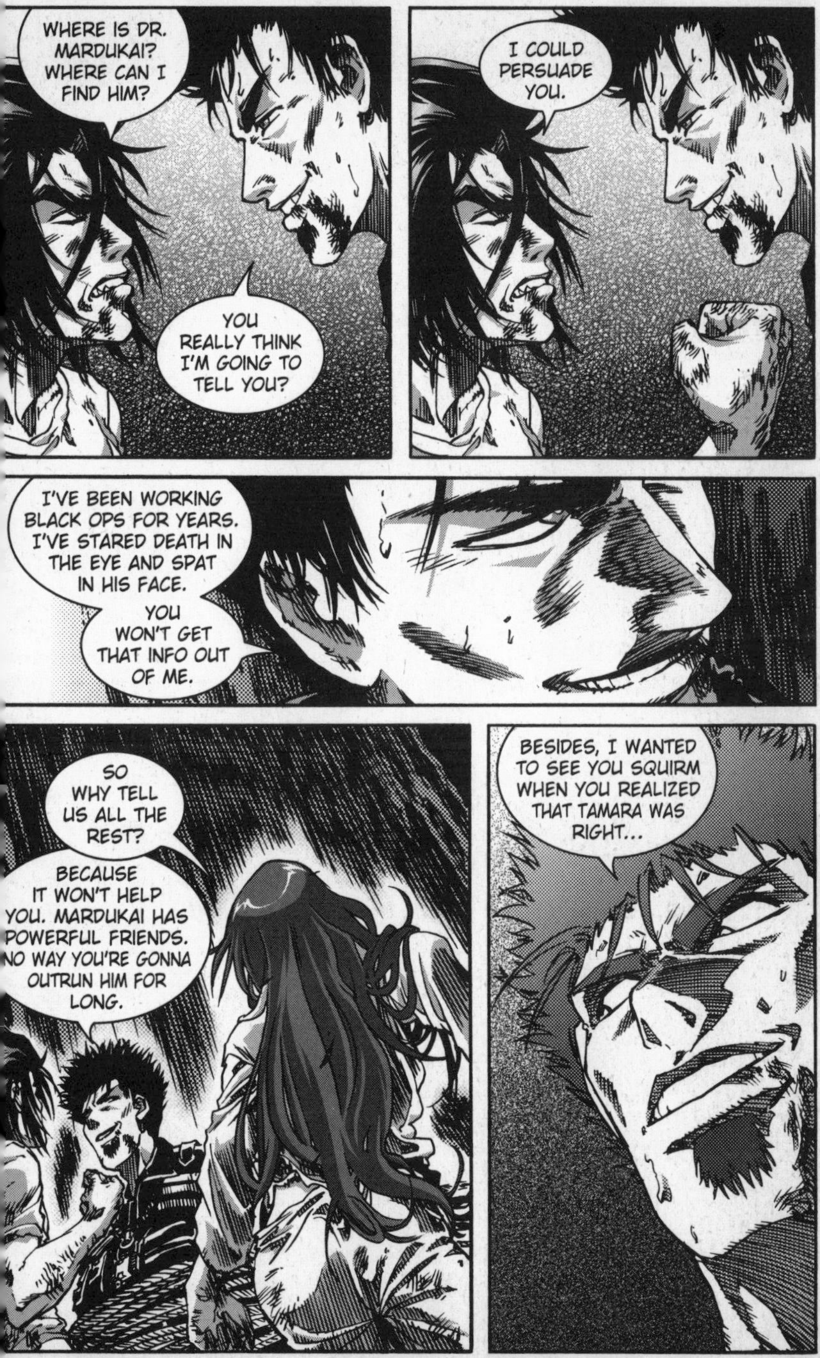
WHERE IS DR. MARDUKAI? WHERE CAN I FIND HIM?
YOU REALLY THINK I'M GOING TO TELL YOU?
I COULD PERSUADE YOU.
I'VE BEEN WORKING BLACK OPS FOR YEARS. I'VE STARED DEATH IN THE EYE AND SPAT IN HIS FACE.
YOU WON'T GET THAT INFO OUT OF ME.
SO WHY TELL US ALL THE REST?
BECAUSE IT WON'T HELP YOU. MARDUKAI HAS POWERFUL FRIENDS. NO WAY YOU'RE GONNA OUTRUN HIM FOR LONG.
BESIDES, I WANTED TO SEE YOU SQUIRM WHEN YOU REALIZED THAT TAMARA WAS RIGHT...

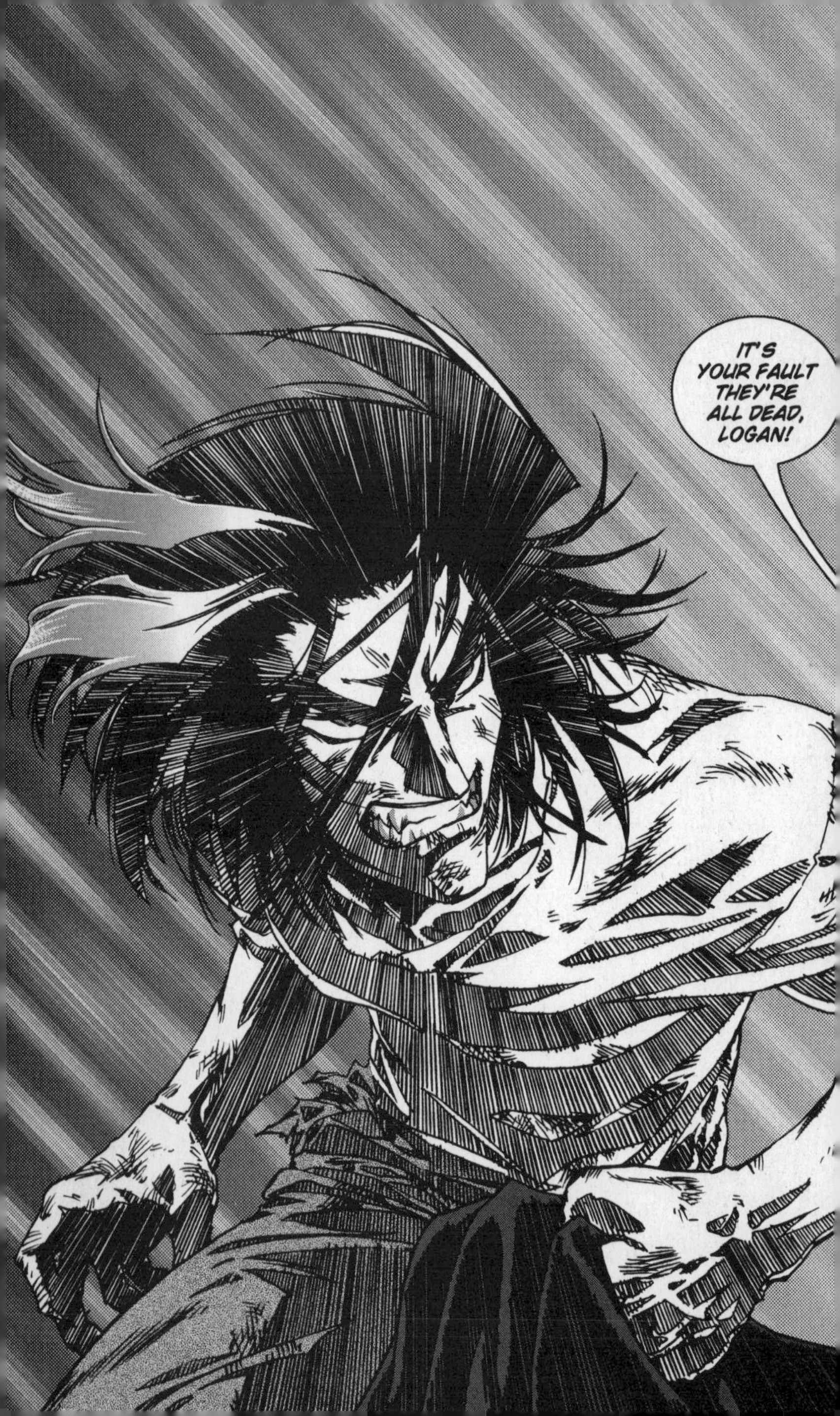
IT'S YOUR FAULT THEY'RE ALL DEAD, LOGAN!

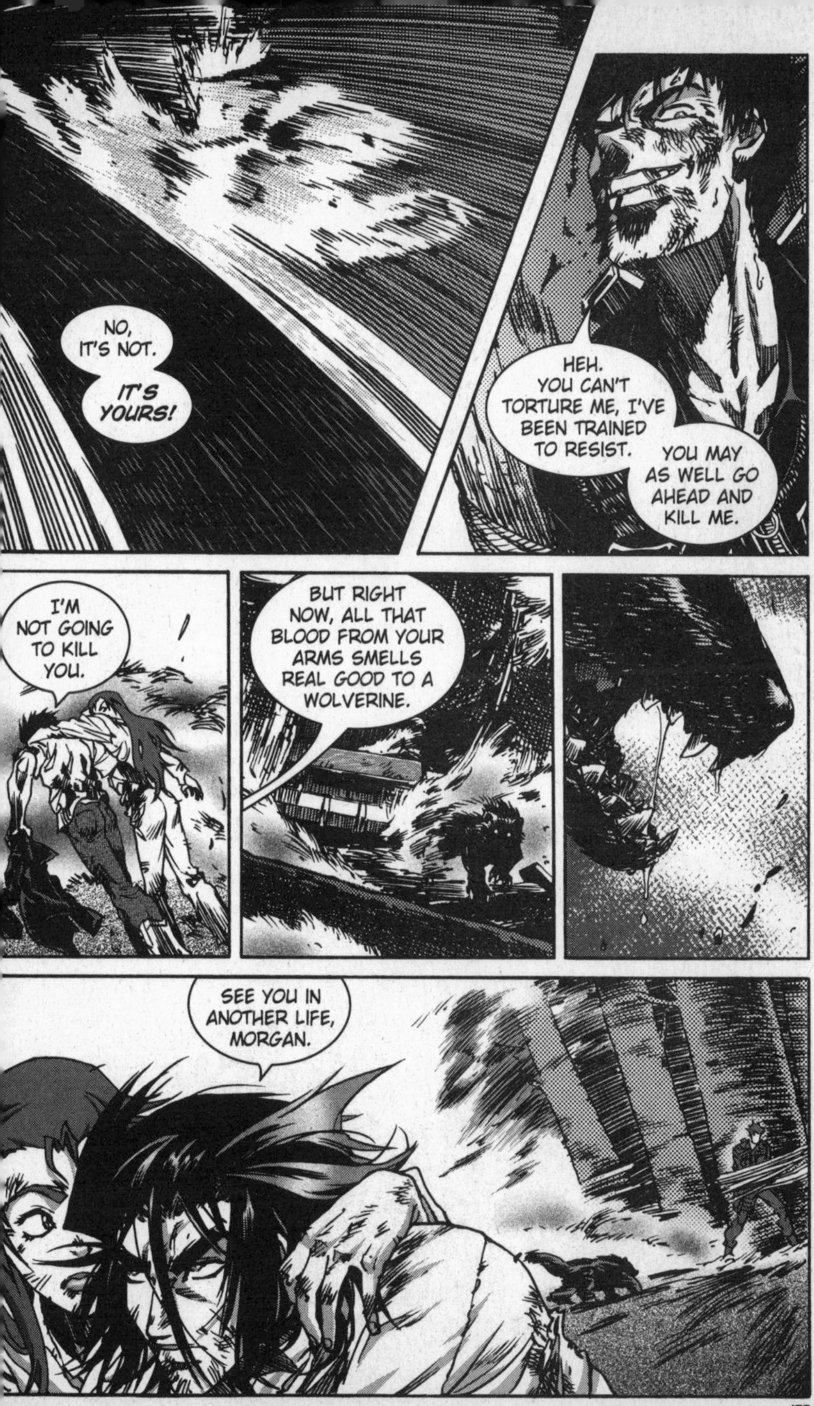

NO, IT'S NOT.
IT'S YOURS!
HEH. YOU CAN'T TORTURE ME, I'VE BEEN TRAINED TO RESIST.
YOU MAY AS WELL GO AHEAD AND KILL ME.
I'M NOT GOING TO KILL YOU.
BUT RIGHT NOW, ALL THAT BLOOD FROM YOUR ARMS SMELLS REAL GOOD TO A WOLVERINE.
SEE YOU IN ANOTHER LIFE, MORGAN.

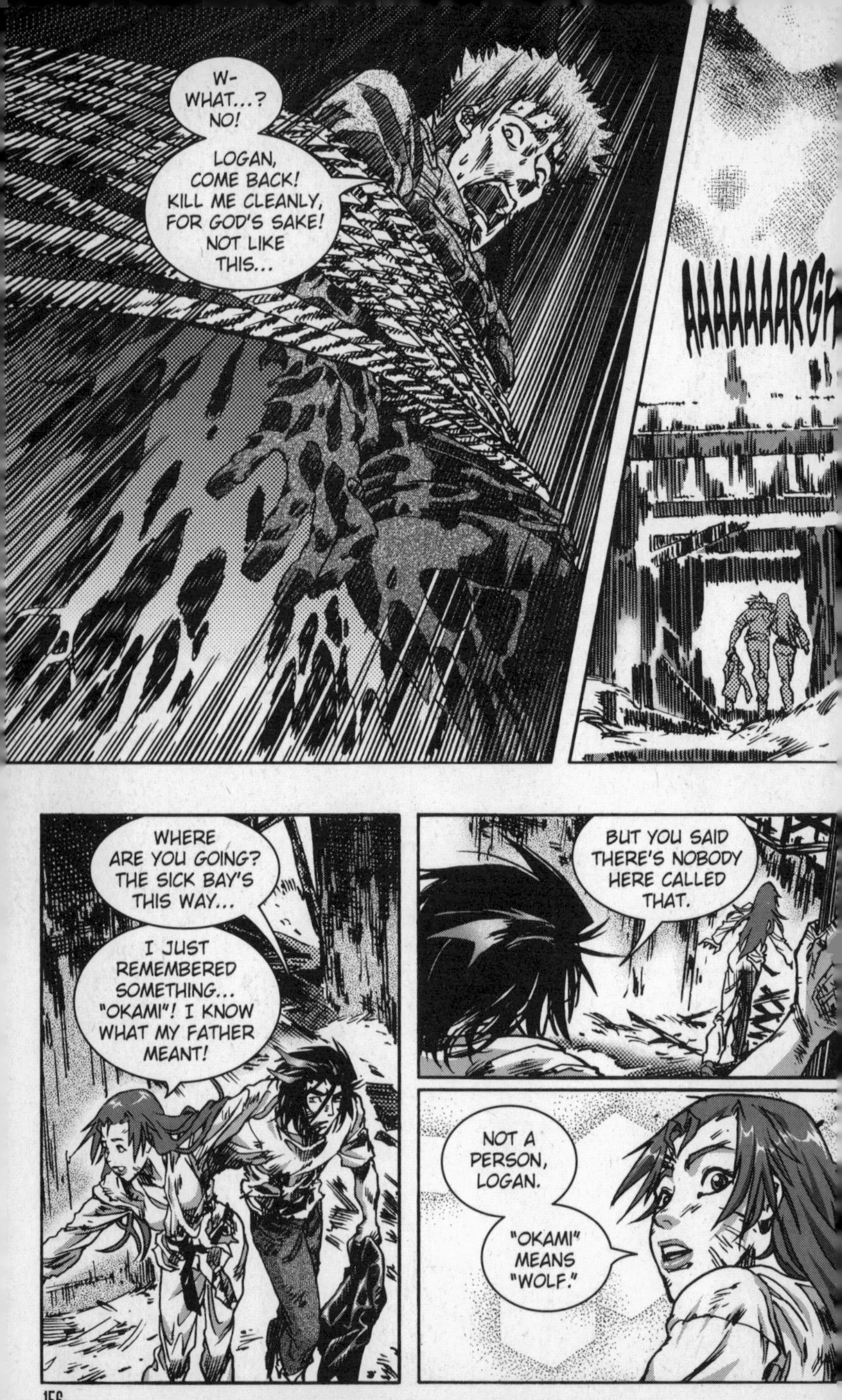
W- WHAT...? NO!
LOGAN, COME BACK! KILL ME CLEANLY, FOR GOD'S SAKE! NOT LIKE THIS...
AAAAAAARGH
WHERE ARE YOU GOING? THE SICK BAY'S THIS WAY...
I JUST REMEMBERED SOMETHING... "OKAMI"! I KNOW WHAT MY FATHER MEANT!
BUT YOU SAID THERE'S NOBODY HERE CALLED THAT.
NOT A PERSON, LOGAN.
"OKAMI" MEANS "WOLF."

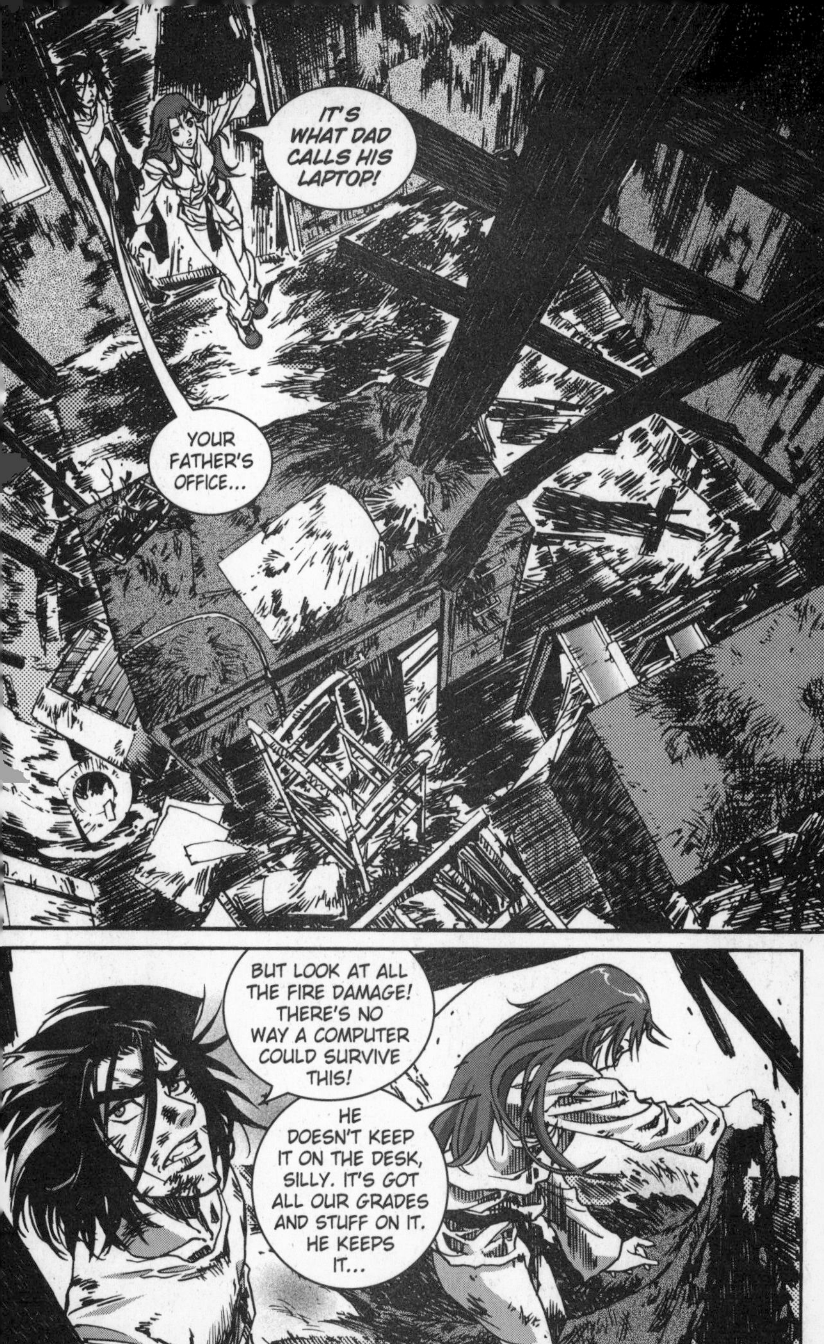
IT'S WHAT DAD CALLS HIS LAPTOP!
YOUR FATHER'S OFFICE...
BUT LOOK AT ALL THE FIRE DAMAGE! THERE'S NO WAY A COMPUTER COULD SURVIVE THIS!
HE DOESN'T KEEP IT ON THE DESK, SILLY. IT'S GOT ALL OUR GRADES AND STUFF ON IT. HE KEEPS IT...

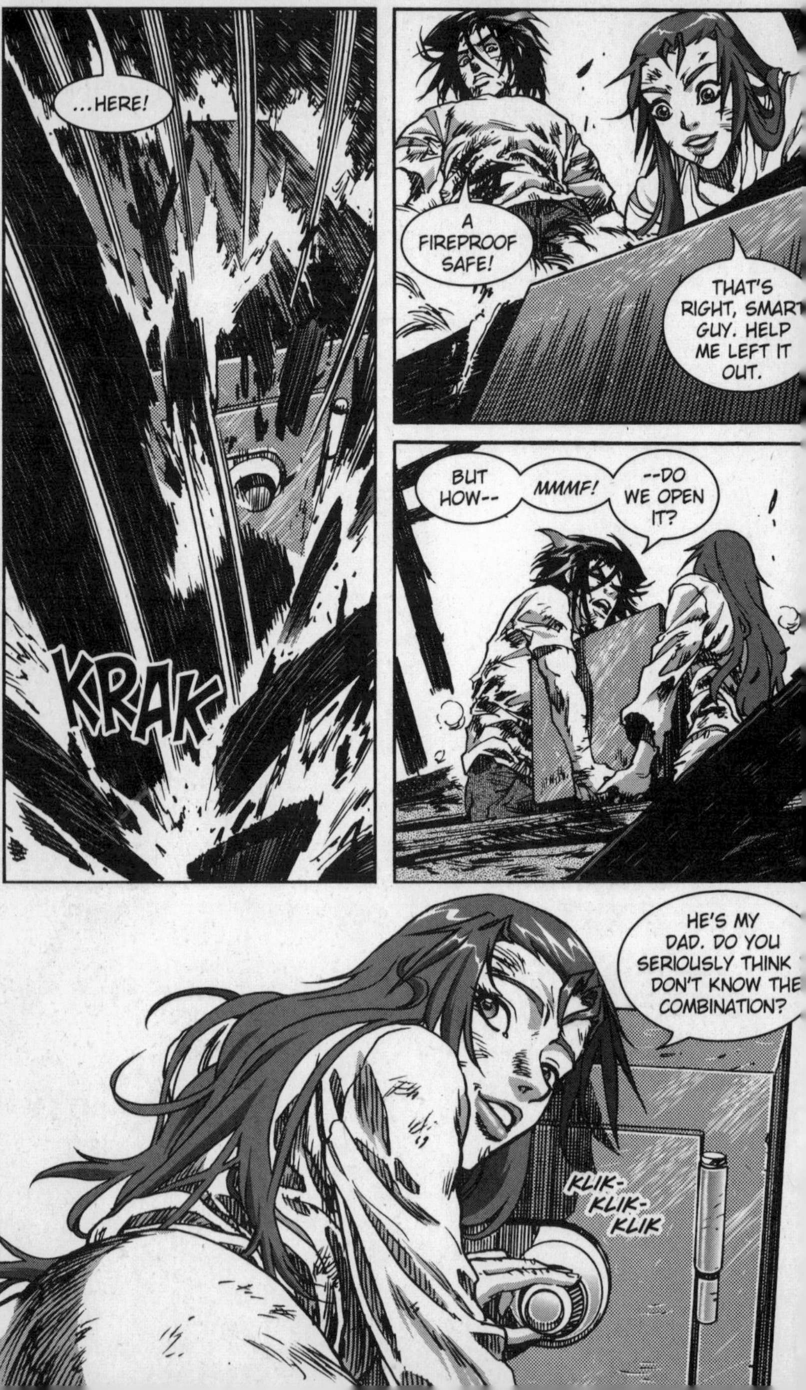
...HERE!
KRAK
A FIREPROOF SAFE!
THAT'S RIGHT, SMART GUY. HELP ME LEFT IT OUT.
BUT HOW--
MMMF!
--DO WE OPEN IT?
HE'S MY DAD. DO YOU SERIOUSLY THINK DON'T KNOW THE COMBINATION?
KLIK-
KLIK-
KLIK

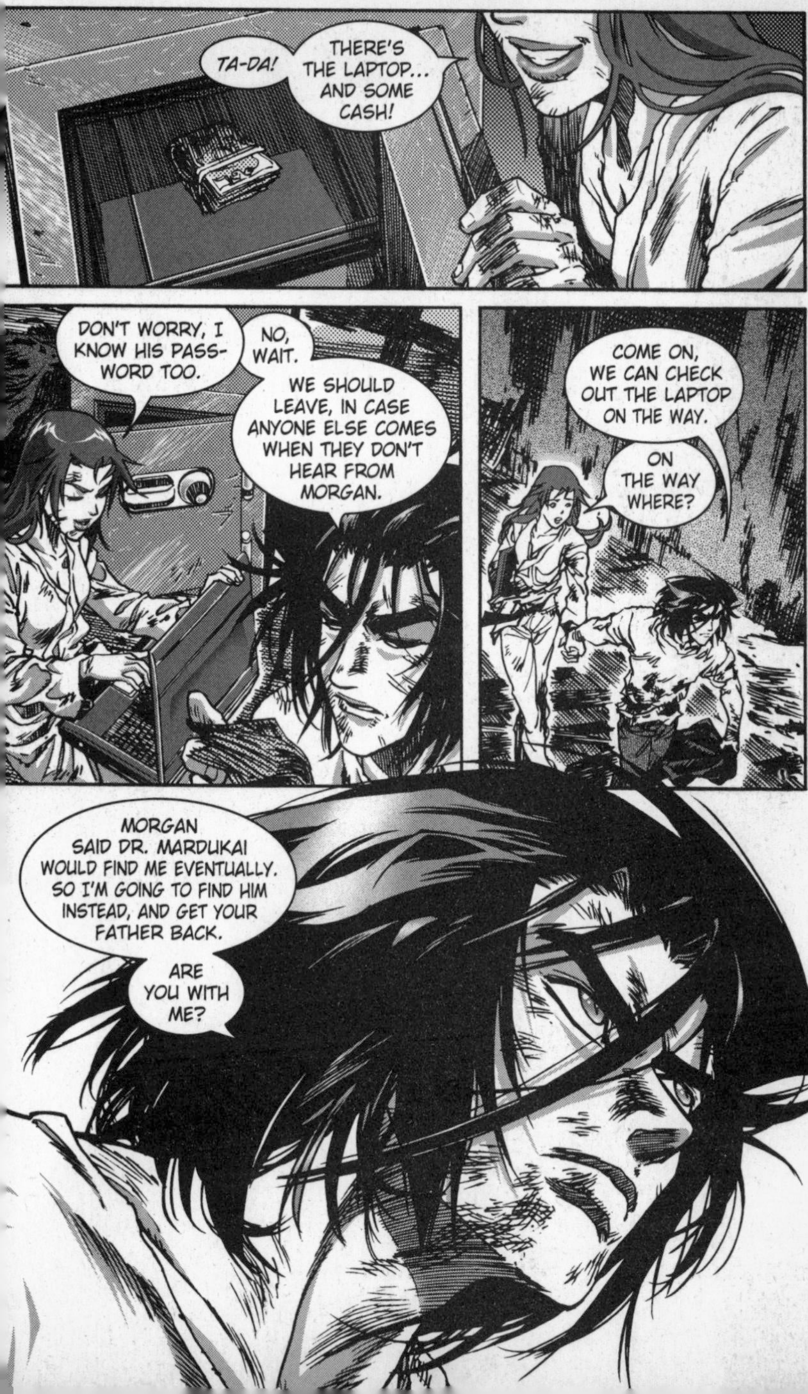

TA-DA!
THERE'S THE LAPTOP... AND SOME CASH!
DON'T WORRY, I KNOW HIS PASS-WORD TOO.
NO, WAIT.
WE SHOULD LEAVE, IN CASE ANYONE ELSE COMES WHEN THEY DON'T HEAR FROM MORGAN.
COME ON, WE CAN CHECK OUT THE LAPTOP ON THE WAY.
ON THE WAY WHERE?
MORGAN SAID DR. MARDUKAI WOULD FIND ME EVENTUALLY. SO I'M GOING TO FIND HIM INSTEAD, AND GET YOUR FATHER BACK.
ARE YOU WITH ME?

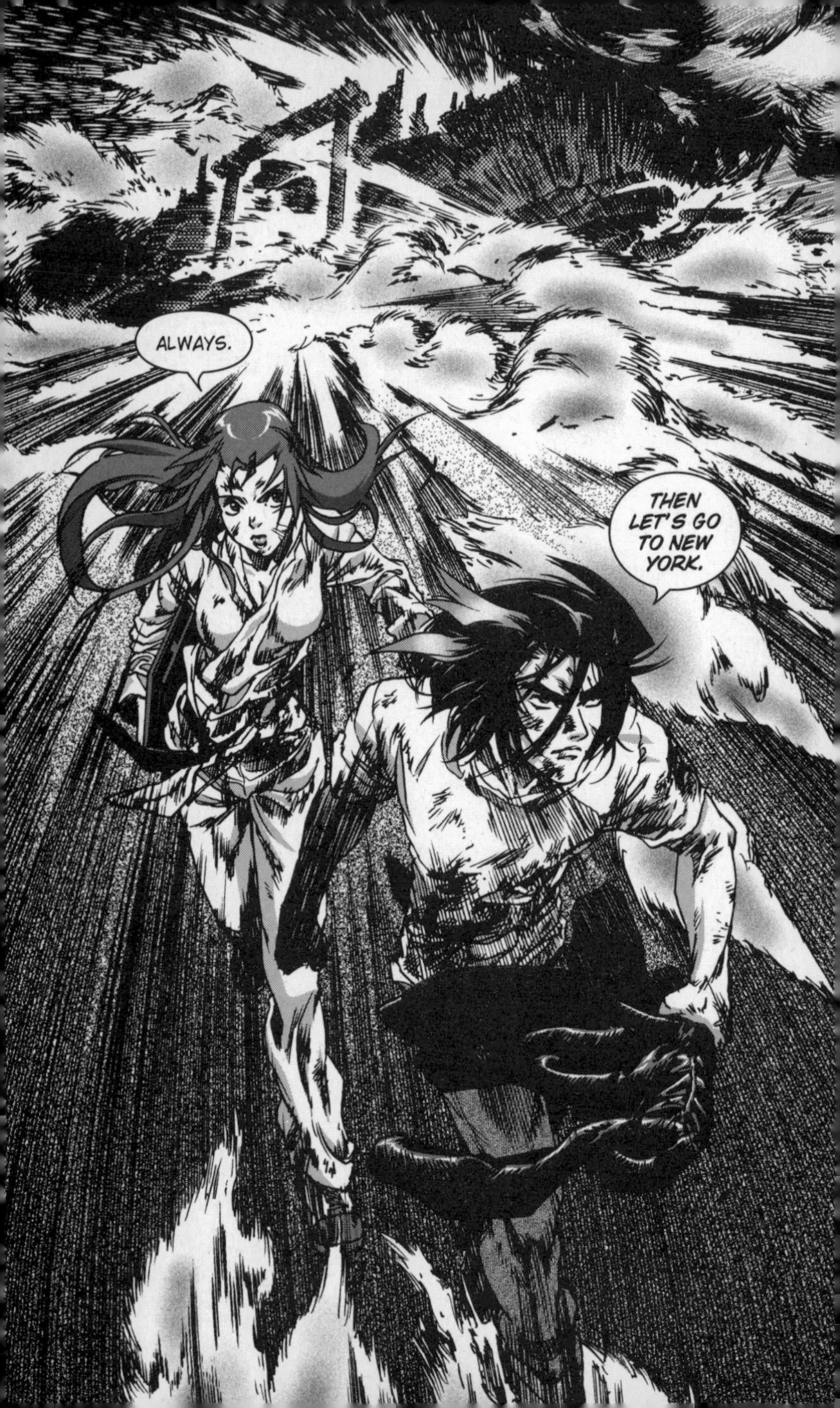
ALWAYS.
THEN LET'S GO TO NEW YORK.

Epilogue

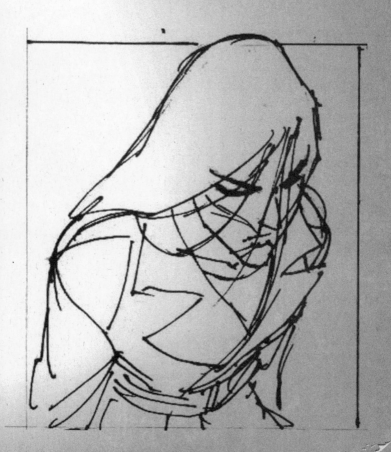

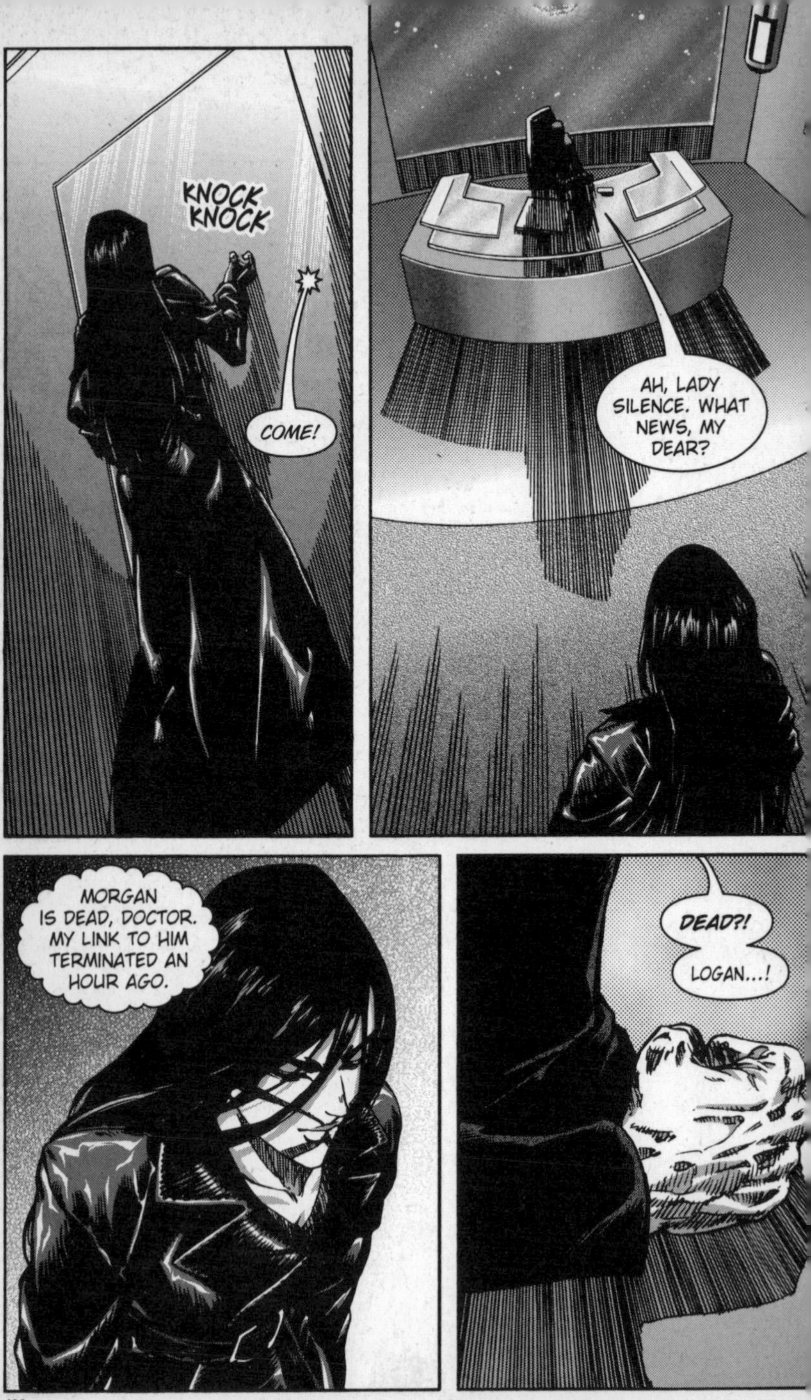
KNOCK KNOCK
COME!
AH, LADY SILENCE. WHAT NEWS, MY DEAR?
MORGAN IS DEAD, DOCTOR. MY LINK TO HIM TERMINATED AN HOUR AGO.
DEAD?!
LOGAN...!

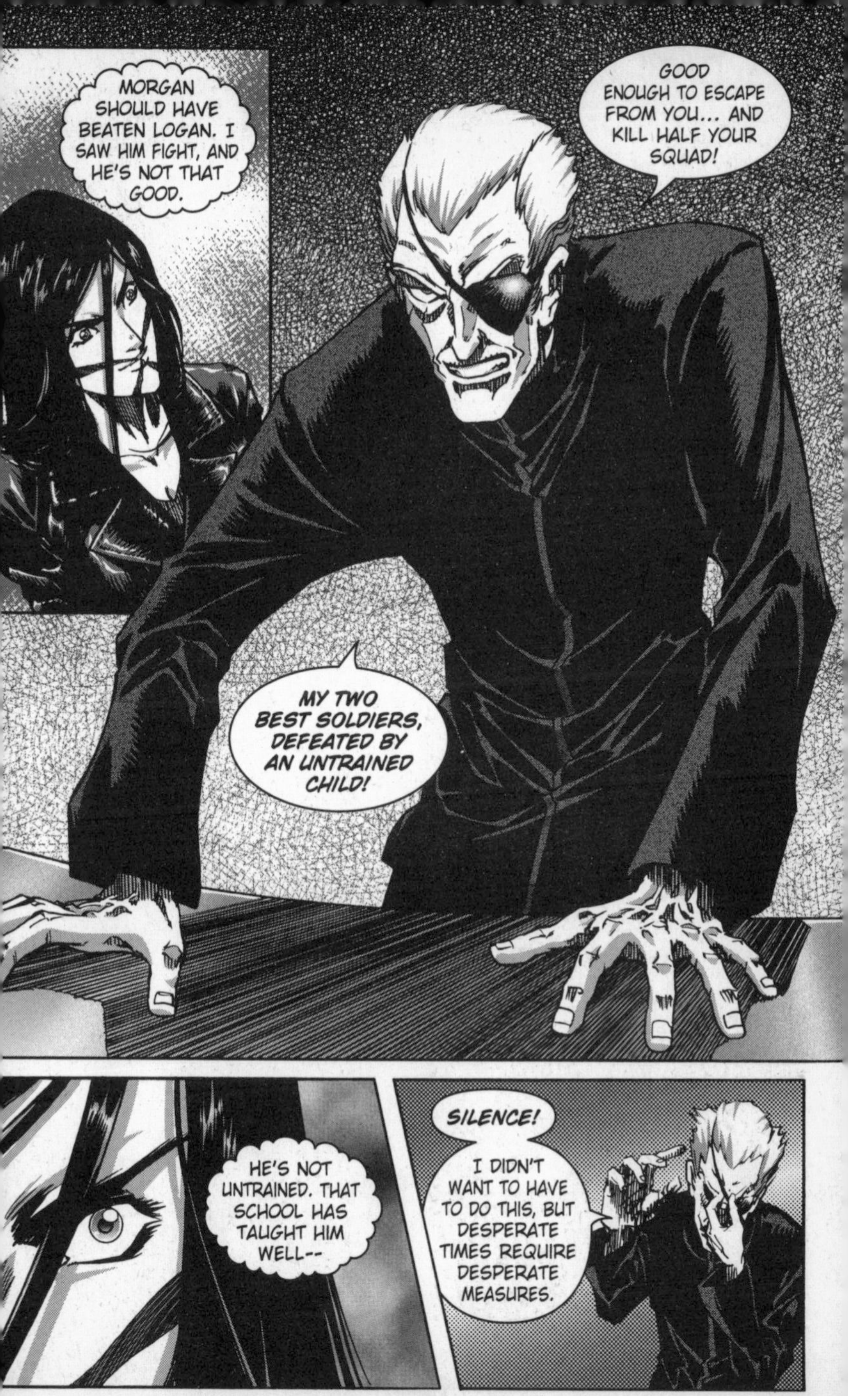
MORGAN SHOULD HAVE BEATEN LOGAN. I SAW HIM FIGHT, AND HE'S NOT THAT GOOD.
GOOD ENOUGH TO ESCAPE FROM YOU... AND KILL HALF YOUR SQUAD!
MY TWO BEST SOLDIERS, DEFEATED BY AN UNTRAINED CHILD!
HE'S NOT UNTRAINED. THAT SCHOOL HAS TAUGHT HIM WELL--
SILENCE!
I DIDN'T WANT TO HAVE TO DO THIS, BUT DESPERATE TIMES REQUIRE DESPERATE MEASURES.

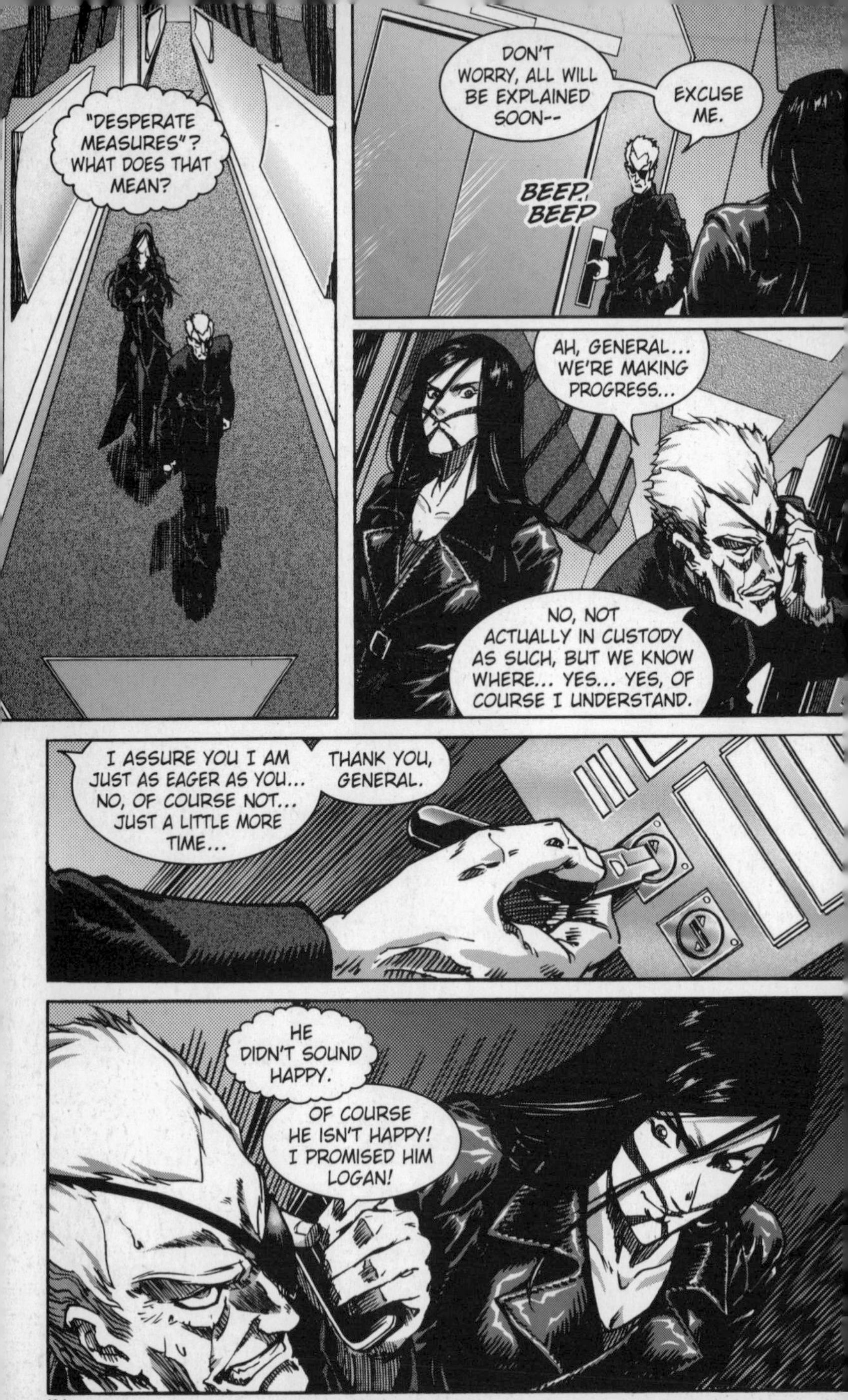
"DESPERATE MEASURES"? WHAT DOES THAT MEAN?
DON'T WORRY, ALL WILL BE EXPLAINED SOON--
BEEP BEEP
EXCUSE ME.
AH, GENERAL... WE'RE MAKING PROGRESS...
NO, NOT ACTUALLY IN CUSTODY AS SUCH, BUT WE KNOW WHERE... YES... YES, OF COURSE I UNDERSTAND.
I ASSURE YOU I AM JUST AS EAGER AS YOU... NO, OF COURSE NOT... JUST A LITTLE MORE TIME...
THANK YOU, GENERAL.
HE DIDN'T SOUND HAPPY.
OF COURSE HE ISN'T HAPPY! I PROMISED HIM LOGAN!

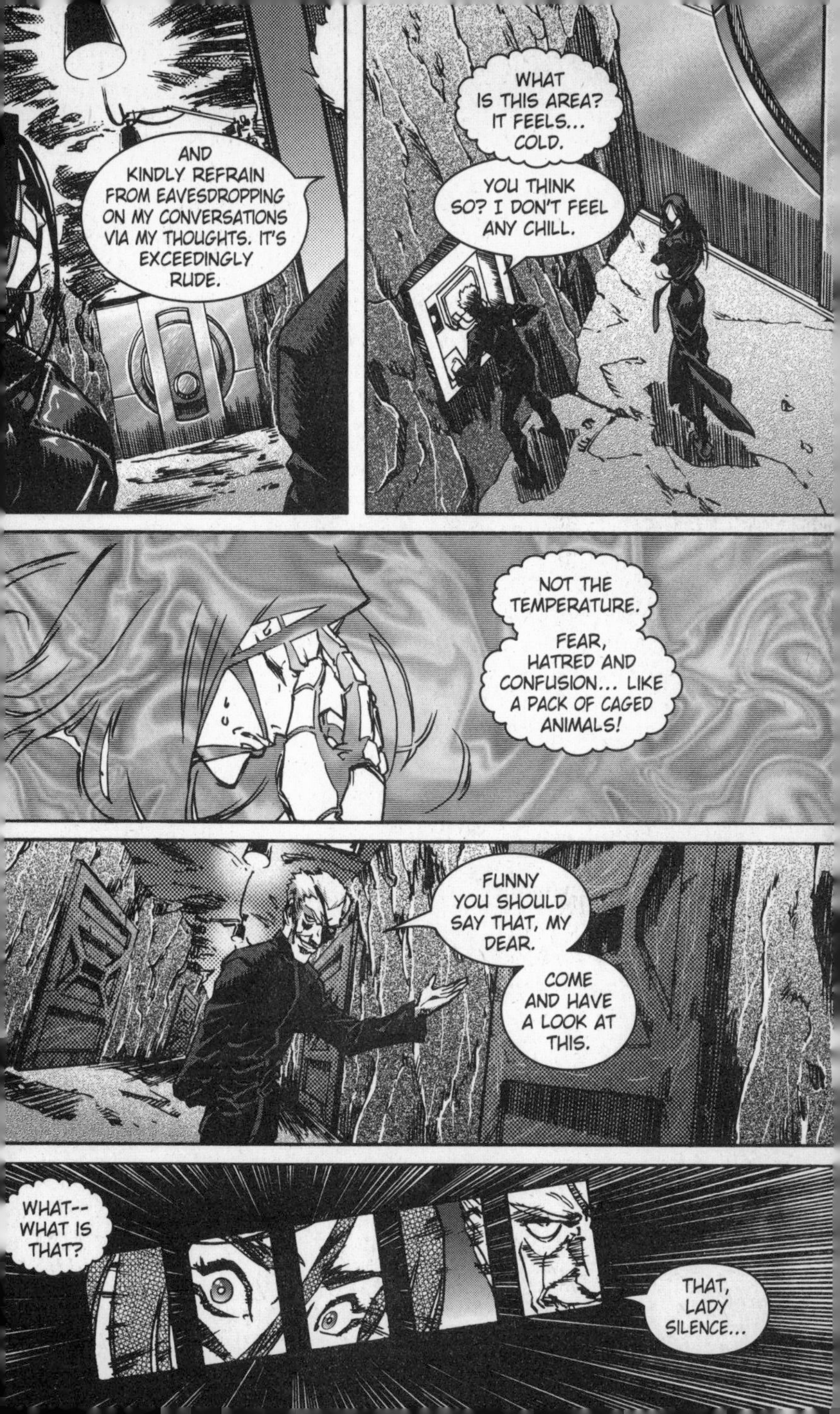
AND KINDLY REFRAIN FROM EAVESDROPPING ON MY CONVERSATIONS VIA MY THOUGHTS. IT'S EXCEEDINGLY RUDE.
WHAT IS THIS AREA? IT FEELS... COLD.
YOU THINK SO? I DON'T FEEL ANY CHILL.
NOT THE TEMPERATURE.
FEAR, HATRED AND CONFUSION... LIKE A PACK OF CAGED ANIMALS!
FUNNY YOU SHOULD SAY THAT, MY DEAR.
COME AND HAVE A LOOK AT THIS.
WHAT-- WHAT IS THAT?
THAT, LADY SILENCE...

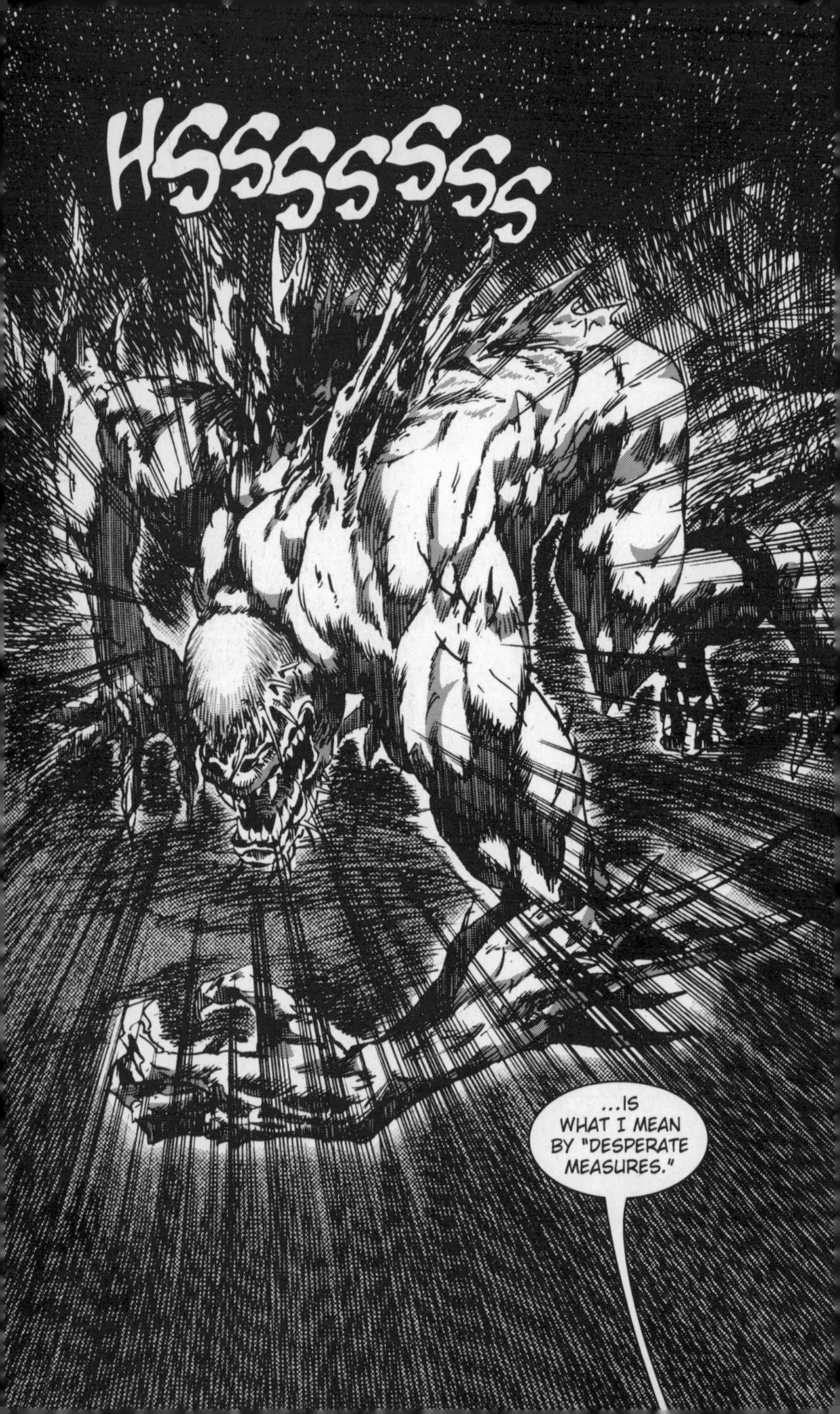
HSSSSSSS
...IS WHAT I MEAN BY "DESPERATE MEASURES."

WOLVERINE

Continues in
WOLVERINE: PRODIGAL SON
Volume 2

Character Design Sketches

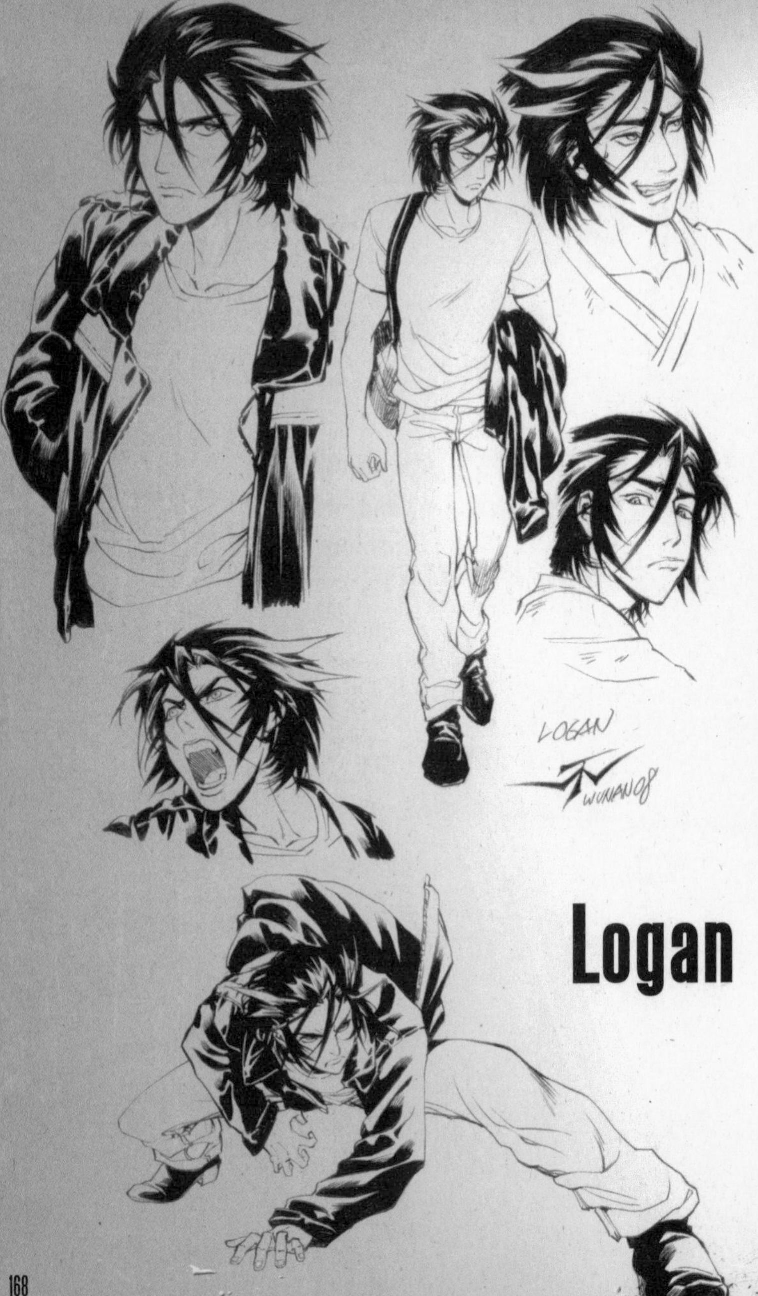
LOGAN
WUNAN 08

Logan

Tamara

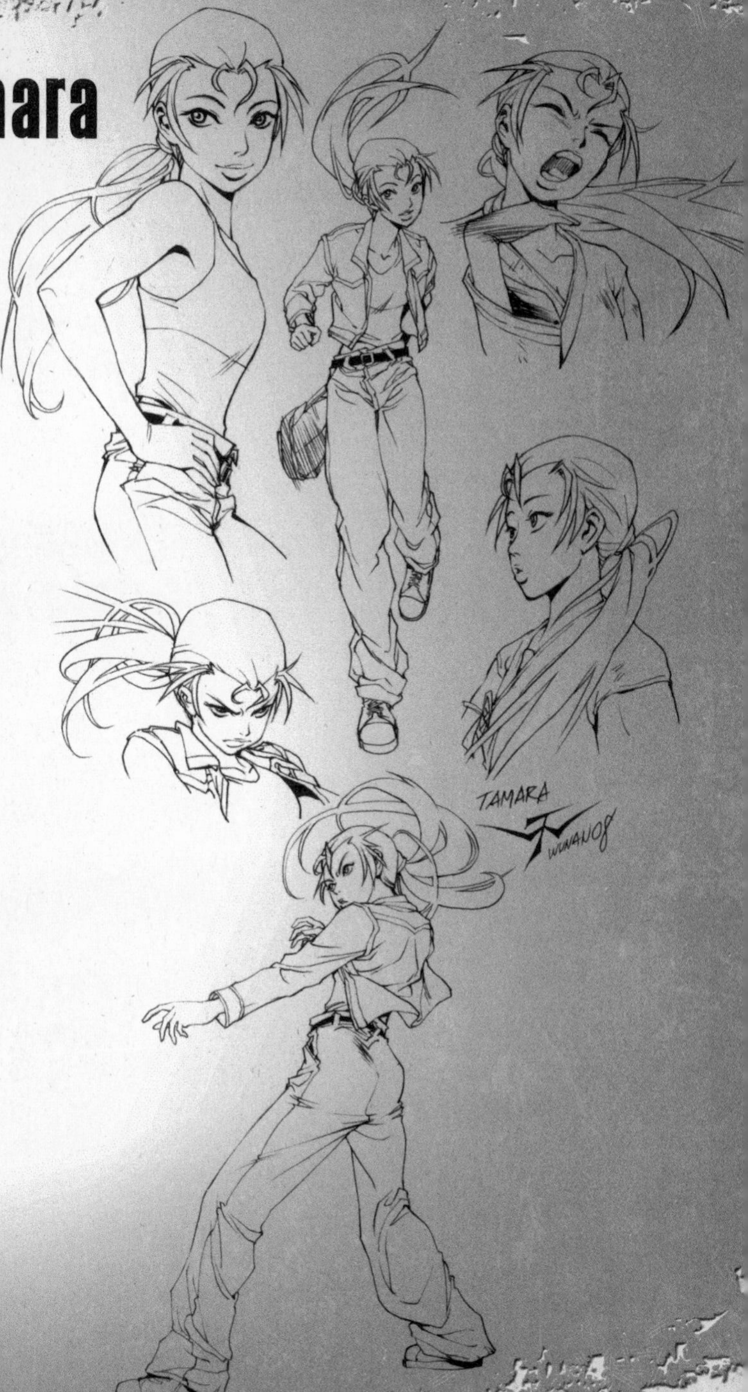
TAMARA

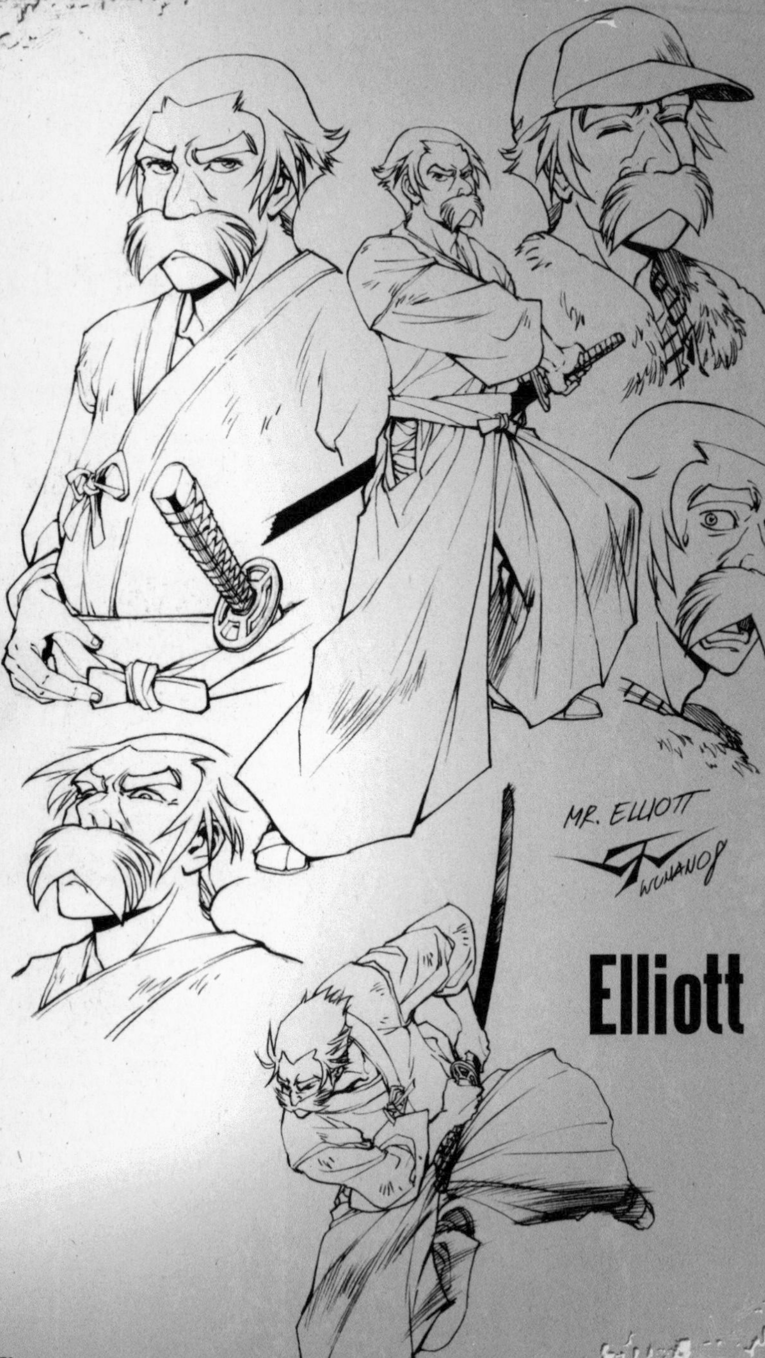
MR. ELLIOTT

Elliott

Jack

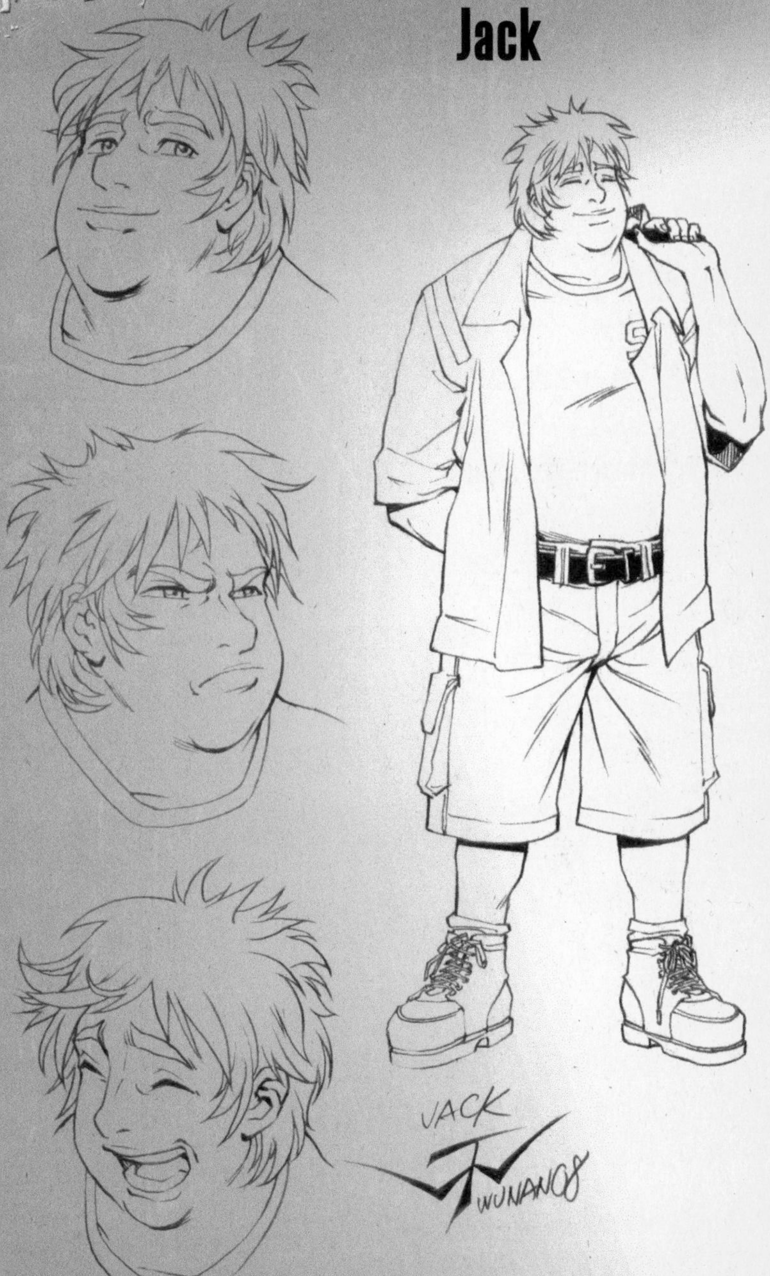
JACK
WUNAN08

Carter version 1

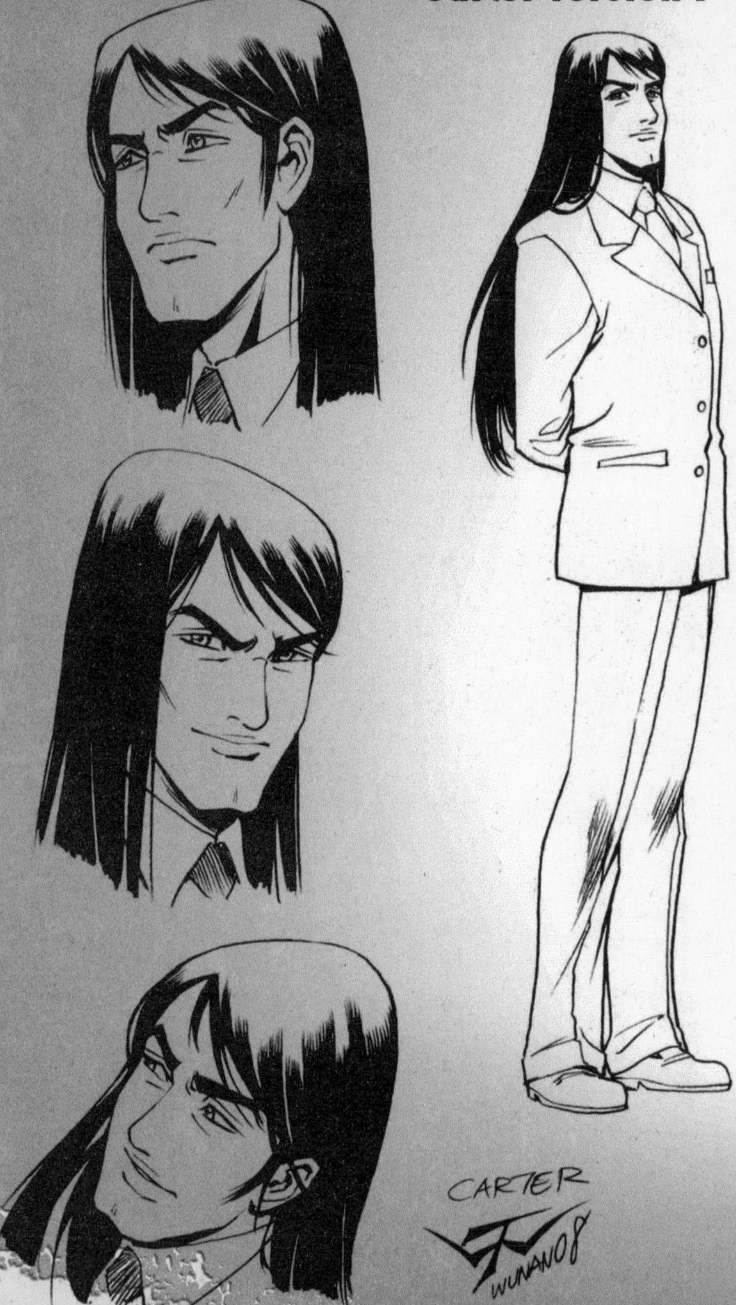
CARTER
WUNAN 08

Carter version 2

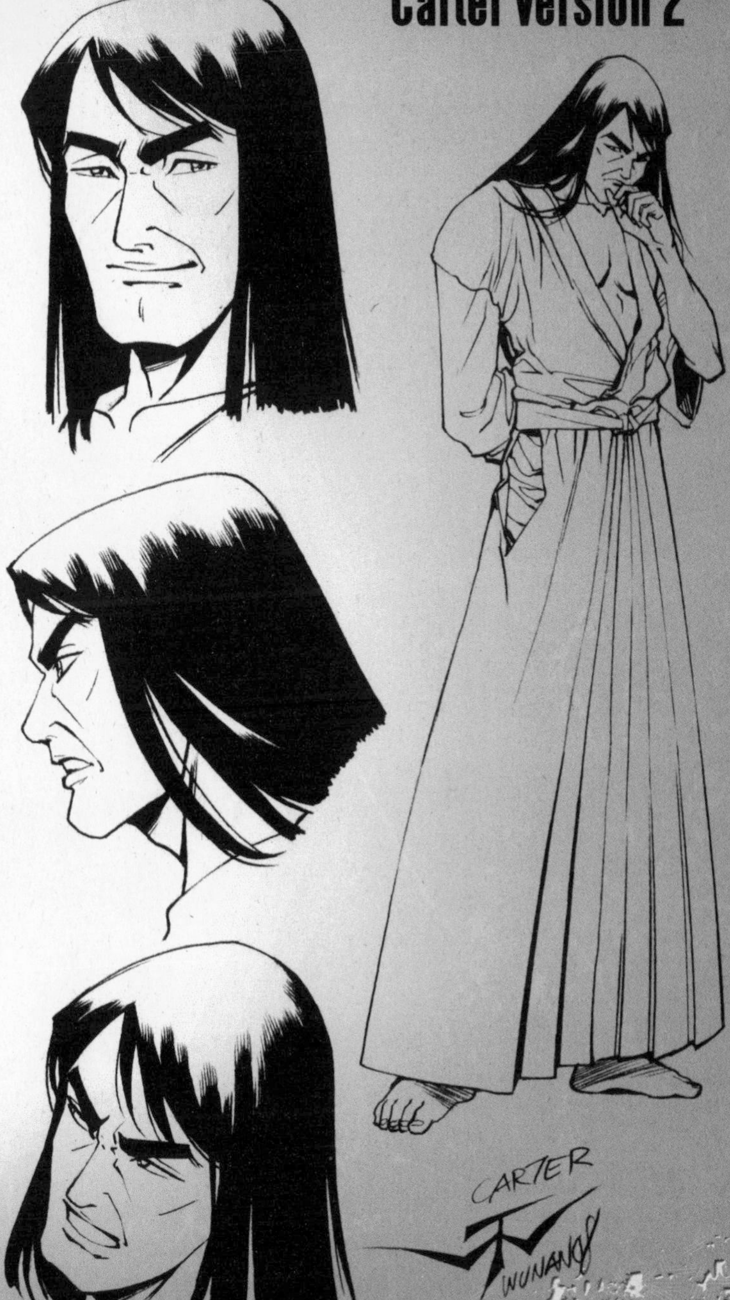
CARTER

Vincent version 1

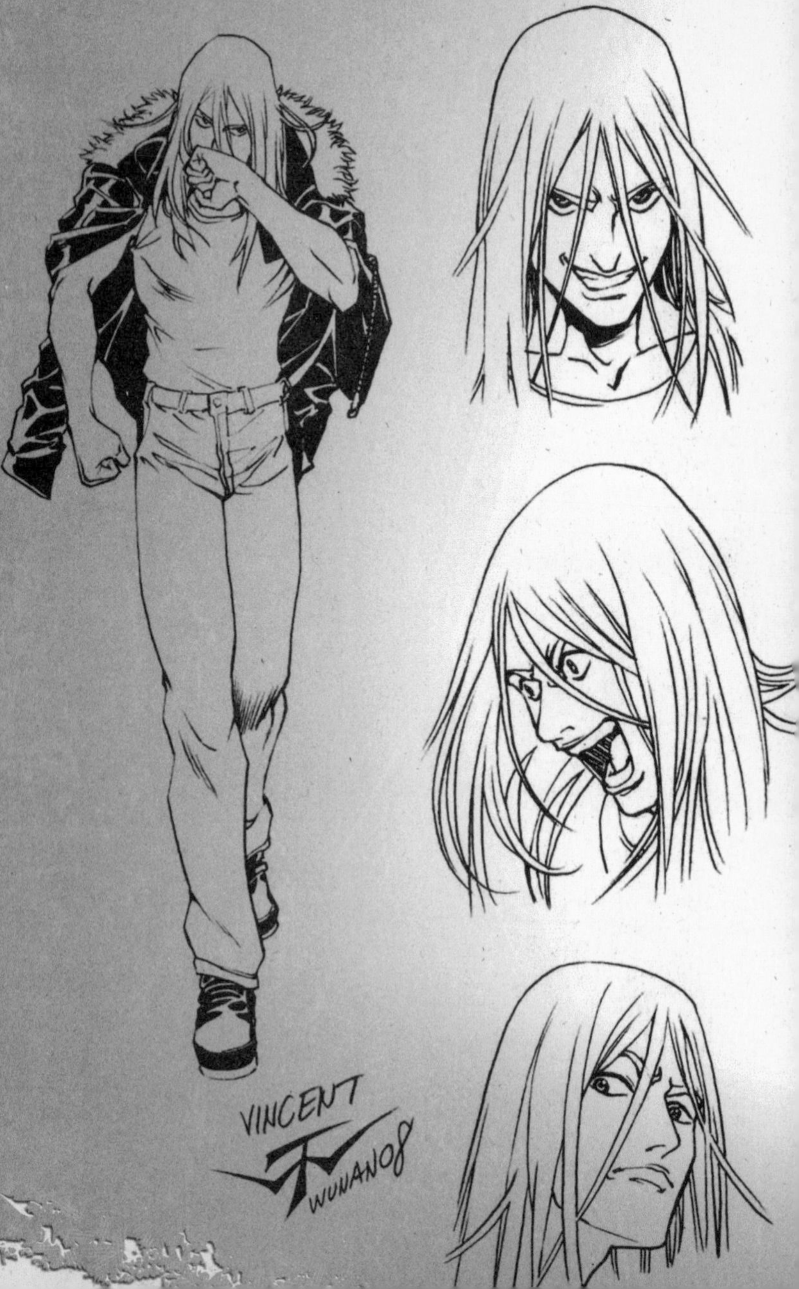
VINCENT
WUNANO8

Vincent version 2

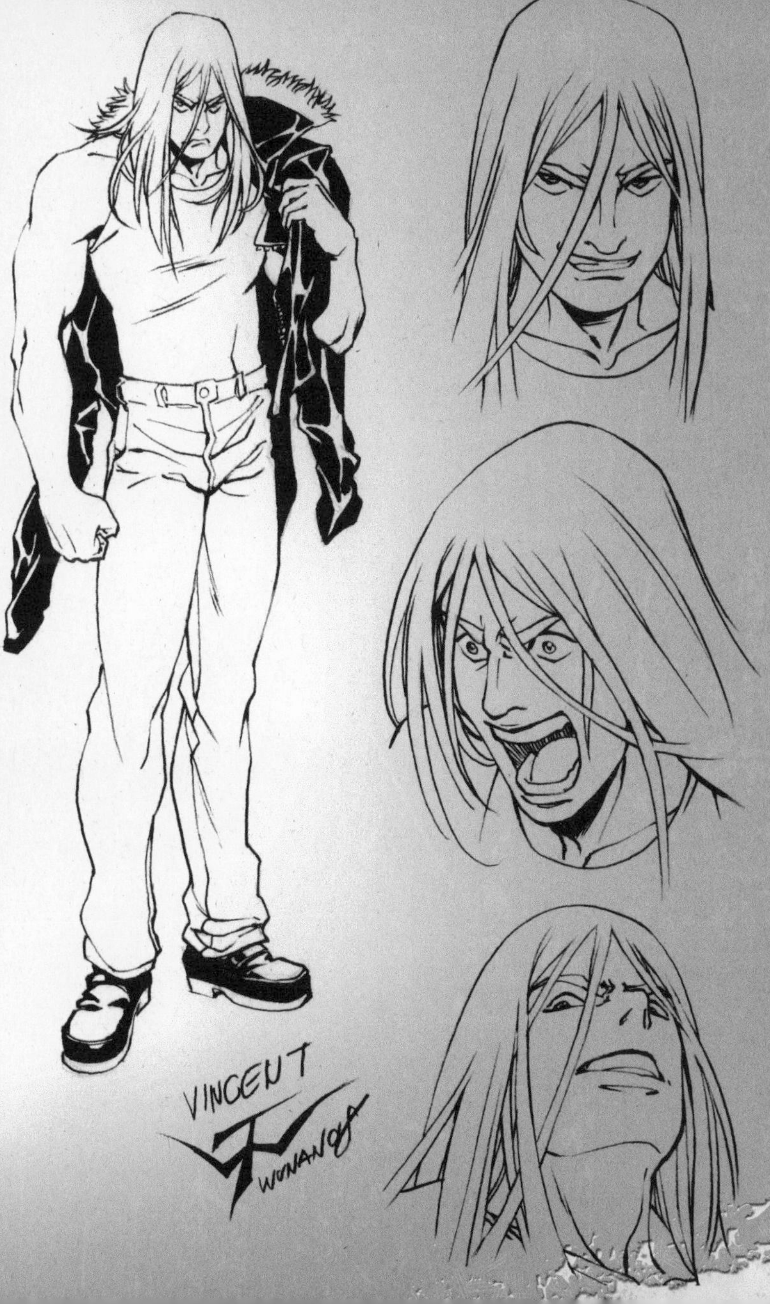
VINCENT
WUNANOYA

Morgan

MORGAN
TWUNANOS

Lady Silence

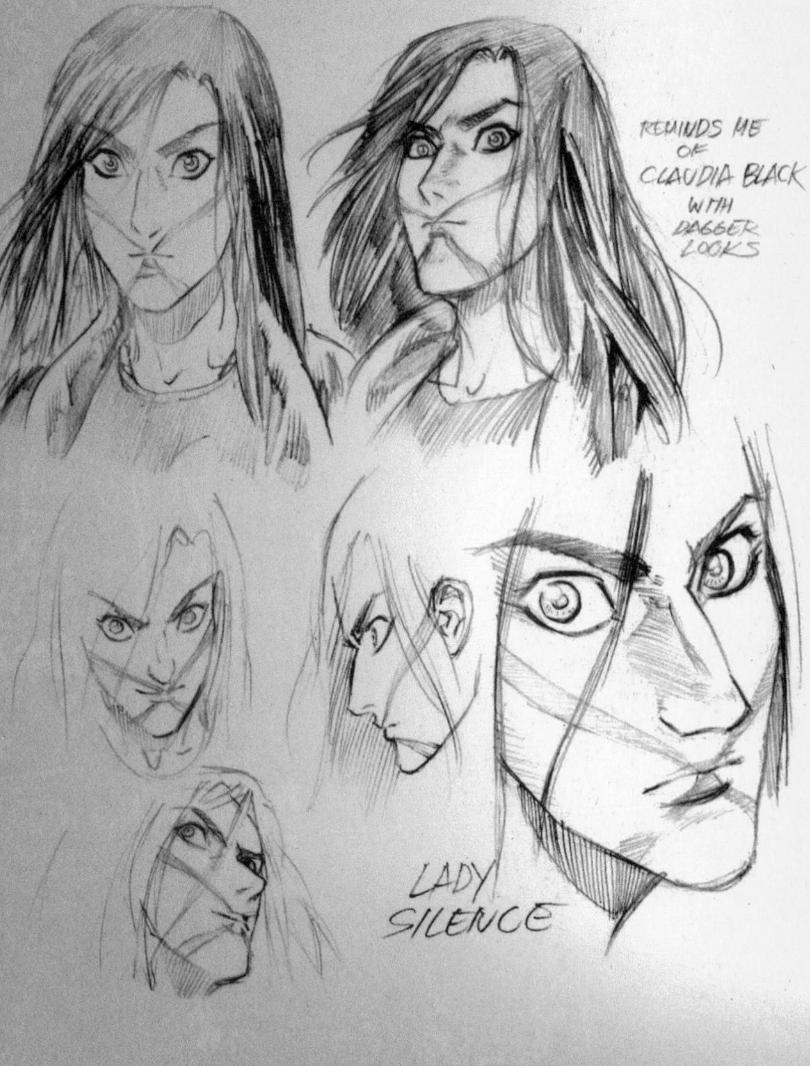
REMINDS ME OF CLAUDIA BLACK WITH DAGGER LOOKS
LADY SILENCE

Lady Silence

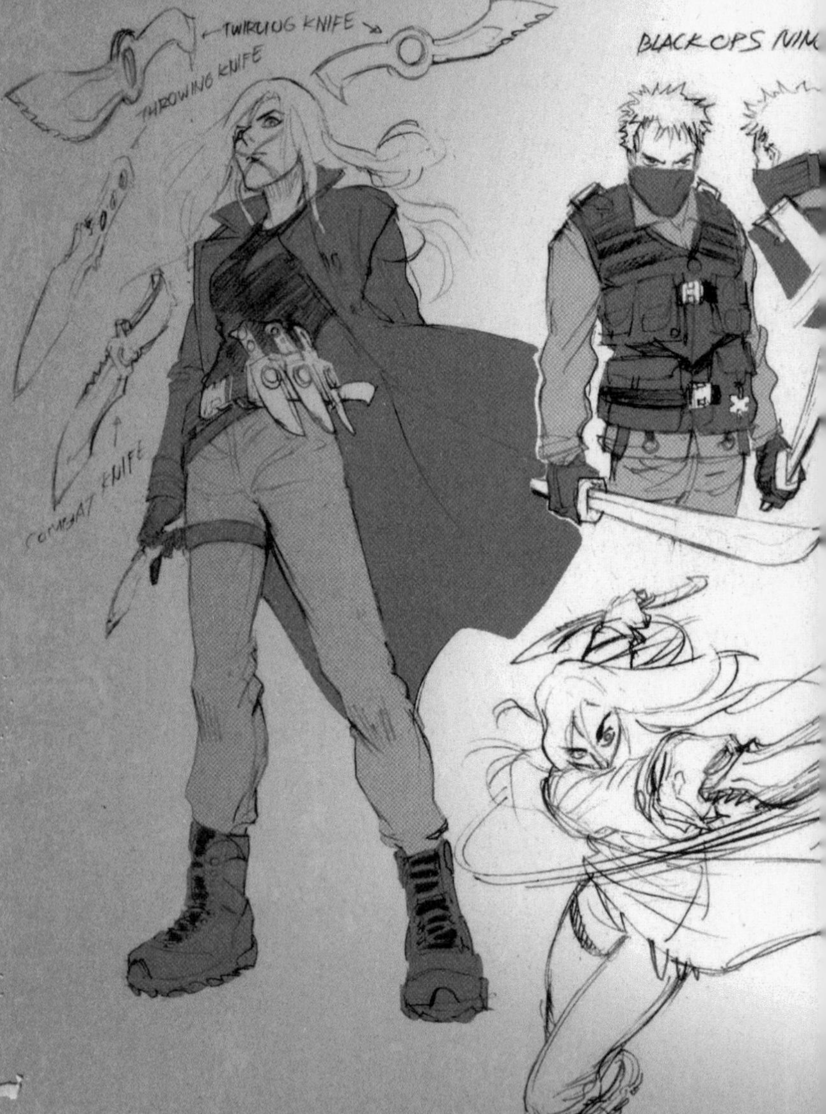
TWIRLING KNIFE
THROWING KNIFE
COMBAT KNIFE
BLACK OPS NIN

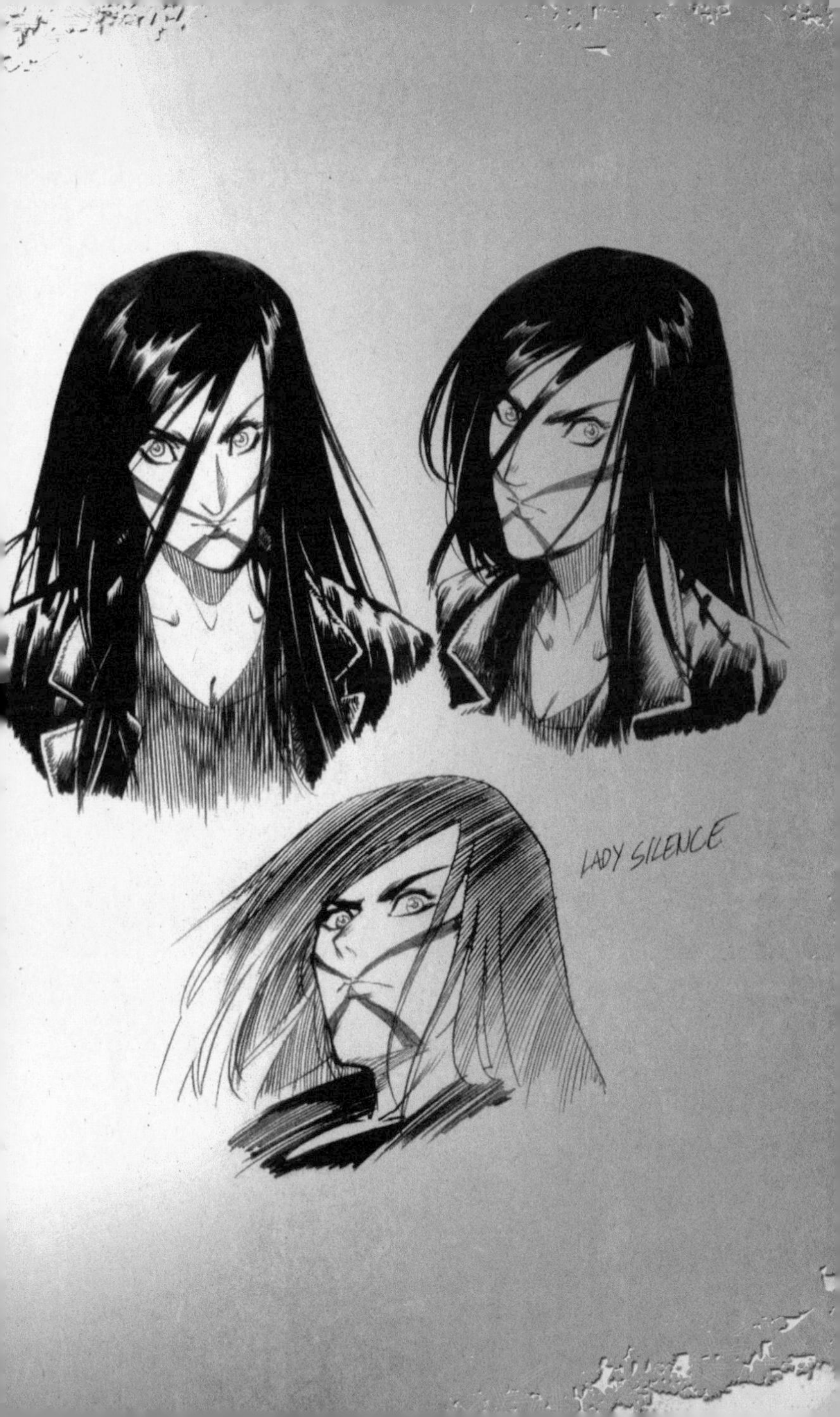
LADY SILENCE

Cover Design Sketches

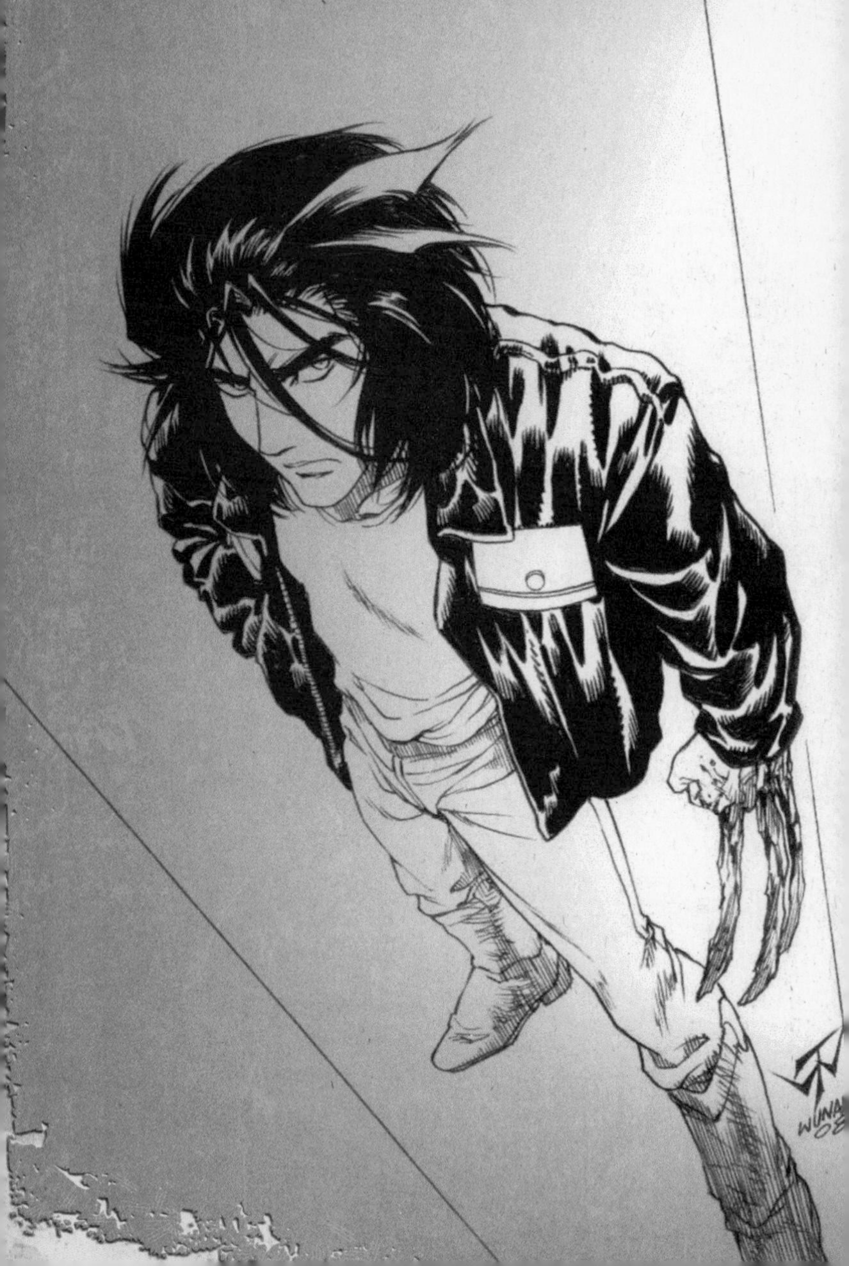

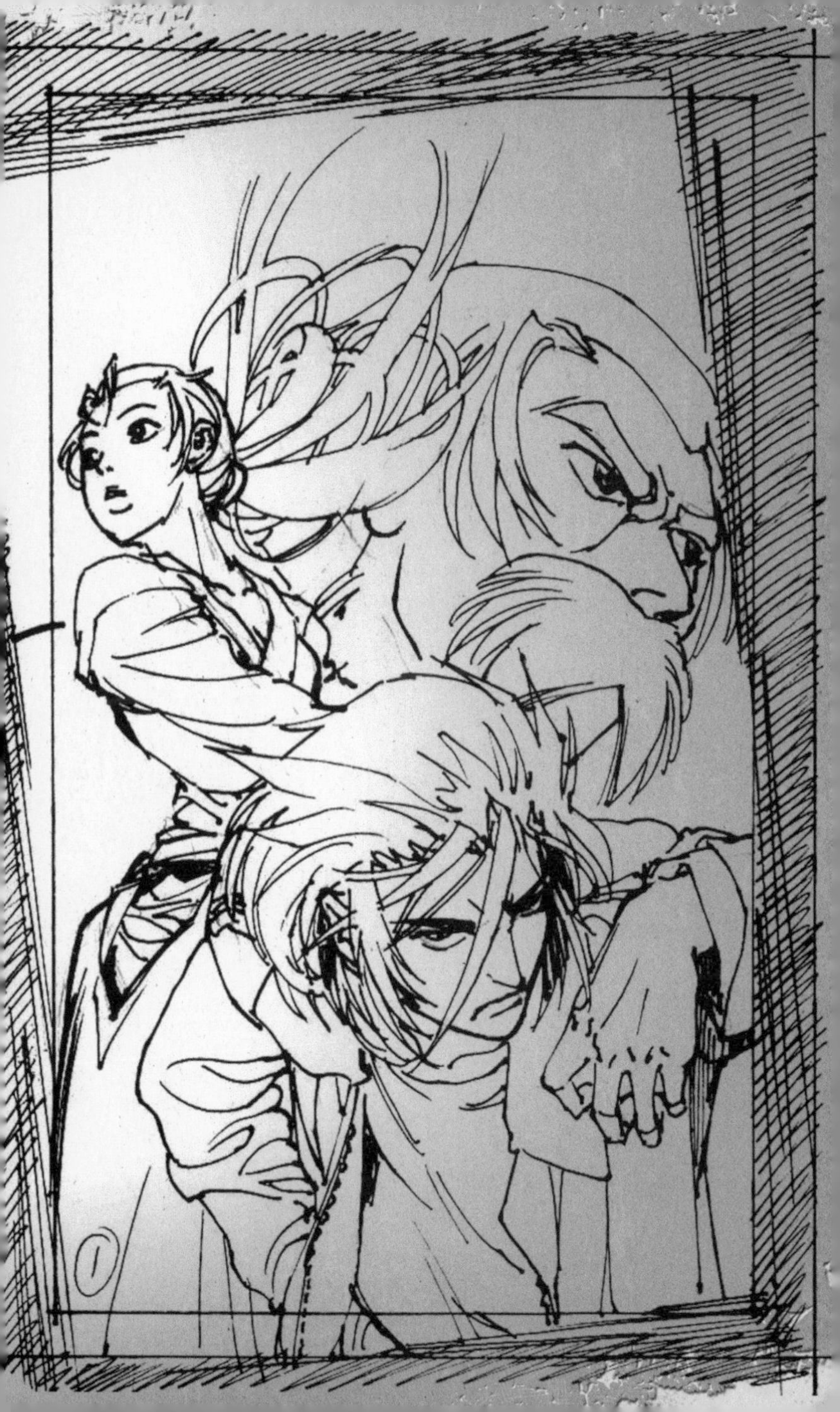

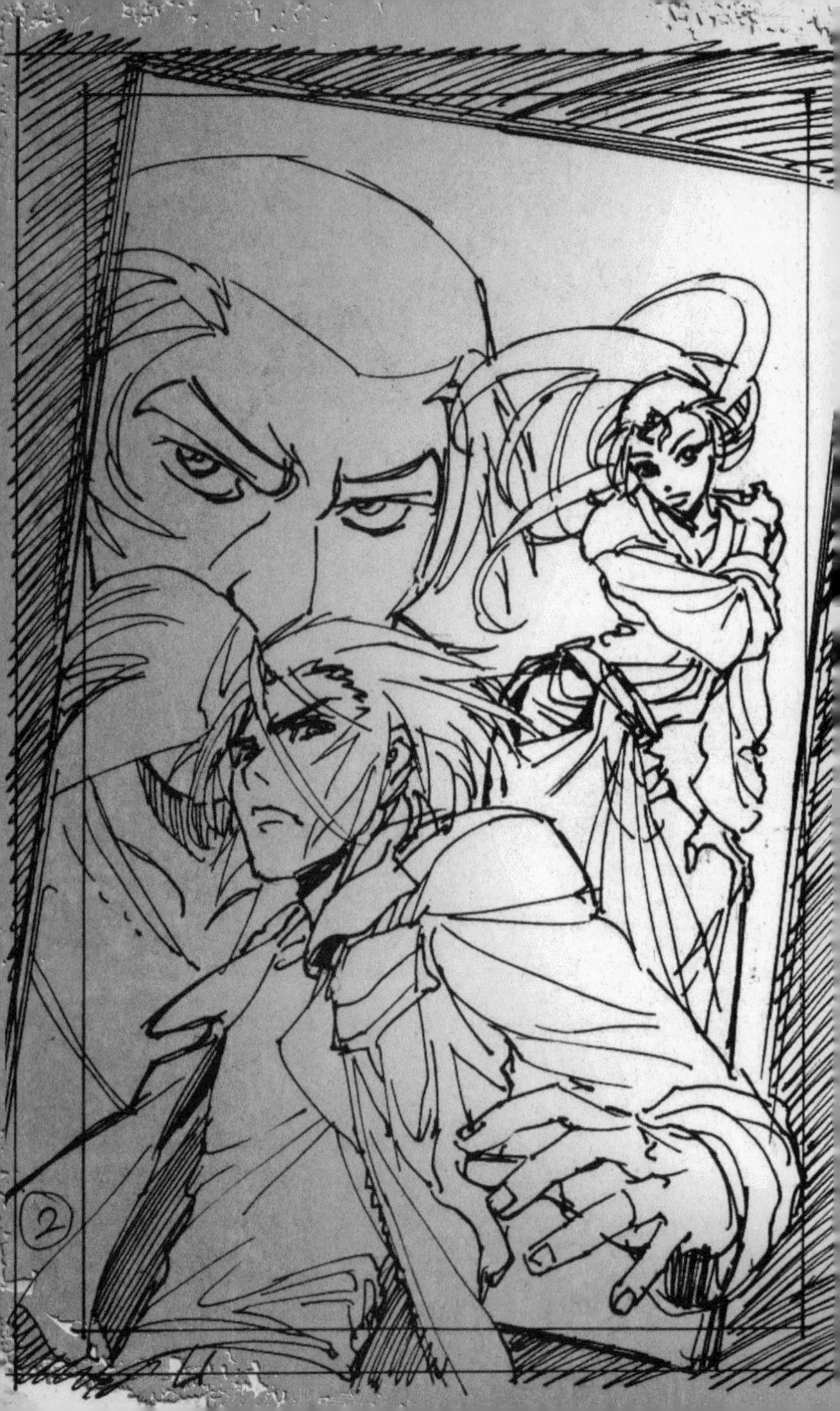
2

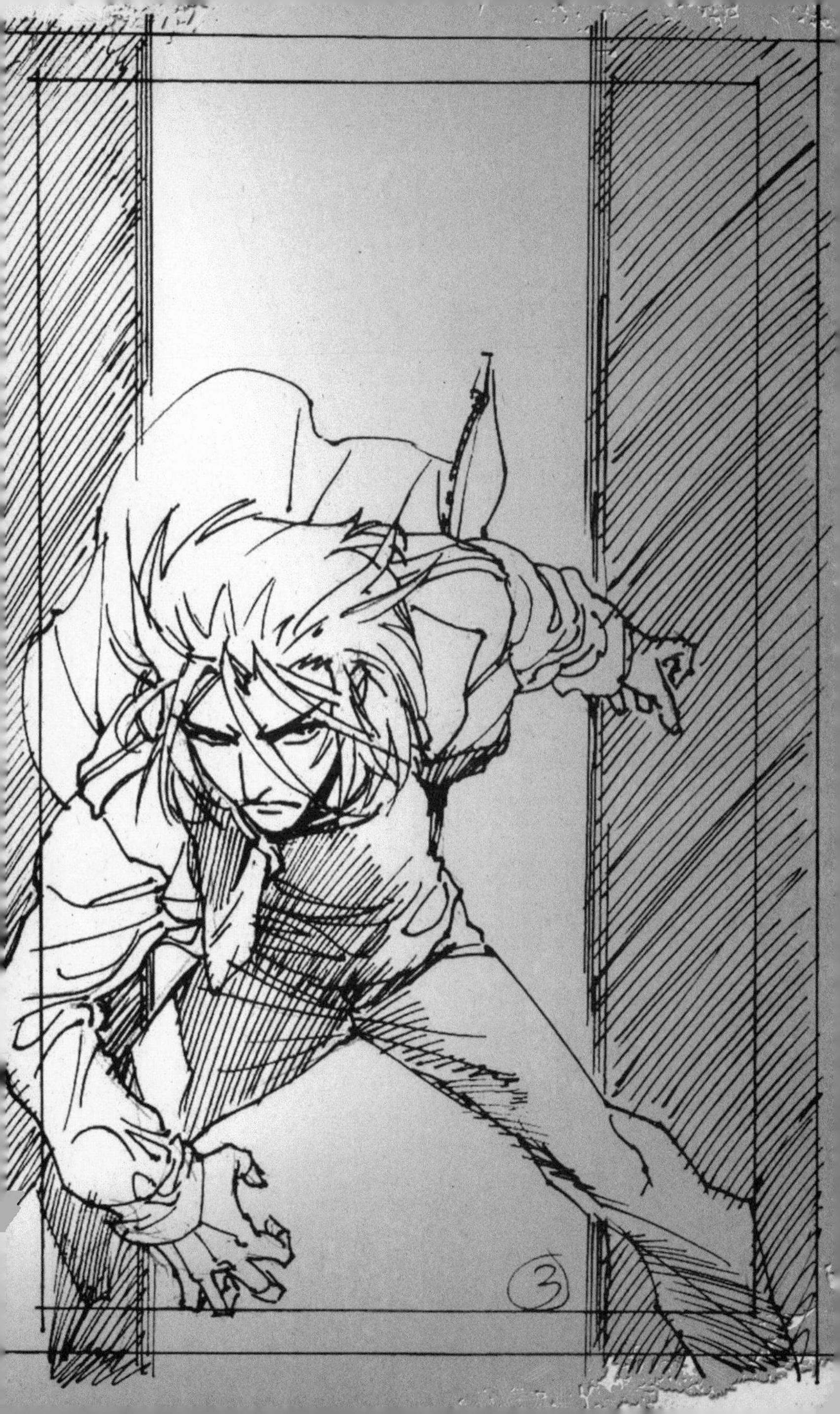
3

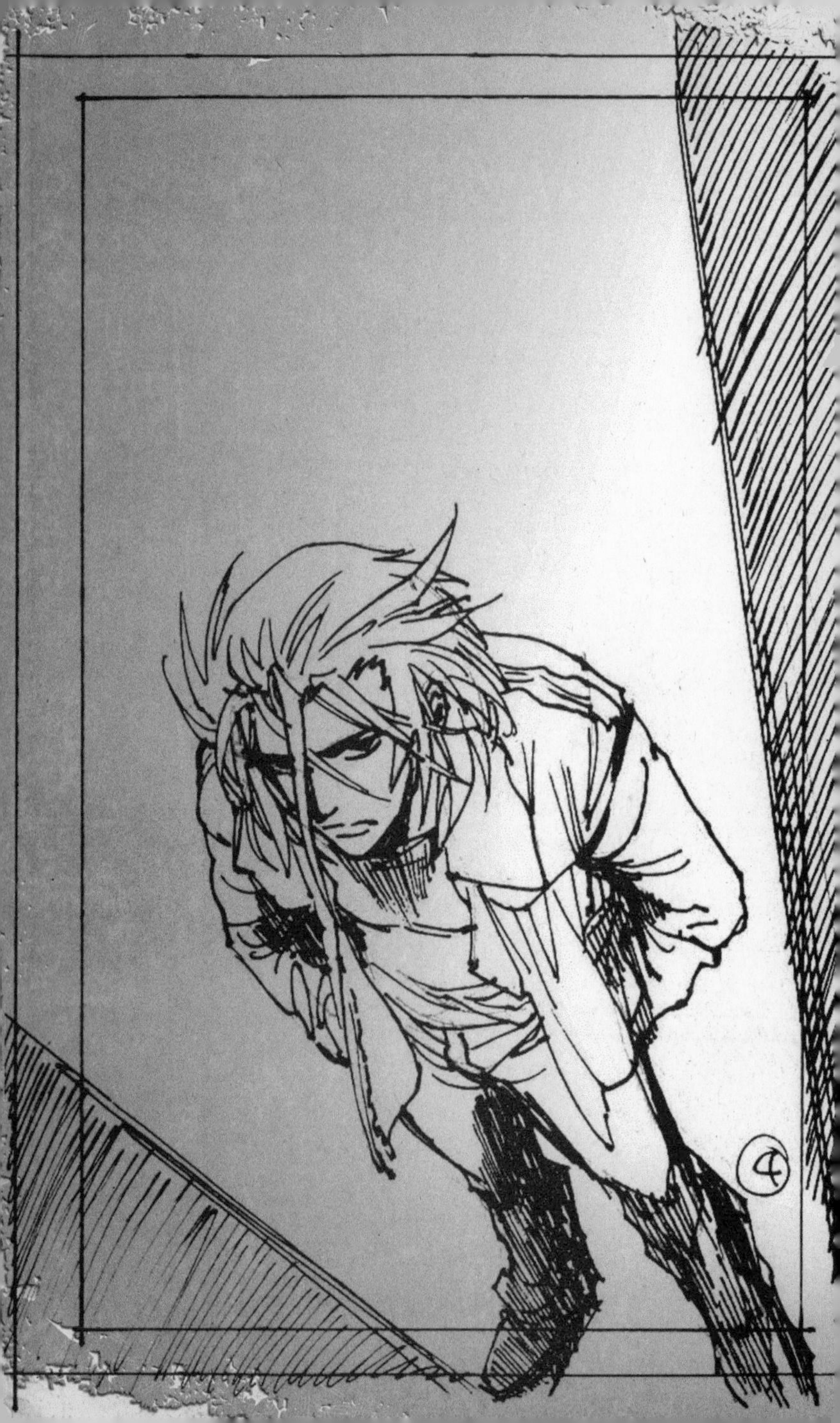

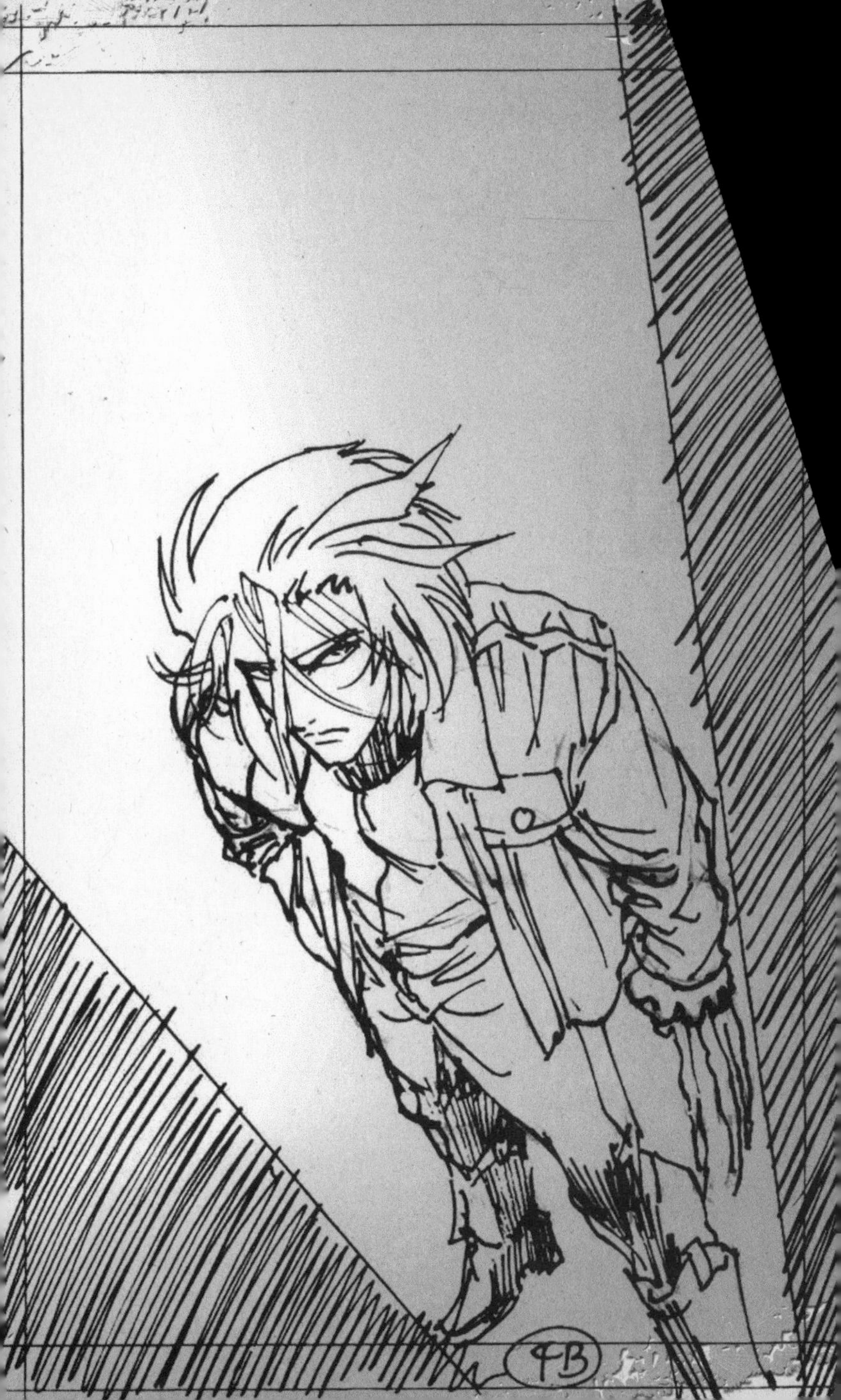